应用型本科院校"十四五"精品教材

商务英语实训系列

商务口译
实训教程

主　编　刘　慧　战秀琴　何文明

副主编　应　虹　王　标　张　艳　石本俊

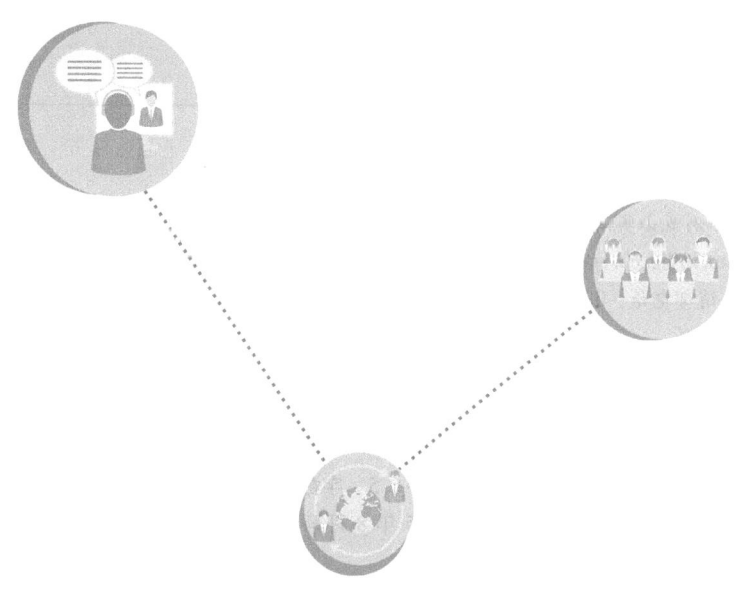

·广州·

图书在版编目（CIP）数据

商务口译实训教程/刘慧，战秀琴，何文明主编. —广州：华南理工大学出版社，2024.10（2025.8重印）
　ISBN 978-7-5623-7632-3

　Ⅰ.①商… Ⅱ.①刘… ②战… ③何… Ⅲ.①商务–英语–口译–教材 Ⅳ.①F7

中国国家版本馆 CIP 数据核字（2024）第 015753 号

商务口译实训教程
刘　慧　战秀琴　何文明　主编

出 版 人：房俊东
出版发行：华南理工大学出版社
　　　　　（广州五山华南理工大学 17 号楼　邮编：510640）
　　　　　http://hg.cb.scut.edu.cn　E-mail: scutc13@scut.edu.cn
　　　　　营销部电话：020-87113487　87111048（传真）
策划编辑：吴翠微
责任编辑：宗　艺　刘　锋
责任校对：梁樱雯
印 刷 者：广州小明数码印刷有限公司
开　　本：787mm×1092mm　1/16　印张：16.5　字数：482 千
版　　次：2024 年 10 月第 1 版　印次：2025 年 8 月第 2 次印刷
定　　价：48.00 元

版权所有　盗版必究　　印装差错　负责调换

前　言

《商务口译实训教程》是专门为应用型本科院校商务英语专业学生编写的口译教材。本书编者均为广东培正学院长期从事商务英语口译教学的一线教师，多位教师具有口译实践经历，并为双师双能型教师。本书旨在为应用型本科院校商务英语专业学生提供具有时代性、实用性、适用性和实效性的商务英语口译实训教材。同时，本教材引入了大量思政素材，将知识、能力和育人相结合，每个单元的教学目标包括知识目标和思政目标，以更好地培养学生的应用能力，促进学生全面发展，适应就业市场需求。本教材既可以作为高等院校商务英语专业教材，也可以作为有一定英语基础、已经或将要从事涉外商务工作的读者的职业培训教材。

一、教材实训项目、内容安排与目标要求

本书共分为口译技巧和商务专题实训项目两大部分。

一是口译技巧（Unit 1）部分。其主要包括 Memory Training（记忆训练）、Note-taking Skills（记录技巧）、Syntactic Linearity（顺句驱动）、Skills for Sight Interpreting（视译技巧）和 Figures Interpreting（数字口译）五大模块。本单元旨在全面提升学生的口译技巧，使其能够在商务领域中胜任口译工作，为应用型本科院校商务英语专业学生的职业发展提供有力支持。本单元具体目标主要包括以下几个方面。

（1）提高学生的记忆能力。通过 Memory Training 部分，培养学生记忆口译材料的能力，使其能够更好地记住口译内容，提高其口译的准确性和流利度。

（2）培养学生的口译记录技巧。通过 Note-taking Skills 部分，使学生掌握如何有效地记录口译过程中的关键信息，提高其听记能力和整理能力，使其口译过程更加顺利，口译结果更加准确。

（3）提升学生的顺句驱动能力。通过 Syntactic Linearity 部分，帮助学生理解和运用语法结构，使其能够更好地理解和表达句子的逻辑关系，提高其口译的连贯性和准确性。

（4）培养学生的视译技巧。通过 Skills for Sight Interpreting 部分，培养学生在没有事先准备的情况下就能够通过观察和理解口译材料的视觉信息进行即时口译的能力，提高其反应速度和应变能力。

（5）提高学生的数字口译能力。通过 Figures Interpreting 部分，培养学生在商务情景中处理数字信息的能力，包括数字的听写、口译和口头表达，提高其在商务口译中的专业性和准确性。

二是商务专题（Unit 2—13）部分。其分为四个实训项目，分别为 Business Reception（商务接待）、Business Presentation（商务陈述）、Business Talks（商务会谈）和 Business Cooperation（商务合作）。每个项目包括三个单元，具体内容及目标如下。

（1）Business Reception：包括 Protocol Routine（迎来送往）、Ceremonial Address（礼仪致辞）和 Business Travel（商务旅游），旨在培训学生涉外商务接待服务方面的口译技能。

（2）Business Presentation：包括 Enterprise Introduction（企业介绍）、Product Presentation（产品介绍）和 Business Strategies（商务策略），旨在通过实训使学生具备企业对外公关、出口产品推荐和商务策略讨论方面的口译能力。

（3）Business Talks：包括 Business Conference（商务会议）、Marketing and Promotion（商务陈述）和 Business Negotiation（商务洽谈），旨在通过实训使学生初步具备国际商务会议、商务演讲和商务谈判方面的口译能力。

（4）Business Cooperation：包括 Investment Invitation（招商引资）、Business Management（经营管理）和 Business Exhibition（商务会展），旨在通过实训使学生具备对外招商、商务管理会议、商务会展方面的口译能力。

二、项目单元模块结构、内容安排与教学要求

本教材共包含 13 个单元。第 1 单元为口译技巧，包括 Memory Training（记忆训练）、Note-taking Skills（记录技巧）、Syntactic Linearity（顺句驱动）、Skills for Sight Interpreting（视译技巧）和 Figures Interpreting（数字口译）五大模块，每个模块均包括 Knowledge and Theory（知识和理论）及 Practical Training（实战操练）两个部分。

第 2 单元至第 13 单元为商务专题，各单元分为三个模块，包括 Interpreting Preparation（口译准备）、Interpreting Practice（口译实训）和 Interpreting Assessment（口译测评），各模块具体内容及目标如下。

（1）Interpreting Preparation：包括 Key Concepts（核心概念），简要介绍各单元涉及的术语概念，并融入思政元素；Sight Interpreting（视译），培养学生的视译能力，引导学生熟悉单元主题内容和相关语言材料，为口译实训做好准备；Memory Practice（记忆训练），旨在提高学生的口译工作记忆能力，为口译

实践打下基础。

(2) Interpreting Practice：由4篇（英汉各两篇）口译材料构成。本教材的每篇材料都提供了译前词语准备（Warm-up Words & Expressions）和参考译文，教师可以根据教学时间、学生语言基础、学习能力或教学实际需要进行选用。该模块是口译实训教学的重点和难点，要求学生通过口译实训掌握口译的基本技能，并能翻译同类主题的语篇。

(3) Interpreting Assessment：旨在考查学生是否拥有单元教学目标所要求的口译能力。2篇口译测评资料的选材和单元主题相同，并附有测试评分标准，供学生自评、互评和教师评价使用。

三、教材使用方法和教学建议

Section 1　Interpreting Preparation

(1) Key Concepts：课前，教师可以引导学生仔细阅读并理解每个单元中出现的核心概念。学生可以通过阅读教材中提供的相关材料，对核心概念进行进一步的学习和思考。学生可以查阅相关资料，拓展自己的知识，并与同学进行讨论和交流。在教学过程中，教师可以将核心概念与思政元素结合起来，引导学生思考概念与社会、经济、文化等方面的关系。思政元素的引入，可以帮助学生更好地理解和应用核心概念。教师还可以设计一些小组讨论或案例分析的活动，让学生运用核心概念来分析和解决实际问题。这样可以提高学生的思维能力和应用能力，并培养他们的团队合作和沟通能力。

(2) Sight Interpreting：视译训练会占用大量课堂时间，因此建议教师安排学生在课前完成单元视译练习，并在课前花几分钟时间随机抽查学生是否完成视译练习，并将检查结果记为学生平时成绩。

(3) Memory Practice：教师播放原文录音，要求学生边听边记忆原文主旨大意。播放完毕后，教师随堂抽查学生用原语复述段落主旨大意。练习目的是训练学生在口译中的记忆能力和复述能力。

Section 2　Interpreting Practice

(1) 该模块包含4篇口译素材，应作为商务口译课堂的重点教学内容，实训时间应不少于单周课时的60%。如果在课堂上不能完成口译实训课文的全部练习，建议教师安排学生两人一组在课外完成口译实训任务，在课堂随机检查并作出相应评价。

(2) 汉译英口译教学的难点是学生的汉译英能力不足，其主要障碍是未掌握汉英转换方法和欠缺英语表达能力。学生需要通过汉英口译训练，掌握汉英转换技巧和积累英语表达方式。教师需要引导学生分析汉语和英语在表达形式和语义特征方面的同一性和差异性，通过汉英口译强化促进语言材料的内化，打好汉英口译语言基本功，逐步提高学生的汉英口译能力。

Section 3　Interpreting Assessment

（1）学生自评：教师需先要求学生合上教材，再打开实验室口译录音设备或有录音功能的手机，播放原文录音，让学生边听边做笔记，然后进行口译。学生完成口译任务后，要求其根据参考译文和口译录音进行对比检查，根据口译评分标准做出客观评价。自评有助于调动学生的学习积极性，培养学生自主学习、自我监控、自我评价的良好学习习惯。

（2）学生互评：教师要求学生两人一组，一名担任发言人按正常速度读原文，另一名担任译员，并录下自己的译文。完成口译后，将录音和参考译文作对比分析，并按口译评分标准对译文质量作出评价。之后两人交换角色，以同样的方式完成第二次口译课文测评。互评有利于培养学生的合作精神，激励学生相互学习、互相帮助、共同进步。

（3）教师评价：教师挑选两名学生，一名担任发言人念原文，另一名担任译员做笔记和口译（需录音）。口译结束后，教师根据教材参考译文对学生的口译录音进行点评。另外，由于教材提供了口译测评参考译文，参加测评的学生的课前预习情况将直接影响测评结果的信度和效度，在一定程度上不能客观、真实地反映学生实际的口译能力。建议教师从课外选择在主题内容和难度上与课文相近的语言材料作为测试题，以便获得客观真实的评价数据，从而为口译教学提供更有价值的反馈信息。

本教材为广东培正学院外国语言文学重点学科专业建设成果。本书的主要结构框架改编自石本俊、战秀琴主编的《商务英语口译实训教程》。第1单元由张艳编写，第2、3、4单元由何文明编写，第5、6、7单元由刘慧编写，第8、9、10单元由应虹编写，第11、12、13单元由王标编写。刘慧、战秀琴、何文明负责本书的框架修订和书稿校对。本教材在编写过程中参考了大量国内外有关著作和资料，在此谨向有关作者、译者表示诚挚的谢意。

因时间仓促和编者能力所限，教材中难免有错漏之处，希望使用本教材的读者能不吝赐予宝贵意见，以便再版时改进。

主编
2024年5月

CONTENTS

Unit 1　Interpreting Skills ········· 1
　Section 1　Memory Training ········· 1
　Section 2　Note-taking Skills ········· 8
　Section 3　Syntactic Linearity ········· 15
　Section 4　Skills for Sight Interpreting ········· 16
　Section 5　Figures Interpreting ········· 22

Project 1　Business Reception

Unit 2　Protocol Routine ········· 29
　Section 1　Interpreting Preparation ········· 29
　Section 2　Interpreting Practice ········· 34
　Section 3　Interpreting Assessment ········· 38
Unit 3　Ceremonial Address ········· 40
　Section 1　Interpreting Preparation ········· 40
　Section 2　Interpreting Practice ········· 46
　Section 3　Interpreting Assessment ········· 49
Unit 4　Business Travel ········· 51
　Section 1　Interpreting Preparation ········· 51
　Section 2　Interpreting Practice ········· 55
　Section 3　Interpreting Assessment ········· 59

Project 2　Business Presentation

Unit 5　Enterprise Introduction ········· 63
　Section 1　Interpreting Preparation ········· 63
　Section 2　Interpreting Practice ········· 66
　Section 3　Interpreting Assessment ········· 71
Unit 6　Product Presentation ········· 73
　Section 1　Interpreting Preparation ········· 73
　Section 2　Interpreting Practice ········· 76
　Section 3　Interpreting Assessment ········· 80

Unit 7　Business Strategies ·· 82
　　Section 1　Interpreting Preparation ·· 82
　　Section 2　Interpreting Practice ·· 85
　　Section 3　Interpreting Assessment ·· 90

Project 3　Business Talks

Unit 8　Business Conference ·· 95
　　Section 1　Interpreting Preparation ·· 95
　　Section 2　Interpreting Practice ·· 98
　　Section 3　Interpreting Assessment ·· 101
Unit 9　Marketing and Promotion ·· 103
　　Section 1　Interpreting Preparation ·· 103
　　Section 2　Interpreting Practice ·· 107
　　Section 3　Interpreting Assessment ·· 110
Unit 10　Business Negotiation ·· 112
　　Section 1　Interpreting Preparation ·· 112
　　Section 2　Interpreting Practice ·· 115
　　Section 3　Interpreting Assessment ·· 118

Project 4　Business Cooperation

Unit 11　Investment Invitation ·· 123
　　Section 1　Interpreting Preparation ·· 123
　　Section 2　Interpreting Practice ·· 126
　　Section 3　Interpreting Assessment ·· 131
Unit 12　Business Management ·· 134
　　Section 1　Interpreting Preparation ·· 134
　　Section 2　Interpreting Practice ·· 137
　　Section 3　Interpreting Assessment ·· 142
Unit 13　Business Exhibition ·· 144
　　Section 1　Interpreting Preparation ·· 144
　　Section 2　Interpreting Practice ·· 148
　　Section 3　Interpreting Assessment ·· 153

参考答案及译文 ··· 155
参考文献 ··· 249

Unit 1　Interpreting Skills

Learning Objectives
- Gain proficiency in the fundamental principles of long-term and short-term memory
- Acquire techniques for enhancing short-term memory
- Develop effective strategies for note-taking
- Learn techniques for interpreting English and Chinese visual content
- Understand the foundational concepts of syntactic linearity
- Acquire skills for interpreting visual figures accurately

Ideological and Political Elements
- Instill a sense of global citizenship by engaging with international political and ideological topics
- Highlight the role of interpreters in promoting international understanding and cooperation
- Comprehend the distinctions between Chinese and Western language expressions, all the while fostering correct values grounded in core socialist values and maintaining a firm political stance
- Look at the changes of differences from the perspective of development, carry forward and inherit the fine traditional Chinese culture, cultivate correct values, and improve cross-cultural communication skills in business communication
- Promote cultural sensitivity and inclusivity in interpretation by exploring the diverse cultural and ideological backgrounds of speakers
- Address the ethical dimensions of interpretation, particularly in politically sensitive situations
- Understand the ethical responsibilities of interpreters when dealing with ideological and political contents
- Provide insights into international relations and diplomacy through the interpretation of political speeches, negotiations, and diplomatic discourse

Section 1　Memory Training

👉 Knowledge and Theory

张威和王克非（2007）提出，口译过程中的记忆机制是口译认知处理过程研究关注的重点，相关研究关注了译员的记忆容量、记忆时长、回忆效果以及记忆与口译专业技能的关系等。译员在口译时虽然需要激活对背景知识等非语言知识的长时记忆，但其在口译的认知处理过程中主要运用的是短时记忆。

Miller（1956）提出，人的短时记忆容量为 $7±2$ 个组块。由于短时记忆容量有限，故译员在口译记忆时往往在记忆单位上做文章。也就是说，通过听辨理解进行信息分析和整合，把相互关联的信息整合为一个信息项。

根据 Gile（1995）提出的认知负荷理论，口译以短时记忆为中心。认知负荷由"多重信息加工"的概念引申而来。Gile 提出口译过程包括两个阶段，即源信息听取理解阶段和信息加工重组阶段。

短时记忆在口译过程中起着非常重要的作用，是口译训练的技巧之一。因此，在口译课程中，学生需要学会正确运用记忆来处理信息。本部分将集中讨论一些信息处理的方法，以便学生学习如何将短时记忆变成长时记忆。通过本部分的学习，学生可以通过正确使用记忆力训练方法记住更多信息。

以下是如何进行语篇分析和短时记忆训练的实例。

例

第一，气候变化是全球性问题，需要各国携手合作，共同保护我们的家园。发达国家应该正视自己的历史责任和当前人均排放水平仍然居高的现实，严格履行《京都议定书》确定的减排目标，在2012年后继续率先减排。发展中国家应该根据自身能力积极采取有效措施，为应对气候变化做出力所能及的贡献。国际社会应该加大对发展中国家的支持，发达国家应该履行对发展中国家的技术转让和资金支持承诺，切实帮助发展中国家提高减缓和适应气候变化能力。

第二，气候变化从根本上说是发展问题。应该把经济增长、社会发展、环境保护统筹协调起来，建立适应可持续发展要求的生产方式和消费方式。为应对气候变化而停滞发展，或者无视气候变化片面追求经济增长都是不可取、不可行的。据估计，今天全球约有24亿人仍以煤炭、木炭、薪柴、农作物秸秆作为主要燃料，有16亿人没有用上电。让贫困人口得到现代能源的服务，进而享受发展的机会，是一种道义责任和社会责任。因此必须强调，应对气候变化的努力应该促进而不是阻碍各国尤其是发展中国家发展经济、消除贫困。

第三，《联合国气候变化框架公约》及其《京都议定书》奠定了应对气候变化国际合作的法律基础，最具权威性、普遍性、全面性。公约确立的"共同但有区别的责任"和公平原则，凝聚了国际社会共识，反映了各国经济发展水平、历史责任、当前人均排放上的差异。我们应该以公约和议定书作为国际合作的基本框架，也欢迎将其他开展务实合作的倡议和机制作为公约框架的有益补充。

第四，技术进步对减缓和适应气候变化具有决定性作用。国际社会要增加资金投入，扩大信息交流，加强节能、环保、低碳能源等技术的研发和创新合作，特别是加强技术推广和利用，使广大发展中国家买得起、用得上。在这方面，不能只强调市场机制的作用，把应对气候变化的任务全部推向市场。发达国家应减少贸易和技术壁垒，支持尽早落实公约关于技术转让的规定，建立切实有效的技术转让和技术合作机制，提高共同应对气候变化的能力。

(https://www.gov.cn/ldhd/2007-11/22/content_812088.htm)

【语篇分析】

这篇文章是说话人在阐述对于气候变化的四点看法和主张。我们可以注意到，每个段落的首句话都是该段落的主题句。具体分析如下：

第一段："气候变化是全球性问题，需要各国携手合作，共同保护我们的家园。"这句话为主题句，主要提出气候变化是世界各国都需要携手合作解决的全球性问题。此后，谈论了不同国家或组织的义务和责任：

①发展中国家需根据自身能力采取力所能及的措施；

②国际社区需要给予发展中国家支持；

③发达国家需要履行对发展中国家的承诺。

第二段：此段表明，气候变化是发展问题，应该统筹协调经济增长、社会发展以及环境保护，建立可持续发展生产和消费方式，还列举了相关的数字说明气候变化与经济社会的问题。

第三段：此段提到了两份具有法律效力的文件及其存在的意义。

第四段：此段提到了技术进步对减缓和适应气候变化的重要性，并指出了应当从两个方面着手采取相应措施，具体如下：

①国际社会加大资金投入，扩大信息交流，加强环保技术研发和创新合作；

②发达国家应该减少贸易和技术壁垒。

【语篇与记忆结合】

1. 主题句和段落标签记忆

学生应关注每个段落的主题句，这些句子通常包含了文章段落的核心思想。例如，第一段的主题句是："气候变化是全球性问题，需要各国携手合作，共同保护我们的家园。"学生可以将这句话视为该段的关键观点，然后记住与之相关的子观点。

每个段落的摘要或标签也可以用于记忆该段的主题。例如，第四段可以标记为"技术进步对减缓和适应气候变化的重要性"。

2. 关联记忆

学生可以考虑如何使不同段落之间的信息相互关联。例如，第一段和第二段都强调了气候变化是全球性问题，但第二段更专注于将气候变化与经济和社会发展联系起来。学生可以记住这两个段落之间的关联，并理解气候变化如何影响全球发展。

3. 使用记忆技巧

在记忆每个段落的内容时，学生可以使用记忆技巧，例如使用关键词或首字母缩写来帮助记忆每个段落的主要观点。例如，针对第三段的"《联合国气候变化框架公约》"，学生可以通过记住"联合国"和"框架公约"这两个关键词来记忆关于这一法律基础的内容。

4. 反复阅读和复述练习

学生应该进行多次阅读和复述练习，尝试在没有文本的情况下简洁而准确地复述每个段落的主要观点。例如，学生可以尝试复述第一段的观点，即全球气候变化需要国际合作，发达国家有历史责任，等等。

5. 应用到实际练习

为了进一步结合语篇分析和记忆，学生可以将这些技巧应用到实际的口译或翻译练习中，尝试记忆口译材料或翻译文本的各个部分，确保在需要时可以精确而流利地运用这些记忆技巧。

Memory Training Methods

根据 Gile（1995）提出的认知负荷理论，口译的过程包括：I = L + M + N。I 代表"interpreting"，即口译；L 代表"listening"，即听，表示在听取过程中分析源信息；M 代表"memory"，即记忆，表示从听取信息起到以笔记形式储存信息需要的短时记忆；N 代表"notes"，即口译笔记。短时记忆主要包括信息输入、信息储存、记忆形态（图形、声音和语义编码）、信息丢失和信息提取。因此，训练短时记忆对于译者翻译结果的产出至关重要。以下是训练短时记忆的主要方法。

源语复述：以播放录音的形式，让学生听一段大约 200 个词的文章，随后让学生用同种语言进行信息复述，听力期间不准记笔记。

目的语复述：以播放录音的形式，让学生听一段大约 200 个词的文章，随后让学生用目的语进行信息复述，听力期间不准记笔记。

影子跟读练习：影子跟读练习是一种有效的语言学习方法，它通过播放录音让学生听取一段大约 200 字的文章，同时要求他们跟读所听到的内容。这种练习不仅有助于提高学生的听力技能，还能够帮助他们提高发音准确度、语音节奏和语调。通过模仿录音中的语速、语调和语音，学生能够更好地理解和掌握语言的运用方式，从而提高口语表达能力。此外，影子跟读练习还可以帮助学生加强对语言结构和词汇的记忆，促进语言的自然习得过程。

信息逻辑整理：以播放录音的形式，让学习者听一段 100 个词左右的文章，并通过以下技巧进行练习。

1. 听辨句子关键词

做好口译的前提是准确听出原文的信息，只有在听懂的基础上才有可能记住信息并进行口译，而抓住句子的关键词是听辨源语的重点。关键词往往包含实际内容以及说话人的意图，强调的是说话人传递的信息。关键词包括动词、名词、形容词、代词、副词等。词语在句子中的成分也对关键词的关联有影响。例如"I am very pleased to inform you that…"，此处的形容词"pleased"为关键词，表示说话人的心情；动词"inform"也是关键词之一，通过抓住关键词"inform"，我们可知道其后的内容也是重要信息。

听辨下列段落，注意用听辨句子关键词的方法来记忆并复述信息。

（1）小米集团成立于 2010 年 4 月，2018 年 7 月 9 日在我国香港上市，是一家以智能手机、智能硬件和 IoT 平台为核心的消费电子及智能制造公司。小米是全球领先的智能手机品牌之一，智能手机出货量稳居全球前三。截至 2023 年 6 月，全球 MIUI 月活跃用户数 6.06 亿。目前，集团业务已进入全球逾 100 个国家和地区。2023 年 8 月，小米集团连续五年入选《财富》"世界 500 强排行榜"（*Fortune* Global 500）。

（2）Amazon is guided by four principles: customer obsession rather than competitor focus, passion for invention, commitment to operational excellence, and long-term thinking. Amazon strives to be Earth's most customer-centric company, Earth's best employer, and Earth's safest place to work. Customer reviews, one-click shopping, personalized recommendations, Prime, Fulfillment by Amazon, AWS, Kindle Direct Publishing, Kindle, Career Choice, Fire tablets, Fire TV, Amazon Echo, Alexa, Just Walk Out technology, Amazon Studios, and The Climate Pledge are some of the things pioneered by Amazon.

2. 听辨句子主干结构

仅仅依靠听辨关键信息的词语或短语，译员无法完全理解说话人的意图，因此译员还需要听辨这些词语是如何组织成一句完整的话的。基于此，译员需要进行听辨句子主干结构的训练。以英语为例，通过听辨"主谓宾"的基本结构，可以理解句子的整体意思。例如，句子"Children are the backbone of the country."中的主语是"children"，谓语是"are"，宾语是"the backbone"，定语是"of the country"，用于修饰宾语"backbone"。

听辨下列段落，注意用听辨句子主干结构的方法来记忆并复述信息。

（1）华为创立于1987年，是全球领先的ICT（信息与通信）基础设施和智能终端提供商。我们的20.7万员工遍及170多个国家和地区，为全球30多亿人口提供服务。我们致力于把每个人、每个家庭、每个组织带入数字世界，构建万物互联的智能世界。华为重视研究与创新，坚持走开放创新的道路，愿意与学术界、产业界一起，共同探索科学技术的前沿，推动创新升级，不断为全行业、全社会创造价值，携手共建美好的智能世界。

（1）The 2023 Global Guangdong Entrepreneurs Conference will be held in Guangzhou from September 21 to 23, and will gather entrepreneurs of leading Guangdong brands and high-profiled scholars to highlight and seize the opportunities in the Guangdong-Hong Kong-Macao Greater Bay Area (GBA). Over 800 representatives will participate in the event, including Guangdong entrepreneurs, representatives of the Guangdong Chamber of Commerce from home and abroad, business representatives of Global 500 enterprises, China 500 enterprises, financial institutions, and experts.

3. 听辨句子逻辑关系

英语句式包括简单句和复杂句，尤其是句子之间有许多衔接用语，这些词语是句子和段落之间的纽带。正确理解句子的逻辑关系是理解句子和话语的关键步骤。在听力训练阶段，学生往往过于关注对单词的理解，而忽略了句子的整体意思，导致无法抓住关键信息和句子的主旨。因此，学生需要集中精力训练句子逻辑关系的听辨，以便全面理解整个句子的意思。

以下例子是对结构相似但逻辑关系词不同的英语句子的理解。

The economy is experiencing a downturn; <u>however</u>, the World Bank has left interest rates <u>unchanged</u>.

The economy is experiencing a downturn; <u>besides</u>, the World Bank has left interest rates <u>unchanged</u>.

在口译练习中，遇到上述例子时，大部分学生通常能够听到画线的关键词。然而，如果漏听或误听了关键的逻辑词"however"和"besides"，就无法正确理解整体信息。因此，掌握逻辑关系是深化信息理解的关键。以下是一些常用的逻辑关系表达方式。

（1）表顺承、补充与递进：and、what's more、besides、moreover、furthermore、in addition、additionally、further（而且，况且）、similarly、also、either、too、again（另外，还有）等。

（2）表转折：but、however、yet、instead、on the other hand（另一方面）、on the contrary

（相反地）、nevertheless（然而）、otherwise、after all（毕竟）等。

（3）表因果。

①引出原因：for、as、since、now that、because、thanks/owing/due to、because of、on account of、as a result/consequence of、in consequence of、result from（由……引起）等。

②引出结果：so、therefore、thus、hence、as a result/consequence、in consequence、consequently、account for（是……的原因）、result in（导致）、lead to（导致）、bring about（导致）、cause（导致）、so that（以致）、(so...) that等。

③（祈使句+）and/or/otherwise（+句子）。

（4）表让步：although、though、while、even if/though、while、as + 倒装句、疑问词-ever、no matter +疑问词、despite、in spite of、however、in any case等。

（5）表目的：in order to/that、so as to、for fear that、so that（以便）、lest、in case（以防，以免）等。

Practical Training

▶ Passage Retelling

Passage 1 乘风破浪潮头立，扬帆起航正当时——刘光源特派员在第四届粤港澳大湾区论坛上的主旨演讲（节选）

Warm-up Words & Expressions

副主席 vice-chairman
社长兼总编辑 publisher and editor-in-chief
副秘书长 deputy secretary-general
粤港澳大湾区论坛 Guangdong-Hong Kong-Macao Greater Bay Area Conference
外交部驻港公署 Commissioner's Office of the Ministry of Foreign Affairs in the HKSAR
以国内大循环为主体、国内国际双循环相互促进的新发展格局 a new development paradigm featuring "dual circulations", with domestic circulation as the mainstay, domestic and international circulations reinforcing each other
营商环境 business environment
创新试验场 innovation pilot zone
一国两制 one country, two systems
新标杆 new benchmark
外商直接投资 foreign direct investment
合作共赢 win-win cooperation

🎧 Listen to the following text, retell it in the source language at the end of each segment for the first time, and retell it in the target language for the second time.

尊敬的梁振英副主席，
尊敬的周树春社长兼总编辑，
尊敬的郑李锦芬副秘书长，

各位嘉宾，女士们、先生们：

大家上午好！很高兴出席第四届粤港澳大湾区论坛。我谨代表外交部驻港公署对论坛召开表示热烈祝贺！

大湾区建设是中国高水平对外开放的新窗口。中国正加快构建以国内大循环为主体、国内国际双循环相互促进的新发展格局，致力于打造更加市场化、法治化、国际化的营商环境。大湾区作为中国开放程度最高、经济活力最强的区域之一，堪称中国构建对外开放新格局的"创新试验场"。随着前海、横琴、南沙等重大合作平台稳步推进，区域内贸易、金融、科技等领域开放举措相继出台，大湾区以实际行动向世界证明，中国扩大高水平开放的决心不会变，同世界分享发展机遇的决心不会变，推动经济全球化朝着更加开放、包容、普惠、平衡、共赢方向发展的决心不会变。

大湾区建设是"一国两制"成功实践的新标杆。大湾区建设的一项基本原则就是坚守"一国"之本、善用"两制"之利，严格依照宪法和基本法办事。对港澳而言，"一国两制"是最大优势，大湾区是最佳舞台。中央政府高度重视港澳长期繁荣稳定和市民福祉，陆续推出一系列支持港澳发展、促进三地合作的政策措施，目的就是推动港澳发挥自身所长、服务国家所需，在融入国家发展大局中开拓新气象、激发新动能、展现新作为，进一步释放区域融合发展的宏阔红利、丰富"一国两制"行稳致远的生动实践。

大湾区建设是中国与世界合作共赢的新平台。大湾区建设对接高标准贸易投资规则，加快培育国际合作和竞争新优势，欢迎各国广泛参与、深化合作，共商共建共赢发展。当前区内国际贸易总额超过14万亿元，外商直接投资额达1037亿美元，数十家全球500强企业总部在此安营，越来越多的国内外人才来此安居乐业，国际一流湾区和世界级城市群的目标正在稳步实现。大湾区已然成为外国来华投资兴业的一片热土、沃土，中国与世界合作共赢的一股清流、暖流，以及全球经济平衡及可持续增长的一针催化剂、强心剂。

最后，预祝本届论坛取得圆满成功！

谢谢大家！

(https://mp.weixin.qq.com/s/nRp5wRhU1n-7ea6ta17pew)

Passage 2　The Opening Speech Delivered by the President of Princeton in 2023（Excerpt）

Warm-up Words & Expressions

Princeton 普林斯顿大学
athletic fields 运动场
myriad 无数，大量
blossom with vibrant life 焕发着勃勃生机
exhilarating and uplifting 振奋和开心
bewildering or disconcerting 困惑和不安

🎧 **Listen to the following text, retell it in the source language at the end of each segment for the first time, and retell it in the target language for the second time.**

I am delighted to greet you today as the University welcomes Princeton's Great Class of 2027 and celebrates the beginning of a new academic year.

One of the marvels of university life is the excitement that comes each fall when our classrooms, athletic fields, dining halls, and myriad other spaces across campus blossom with vibrant life and we welcome new members of our community. I am so glad that you are here!

I realize that, if the year's beginning can feel exhilarating and uplifting, so too can it feel bewildering or disconcerting. It is often all of these things at once, and that combination will likely persist during your time here.

Indeed, when I speak to Princeton alumni about their education, the word they use most often is "transformative". I would say that about my own undergraduate career at Princeton, and Anthony Romero said that about his time here. I want it to be true of yours.

Transformation is a wonderful thing. It's also very demanding. It brings worry along with joy, frustration along with happiness. That's okay, indeed, it's part of what it means to get a great education.

Professor Toni Morrison, one of the world's greatest novelists, wrote that at Princeton "Every doorway, every tree and turn is haunted by peals of laughter, murmurs of loyalty and love, tears of pleasure and sorrow and triumph."

I like this passage very much, partly because it recognizes that learning and growth are not easy, not for anyone. There will inevitably be not just triumphs but also sorrows, not just laughter but also tears, when we challenge ourselves, when we develop and change, and when we care deeply—as we should, as we must—about our academic and co-curricular endeavors and our community.

(https://mp.weixin.qq.com/s/M2IanIJAaanYMF7aK7G_MA)

Section 2　Note-taking Skills

Knowledge and Theory

在正式场合或会议场合的口译中，仅仅依靠短时记忆和长时记忆是不够的。译员通常需要在有限的时间内记下讲话人传达的信息，并用另一种语言准确、完整、迅速地传达讲话人的意思。这时，口译笔记起到了至关重要的作用。口译笔记可以帮助译员在听取信息的同时，用符号记录下关键信息，从而弥补短时记忆的不足。口译笔记具有以下特点：在理解讲话人意思的基础上进行速记；口译笔记只是辅助记忆的工具，不是口译的核心，主要还是依靠大脑记忆；口译笔记不需要记录所有内容，只需记录具有提示作用的文字、符号、数字、单词缩写、逻辑词等。

我们可以通过听一小段音频，边记忆边做笔记来练习口译笔记。首先，在音频播放结束后，依靠自己的大脑记忆和笔记用源语复述。复述时可以录音，然后回放，检查记忆的准确性。要不断练习，直到能够在边浏览、边记忆、边做笔记的情况下，完整地复述原文的内容和意思。其次，加上翻译进行训练，数量也要按照上述方法逐步增加。要练习到在边听、边记忆、边做笔记的情况下，能够完整地口译出所听到的内容。

口译常用的笔记符号是一种简单、方便、省时的工具。例如，联合国可以用"UN"代表，中国全称可以用"PRC"表示，美国全称用"USA"，英国全称可以用"B"或中文"英"字表示，加拿大可用"CA"或"加"表示等。汉语地名可以用拼音缩写代替，例如,广东可以写成"GD",北京可以写成"BJ",粤港澳大湾区可以用"GBA"表示。以下是一些常用的笔记符号。

1. 数学和标点符号

符号	中文	英文
√	正确的,好的,积极的,优秀的,肯定的	correct, good, positive, excellent, affirmative
>	大于,超出,多于,优于	surpass, exceed, more than, superior to, greater than
<	少于,不如,次于	less than, inferior to
+	更多,加上	plus, more
-	减去,减少	reduce
÷	除了	except
≠	不等于,不同,差别	unequal, difference
=	相等,相同	the same as, equal to
≈	大约,差不多,接近	about, approximate, near, roughly, approach
?	问题	problem, issue
!	吃惊,值得注意的,引人注目的	surprised, astonished, notable, noticeable
&	而且	and
……	等等,不断地,连续地	so on, constantly, continuously
( )	包括,包含	include, contain

2. 图形符号

符号	中文	英文
□	国家,组织,公司	country, organization, company
○	全球的,国际的,全部的	global, international, whole
↑	上升,上涨,发展,促进,增进	increase, go up, develop, promote, improve, enhance
↗	逐步增加,逐步发展	increase gradually, develop step-by-step
→	导致,造成,结果	lead to, result in
↘	逐步减少,逐渐放缓	decrease gradually
↓	下降,下跌,滑坡,恶化	decrease, fall, slip, worsen
:	源于,产生于	originate from, result from, as a result of
∵	因为,由于	because, owing to, thanks to
∴	因此	so, therefore, thus
⊙	会议	conference, meeting
∪	大学,学院	university, college
△	城市,城镇,都市	city, town, metropolis
▽	乡村,农村	countryside
∈	属于	belong to
∉	不属于	not belong to

续表

符号	中文	英文
∅	不完整的，不完美的	incomplete, imperfect
⊥	依赖，基于	rely on, depend on
><	对立，冲突，矛盾	conflict, confrontation, clash
β	变化，改变	change, alter, transform
$	美元，财富，富裕	dollar, wealth, rich
^	领导，管理，控制，掌控	lead, manage, control, manipulate
☆	重点，重要的，关键的，优秀的	key, important, crucial, critical, essential, excellent, brilliant
*	特点，特征，代表	representative, feature, characteristic, on behalf of
‖	道路，渠道，方式，途径	way, road, channel, method
Σ	总计	total
∞	无穷的，无止境的，无限的	endless, boundless, limitless

Note-taking Examples

Chinese to English Note-taking

为了能更好地理解运用上述笔记方法和符号，以下是一些汉译英笔记练习的例句。

（1）新形势、新趋势、新技术促进了生产力的发展，促进了各国之间的合作与交流。世界联系变得更加紧密。爱好和平与渴望发展的各国人民，正奋力推动世界走向进步和光明的未来。

【参考笔记与分析】

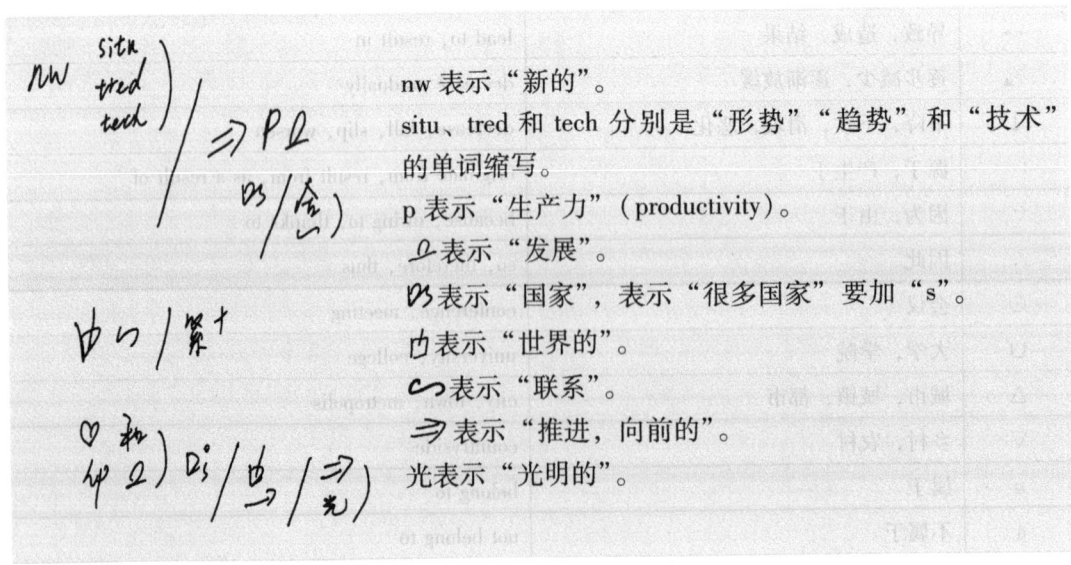

nw 表示"新的"。
situ、tred 和 tech 分别是"形势""趋势"和"技术"的单词缩写。
p 表示"生产力"（productivity）。
↗ 表示"发展"。
σs 表示"国家"，表示"很多国家"要加"s"。
凸 表示"世界的"。
∽ 表示"联系"。
⇒ 表示"推进，向前的"。
光 表示"光明的"。

【参考译文】

New situation, new trends and new technologies have helped expand productive forces, enhanced cooperation and cultural relations, and exchanges among countries and forged closer global ties. All people who love peace and long for development are working hard to create a more progressive world with a bright future.

(2) 我们要积极有效地利用外资,进一步扩大对外开放的领域和地域。逐步推进商业、外贸、银行、保险、证券、电信、旅游和中介服务等领域的对外开放。放宽外商投资在技术转让、内销比例和一些行业持股比例的限制。

【参考笔记与分析】

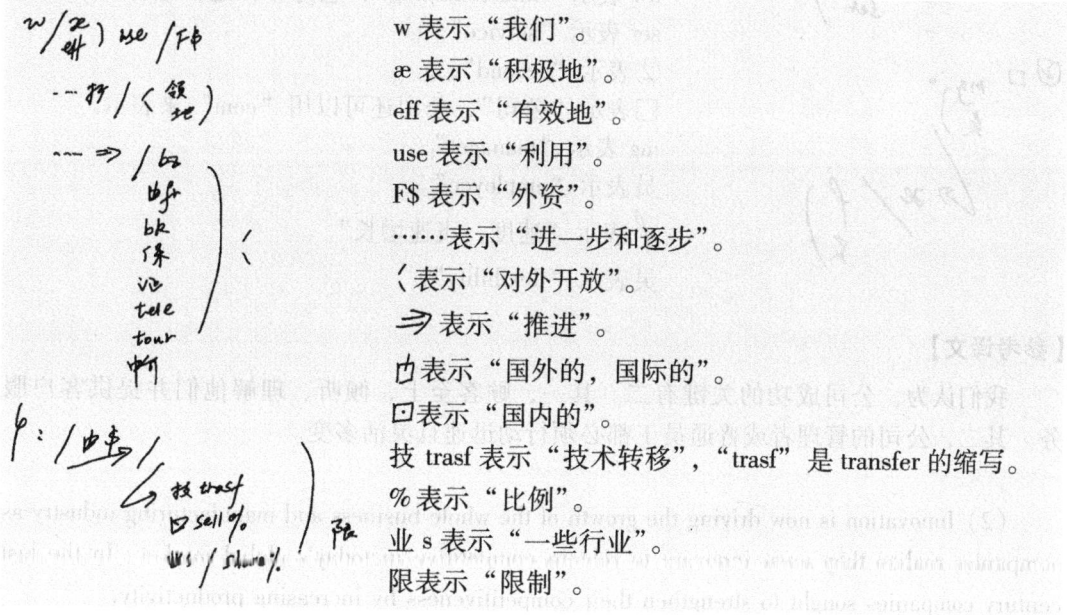

w 表示"我们"。
æ 表示"积极地"。
eff 表示"有效地"。
use 表示"利用"。
F$ 表示"外资"。
…… 表示"进一步和逐步"。
< 表示"对外开放"。
⇒ 表示"推进"。
凸 表示"国外的,国际的"。
凹 表示"国内的"。
技 trasf 表示"技术转移","trasf"是 transfer 的缩写。
% 表示"比例"。
业 s 表示"一些行业"。
限 表示"限制"。

【参考译文】

We will utilize foreign funds more effectively. The areas of operation and geographical regions open to foreign businesses will be expanded. Commerce, foreign trade, banking, insurance, securities, telecommunications, tourism and intermediary services will gradually be opened to the outside world. Restrictions will be relaxed on foreign investment pertaining to technology transfer, the proportion of products to be sold domestically and share of holdings in some industries.

English to Chinese Note-taking

为了能更好地理解运用上述笔记方法和符号,以下是一些英译汉笔记练习的例句。

(1) We believe that a business must do two things to be successful. First, it must put the customer first—by listening, understanding, and providing customer service. Second, a company—both its managers and employees—must act with speed and flexibility.

【参考笔记与分析】

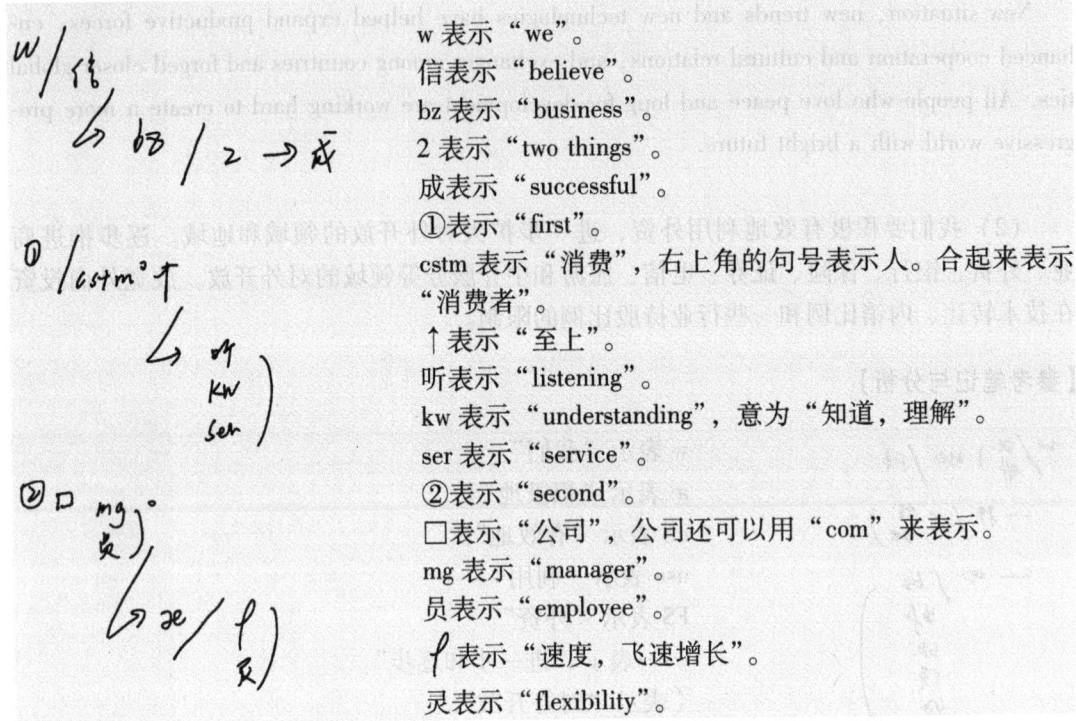

w 表示 "we"。
信 表示 "believe"。
bz 表示 "business"。
2 表示 "two things"。
成 表示 "successful"。
① 表示 "first"。
cstm 表示 "消费",右上角的句号表示人。合起来表示"消费者"。
↑ 表示 "至上"。
听 表示 "listening"。
kw 表示 "understanding",意为 "知道,理解"。
ser 表示 "service"。
② 表示 "second"。
□ 表示 "公司",公司还可以用 "com" 来表示。
mg 表示 "manager"。
员 表示 "employee"。
ʃ 表示 "速度,飞速增长"。
灵 表示 "flexibility"。

【参考译文】

我们认为,公司成功的关键有二。其一,顾客至上,倾听、理解他们并提供客户服务。其二,公司的管理者或普通员工都必须行动迅速且灵活多变。

(2) Innovation is now driving the growth of the whole business and manufacturing industry as companies realize they must innovate to remain competitive in today's global market. In the last century companies sought to strengthen their competitiveness by increasing productivity.

【参考笔记与分析】

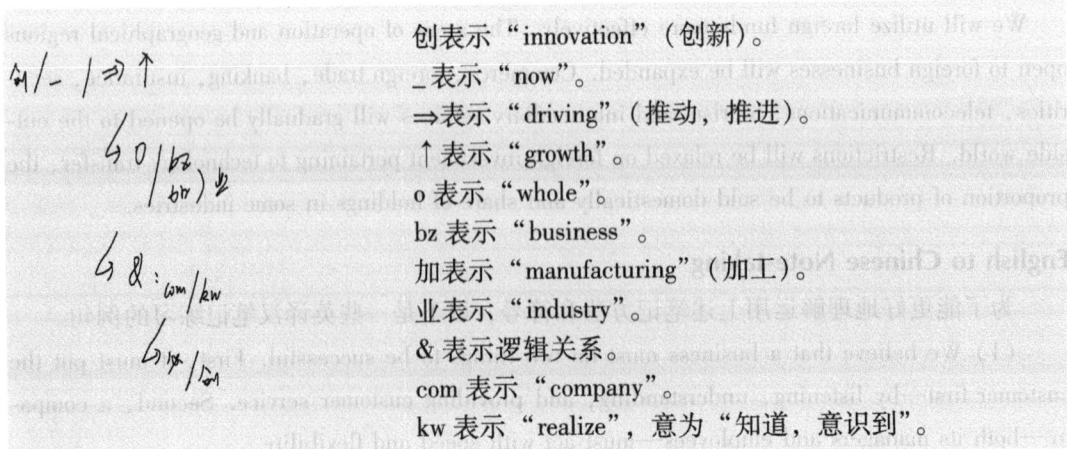

创 表示 "innovation"(创新)。
_ 表示 "now"。
⇒ 表示 "driving"(推动,推进)。
↑ 表示 "growth"。
o 表示 "whole"。
bz 表示 "business"。
加 表示 "manufacturing"(加工)。
业 表示 "industry"。
& 表示逻辑关系。
com 表示 "company"。
kw 表示 "realize",意为 "知道,意识到"。

_ 表示 "remain"。
θ力表示 "竞争力"。
市表示 "market"。
⌐ 表示 "过去"。
c 表示 "世纪"。
com 表示 "company"。
+ 表示 "strengthen"（加强）。
↳表示 "by"（通过）。
↑ 表示 "increasing"。
p 表示 "productivity"。

【参考译文】

由于各公司都意识到要想在今天的国际市场上保持竞争力就必须创新，所以创新正在推动整个工商业的发展。在上世纪，公司通过提高生产力来加强自己的竞争能力。

Practical Training

Note-taking Training

Passage 1 China-CELAC Private Sector Forum held in Dongguan, Guangdong

Warm-up Words & Expressions

China-CELAC Private Sector Forum 中拉民营经济合作论坛
trade volume 贸易额
the Community of Latin American and Caribbean States (CELAC) 拉美和加勒比国家共同体
friendly exchanges, economic cooperation and trade cooperation 友好交往和经贸合作与交流
build a market-oriented, law-based and internationalized business environment 构建市场化、法治化、国际化的营商环境
consulates general 总领事馆

📖 Please read the following passage, try to practice note-taking symbols with the methods learned, and interpret it into the target language.

The trade volume between south China's Guangdong Province and the Community of Latin American and Caribbean States (CELAC) exceeded 65.5 billion U.S. dollars in 2022, up 9.5 percent year on year, according to the China-CELAC Private Sector Forum held on May 24 in Dongguan, Guangdong.

In 2022, China-LAC trade reached 485.7 billion U.S. dollars, up 7.7 percent year on year.

With the active participation of private enterprises, Guangdong has continuously strengthened its friendly exchanges, economic cooperation and trade cooperation with Latin American and Caribbean countries in recent years. The province and CELAC have paired 18 cities with sister cities, and 11 Latin American countries have established consulates general in Guangzhou, capital of Guangdong.

In 2022, the added value of Guangdong's private economy was 6.98 trillion yuan, and the total import and export value of the province's private economy was 4.87 trillion yuan, according to the provincial government.

Guangdong will continue steadfastly promoting high-level opening-up, and building a market-oriented, law-based and internationalized business environment to deepen its private economic cooperation with Latin American and Caribbean countries.

（https://language.chinadaily.com.cn/a/202305/26/WS6470509da310b6054fad5493.html）

Passage 2 第134届广交会吸引15万采购商

Warm-up Words & Expressions

广州国际会展中心（琶洲展馆）Pazhou International Convention and Exhibition Center in Guangzhou
陶瓷产品 ceramic products
广东四通集团 Guangdong Sitong Group Co., Ltd.
"一带一路" the Belt and Road Initiative
附加值 added value
达伦特集团 Talent Group
乳木果油 shea butter
蜡烛和香薰 candle and aromatherapy
低碳原料 a low-carbon material

📖 **Please read the following passage, try to practice note-taking symbols with the methods learned, and interpret it into the target language.**

在广州国际会展中心（琶洲展馆）的一个展位上，销售经理徐亚杰一整天都在忙着向来自阿拉伯联合酋长国的买家介绍五颜六色的陶瓷产品。

徐亚杰是广东四通集团的一名员工，他说："越来越多的海外买家，特别是共建'一带一路'国家和地区的买家，对创新产品感兴趣。"

广东四通是一家位于广东潮州的陶瓷公司。在第134届广交会第二期，9674家公司展示最新的创新产品和服务。

第134届广交会第二期于10月23日开展，本期展览面积为51.5万平方米，展览以建筑材料、家具、家居装饰、礼品和家居用品等产品服务为主。

徐亚杰说，广东四通的产品出口到全球90多个市场，他在展会上展示了特别定制的陶瓷产品。

徐亚杰说："由于前期做足准备，特别是在新产品设计和研究方面加大了投资，来自中东、欧美等海外市场的买家表现出了强烈的订购意愿。"

她说，多年来凭借设计和工艺升级，公司的陶瓷制品在全球市场上获得了更高的附加值，尤其是在德国、中东和中亚。"我们发现德国的买家越来越多，德国在陶瓷制品的设计和工艺方面有更严格的市场标准。这表明了我们的产品在海外市场的竞争力。"

据活动组织者介绍，截至10月25日，第134届广交会吸引了来自214个国家和地区的约15万境外采购商到会，人数比上届同期增幅超50%。

辽宁省大连市高端香氛生产商达伦特集团在展会上展示了其最新的创新蜡烛和香薰产品。

达伦特集团董事长王立新表示，Restore系列主要由乳木果油制成，在国际市场上更具竞争力，乳木果油是一种用于蜡烛和香薰的低碳原料。

王立新说："采用低碳原料，在设计中融入中国传统文化元素，极大地提高了我们产品在全球市场的价值。在展会期间，我们的产品受到了海外买家的广泛赞誉，尤其是来自发达市场的买家。"

（https://language.chinadaily.com.cn/a/202310/26/WS653a30cea31090682a5eaefe.html）

Section 3　Syntactic Linearity

Knowledge and Theory

在口译过程中，译员会按照听到的源语句子的顺序，将整个句子分割成若干个意群或信息单位，然后使用连接词将这些单位自然地连接起来，以传达整体的意思。这种翻译方法被称为"顺句驱动"。

【例1】I come to China at an important time.
笔译：我在一个重要的时刻来到中国。
口译：我到中国来访问，正逢一个重要的时刻。

【例2】They built the bridge in two months.
笔译：他们花了两个月建这座桥。
口译：他们建这座桥，花了两个月。

【例3】Aristotle, the greatest of the ancient Greek writers, had written a work containing all the knowledge of his time.
笔译：最伟大的古希腊作家亚里士多德写过一部关于他同时代所有知识的著作。
口译：亚里士多德是最伟大的古希腊作家，曾写过一部囊括同时代所有知识的著作。

【例4】It is nevertheless many years since our two worlds first touched.
笔译：然而，我们两个世界的第一次接触已经有很多年了。
口译：但是，很久以前我们两个世界就开始接触了。

Practical Training

▶ Sentence Interpreting

📖 Use the strategy of Syntactic Linearity to interpret the following sentences.

1. I was surprised at what he said.
2. Governments have a crucial role to play in promoting social human development and in

providing the poor with the necessary working skills.

3. They have been working busily since 8 o'clock in the morning.
4. They will get the preparation done before considering other proposals.
5. My country will submit its report between now and Kyoto.

Section 4　Skills for Sight Interpreting

Knowledge and Theory

Chinese to English Sight Interpreting

视译在口译训练中扮演着非常重要的角色。在进行视译时，我们需要遵循一些基本原则，即符合英语的表达习惯和句式结构要求。此外，我们还需要掌握一些基本技巧，李长栓（2008）提出"抓住主干，搭好架子，添加细节，以及注意运用动词句型"。因此，在进行视译时，我们不能固守汉语原文的词序，而是要按照英语句法的要求来安排短语的位置。通过运用各种连接手段，比如从句、分词结构等，我们可以将有内在逻辑关系的几个短句合并成一个较长的英文句子，这样的句子长短结合富于变化，符合英语的表达习惯。

在进行译前准备时，我们可以多次推敲那些难句，寻找能够充当主语的短语或名词，以确定英义句子的主干。对于意思晦涩、结构不清的句子，我们需要反复思考，理清逻辑关系，找出主干和句子成分。

英语基本句型

1. 主语 + 系动词 + 表语（主系表结构，SVP）

【例】中国与中亚国家是同处于欧亚大陆桥上的友好邻邦。

China and countries in Central Asia are friendly neighbors in Eurasia Continent.

2. 主语 + 及物动词 + 宾语（主谓宾结构，SVO）

【例】国际直接投资持续升温，全球跨国并购日益强劲，带来了新的历史机遇和挑战。

The growing international direct investments as well as the ever-increasing transnational merges and acquisitions have brought about new historic opportunities and challenges.

3. 主语 + 不及物动词（主谓结构，SV）

【例】中国经济在过去30年里持续高速发展，创造了一个又一个奇迹。

China's economy has been developing very fast for the past 30 years, creating a number of miracles.

4. 主语 + 及物动词 + 双宾语（双宾语结构，SVOO；间接宾语指物，直接宾语指人）

【例】借此机会，我简要介绍一下中国国内经济和中法关系的情况。

Taking this opportunity, I would like to give you some information on China's economic development and the current China-French relations.

5. 主语 + 及物动词 + 宾语 + 宾语补足语（宾补结构，SVOC）

【例】因此，中国要赶上西方发达国家的经济发展与生活水平还有很长的路要走。

Therefore, China still has long way to go in order to catch up with the Western economic development and its living standards.

6. There + 系动词 + 主语（there be 结构）

【例】自由市场经济国家的企业有多种多样。

There are many types of businesses in free-market economies.

在进行视译时，首先要对汉语进行分析，抓住其大意，并迅速为译语的句子找到合适的主语和谓语，按照英语句型来组织相关成分。也就是说，我们需要选取适当的句型，抓住句子中的主要成分（主谓宾表），然后通过使用介词、连词或从句等手段来搭建好句子的结构。接下来，我们需要添加细节，即按照英语的习惯和语法规则将主要部分以外的其他部分添加到句子的主干上。

汉英视译例句解析

【例1】海洋是人类生存和发展的重要基础。

【解析】第一步，先寻找该句子的主语、谓语、宾语。主语是"海洋"，谓语是"是"，宾语是"基础"。

稿1：Ocean is a foundation.

第二步，把句子中的其他信息，如定语、状语、补语补充完整。

稿2：Ocean is an important foundation for human existence and development.

【参考译文】Ocean is an important foundation for human existence and development.

【例2】当今世界正在经历百年未有之大变局。

【解析】第一步，先寻找该句子的主语、谓语、宾语。主语是"世界"，谓语是"经历"，宾语是"变局"。

稿1：The world experiences changes.

第二步，把句子中的其他信息，如时态、定语、状语、补语补充完整。

稿2：Today's world is experiencing great changes unseen in a century.

【参考译文】Today's world is experiencing great changes unseen in a century.

【例3】中国是负责任的发展中大国，是全球气候治理的积极参与者。

【解析】第一步，先寻找该句子的主语、谓语、宾语。主语是"中国"，谓语是"是"，宾语是"大国"和"参与者"。

稿1：China is a major power and participant.

第二步，把句子中的定语补充完整。

稿2：China is a responsible developing major power and an active participant in global climate governance.

【参考译文】China is a responsible developing nation and an active participant in global climate governance.（major power 在此句子中表现累赘，因此用 nation 表示。）

English to Chinese Sight Interpreting

由于中英句子结构不同，英汉视译和汉英视译的技巧也不同。以下是一些关于英汉视译的技巧：

（1）基本按照原文语序进行原文意思的翻译（局部调整）；

（2）采用带稿同传的基本形式，有一定的原文阅读时间；

（3）视译的译文相对紧凑、复杂、繁琐（不要用笔译的标准去看待视译）；

（4）添加或者减少词汇，衔接前后意思。

英文句子往往比较长，因此划分意群在英汉视译中起着非常关键的作用。视译时，主要依据意群划分原文的层次关系。意群是指具有相对独立意义的词组或者短语（可以断开的地方）；意群切分的主要依据为介词、从句引导词、连词、标点符号等；视译速度取决于意群的切分方式，以及个人的阅读、表达能力。

视译过程包括以下四个步骤。

看：在有限的时间内，快速阅读原文意思。

切：原文意群切分（"看"和"切"同时进行）。

编：编辑意群（涉及添加或者减少词汇）。

说：组织语言输出（语速适中，减少自我修正）。

【例1】There will come a day when people the world over will live a happy life under the sun of socialism.

【解析1】There will come a day// when people the world over will live a happy life under
　　　　　　　　　　　　　①　　　　　　　　　　　　　　　　　　　②
the sun of socialism.

【译文1】全世界人民在社会主义的阳光下过着幸福生活的一天//是会来的。
　　　　　　　　　　　　　　　②　　　　　　　　　　　　　　　　①

【解析2】There will come a day// when people the world over will live a happy life under
　　　　　　　　　　　　　①　　　　　　　　　　　　　　　　　　　②
the sun of socialism.

【译文2】终究会有一天//世界人民将在社会主义阳光下过着幸福的生活。
　　　　　　　①　　　　　　　　　　②

【解析3】

There will come a day	终有一天
when people the world over	全世界人民
will live a happy life	会过上幸福的生活
under the sun of socialism	沐浴着社会主义的阳光

【译文3】终有一天，全世界人民会过上幸福的生活，沐浴着社会主义的阳光。

词性转换是英汉翻译的重要方法之一，翻译中的词性转换研究，以美国翻译理论家尤金·奈达的研究最具代表性。

1. 将英文中的名词译为汉语中的动词（名词→动词）

相比于汉语，英语在语言词性使用中，使用频率较高的是名词。因此，在英译汉时，为了实现既尊重原文的语义，又迎合译文的语言习惯这一目标，往往会将英文中的某些名词转换为汉语的动词。例如：

Mastery of a language is not easy.

掌握一门语言并非易事。

Those small factories are also lavish consumption and waster of raw materials.

这些小工厂同时大量地消耗和浪费原材料。

2. 将英文中的介词译为汉语中的动词（介词→动词）

在英文中，只有一个谓语动词，为了使语义连贯，会将介词作为连接手段。为了使译文信息准确、语义流畅，在翻译实践中往往会将英文中的介词或介词短语转换成汉语中的动词及其组成成分。例如：

Hoping to amend his condition, he left Vietnam for the United State.

为了改善生活，他离开越南，前往美国。

We need to end poverty and protect the environment for future generation.

我们要消除贫困，保护环境，造福子孙后代。

3. 英语中的有些形容词可转换为汉语动词（形容词→动词）

在英语句子中充当复合谓语成分的某些形容词，在英译汉时可将其转换为汉语动词，这些词往往是描述情绪、感知、想法等状态的形容词，如 indulgent、sorry、ignorant、kind、sweet、afraid、uneasy 等。例如：

His indulgent mother was willing to let him do anything he wanted.

他的母亲很宠他，什么事情都由着他。

The world had almost 1.1 billion fewer poor in 2013 than in 1990.

相比于1990年，2013年，世界减少了11亿贫困人口。

Practical Training

Sentence Interpreting

Please sight interpret the following sentences into the target language.

1. 实现各国人民对美好生活的向往，是共建"一带一路"的初心。
2. 现在许多西方人都知道，与别国人相比，中国人一向是最不关心宗教的。
3. 在中国文化中，虎是勇敢和力量的象征。
4. 2022届高校毕业生规模预计1076万人。
5. 2021年北京地区生产总值比上年增长8.5%。
6. Jo's quarrel with her friend Laurie finally reaches a peaceful settlement.
7. For Westerners in China, the establishment of an effective team of managers means attracting local management talent.
8. With a rifle across his shoulder the boy was playing the soldier.
9. *Pilgrim's Progress* is an allegory of the temptations and victories of man's soul.
10. Americans remain split （分裂的、分歧的）on whether NAFTA（North American Free Trade Area）is beneficial for the United States.

Passage Interpreting

Passage 1　APEC 经济体应秉持开放态度（节选）

Warm-up Words & Expressions

商务部 Ministry of Commerce
亚太经济合作组织（APEC）部长级会议 Asia-Pacific Economic Cooperation Ministerial Meeting
多边贸易体制 multilateral trade system
区域经济一体化、供应链合作、数字经济 regional economic integration, supply chain cooperation, digital economy
自由贸易协定 free trade agreement
亚太自贸区 Free Trade Area of the Asia-Pacific (FTAAP)
《区域全面经济伙伴关系协定》（RCEP）Regional Comprehensive Economic Partnership Agreement
《全面与进步跨太平洋伙伴关系协定》（CPTPP）Comprehensive and Progressive Agreement for Trans-Pacific Partnership
国际货币基金组织 International Monetary Fund
大型物流企业 logistics conglomerate
叶水福集团 YCH Group

Please sight interpret the following text into the target language.

商务部 11 月 16 日在一份网上声明中称，亚太经济合作组织（APEC）部长级会议围绕支持多边贸易体制、区域经济一体化、供应链合作、数字经济、促进包容、可持续贸易投资等议题进行了讨论。

王受文呼吁在世贸组织第十三届部长级会议之前再次举行高官会，凝聚共识。他提出，APEC 要秉持开放态度，推动投资便利化等联合声明倡议取得成果并纳入多边框架。

商务部数据显示，2022 年我国与 APEC 成员的进出口总额达到 3.74 万亿美元，占我国进出口总额的 59.7%。在中国前十大贸易伙伴中有 8 个是 APEC 成员。

中国是 13 个 APEC 经济体的第一大贸易伙伴。有 15 个 APEC 经济体和我国签署了自由贸易协定。

根据商务部数据，2022 年我国利用的其他 APEC 经济体的直接投资占我国外商直接投资总额的 86.6%；在我国前十大外资来源地中，有 5 个是 APEC 成员。

王受文指出，APEC 要坚持亚太自贸区的主渠道地位。《区域全面经济伙伴关系协定》（RCEP）和《全面与进步跨太平洋伙伴关系协定》（CPTPP）是 APEC 领导人共同确定的亚太自贸区的两条可能路径，要坚持开放包容、不断推进扩员进程，以惠及更多经济体。

王受文表示，要坚持发展优先，充分照顾发展中经济体的利益。中方愿与更多 APEC 经济体加强数字经济和绿色发展领域的务实合作。

国际货币基金组织近日将 2023 年中国经济的增长预期从 5% 上调为 5.4%。王受文表示，中方将进一步扩大高水平对外开放，愿与 APEC 经济体和全球分享中国大市场发展机遇，共同推进高质量发展与繁荣。

新加坡大型物流企业叶水福集团的执行主席叶进国表示，叶水福集团将在亚太地区提供更多供应链解决方案，成为中国区域贸易和供应链的重要纽带。

11月早些时候，叶水福集团在上海举行的第六届中国国际进口博览会上宣布和两家中国企业达成了战略合作伙伴关系。

叶进国表示：“这些合作超越了传统的业务拓展，将着力于提供创新化解决方案，帮助中国企业克服在国际业务扩张时所面临的运营方面的挑战，助力中国企业进入东盟国家市场。”

（https://language.chinadaily.com.cn/a/202311/17/WS655718c5a31090682a5eecc7.html）

Passage 2 Opening Assembly Address, Yale College Class of 2027 (Except)

Warm-up Words & Expressions

academic distinction 学术造诣
leadership savvy 领导才能
outstanding motivation 出色的驱动力
Bright College Years《美好校园年华》

Please sight interpret the following text into the target language.

Good morning!

It gives me a great pleasure to welcome you, our entering students, and your family members to campus, and to mark officially the start of your undergraduate education. I'm glad this day has arrived and I'm so glad you are here.

It is evident why you belong at Yale. Your academic distinction, leadership savvy, and outstanding motivation solidify your standing among students who have sat for centuries where you are sitting today. What is more, the richness of your diversity—across every dimension—reflects Yale's commitment to creating an inclusive educational environment.

Now, as you prepare to enter Yale—and leave your unique imprint on it—allow me to alert you to a perennial observation among our alumni. Many of your predecessors, I must caution, have marveled at the breakneck clip at which today's festivities give way to your graduation.

It's a hard truth codified in one of Yale's most celebrated traditions, the singing of our unofficial alma mater, "*Bright College Years*". Your time here is described as the "shortest, gladdest years of life", and as "gliding by" "swiftly" in fact.

So I encourage you to savor the qualities that drew you to this remarkable place.

（https://mp.weixin.qq.com/s/DyWgbwY8jqcGWUba27HVEg）

Section 5　Figures Interpreting

Knowledge and Theory

数字口译是英汉口译的难点，也是口译中非常重要的一部分。汉英数字常用单位存在差异，因此了解中英文读数体系的差别对于语言转换至关重要。下表对比了英汉两种语言的数字单位。

英语数字三位数分法

第一段位	one	ten	hundred
第二段位	thousand	ten thousand	hundred thousand
第三段位	million	ten million	hundred million
第四段位	billion	ten billion	hundred billion
第五段位	trillion		

汉语数字四位数分段法

第一段位	个	十	百	千
第二段位	万	十万	百万	千万
第三段位	亿	十亿	百亿	千亿
第四段位	兆（万亿）			

Comparison of English and Chinese Numerical Expressions

在汉语中，我们通常将每四个数字划分为一个单位，用一些具体的词如"个""万""亿"来代表这些单位。在处理成英语数字时，"个"对应的表述是"one"，"万"对应的表述是"ten thousand"，"亿"对应的表述是"a hundred million"。在英语中，我们通常将每三个数字划分为一个单位，如"thousand"是"千"，"million"是"百万"，"billion"是"十亿"。下表给出了英汉数字表达对比示例。

Comparison of English and Chinese Number Expressions

数字	英语	汉语
1	one	个
10	ten	十
100	one hundred	百
1,000	one thousand	千
10,000	ten thousand	万
100,000	one hundred thousand	十万

续表

数字	英语	汉语
1,000,000	one million	百万
10,000,000	ten million	千万
100,000,000	one hundred million	亿
1,000,000,000	one billion	十亿
10,000,000,000	ten billion	百亿
100,000,000,000	one hundred billion	千亿
1,000,000,000,000	one trillion	万亿

The Method of "Commas and Slashes"

此方法即用逗号","进行三位数分段，斜杠"/"进行四位数分段。

【例1】三十亿零七万九千八百四十二

【解析】在处理中文译文时，我们通常每隔四个数字使用一个斜杠来记录，例如：30/0007/9842。

【例2】3000079842

【解析】在处理英文译文时，我们通常每隔三个数字使用一个逗号来记录，例如：3,000,079,842，也就是"three billion seventy-nine thousand eight hundred and forty-two"。

要想做好英汉数字口译，必须进行大量的训练，要让转换成为一种自然而然的能力，这样才能够在翻译的数字比较多时从容不迫。

Skills for Expressing Multiples

甲是乙的两倍 $\begin{cases} \text{A is twice as...as B} \\ \text{A is twice the amount/number/size/length of B} \\ \text{A increases by 100\%/double} \end{cases}$

【例1】他们今年的产量是去年的两倍。

译文：Their output this year is twice as much as what it was last year.

【例2】他们今年的产量比去年增加了一倍。

译文：Their output this year is twice the amount of what it was last year.

【例3】他们今年的产量比去年翻了一番。

译文1：Their output this year is double what it was last year.

译文2：Their output this year has increased by 100% over last year.

Expressing the Decrease in Quantity

数量减少的表达与介词息息相关，不同的介词搭配表示的意思不同。以下表格提供了一些表达数量减少的例子。

Expressing the Decrease of Quantity

汉语	英语
降到20%/减少80%	reduce to 20%
减少20%（只有80%）	reduce by 20%
下降30%	fall by 30%/drop by 30%
使……缩短为原来的五分之一（缩短五分之四）	shorten...5 times...
减少四分之三	reduce by three forths

Fractions

(1) The numerator is one.

If the numerator is one, the numerator should be unchanged and the denominator should be the ordinal numeral form. As for special expressions of figure, such as half and quarter, the numerator can use a as well as one.

  e.g. 1/5 五分之一 one-fifth
     1/2 二分之一 a/one half
     1/4 四分之一 a/one quarter

(2) The numerator is not one.

If the numerator is not one, the plural form should be used for the denominator.

  e.g. 3/5 五分之三 three-fifths
     9/10 十分之九 nine-tenths

(3) Pronouncing fractions with big numerator and denominator.

In case the numerator and denominator are big numbers, both are pronounced as cardinal numbers, but they are joined by the word "over" in between.

  e.g. 53/79 七十九分之五十三 fifty-three over seventy-nine
     26/95 九十五分之二十六 twenty-six over ninety-five

Decimals

The decimal point is read as "point" or "o" or "zero".

  e.g. 0.8 point eight, zero/naught point eight
     98.53 ninety-eight point five three

👉 Practical Training

▶ **Sentence Interpreting**

🎧 Listen to the following sentences and interpret them from the source language into the target language. You may take notes while listening.

1. 2023年第一季度，广东一般贸易进出口1.06万亿元，增长3.8%，占广东外贸进出口总值的57.5%。

2. 跨境物流的全面恢复促进了保税业务发展，第一季度广东保税物流进出口3 156.4亿元，增长14.8%。

3. 广东对共建"一带一路"国家的进出口增长10.9%，占进出口总值的29.4%；对RCEP其他成员国进出口增长2.8%。

4. Gross imports in 2007 are expected to increase by 6.5 percent over 2006 levels while exports are expected to decrease by 4.0 percent. Net imports are expected to increase by about 8.6 percent in 2007, followed by a 1.4 percent decrease in 2008.

5. Based on reports from underground storage facilities for December 1, natural gas in storage reached an all-time record of 35,450. This is 8.9 percent above the 5-year (2002—2006) average of 32,540 billion cubic feet.

6. In 1978 China built only 149 thousand vehicles. Annual vehicle production reached 1 million units in 1992; 2 million units in 2000; 5 million units in 2004 and more than 9 million units in 2008.

▶ Passage Interpreting

🎧 **Listen to the following passages and interpret them from the source language into the target language. You may take notes while listening.**

Passage 1

10月我国工业企业利润连续3个月实现正增长，表明经济进一步企稳向好。国家统计局11月27日发布的数据显示，10月全国规模以上工业企业（年主营业务收入在2000万元及以上的工业企业）利润同比增长2.7%，9月规模以上工业企业利润同比增长11.9%。

国家统计局统计师于卫宁将工业企业利润持续恢复向好归功于宏观政策效果持续显现，工业生产稳定增长，工业企业营收加快回升。统计局称，1—10月，全国规模以上工业企业实现利润总额61 154.2亿元，同比下降7.8%，降幅较1—9月（9%）收窄。

值得注意的是，随着下游需求不断恢复，10月原材料制造业利润实现大幅增长，增速达到22.9%。随着扩内需促消费政策逐渐生效，10月消费品制造业利润增长2.2%，连续3个月增长。国家统计局的数据显示，1—10月，装备制造业利润同比增长1.1%。

(https://language.chinadaily.com.cn/a/202311/28/WS6565ab0fa31090682a5f06ed.html)

Passage 2

China's total import and export value of goods amounted to 37.96 trillion yuan from January to November 2023, remaining consistent with the corresponding period from the previous year, data from the General Administration of Customs showed on December 7.

The country's exports grew by 0.3 percent year-on-year to 21.6 trillion yuan during the 11-month-period, while imports stood at 16.36 trillion yuan, experiencing a 0.5 percent fall on a yearly basis. Its trade surplus reached 5.24 trillion yuan, expanding by 2.8 percent year-on-year.

In November alone, China's import and export value reached 3.7 trillion yuan, showing a 1.2

percent growth year-on-year, according to the General Administration of Customs.

China exported 12.66 trillion yuan of mechanical and electrical products in the first 11 months, an increase of 2.8 percent year-on-year, accounting for 58.6 percent of the country's total export value.

(https://language.chinadaily.com.cn/a/202312/08/WS6572ca95a31040ac301a6ddb.html)

Project 1
Business Reception

Unit 2 Protocol Routine

Learning Objectives

- Gain some cultural background knowledge about protocol routine
- Master the frequently used words, phrases, sentence patterns, etc. in protocol routine
- Understand what and how to prepare for the interpreting tasks in the long run

Ideological and Political Objectives

- Value moral principles and carry on etiquette traditions
- Be humble, polite, and genuine with others to cultivate a good image
- Be confident yet modest, inclusive and magnanimous, demonstrating the poise of a great nation
- Maintain a rigorous work ethic and professionalism

Section 1 Interpreting Preparation

Key Concepts

1. China-Africa community with a shared future 中非命运共同体

At the Forum on China-Africa Cooperation (FOCAC) Beijing Summit on September 3, 2018, President Xi Jinping further proposed building a closer China-Africa community with a shared future. He called on both sides to assume joint responsibility, pursue win-win cooperation, deliver happiness for all, enjoy cultural prosperity and common security, and promote harmony between man and nature.

2. Cantonese cuisine 粤菜

Cantonese cuisine ranks among China's top four cuisines and is comprised of Guangzhou cuisine, Chaozhou cuisine, and Dongjiang cuisine. Guangzhou cuisine is the quintessential form of Cantonese cuisine.

Guangzhou cuisine has evolved into its unique form by integrating folk delicacies throughout Guangdong Province, absorbing the strong points of all major Chinese cuisines and drawing on selected strengths of Western recipes. It is characterized by the diversity of the ingredients used, the rigor of their selection, the polished culinary skills applied and a seemingly endless variety of dishes. The Guangzhou Renowned Dishes and Delicacies Expo in 1956 featured more than 5,447 dishes as well as 815 dim sum platters and hundreds of snacks.

3. Tao Tao Ju 陶陶居

Tao Tao Ju, originating in 1880, is a historic Chinese time-honored brand in Guangdong. Not only is it a Cantonese restaurant where you can enjoy "a nice cup of tea and two kinds of dim sum", but also can participate in and witness Lingnan culture. Now, Tao Tao Ju actively meets the needs of youngsters and adds the elements of China-chic, which has become a major force in renovating old towns.

4. Cantonese opera 粤剧

As one of the local operas in Guangdong, Cantonese opera is very popular among Cantonese-speaking people and overseas Chinese. The opera enjoys a good reputation of being "Southern Red Bean". In 2009, Cantonese opera was listed as a world intangible cultural heritage.

5. COP26 第26届联合国气候变化大会

The UN Climate Change Conference in Glasgow (COP26) brought together 120 world leaders and over 40,000 registered participants, including 22,274 party delegates, 14,124 observers and 3,886 media representatives. For two weeks, the world was riveted on all facets of climate change—the science, the solutions, the political will to act, and clear indications of action.

The outcome of COP26—the *Glasgow Climate Pact*—is the fruit of intense negotiations among almost 200 countries over the two weeks, strenuous formal and informal work over many months, and constant engagement both in-person and virtually for nearly two years.

Cuts in global greenhouse gas emissions are still far from where they need to be to preserve a livable climate, and support for the most vulnerable countries affected by the impacts of climate change is still falling far short. But COP26 did produce new "building blocks" to advance implementation of the *Paris Agreement* through actions that can get the world on a more sustainable, low-carbon pathway forward.

6. Absolute poverty 绝对贫困

Absolute poverty has two criteria. First, the baseline for poverty is absolute, it refers to the basic living standards or basic needs for human subsistence. Second, it means a condition of extreme poverty, with a severe shortage of basic necessities of life or extreme deprivation of basic human needs. Absolute poverty is also called "subsistence poverty" or "basic needs poverty" in some developing countries.

To determine whether an individual or family is living under absolute poverty, an acceptable wellbeing line (absolute poverty line) is set for basic needs or minimum living conditions for subsistence, and the individual or family will be defined as suffering absolute poverty if their wellbeing (income or consumption) falls below this line.

There are a number of ways to define the absolute poverty line, such as the Market Basket Method, Engle's Ratio Method and Martin Method.

7. Green development 绿色发展

As one of the Five Concepts for Development, green development highlights the importance of harmony between man and nature.

The report to the 19th CPC National Congress pointed out that China will step up efforts to establish a legal and policy framework that promotes green production and consumption, and promote a sound economic structure that facilitates green, low-carbon, and circular development. China will create a market-based system for green technology innovation, develop green finance, and encourage the development of energy-saving and environmental protection industries as well as clean production and clean energy industries. China will promote a revolution in energy production and consumption, and build an energy sector that is clean, low-carbon, safe and efficient.

China will encourage conservation across the board and promote recycling, take action to ensure that everyone conserves water, cut consumption of energy and materials, and establish linkages between the circular use of resources and materials in industrial production and in everyday life. China encourage simple, moderate, green, and low-carbon ways of life, and oppose extravagance and excessive consumption. China will launch initiatives to make Party and government offices do better when it comes to conservation, and develop eco-friendly families, schools, communities, and transport services.

8. Global Development Initiative 全球发展倡议

The Global Development Initiative (GDI) was proposed by Chinese President Xi Jinping at the 76th Session of the UN General Assembly in September 2021. It was put forward with the hope that countries would work together to overcome the impact of COVID-19 on global development, accelerate the implementation of the 2030 Agenda for Sustainable Development, and build a global community of development with a shared future.

9. Global Security Initiative 全球安全倡议

President Xi Jinping, with the future of all humanity in mind, proposed the Global Security Initiative (GSI) for the first time at the opening ceremony of the Boao Forum for Asia Annual Conference 2022. This initiative gives explicit answers to questions of our times such as what security concept the world needs and how countries can achieve common security, providing important guiding principles for resolving security dilemmas faced by humanity.

The GSI stresses that we humanity are living in an indivisible security community. It has six core tenets: stay committed to the vision of common, comprehensive, cooperative and sustainable security, and work together to maintain world peace and security; stay committed to respecting the sovereignty and territorial integrity of all countries, uphold non-interference in internal affairs, and respect the independent choices of development paths and social systems made by people in different countries; stay committed to abiding by the purposes and principles of the UN Charter, reject the Cold War mentality, oppose unilateralism, and say no to group politics and bloc confrontation; stay committed to taking the legitimate security concerns of all countries seriously, uphold the principle of indivisible security, build a balanced, effective and sustainable security architecture, and oppose the pursuit of one's own security at the cost of others' security; stay committed to peacefully resolving differences and disputes between countries through dialogue and consultation, support all efforts conducive to the peaceful settlement of crises, reject double standards, and oppose the wanton use of unilateral sanctions and long-arm jurisdiction; stay committed to maintaining security in both traditional and non-traditional domains, and work together on regional disputes and global challenges such as terrorism, climate change, cybersecurity and biosecurity. These six tenets not only demonstrate macro thinking of top-level design, but also contain micro perspective of solving practical problems. They chime with the shared aspiration of the international community for peace, cooperation and development.

10. Global Civilization Initiative 全球文明倡议

Confronted with the questions of the world, the history and the era, President Xi Jinping put forward the Global Civilization Initiative in March 2022 after presenting the Global Development Initiative and the Global Security Initiative. Through these initiatives, China has made its own devotion to the international community to cope with the common challenges and helped build strong support for the promotion of the community with a shared future for mankind.

The core concepts of the Global Civilization Initiative are to advocate the respect for the diversity of civilizations, advocate the common values of humanity, advocate the importance of inheritance and innovation of civilizations, and advocate robust international people-to-people exchanges and cooperation.

The Global Civilization Initiative advocates that countries need to uphold the principles of equality, mutual learning, dialogue and inclusiveness among civilizations, and let cultural exchanges transcend estrangement, mutual learning transcend clashes, and coexistence transcend feelings of superiority. This reflects China's outlook on civilization in working with other countries to promote the concept that each country has its own beauty and beauties of all countries should be cherished and respected by all.

Sight Interpreting

Passage 1 A Welcoming Speech for the Chinese Delegation

Warm-up Words & Expressions

vineyard 葡萄园
heartfelt gratitude 衷心的感谢
showcase 展示
excellence 卓越
avenue 选择；途径；渠道
esteemed 受尊敬的；受敬重的
milestone 里程碑
winemaking 酿酒

dedication 献身；奉献
catalyst 催化剂
forge long-lasting partnership 建立长期的伙伴关系
blend（不同事物的）和谐结合，融合
embody the essence 体现本质
exceptional 杰出的；优秀的；独特的
sustainability 可持续性

Read Passage 1 and interpret it from English into Chinese.

Ladies and gentlemen,

Good evening!

I'm truly honored to be here to extend a warm welcome to our distinguished guests from China.

On behalf of Simon Vineyard, I would like to express our heartfelt gratitude for your presence here today.

We are truly delighted to have this opportunity to showcase the beauty and excellence of our vineyard, and to explore potential avenues for business cooperation with our esteemed Chinese partners. This visit marks a significant milestone in our journey towards fostering stronger ties between our two countries.

As we gather here at our vineyard, I am reminded of the shared passion and appreciation for the art of winemaking that unites us. Our vineyard, nestled in the heart of Australia's renowned wine region, has been nurtured with love and dedication for generations. We take immense pride in producing some of the finest wines that have gained recognition both locally and internationally.

Today, we are privileged to have our Chinese friends here with us. Your presence shows that there is an increasing interest and demand for Australian wines in the Chinese market. We firmly believe that this visit will serve as a catalyst for forging long-lasting partnerships and opening new avenues for collaboration.

Our vineyard stands as a testament to the harmonious blend of tradition and innovation. We have embraced modern techniques while staying true to the time-honored practices that have been passed down through generations. This unique combination has allowed us to create wines that embody the essence of our land, capturing the flavors and aromas that make Australian wines truly exceptional.

We are confident that our vineyard's commitment to quality, sustainability, and innovation will resonate with you. We believe that by joining forces, we can create a partnership that will not only benefit our respective businesses but also contribute to the cultural exchange and mutual understanding between our nations.

Once again, I extend my warmest welcome to you all. May this visit be the beginning of a fruitful partnership, one that will bring our nations closer together and create a legacy of shared success.

Thank you.

Passage 2 习近平在中法企业家委员会第六次会议闭幕式上的致辞（节选）

Warm-up Words & Expressions

亚欧大陆 Eurasian continent
地缘政治矛盾 geopolitical conflicts
根本利益冲突 clashes of fundamental interests
务实合作 result-oriented cooperation
全方位交流合作 all-round exchanges and cooperation
全面战略伙伴关系 comprehensive strategic partnership
经贸内涵 economic and trade dimensions
免签政策 visa exemption entry
人员往来 people-to-people exchanges
政治互信 political mutual trust
化解分歧 resolve differences

Read Passage 2 and interpret it from Chinese into English.

女士们、先生们、朋友们！

中法两国同属亚欧大陆，一个在东端，一个在西端；一个是东方文明的重要代表，一个是西方文明的重要代表。中法两国没有地缘政治矛盾，没有根本利益冲突，有着独立自主的精神共鸣，有着灿烂文化的彼此吸引，更有着利益广泛的务实合作。有历史可鉴，有现实可依，中法两国没有理由不发展好双边关系。站在人类发展新的十字路口，面对世界百年变局的风云际会，中方愿同法方密切全方位交流合作，推动中法关系迈上更高水平，取得更大成绩。

——面向未来，我们愿同法方一道充实中法全面战略伙伴关系的经贸内涵。法国是最早参与中国改革开放进程的国家之一，为中国现代化建设作出了贡献并从中受益。深化友谊就要经常来往、加强合作。我们始终视法国为优先和可信赖的合作伙伴，致力于拓展双边经贸关系的广度和深度，开辟新领域、创造新模式、培育新增长点。中方愿继续积极利用"从法国农场到中国餐桌"全链条快速协同机制，让奶酪、火腿、葡萄酒等更多法国优质农产品出现在中国老百姓餐桌上。中方决定，将对法国等12国公民短期来华的免签政策延长至2025年年底，这将有利于促进两国人员往来。

——面向未来，我们愿和法方共同推动中欧互利合作。中欧是推动多极化的两大力量、支持全球化的两大市场、倡导多样性的两大文明，中欧关系关乎世界和平、稳定、繁荣。双方要坚持全面战略伙伴关系正确定位，不断增强政治互信，排除各种干扰，共同反对经贸问题政治化、意识形态化、泛安全化。期待欧方同中方相向而行，以对话增进理解，以合作化解分歧，以互信消除风险，将中欧打造成为彼此经贸合作的关键伙伴、科技合作的优先伙伴、产业链供应链合作的可信伙伴。中方将自主扩大电信、医疗等服务业对外开放，进一步开放市场，为包括法国和欧洲企业在内的各国企业创造更多市场机遇。

（https://www.gov.cn/yaowen/liebiao/202405/content_6949484.htm）

Memory Practice

Listen to the following paragraphs carefully without taking notes and then retell the main ideas in the source language based on your memory.

1. What is the main idea of Paragraph 1?
2. What is the main idea of Paragraph 2?

Section 2　Interpreting Practice

Dialogue 1　Receiving the Guest at the Airport

Warm-up Words & Expressions

市场部经理 marketing manager
claim one's luggage 取某人的行李
jet-lag 时差
小吃 snack

thoughtful 体贴的；关心别人的；周到的
带……逛逛 show sb. around
Cantonese cuisine 粤菜；广东菜

🎧 **Listen to Dialogue 1 and interpret it into the target language.**

A: 请问，您是从新西兰来的布朗先生吗？

B: Yes, I'm Tony Brown from Summer Import and Export Company. You must be Mr. Li, if I'm not mistaken.

A: 是的，我叫李明，是广州市自然美化妆品有限公司市场部经理。布朗先生，很高兴认识您，欢迎来到广州！

B: It's a pleasure to meet you. Thank you for coming to meet me at the airport.

A: 不客气，旅途还顺利吧？

B: It was pleasant all the way. By the way, where should I claim my luggage?

A: 这边请。

B: Thank you so much.

A: 长途旅行后一定很累了吧。

B: I'm a bit tired after such a long journey. I'm very bad with a jet-lag. But I'll be all right tomorrow morning.

A: 好的，行李都齐了，我先开车送您回酒店。酒店位于湖边，风景优美。离机场只有半小时的车程，相信您一定会喜欢的。

B: That's wonderful. I love living in the hotel with a good view.

A: 我们已经在酒店房间为您准备了一些小吃，希望能为您补充一点能量。

B: It's really thoughtful of you. Thank you so much.

A: 不用谢，明天晚上7点我们将设宴为您接风洗尘！对了，您有想去观光的地方吗？我非常乐意带您逛逛。

B: Well, it depends. If everything goes well, I'd leave a day for sightseeing. I'm very interested in Cantonese cuisine and culture. I really want to visit some must-see attractions. And I hope to gain a deeper understanding of Guangzhou.

A: 没问题，观光的事情我来安排。广州的确有着丰富的文化遗产和许多值得逛的景点。

B: Thank you very much. I'm really looking forward to it.

A: 不客气。希望您玩得开心。明天见！

B: See you!

Dialogue 2 Hotel Check-in

Warm-up Words & Expressions

check in 办理入住   extra charge 额外费用
豪华套房 deluxe suite   regular rate 常规费用

🎧 **Listen to Dialogue 2 and interpret it into the target language.**

A: 下午好，欢迎来到新世纪酒店。有什么可以帮到您的吗？

B: Yes, I'd like to check in, please.

A: 好的，先生，请问您尊姓大名？有没有预订房间？

B: Yes, it's Tony Brown. I suppose someone has made a reservation for me.

A: 稍等，我这就帮您查一下。让您久等了，先生。不过，这里查不到您的预订记录。请问您预订的日期是？

B: I booked for today through Friday this week, 4 nights in total.

A: 我明白了。让我再仔细看一下……原来如此，我们的预订系统最近升级了，可能出现了一些小问题。非常抱歉给您造成不便。

B: No problem, these things happen.

A: 您放心，我们还有空房间。我查一下，哦，还有一间双人间和一间豪华套房没人入住。不知您要哪一套呢？

B: Many thanks. I prefer the double room. How long can I keep it? Is there any extra charge besides the regular rate?

A: 您可以一直住到周五，房费保持原定价格，我们会免费提供早餐以示歉意。

B: That's very kind of you! I was a bit worried I wouldn't have a room.

A: 不用谢，这是我们应该做的。希望您在新世纪酒店度过愉快的时光。有任何需要都请直接与我联系。

B: Great, thank you so much for your help!

Dialogue 3 Discussing the Schedule

Warm-up Words & Expressions

metropolis 大都市
schedule 日程安排
生产车间 production plant
美食 delicacy
give insights into 深入了解……
广府文化 Guangzhou culture
marketing team 营销团队

immerse oneself in 沉浸于……
总结会议 wrap-up meeting
告别午宴 farewell luncheon
安排 arrangement
thoughtful itinerary 周到的行程规划
partnership opportunities 合作机会

🎧 **Listen to Dialogue 3 and interpret it into the target language.**

A: 布朗先生，您之前来过广州吗？

B: No. This is my first visit to the city, but I heard a lot about it. Guangzhou is a historically and culturally rich metropolis that serves as one of China's most important economic and transportation centers. I'm very much looking forward to exploring the city.

A: 太好了。布朗先生，我已经安排了您这几天在广州的行程。如果有哪里需要修改的话，请一定告诉我。

B: OK. Could you brief me on the schedule first?

A: 当然可以。今天下午没有任何安排，您可以好好休息调整时差。晚上5点半，我们总经理会在广州酒家设宴欢迎您。

B: Wonderful, that will give me time to rest up from the flight. What's on the agenda for tomorrow?

A: 明天上午9点至11点，安排了参观我们的生产车间和实验室。这可以让您更全面地了解我们的产品质量和生产流程。中午12点在希尔顿酒店用餐。下午我们会进行一场商务会议来讨论合作细节和市场策略。晚上我们会一起品尝地道的广州美食。

B: That sounds fantastic. I'm particularly interested in seeing your production facility and having the business meeting. It will give me valuable insights into your company and products.

A: 很高兴您对我们的工厂感兴趣。后天上午，我们会先在陶陶居吃早餐，陶陶居是一家历史悠久的中华老字号餐厅。然后参观广州的一些零售商和美容院，感受我们产品的市场推广情况和受欢迎程度。下午，我们会与营销团队见面，讨论营销策略。晚上，我们会带您欣赏一场粤剧表演，领略广府文化的魅力。

B: That agenda sounds great. I look forward to seeing your marketing in action and hearing from your marketing team. The cultural experience will be an excellent opportunity to immerse myself in Guangzhou's heritage.

A: 最后一天，我们会进行一次总结会议，确定合作细节。之后会举办告别午宴，庆祝我们的合作。您乘坐的是会议结束后第二天早上10点的航班，我会在早上8点来酒店接您，送您去广州白云国际机场。您觉得这些安排可以吗？

B: It looks like very productive and enriching days. Thank you for planning such a thoughtful itinerary, Mr. Li. I'm very excited about the partnership opportunities ahead.

A: 不用谢，布朗先生。这都是我应该做的。非常期待与您的合作！

Dialogue 4 Seeing off at the Airport

Warm-up Words & Expressions

战略合作关系 strategic partnership
研发实力 R&D (research and development) capability
直观的 intuitive
production facility 生产设备

魅力 charm
vibrant 充满活力的
机场航站楼 airport terminal
值机柜台 check-in counter
stay in touch 保持联系

🎧 Listen to Dialogue 4 and interpret it into the target language.

A: 布朗先生，参观即将结束，感谢您的到访。这次合作让我们获益良多，非常高兴可以与贵公司建立战略合作关系。

B: Mr. Li, I would also like to express my gratitude for your company's warm hospitality. This has been a very successful business visit. I have been deeply impressed by your company's products and services.

A: 希望通过这次对工厂和实验室的参观，能让您对我们的产品质量和研发实力有更直观的了解。未来我们可以在多个领域开展合作。

B: Yes, I'm truly impressed by your production facilities and R&D capabilities. I'm confident we can build a strong partnership across multiple regions. The business meetings were also very productive.

A: 广州是一座历史悠久的城市，非常欢迎您日后再次光临，继续探索这座城市的文化魅力。

B: Guangzhou is such a vibrant city with rich history and culture. I thoroughly enjoyed exploring the sights and experiencing the local cuisine and customs. This was a truly memorable visit.

The more I know about Guangzhou, the more I want to learn. There are still so many places that I'd like to visit.

A: 是的，衷心祝愿我们的合作之路一帆风顺。欢迎您随时再访问广州。

B: Thank you. I hope our partnership will continue to prosper. I look forward to future visits to Guangzhou and your company!

A: 我们已经到了机场航站楼。您乘坐的是哪家航空公司的航班？

B: China Southern Airlines.

A: 南方航空的航班在1号航站楼。请您直走，穿过前面几道门，然后向右转，就能看到值机柜台了。

B: Thanks for spending the afternoon with me. Although this was a short trip, it was very productive. Thank you again for all your assistance. I will cherish this experience. Let's stay in touch.

A: 当然！期待您的下一次广州之行。

B: Certainly, I will. That's a promise.

A: 再见，一路平安。

Section 3 Interpreting Assessment

Passage 1 A Speech by Her Majesty the Queen Delivered via Video Message to the COP26 Evening Reception (Excerpt)

Warm-up Words & Expressions

fitting 合适的
Glasgow 格拉斯哥
address 应对；解决
discharge 履行
close to the heart 牵挂；关心
late 已故的
the Duke of Edinburgh 爱丁堡公爵
draw comfort 获得慰藉

play one's part (在……中) 发挥作用
insurmountable 无法克服的
triumph over 战胜
adversity 困境
rise above 超越
pass up 错过
follow in sb.'s footsteps 效仿

🎧 Listen to Passage 1 and interpret it from English into Chinese.

评价项目	评价标准	原始赋分	学生得分
内容准确	忠实于原文，知识点准确，用词得当，句式合理。	30分	
内容完整	完整传达原文的内容和含义，没有漏译。	20分	
语言标准	语音语调标准，符合目标语言的地道表达方式，能够传达出原文的语气和情感。	20分	

续表

评价项目	评价标准	原始赋分	学生得分
表达流利	口译流畅自然，无重译、停顿或修正现象。	20 分	
职业素养	听力反应敏捷，仪态大方，临场反应能力强。	10 分	
合计		100 分	
被评人			
评价人			
教师评价			

Passage 2 驻欧盟使团团长傅聪大使在庆祝中华人民共和国成立七十四周年国庆招待会上的致辞（节选）

Warm-up Words & Expressions

使节 excellency
中国驻欧盟使团 Chinese Mission to the European Union
中欧友好合作 China-EU friendship and cooperation
共产党 Communist Party
绝对贫困 absolute poverty
社会保障 social security

稳定 stability
改革开放 reform and opening-up
国内生产总值 gross domestic product (GDP)
韧性 resilience
倡议 initiative
求同存异 seek common ground while reserving differences
幸福安康 happiness and good health

🎧 **Listen to Passage 2 and interpret it from Chinese into English.**

评价项目	评价标准	原始赋分	学生得分
内容准确	忠实于原文，知识点准确，用词得当，句式合理。	30 分	
内容完整	完整传达原文的内容和含义，没有漏译。	20 分	
语言标准	语音语调标准，符合目标语言的地道表达方式，能够传达出原文的语气和情感。	20 分	
表达流利	口译流畅自然，无重译、停顿或修正现象。	20 分	
职业素养	听力反应敏捷，仪态大方，临场反应能力强。	10 分	
合计		100 分	
被评人			
评价人			
教师评价			

Unit 3 Ceremonial Address

Learning Objectives
- Understand the importance of ceremonial address
- Know the basic manners in ceremonial address
- Master the frequently used words, phrases, sentence patterns, etc. in ceremonial address

Ideological and Political Objectives
- Understand the solemnity and propriety of ceremonial speeches
- Learn about major domestic and global events and exemplary spirits
- Foster confidence in regional growth and national pride

Section 1 Interpreting Preparation

☞ Key Concepts

1. World Economic Forum 世界经济论坛

The World Economic Forum (WEF, also known as Davos Forum) is an international non-governmental and lobbying organization for multinational companies based in Geneva, Switzerland. It was founded in 1971 by Swiss engineer Klaus Schwab. The foundation, which is mostly funded by its 1,000 member companies—typically global enterprises with more than $5 billion in turnover—as well as public subsidies, views its own mission as "improving the state of the world by engaging business, political, academic, and other leaders of society to shape global, regional, and industry agendas".

The WEF is mostly known for its annual meeting at the end of January in Davos, a mountain resort in the eastern Alps region of Switzerland. The meeting brings together some 3,000 paying members and selected participants—among whom are investors, business leaders, political leaders, economists, celebrities and journalists—for up to five days to discuss global issues across 500 sessions.

2. Unilateralism 单边主义

Unilateralism is any doctrine or agenda that supports one-sided action. Such action may be in disregard for other parties, or as an expression of a commitment toward a direction which other parties may find disagreeable. As a word, unilateralism is attested from 1926, specifically relating to unilateral disarmament. The current, broader meaning emerges in 1964. It stands in contrast with multilateralism, the pursuit of foreign policy goals alongside allies.

3. Protectionism（贸易）保护主义

Protectionism, sometimes referred to as trade protectionism, is the economic policy of restricting imports from other countries through methods such as tariffs on imported goods, import quotas, and a variety of other government regulations. Proponents argue that protectionist policies shield the producers, businesses, and workers of the import-competing sector in the country from foreign competitors. Opponents argue that protectionist policies reduce trade and adversely affect consumers in general (by raising the cost of imported goods) as well as the producers and workers in export sectors, both in the country implementing protectionist policies and, in the countries, protected against.

4. Deglobalization 逆全球化

Deglobalization or deglobalisation is the process of diminishing interdependence and integration between certain units around the world, typically nation-states. It is widely used to describe the periods of history when economic trade and investment between countries decline. It stands in contrast to globalization, in which units become increasingly integrated over time, and generally spans the time between periods of globalization. While globalization and deglobalization are antitheses, they are not mirror images.

5. A community with a shared future for mankind 人类命运共同体

A community with a shared future for mankind, as the word suggests, is that the future and destiny of each nation and country are closely connected. Everyone should pull together for a common cause, share weal and woe, and strive to build earth into a harmonious big family, making the wish for a better life of people all over the world into reality.

Although different countries have different histories, cultures, and systems, they should all live in harmony and treat each other as equals. They should respect and learn from each other, and abandon all arrogance and prejudice. All countries should transcend national, ethnical, cultural, and ideological boundaries, adhere to the common values of peace, development, fairness, justice, democracy, and freedom for all mankind, in building a community with a shared future as to achieve win-win, shared benefits and common development.

6. Entrepreneurship 创业

An entrepreneur is an individual who creates a business, bearing most of the risks and enjoying most of the rewards. The process of setting up a business is known as entrepreneurship.

Entrepreneurs play a key role in any economy, using the skills and initiative necessary to anticipate needs and bring new ideas to market. Entrepreneurship that proves to be successful in taking on the risks of creating a startup is rewarded with profits and growth opportunities.

7. G20 二十国集团

The G20 or Group of 20 is an intergovernmental forum comprising 19 sovereign countries and the European Union (EU). It works to address major issues related to the global economy, such as international financial stability, climate change mitigation and sustainable development.

The G20 is composed of most of the world's largest economies' finance ministries, including both industrialized and developing countries; it accounts for around 80% of gross world product (GWP), 75% of international trade, two-thirds of the global population, and 60% of the world's land area.

The G20 was founded in 1999 in response to several world economic crises. Since 2008, it has convened at least once a year, with summits involving each member's head of government or state, finance minister, or foreign minister, and other high-ranking officials; the EU is represented by the European Commission and the European Central Bank. Other countries, international organizations, and nongovernmental organizations are invited to attend the summits, some permanently.

In its 2009 summit, the G20 declared itself the primary venue for international economic and financial cooperation. The group's stature has risen during the subsequent decade, and it is recognized by analysts as exercising considerable global influence; it is also criticized for its limited membership, lack of enforcement powers, and for the alleged undermining of existing international institutions. Summits are often met with protests, particularly by anti-globalization groups.

8. Chevening Scholarship 志奋领奖学金

Funded by the Foreign, Commonwealth & Development Office and partner organizations, Chevening Scholarships are awarded to individuals with demonstrable leadership potential and strong academic backgrounds. The scholarship offers full financial support to study for any eligible master's degree at any UK university while gaining access to a wide range of exclusive academic, professional, and cultural experiences.

Since the program was created in 1983, over 50,000 outstanding professionals, have had the opportunity to develop in the UK through Chevening. There are more than 1,500 scholarships on offer globally for the 2023—2024 academic year, demonstrating the UK's ongoing commitment towards developing the leaders of tomorrow.

9. Biodiversity loss 生物多样性丧失

Biodiversity loss, also called loss of biodiversity, a decrease in biodiversity within a species, an ecosystem, a given geographic area, or Earth as a whole. Biodiversity, or biological diversity, is a term that refers to the number of genes, species, individual organisms within a given species, and biological communities within a defined geographic area, ranging from the smallest ecosystem to the global biosphere. (A biological community is an interacting group of various species in a common location.) Likewise, biodiversity loss describes the decline in the number, genetic variability, and variety of species, and the biological communities in a given area. This loss in the variety of life can lead to a breakdown in the functioning of the ecosystem where decline has happened.

10. Data For Now 为现在服务的数据

The Data For Now initiative (Data4Now), aims to develop countries' capacities to deliver the information needed by local and national policy and decision makers to design effective development strategies and policy programs to achieve the 2030 Agenda and make a positive difference in people's lives. To this end, it supports members of the National Statistical Systems in participating countries to leverage innovative sources, technologies and methods for the streamlined production and dissemination of better, more timely and disaggregated data for sustainable development. In this context, it also supports effective collaboration between members of the National Statistical System, local, national, and global partners from intergovernmental organizations, academia, civil society, and the private sector.

Data4Now initiative was launched by UN Deputy-Secretary General Amina Mohammed on the side-lines of the UN General Assembly, in September 2019. The initiative is co-led by the United Nations Statistics Division (UNSD), the World Bank, the Global Partnership for Sustainable Development Data (GPSDD), and the Sustainable Development Solutions Network (SDSN). A set of eight countries from three continents initially joined the initiative in 2019. Since then, many more have joined.

11. Low-carbon development 低碳发展

Low-carbon development is a holistic approach to design and construction that comprises evolving, energy-efficient, and environmentally friendly practices used to build a better future. Broadly defined, it's development "that meets the needs of the present without compromising the ability of future generations to meet their own needs", according to the Brundtland Commission, a mid-1980s global conference that first defined core concepts for the renewable vision now embraced in principle by industry leaders worldwide.

As technology evolves and climate change reinforces the urgency of sustainable solutions, low-carbon development isn't just the future, it's the present. There's simply no way to achieve overall sustainability in the architecture, engineering, and construction (AEC) industry without radically changing the way projects are designed and built. Buildings account for 38% of annual carbon emissions worldwide—28% from operational emissions via heating, cooling, and power and 10% from materials and construction. Reducing those numbers will be more challenging due to an expected wave of urbanization.

Sight Interpreting

Passage 1 A Speech by the King at the State Banquet of the State Visit of the President of the Republic of South Africa (Excerpt)

state visit 国事访问
G20 二十国集团
Chevening Scholarship 志奋领奖学金
biodiversity loss 生物多样性丧失

Global Biodiversity Framework 全球生物多样性框架
archbishop 大主教

Read Passage 1 and interpret it from English into Chinese.

President Ramaphosa,

My wife and I are delighted to welcome you to Buckingham Palace this evening.

South Africa, like the Commonwealth, has always been a part of my life. My mother often recalled her visit in 1947, the year before I was born, when, from Cape Town on her twenty-first birthday, she pledged her life to the service of the people of the Commonwealth.

It is therefore particularly moving and special that you are our guest on this, the first state visit we have hosted.

The determination of people in South Africa to continue the legacy of the great men and women who have built your democracy is truly inspiring. It is our responsibility as leaders, and as partners in the U. N. and G20 as well as the Commonwealth, to create the opportunity, prosperity and security that will allow them to do so. This is what I know you are seeking to achieve, Mr. President, through your Adopt A School Foundation and what the United Kingdom seeks to support through our Chevening Scholarship programme which enables South African students to further their studies in universities across the United Kingdom.

It is only by working together across our countries and our generations that we will tackle some of the greatest challenges of our times. For instance, our collaboration in science and innovation is literally vital in order to protect our people's health by preparing for future pandemics. Perhaps, above all, we must find and implement practical solutions to the twin, existential threats of climate change and biodiversity loss. To this end, I am proud that the United Kingdom, along with France, Germany, the United States of America and the European Union, have established a lasting partnership with South Africa by supporting your ambitions for a Just Energy Transition to a sustainable, green, economically vibrant future, and that our countries are committed to ensuring an ambitious Global Biodiversity Framework in Montreal this December. These are examples of our crucial modern relationship.

Mr. President, your visit offers an opportunity for us to chart a path forward together, investing in each other's potential, and facing the challenges of our world together, as partners, and as friends, striving for equality, justice and fairness for all.

At the turn of the year the world paid tribute to the life and legacy of a great South African, former Archbishop Desmond Tutu. Amongst his many memorable teachings, I am often reminded of one saying in particular— "My humanity is bound up in yours, for we can only be human together." I believe that is a vital lesson for us all, and an important thread in the partnership between our countries.

Ladies and gentlemen, as we commit to continuing on that journey, I invite you all to rise and drink a toast to President Ramaphosa, and to the people of South Africa.

(https://www.royal.uk/speech-king-state-banquet-state-visit-president-republic-south-africa)

Passage 2 李强在第十四届夏季达沃斯论坛开幕式上的致辞（节选）

Warm-up Words & Expressions

旗帜 banner
国际秩序 the international order
小康社会 a moderately prosperous society
全面建设社会主义现代化国家 build a modern socialist country in all respects
坚定的力量 staunch force
货物贸易总额 trade in goods
主要经济体 major economy
物美价廉 quality yet inexpensive
动力源 source of impetus

Read Passage 2 and interpret it from Chinese into English.

女士们，先生们，朋友们！

中国作为一个负责任的大国，长期以来，我们始终坚定站在历史正确的一边、站在人类文明进步的一边，高举和平、发展、合作、共赢的旗帜，坚决做世界和平的建设者、全球发展的贡献者、国际秩序的维护者。特别是中共十八大以来，我们着力推动高质量发展，如期实现了全面建成小康社会目标，历史性地解决了绝对贫困问题，现在已经踏上了全面建设社会主义现代化国家新征程。中国经济发展到今天，已与世界经济深度融合。我们在全球化中发展了自己，也成为了维护全球化最坚定的力量。

在过去的十年里，中国一直是世界经济稳定增长的重要动力源。中国十年年均经济增长达到6.2%，经济总量占全球比重由2012年的11.3%提升到18%左右，货物贸易总额连续6年位居世界第一，对世界经济增长的平均贡献率超过30%，一直是推动世界经济增长的最大引擎。疫情暴发当年，中国是全球唯一实现经济正增长的主要经济体，最近三年中国经济年均增长达到4.5%，高于世界平均增速2.5个百分点左右，在主要经济体中居于前列。在与各国联动发展过程中，中国严格履行入世承诺，主动向世界开放市场，与世界各国共享发展机遇，已经成为140多个国家和地区的主要贸易伙伴。中国不仅用自己的发展改善了本国人民的生活，也为各国人民提供了大批物美价廉的产品，为促进国际自由贸易、稳定世界经济增长发挥了重要"压舱石"和动力源的作用。

(https://www.mfa.gov.cn/web/zyxw/202306/t20230627_11104618.shtml)

Memory Practice

Listen to the following paragraphs carefully without taking notes and then retell the main ideas in the source language based on your memory.

1. What is the main idea of Paragraph 1?
2. What is the main idea of Paragraph 2?

Section 2 Interpreting Practice

Passage 1 A Keynote Speech for a Technology Conference

Warm-up Words & Expressions

natural language processing 自然语言处理
computer vision 计算机视觉
voice command 语音指令
medical image 医学图像

fraud 欺诈
common sense reasoning 常识推理
transfer learning 迁移学习

🎧 **Listen to Passage 1 and interpret it into the target language.**

Good morning, everyone. It's an honor to be here at the World Technology Conference to share some thoughts on the latest trends and innovations happening in artificial intelligence (AI).

We are truly living in the age of AI. It's hard to believe how rapidly AI has advanced in just the past few years. We've gone from AI being mostly academic research to now being an everyday reality. AI is embedded in our smartphones, powering our social media feeds, helping us shop online, and so much more.

Some of the most exciting recent advances are in natural language processing and computer vision. We now have AI assistants like Siri and Alexa that can understand and respond to voice commands. Chat-bots can have increasingly natural text conversations with humans. And AI imaging algorithms can describe photos and videos in great detail.

In computer vision, AI is powering new capabilities like facial recognition, which has many applications from security to organizing photo albums. Self-driving car companies are using AI to understand complex environments. This technology is still early but will eventually transform transportation.

AI is also making great strides in specific industries like healthcare and financial services. In healthcare, AI is analyzing medical images to support diagnostics and even suggest treatment plans. AI chat-bots are becoming virtual medical assistants. In finance, AI algorithms are managing investments, detecting fraud, and enabling personalized banking.

Of course, with all new technology, we must ensure AI is deployed ethically and responsibly. AI has potential risks and biases that must be proactively addressed. But if harnessed properly, AI can greatly benefit humanity.

Looking to the future, some truly fascinating AI capabilities are on the horizon. For example, deep learning algorithms are making strides in natural language understanding and generation. We may soon have AI that can really converse like humans and be helpful assistants. In computer vision, algorithms are moving toward common sense reasoning about images and videos. Transfer learning techniques will enable AI systems to adapt quickly to new tasks and environments.

The companies and researchers represented here at the World Technology Conference are at the forefront of these exciting innovations. I look forward to the rest of the conference and hearing about the amazing work you all are driving forward. The future of AI is bright, and by working together responsibly, we can build an AI-enabled world that enhances our lives. Thank you.

Passage 2　王树国校长在西安交通大学 2023 届学生毕业典礼上的寄语（节选）

Warm-up Words & Expressions

家国情怀 the duty to country　　　重构 reconstruct
毅力 perseverance　　　　　　　　赛道 track

🎧 **Listen to Passage 2 and interpret it into the target language.**

今天我想讲三点感悟。

第一点，情怀。人的一生不能没有情怀。什么是最大的情怀？家国情怀。这个话题我讲过若干次，为什么今天我还要讲？因为家国情怀是支撑一个人一生事业之基础，没有这个情怀，任何一个个体都难以成大事；没有这个情怀，你无法在人生的道路上一路走得顺畅；没有这个情怀，你将会失去灵魂，茫然无所应对，不知人生的方向在哪里。

第二点，毅力。刚才同学们在发言之中，已经表达了他们在学习之中遇到的各种各样的困难。那位携笔从戎的同学在部队锻炼的时候也经受了深刻的磨炼。这些磨炼都比他们日常生活所能够忍受的限度要高，但是他们坚持下来了。靠的是什么？毅力。一个没有毅力的人，不足以长期地走下去；一个没有毅力的人，不足以完成伟大的事业；一个没有毅力的人，不足以书写自己的无悔人生。

做事要靠毅力，但是没有困难是不可能的，没有挑战是不可能的，人的一生就是伴随着困难和挑战一路走来，生活的价值大概就是如此。我们要不断地面对新问题、解决新问题，然后又面对新问题。当你们走向社会的时候，一定会遇到若干个你们未曾想过的困难，会遇到若干个你们未曾遇到的问题，你们需要直面这些问题，勇敢地面对它们、解决它们。

第三点，创新。这个时代、这个社会是一个变化的、转折的时代。新技术之发展，超乎我们之想象。社会在重构，知识在重构，整个体系结构都在重构。正是因为这样，所以才给了你们施展才能的无限空间。你们赶上了一个好时代，这个时代具有无限之可能，关键看你们能否在新的赛道上把握住机遇，勇立潮头。

我们校歌当中有一句话，是"为世界之光"，让我感触万千。希望大家永远记住，家国情怀、坚韧不拔的毅力、改革创新的精神，将会伴随你们一生，它是你们的精神财富，是埋藏在你们内心深处的一束光，它将照亮你们的人生，让你们成为顶天立地的民族之脊梁，让你们成为世界之光！

由衷地祝福同学们，毕业快乐！

（https://news.xjtu.edu.cn/info/1033/198329.htm）

Passage 3 A Farewell Speech for a Retiring Colleague

Warm-up Words & Expressions

integral 不可或缺的
dedication 奉献
expertise 专业素养
poise 沉着自信；稳重；自若

spearhead 领导；带领
surpass 超出
mentor 导师
uplift 鼓舞

Listen to Passage 3 and interpret it into the target language.

Good evening, everyone. As we gather today, it is with mixed emotions that we celebrate the retirement of our dear friend and colleague, Mary.

Mary, in your 30 years at our company, you have been an integral part of our success. Your passion, dedication, and expertise have made an immeasurable impact on all of us.

I still remember when you first joined us back in 1992. Even as a young graduate, you demonstrated remarkable skill and poise. Over the years, you quickly rose through the ranks due to your top-notch work ethic and leadership capabilities.

Mary, you led some of our most challenging and important projects. You spearheaded our expansion into new markets and helped us adapt through periods of rapid change in the industry. Time after time, you motivated your team and delivered results that far surpassed expectations. Your technical knowledge and strategic mindset have been invaluable.

Beyond your contributions to our business, your kindness and warmth have touched us deeply. You have been a mentor, guiding and developing our new hires. And you have been a caring friend, always willing to listen and uplift your colleagues. I speak for everyone when I say it has been a true joy working with you.

As you step into retirement, we will certainly miss your presence in our office. But we are excited for you to have more time with your family, to travel, and pursue new adventures. You have given so much of yourself to this company—now go out and enjoy.

We wish you all the best in this next chapter of your life. Thank you for everything you have done for our team. You will always be part of our team. We love you!

Congratulations and happy retirement!

Passage 4 晚宴致辞

Warm-up Words & Expressions

考察团 delegation
推广 promote
立足 gain a foothold in
赢得……的青睐 earn the favor of...

护肤 skincare
产品本地化策略 localization strategy
务实的 pragmatic
优质产品 quality product

🎧 **Listen to Passage 4 and interpret it into the target language.**

尊敬的各位来宾,女士们、先生们,

非常荣幸今晚能与大家相聚在此,共同参加我们为澳大利亚 Facial 化妆品销售公司考察团举办的欢迎晚宴。请允许我代表广州自然美化妆品有限公司,向从澳大利亚远道而来的朋友们表示最热烈的欢迎!有朋自远方来,不亦乐乎!

多年来,澳大利亚 Facial 化妆品销售公司为我司产品在澳大利亚市场的推广作出了巨大贡献。我谨代表公司全体员工,向贵公司长期以来给予我们的大力支持和帮助表示衷心的感谢!正是有了贵公司对我们品牌的认可和推广,才使我们得以在澳大利亚市场立足,并赢得了澳大利亚消费者的青睐。

记得在 5 年前,贵公司决定引入我司旗下的护肤产品。为了确保产品顺利在澳大利亚市场推出,双方团队进行了充分讨论和细致准备,并共同制定了产品本地化策略。最终,该产品获得澳大利亚消费者的一致好评,销量不断增长。这充分证明了中澳两国企业务实合作的巨大成果。

展望未来,我相信我们两家公司必将继续携手合作,为消费者带来更多优质产品,助力两国经济和社会发展。在此,我谨代表广州自然美化妆品有限公司管理层,向澳大利亚的朋友表示衷心的祝福,预祝各位新年快乐,万事如意!

最后,我诚挚地邀请各位嘉宾举杯,为中澳友谊与合作干杯!

Section 3　Interpreting Assessment

Passage 1　UN Secretary-General's Message to the Opening of the United Nations World Data Forum

Warm-up Words & Expressions

the United Nations Data Strategy 联合国数据战略
stall 暂缓;搁置;停滞
turbocharge 用涡轮增压;促进;推动
bedrock 基石;基本事实;基本原则
harness 控制;利用

🎧 **Listen to Passage 1 and interpret it from English into Chinese.**

评价项目	评价标准	原始赋分	学生得分
内容准确	忠实于原文,知识点准确,用词得当,句式合理。	30 分	
内容完整	完整传达原文的内容和含义,没有漏译。	20 分	
语言标准	语音语调标准,符合目标语言的地道表达方式,能够传达出原文的语气和情感。	20 分	
表达流利	口译流畅自然,无重译、停顿或修正现象。	20 分	
职业素养	听力反应敏捷,仪态大方,临场反应能力强。	10 分	
合计		100 分	

续表

评价项目	评价标准	原始赋分	学生得分
被评人			
评价人			
教师评价			

Passage 2　李强在二十国集团领导人第十八次峰会第一阶段会议上的讲话（节选）

Warm-up Words & Expressions

二十国集团 G20
新德里峰会 New Delhi Summit
人类命运共同体 a community with a shared future for mankind
地球村 global village
全局的视野 a broader view
全球发展倡议 Global Development Initiative
世界经济复苏 global recovery
可持续发展 sustainable development

🎧 **Listen to Passage 2 and interpret it from Chinese into English.**

评价项目	评价标准	原始赋分	学生得分
内容准确	忠实于原文，知识点准确，用词得当，句式合理。	30分	
内容完整	完整传达原文的内容和含义，没有漏译。	20分	
语言标准	语音语调标准，符合目标语言的地道表达方式，能够传达出原文的语气和情感。	20分	
表达流利	口译流畅自然，无重译、停顿或修正现象。	20分	
职业素养	听力反应敏捷，仪态大方，临场反应能力强。	10分	
合计		100分	
被评人			
评价人			
教师评价			

Unit 4 Business Travel

Learning Objectives

- Understand the importance of business travel
- Know the basic manners in business travel
- Master the frequently used phrases, sentence patterns, etc.

Ideological and Political Objectives

- Further explore regional cultures
- Enhance interpretation of traditional and current popular travel routes, red tourism sites, and their historical narratives in the Greater Bay Area
- Cultivate profound connection to the hometown and dedication to serve it

Section 1 Interpreting Preparation

Key Concepts

1. Red tourism 红色旅游

Red tourism is not only about the joy of visiting a new place and taking in the wonderful sights. It is also about gaining knowledge about history and being inspired by the stories of the people who contributed to the founding of the People's Republic of China in 1949 and worked for the wellbeing of the Chinese people.

By rediscovering history and passing on the stories of the Chinese revolution and its heroes to the next generations, people can uplift their spirit.

Red tourism can also be used as a leverage to revitalize rural areas because most of the revolutionary bases and red tourism sites are in the countryside. By exploiting such sites to raise the incomes of rural residents, the authorities can create a new driving force for integrated rural development. Since red tourism is a labor-intensive sector involving catering, accommodation, entertainment and other related businesses, which creates jobs and helps increase farmers' incomes, it can boost local development.

2. Orange Isle 橘子洲

As the world's longest inland river isle, Orange Isle connects the Mount Yuelu in the west and the downtown in the east, with a length of 5 km and a width of 50 – 200 meters and a total area of

91.64 hectares. Orange Isle comprises three nearly-connected isles: upper isle, middle isle and lower isle. The upper isle is called Ox-head Isle and middle isle is called Land-and-water Isle, while the lower isle is called Fujia Isle. Orange Isle includes Ox-head Isle and Land-and-water Isle at present.

The isle has been a popular site for summer vacation for a long time. During his youth, Mao Zedong spent a lot of time walking on the beach, swimming and sunbathing. There is also a grand white marble monument, on which there are two seal cuttings: four Chinese characters Ju Zi Zhou Tou (Orange Isle) and a classical Chinese poem *Changsha—to the tune of Qin Yuan Chun*, both of which are Mao Zedong's works. The Statue of Young Mao Zedong is erected on the Orange Isle.

3. The Statue of Young Mao Zedong 毛泽东青年艺术雕塑

The Statue of Young Mao Zedong is located on Orange Isle, Changsha. The statue was created based on the image of Mao Zedong when he was a young man in 1925. It is 83 meters long, 41 meters wide and 32 meters high, with the base covering 3,500 square meters. It is made of more than 8,000 Yongding red granite boulders collected from high mountains in Fujian Province, with a total weight of about 2,000 tons.

4. The Tongguan Kiln 长沙铜官窑遗址

As a major porcelain producer during the Tang Dynasty (618 – 907), the Tongguan Kiln is well-known for developing a colored glaze technique. Its porcelain products were sought throughout China and Southeast Asia at that time.

5. Dim sum 点心

In Cantonese cuisine, dim sum is snack-like food traditionally served for breakfast and lunch in restaurants. In modern establishments they might be served from rolling trolleys that pass by diners in a constant procession to be served up when ordered, or diners might select them as they move past on conveyor belts. Another delivery technique is for the diner to tick off desired items on a printed card. All this results in quick service, which makes dim sum a favourite of people with only a short time for a meal break.

Dim sum—whose name derives from the Cantonese word for "appetizer" (the Mandarin word for "dianxin")—is thought to have originated in tea houses along the Silk Road as long ago as 2,500 years as a light accompaniment to appetite-stimulating tea as travelers stopped to rest along the way. There are two broad categories of dim sum: steamed and fried, each embracing dozens of dishes. Examples of the first category are char siu bao (a kind of soft pork bun), and siu mai (a kind of cup-shaped rice-flour wrappers containing pork, shrimp, and vegetables). An example of the second category is the ubiquitous egg roll or spring roll, a kind of deep-fried dumpling containing minced meat and vegetables or, often, vegetables alone. Steamed dishes are traditionally served in bamboo baskets. Alongside these dumplings and rolls are served small dishes such as pork spareribs and chicken feet.

6. Smart tourism 智慧旅游

Smart tourism is an important component of a smart city. Tourism is one of the major components of economic growth for communities worldwide. A key requirement of tourism has been to attract more and more tourists from different parts of the world. Smart tourism refers to the application of information and communication technology (ICT), such similar to the smart cities, for developing innovative tools and approaches to improve tourism. Smart tourism is reliant on core technologies such as ICT, mobile communication, cloud computing, artificial intelligence, and virtual reality. It supports integrated efforts at a destination to find innovative ways to collect and use data derived from physical infrastructure, social connectedness and organizational sources (both government and non-government), and users in combination with advanced technologies to increase efficiency, sustainability, experiences. The information and communication technology tools used for smart tourism include IoT (Internet of Things), mobile communication, cloud computing, and artificial intelligence. It combines physical, informational, social, and commercial infrastructure of tourism with such tools to provide smart tourism opportunities. The principles of smart tourism lie at enhancing tourism experiences, improve the efficiency of resource management, maximize destination competitiveness with an emphasis on sustainable aspects. It should also gather and distribute information to facilitate efficient allocation of tourism resources and integrate tourism supplies at a micro and macro level ensuring that the benefits are well distributed. They are observed to be effective in technologically advanced destinations such as smart cities.

7. Augmented reality 增强现实

Augmented reality (AR) is an interactive experience that combines the real world and computer-generated content. The content can span multiple sensory modalities, including visual, auditory, haptic, somatosensory and olfactory. AR can be defined as a system that incorporates three basic features: a combination of real and virtual worlds, real-time interaction, and accurate 3D registration of virtual and real objects. The overlaid sensory information can be constructive (i.e. additive to the natural environment), or destructive (i.e. masking of the natural environment). This experience is seamlessly interwoven with the physical world such that it is perceived as an immersive aspect of the real environment. In this way, augmented reality alters one's ongoing perception of a real-world environment, whereas virtual reality completely replaces the user's real-world environment with a simulated one.

Sight Interpreting

Passage 1 "Red tourism" Becomes Increasingly Popular Among Gen Z (Excerpt)

Warm-up Words & Expressions

millennium 一千年；千年期（尤指公元纪年）
normalized 常态化的
commemorate （用……）纪念；铭记
memorabilia 收藏品；纪念品

Read Passage 1 and interpret it from English into Chinese.

In the center of Changsha, capital of central China's Hunan Province, Orange Isle is where Mao Zedong carried out revolutionary activities in his youth. The Statue of Young Mao Zedong on the isle is one of China's most attractive and influential "red" scenic spots. The area has become an important window to promote the city's image and a must-visit place in Changsha.

Due to its unique geographical location and rich historical background, Changsha has become a top choice for many young people to visit and "check-in". "Red tourism", as the name implies, includes both patriotic education through reviewing history and leisurely sightseeing. The combination of these two elements gives red tourism its unique charm.

Be it the Yuelu Mountain with its millennium-long academic history, the Orange Isle where young Mao Zedong wrote poetry, or the Tongguan Kiln that witnessed the legendary Maritime Silk Road, the unique Hunan culture provides a solid foundation for these attractions, and with the careful integration of culture and tourism, they bring to life diverse and multi-dimensional tourism resources, increasing the popularity of Changsha.

Red tourism is gradually becoming a normalized travel experience. Data from Ctrip shows that in the first half of 2022, 88 percent of tourists booked tickets for local or nearby red tourism attractions. Young people enjoy visiting sites that combine red tourism with national trend culture and creative products, commemorating history in a more fashionable way and expressing patriotic enthusiasm.

For people born after 1960 and 1970, traveling to red scenic spots is a symbol of honor and a reminder of their youth. But for more young people, red tourism is a way for them to learn history, expand their knowledge and shape their way of life. According to the newly released "Generation Z Red Tourism Consumption Preference Survey Report in 2021", Generation Z aged between 13 and 27 have become the major participants of red tourism. They prefer red tourism products such as historical sites and relics, revolutionary memorabilia and museums, in-depth tours of old revolutionary areas and performing arts.

Not only are Chinese young people interested in Chinese culture and history, but also foreigners. When two exchange students from Russia showed up at Orange Isle, they quickly become the spotlight. They said they have been in China for three years and have a strong interest in Chinese history. After the pandemic eased, they consulted their Chinese friends about which place best represents Chinese history and culture, and the answer was Changsha.

(https://www.globaltimes.cn/page/202304/1288652.shtml)

Passage 2 食在广州

Warm-up Words & Expressions

口味清淡 be of light taste
夜宵 late-night snacks
百年老字号 time-honored
大排档 food stall
亚热带 subtropical zone
木瓜 papaya
杨桃 starfruit
石榴 pomegranate
黄皮 wampee
杨梅 bayberry
菠萝蜜 jackfruit

Read Passage 2 and interpret it from Chinese into English.

"食在广州"历史悠久、闻名遐迩,据考证,该美誉已经有2000年的历史。粤菜是中国八大菜系之一,其食材多样丰博、制作精细,讲求色、香、味、形、鲜。粤菜的口味较为清淡,配合季节性变化,突出其新鲜与营养科学的特点。广州的北京路、上下九步行街、西关美食街一带,随处可见广州著名的小吃、点心和风味食品。煲汤、饮茶、吃夜宵也是广州饮食文化的一部分。

广州有一大批百年老字号的粤菜酒楼、潮菜酒楼,以及经营其他中国菜系的酒楼,例如湘菜馆、川菜馆、鲁菜馆、淮扬菜馆等。广州也有许多吃西方美食的好去处,例如西餐厅、咖啡馆、西式快餐店等,同时还有不少平民化的小餐馆、大排档、传统小吃店等经营特色小菜、火锅、烧烤和小吃的地方。

广州地处亚热带,一年四季都有新鲜水果上市,被誉为"水果之乡"。广州的水果有数百种之多,其中以荔枝、香蕉、木瓜、菠萝著名,并称"岭南四大名果"。此外,芒果、杨桃、石榴、龙眼、白榄、乌榄、黄皮、杨梅、菠萝蜜、三华李、西瓜等水果也颇受欢迎。

(www.gzfao.gov.cn/attachment/0/1/1529/227314.pdf)

Memory Practice

🎧 **Listen to the following paragraphs carefully without taking notes and then retell the main ideas in the source language based on your memory.**

1. What is the main idea of Paragraph 1?
2. What is the main idea of Paragraph 2?

Section 2 Interpreting Practice

Dialogue 1 到广州出差

Warm-up Words & Expressions

upcoming 即将发生(或来临)的　　　　珍稀动物 rare animal
前沿 frontier　　　　　　　　　　　　金刚鹦鹉 macaw
繁华 prosperity

🎧 **Listen to Dialogue 1 and interpret it into the target language.**

A: Hello, Miss Zhang. I'm very glad to be here in Guangzhou for this business trip.
B: 史密斯先生,欢迎您来到广州。
A: Thank you. I'm looking forward to the upcoming meetings, and also to seeing more of this city during my stay. I haven't visited Guangzhou before. Could you tell me more about the city?
B: 听到您对广州之行充满期待,我很开心。广州是一座历史悠久的城市,也是中国改革开放的前沿城市,经济发展非常迅速。这里有许多必看的景点,如珠江夜游,沿着珠江两岸欣赏壮观的夜景,感受这座城市的繁华与魅力;长隆野生动物世界,可以看到许多珍稀动物，如大熊猫、白虎、金刚鹦鹉等；中山纪念堂，纪念中国民主革命先行者孙中山先生的建筑；还有很多可以尝试地道的广州美食的地方。我会帮您安排行程，让您感受这座城市的魅力。

A: That sounds wonderful! A river cruise at night to see the city lights, Chimelong Safari Park, the Sun Yat-sen memorial hall, and Cantonese cuisine—I'm looking forward to experiencing it all. I really appreciate you taking the time to show me around. This will make my trip much more enjoyable.

B: 很高兴能成为您的导游，一起游览广州这座美丽的城市。相信通过这次游览，您会对广州有更深的了解，也会引导我们的合作向前发展。期待与您共同度过几天的美好时光！

A: As do I. Thank you again, Miss Zhang! I know under your guidance, this will be a fruitful and memorable trip.

Dialogue 2 疫情后的商务旅行

Warm-up Words & Expressions

英国航空公司 British Airways
运营 operation
flight route 飞行路线

rebound 回升；反弹
customizable 可定制的；可定做的

🎧 **Listen to Dialogue 2 and interpret it into the target language.**

A: 安娜女士，新冠疫情对全球经济造成了非常大的影响，许多企业都在缩减商务旅行预算，您作为英国航空公司的业务经理，是否也感受到了这一点？

B: Yes, the COVID-19 pandemic has led many companies globally to reduce their business travel budgets. We have certainly experienced decreased corporate travel demand over the past two years.

A: 英国航空公司为应对这种形势付出了哪些努力？公司的运营和前景是否受到了很大冲击？

B: To adapt, we have taken measures such as optimizing flight routes, reducing aircraft sizes, and cutting operational costs where possible. It's undoubtedly been a very challenging time for our industry. However, we believe business travel will rebound steadily as vaccines roll out and economies recover.

A: 公司还做了哪些努力来保留客户和业务量？

B: We truly value our business travelers. To keep providing great service, we've launched more flexible ticket policies and enabled free date changes.

A: 我们注意到，尽管企业在缩减商旅支出，但在很多情况下，还是很有必要进行商务交流和拓展。您认为疫情过后的商旅市场将呈现什么趋势？

B: Yes, business will always require some face-to-face meetings and events. As we move beyond this pandemic, I think business travel will resume but not completely go back to pre-COVID levels. Some virtual collaboration will remain commonplace. Flexibility will be key—companies will want a mix of online and offline options. At British Airways, we aim to provide

customizable travel solutions to meet this evolving corporate demand.
A: 非常感谢安娜女士接受我们的采访!
B: You're welcome.

Passage 1 Embrace Smart Tourism for Adopting Trends in the Industry (Excerpt)

Warm-up Words & Expressions

resilient 有弹性（或弹力）的；能复原的
the Internet of Things 物联网
augmented reality 增强现实
spillover effect 溢出效应
superimpose 使重叠；使叠加；使附加于
align 校正；调整
block chain 区块链
mitigate 减轻；缓和

🎧 **Listen to Passage 1 and interpret it into the target language.**

While traditional tourism has been the mainstay for many economies, smart tourism is the way forward post-COVID. COVID-19 is an opportunity to rethink tourism for the future—a shift from traditional tourism to adopting futuristic trends in the industry to ensure it's resilient in future crises.

The pandemic saw a 60 percent decline in international tourism in 2020, affecting millions of jobs, primarily those held by women and those in the informal economy. Global GDP also took a significant hit. The way forward may be through adopting smart tourism and smart destination strategies.

Smart tourism is the evolution of traditional tourism and e-tourism, involving technology-driven innovation and extensive adoption of information and communication technology and the Internet of Things (IoT). For example, smart ticketing, smart security services, virtual reality tours, and robot city guides.

Should large-scale travel and mobility be restricted again, augmented or virtual reality may offer tourists an alternative memorable and unique tourism experience. Greater investment in such digital technologies could have spillover effects on the economic development of these destinations. Augmented reality enables information to be superimposed via an interface onto the real world, integrating physical and virtual objects to create enhanced experiences. Augmented reality has been used in visitor attractions such as museums, art galleries, theme parks, and UNESCO sites. One example is the Archeoguide in Olympia, Greece, which has adopted augmented reality to digitally reconstruct Greek heritage ruins.

Digital technologies also allow for human capital development, upgrading the mostly low-skilled jobs that dominate the traditional tourism industry to higher-end jobs. Technological development enhances the innovation and competitiveness of tourism destinations for a more resilient and sustainable future.

Importantly, designing and aligning tourism for digitization ensures that the tourism destination is sustainable and resilient. Smart solutions and technologies such as IoT, artificial intelligence, big data, augmented reality and block chain technology allow cities to be more responsive in handling disasters and risks and also mitigate those risks to the tourism sector. For example, with free Wi-Fi and big data, social networking platforms can provide up-to-date information on areas affected by disaster, disease and risks flag to the authorities where to direct their resources, and flag to tourists where to avoid.

(https://codeblue.galencentre.og/2022/10/06/futureproofing-tourism-via-digitalisation/)

Passage 2　"天然影棚"助推侨乡文旅产业"狂飙"

Warm-up Words & Expressions

电视剧 TV drama
拍照"打卡" take photos to tick off
华侨 overseas Chinese
拱券 arch
镌刻 engrave
侨批馆 Overseas Chinese Postal Relics Museum
手信 souvenir
《粤港澳大湾区发展规划纲要》 Outline Development Plan for the Guangdong-Hong Kong-Macao Greater Bay Area

🎧 **Listen to Passage 2 and interpret it into the target language.**

电视剧《狂飙》的热播，带火了剧中主要取景地广东江门。

作为中国著名侨乡，江门既保留了传统的老洋楼，也有浓厚的都市气息，不同年代的元素在这里兼容并蓄，素有"天然影棚"的美称，吸引了多部影视剧来此取景。

江门长堤历史文化街区是电视剧《狂飙》的取景地之一，被该电视剧带火了之后，街区里每天游人如织，大家争相拍照"打卡"，热闹非凡。

距离墟顶老街几百米之外的是1914年由海外华侨集资兴建而成的启明里片区，最近也显得更加热闹。启明里片区的房屋外观在传统岭南民居风格的基础上，大量融合了西方的圆柱、拱券等元素，整体结构轻巧通透、淡雅素净而又充满西方文化的浪漫气息，极具侨乡特色。

启明里的每栋建筑都会有一个门牌，在门牌的上部刻有这栋建筑物的地址和门牌号码，在门牌的下部镌刻着一段文字，对建筑物的历史以及屋主的来历做一个详细的介绍。

在启明里，除了侨批馆、江门非遗手信馆等侨乡文化展览项目，许多由侨屋改造而成的咖啡店也引来不少游客驻足。江门作为中国著名侨乡，五邑先辈从海外带回来的咖啡文化，也融入了当地的日常生活中。

旅游平台数据显示，受益于影视剧热播及春节旅游热潮，春节假期江门接待游客量和旅游收入同比增长34.48%和29.47%，相关景区消费人次环比增长近5倍，江门搜索热度月环比增长近130%。

接下来江门市委宣传部将按照《粤港澳大湾区发展规划纲要》赋予江门建设华侨华人重要文化交流平台的历史使命，致力于华侨文化资源的挖掘整合与活用，努力将江门打造成为全国著名的网红打卡地、华侨华人寻根地以及影视产业集结地。

(http://www.gqb.gov.cn/news/2023/0210/56254.shtml)

Unit 4 Business Travel

Section 3　Interpreting Assessment

Passage 1　Chinese Cities to See Tourism Peak in New Year's Day Holiday

Warm-up Words & Expressions

ticket booking platform 售票平台
sell out 售罄
travel demand 出行需求
visit relative 探亲
home stay 民宿

🎧 Listen to Passage 1 and interpret it from English into Chinese.

评价项目	评价标准	原始赋分	学生得分
内容准确	忠实于原文，知识点准确，用词得当，句式合理。	30 分	
内容完整	完整传达原文的内容和含义，没有漏译。	20 分	
语言标准	语音语调标准，符合目标语言的地道表达方式，能够传达出原文的语气和情感。	20 分	
表达流利	口译流畅自然，无重译、停顿或修正现象。	20 分	
职业素养	听力反应敏捷，仪态大方，临场反应能力强。	10 分	
合计		100 分	
被评人			
评价人			
教师评价			

Passage 2　寻味顺德（节选）

Warm-up Words & Expressions

烧猪 roasted pig
祠堂 ancestral shrine/hall/temple
祭祖 worship ancestors
族谱 family pedigree
集资 pool the money

🎧 Listen to Passage 2 and interpret it from Chinese into English.

评价项目	评价标准	原始赋分	学生得分
内容准确	忠实于原文，知识点准确，用词得当，句式合理。	30 分	
内容完整	完整传达原文的内容和含义，没有漏译。	20 分	

续表

评价项目	评价标准	原始赋分	学生得分
语言标准	语音语调标准，符合目标语言的地道表达方式，能够传达出原文的语气和情感。	20分	
表达流利	口译流畅自然，无重译、停顿或修正现象。	20分	
职业素养	听力反应敏捷，仪态大方，临场反应能力强。	10分	
合计		100分	
被评人			
评价人			
教师评价			

Unit 5 Enterprise Introduction

Learning Objectives

- Master the basic words and expressions of enterprise introduction
- Acquire cultural background knowledge about enterprise introduction
- Find ways to improve the interpreting skills and performance on the speech of enterprise introduction

Ideological and Political Objectives

- Cultivate proper value orientation and integrity principle
- Motivate social responsibility and a sense of national pride
- Foster innovation spirit and creativity
- Hone critical thinking skills and discerning ethical distinctions

Section 1 Interpreting Preparation

☞ Key Concepts

1. Corporate social responsibility 企业社会责任感

The concept of corporate social responsibility is based on the concept that business operation must be correspondent to sustainable development concept. The enterprises should not only care about their financial and operating status, but they have to consider their influence on the society and environment that they are in. The corporate responsibility of an enterprise embodies in the business and management comforting to laws and morality, the investment on community welfare, the social charity and the protection to the environment.

2. Innovation spirit 创新精神

Innovation spirit is the driving force behind many of the world's most successful businesses and individuals. It is the ability to think outside of the box, come up with new ideas, and push boundaries to achieve greatness. With the rapid pace of technological advancements and the ever-changing global landscape, innovation has become more important than ever before. One of the key elements of fostering an innovation spirit is to encourage creativity. Creativity is the foundation of innovation and it is essential for generating new ideas. This can be achieved by creating a culture of open communication, where everyone is encouraged to share their thoughts and ideas freely. It is important to create an environment where people feel comfortable sharing their ideas without fear of judgment or criticism. Another important element of innovation is the ability to take risks. Innovation requires taking calculated risks, trying new things, and not being afraid of failure. Failure is an inevitable part of the innovation process, but it can also be a valuable learning experience. It is essential to create a culture that a failure is a stepping stone to success, rather than a reason for defeat.

3. Business ethics 商业伦理

One of the most important attributes for small business success, is the distinguishing quality of practicing admirable business ethics. Business ethics, practiced throughout the deepest layers of a company, become the heart and soul of the company's culture and can mean the difference between success and failure. Business ethics examines ethical principles and moral problems that can arise in a business environment. In the increasingly conscience-focused marketplaces, the demand for more ethical business processes and actions is increasing.

4. Strategy for sustainable development 可持续发展战略

China has a large population and limited resources. Ever since the policy of reform and opening-up was initiated, the CPC Central Committee and the State Council have been attaching great importance to the issue of sustainable development. Sustainable development is key to the survival of our nation and to the wellbeing of generations to come. It is a cross-cutting, long-term issue of fundamental importance. A sustainable development strategy was identified in the report to the 19th CPC National Congress as one of the seven strategies for realizing the goal of building a moderately prosperous society.

Sight Interpreting

Passage 1 Alibaba Cloud

Warm-up Words & Expressions

subsidiary 子公司	health passport system 健康通行证系统
cloud infrastructure 云基础设施	digital quarantine measure 数字检疫方法
COVID-19 新冠疫情	steer 引导
cloud computing service 云计算服务	major driver 主动力
chip development 芯片研发	CNBC (Consumer News and Business Channel)
coronavirus infection 新冠病毒传播	美国消费者新闻与商业频道
Dingtalk 钉钉	

Read Passage 1 and interpret it from English into Chinese.

Alibaba Cloud, a subsidiary of Chinese e-commerce giant Alibaba, will spend RMB 200 billion on its cloud infrastructure over the next three years following an increase in demand for digital services in the aftermath of the COVID-19 outbreak in China. Alibaba's cloud revenue grew 62%

in the quarter ended December 2019 compared with the same quarter a year earlier, the company said in February.

The COVID-19 pandemic has resulted in extra demand for digital services, which are typically reliant on cloud computing services and data centers to function. Alibaba Cloud is the largest provider of cloud computing services in China, but falls behind Amazon and Microsoft globally. Alibaba's investment will focus on operating system and chip development, as well as on its network of data centers, where the technologies will be deployed.

Alibaba has seen a marked increase in the use of its technology since the beginning of the year. As many businesses requested that their employees work from home to reduce the risk of coronavirus infections, companies across China relied more heavily on tools like Dingtalk, Alibaba's enterprise communications App. Dingtalk also provided a platform for online learning after schools were closed due to the outbreak. Meanwhile, the company helped the Chinese government roll out a health passport system, a digital quarantine measure that assigned users a red, yellow, or green rating based on their health status and travel history.

"The COVID-19 pandemic has posed additional stress on the overall economy across sectors, but it also steers us to put more focus on the digital economy," Jeff Zhang, president of Alibaba Cloud Intelligence, said in a statement on Monday. Alibaba has increased its focus on cloud computing over the past two years, seeing the business as a major driver of growth. Daniel Zhang, Alibaba's CEO, said previously in an interview with CNBC that cloud computing could become the e-commerce giant's "main business".

(http://yingyu.xdf.cn/yd/tech/202004/11055281.html)

Passage 2 华为公司简介（节选）

Warm-up Words & Expressions

基础设施 infrastructure
智能终端 intelligent terminal
万物互联的智能世界 a fully connected, intelligent world
有效授权专利 active patent
商业蓝图 business blueprint

场景化解决方案 scenario-based solution
政务一网通 Government Public Services Digitalization BU (Business Unit)
超级终端 Super Device
数字联盟 digital alliance
价值链 value chain

Read Passage 2 and interpret it from Chinese into English.

华为是谁

华为创立于1987年，是全球领先的ICT（信息与通信）基础设施和智能终端提供商。我们的20.7万名员工遍及170多个国家和地区，为全球30多亿人口提供服务。我们致力于把数字世界带给每个人、每个家庭、每个组织，构建万物互联的智能世界。

研究与创新

科学探索与技术创新是推动人类文明进步和社会发展的主要力量。华为重视研究与创新，坚持走开放创新的道路，愿意与学术界、产业界一起，共同探索科学技术的前沿，推动创新升级，不断为全行业、全社会创造价值，携手共建美好的智能世界。

华为近十年累计投入的研发费用超过人民币 9773 亿元。2022 年，研发费用支出约为人民币 1615 亿元，占全年收入的 25.1%。2022 年底，研发员工约 11.4 万名，占总员工数量的 55.4%。截至 2022 年底，华为在全球共持有有效授权专利超过 12 万件。

发展历程

5G 行业应用迈入黄金发展时期，落地创新应用案例累计超过 2 万个。华为提出 GUIDE 商业蓝图，发布了"全面迈向 5.5G 时代"的理念。打造 100 多个场景化解决方案，成立煤矿、智能公路、公路水运口岸、政务一网通、电力数字化、数字金融、机场与轨道等业务部门。发布 Harmony OS 3，对超级终端进行全面扩容。华为云布局了全球 29 个地理区域，逐渐成为金融、制造等行业客户上云的首选。

华为 TECH4ALL 教育项目在全球 600 多所学校落地，逾 22 万名师生及青少年从中受益。加入国际电联 Partner2Connect 数字联盟，承诺到 2025 年将帮助全球 80 多个国家的 1.2 亿偏远地区人口连接数字社会。

质量方针

时刻铭记质量是华为生存的基石，是客户选择华为的理由。

我们把客户要求与期望准确传递到华为整个价值链，共同构建质量。

我们尊重规则流程，一次把事情做对。

我们发挥全球员工潜能，持续改进。

我们与客户一起平衡机会与风险，快速响应客户需求，实现可持续发展。

我们承诺向客户提供高质量的产品、服务和解决方案，持续不断让客户体验到我们致力于为每个客户创造价值。

（https://www.huawei.com/cn/corporate-information）

Memory Practice

Listen to the following paragraphs carefully without taking notes and then retell the main ideas in the source language based on your memory.

1. What is the main idea of Paragraph 1?
2. What is the main idea of Paragraph 2?

Section 2　Interpreting Practice

Passage 1　The Top 500 List

Warm-up Words & Expressions

Fortune Global 500 list《财富》世界 500 强企业榜单

new energy 新能源

global stage 全球舞台

the fifth consecutive year 连续第五年

top the list 位居榜首
electric vehicle battery maker 电动汽车电池制造商
Beijing Academy of Social Sciences 北京社科院
NEV-related (new energy vehicle) technologies and products 新能源汽车相关技术和产品
China Association of Automobile Manufacturers 中国汽车工业协会
market consultancy SNE Research 市场咨询机构 SNE 研究中心
Chinese Academy of International Trade and Economic Cooperation 商务部国际贸易经济合作研究院
global industrial chain 全球产业链
restructure 重组

🎧 Listen to Passage 1 and interpret it from English into Chinese.

Chinese companies have overtaken their United States counterparts in terms of number on this year's *Fortune* Global 500 list, which was unveiled on August 2, 2023 and tracks the world's richest enterprises in terms of revenue. Industry experts said the list shows China's growing prowess in emerging sectors, such as new energy, on the global stage.

A total of 142 Chinese companies, including those in Taiwan, made it to the annual list, marking the fifth consecutive year that Chinese companies topped the list in terms of number. The US and Japan followed with 136 and 41 enterprises, respectively.

China's Contemporary Amperex Technology Co., Ltd. —the world's largest electric vehicle battery maker—debuted on the list this year and ranked 292nd. Another Chinese company, new energy vehicle manufacturer BYD, jumped 12 spots compared with last year to rank 212th. In total, nine Chinese vehicle manufacturers have made it to the list, with most of them gaining ground with new energy vehicle technologies.

Wang Peng, a senior researcher at the Beijing Academy of Social Sciences, said this collective performance of Chinese companies demonstrated China's increasing international influence on the new energy sector. China has gained momentum in NEV-related technologies and products in recent years.

Many Chinese NEV companies have taken the lead globally with their technological breakthroughs in the new energy sector, according to Wang. He said that given the country's huge market, Chinese companies in the new energy sector are expected to have more presence on the global stage in the coming years. China sold about 6.89 million NEVs last year, an increase of more than 93 percent year-on-year, according to the China Association of Automobile Manufacturers.

A report released by market consultancy SNE Research last year showed that Chinese companies accounted for six of the top 10 NEV battery makers globally in terms of installation. However, Wang Zhile, a former senior researcher at the Chinese Academy of International Trade and Economic Cooperation, said in a note that the ranks of many leading Chinese companies have declined this year, and the gap between their average profit and that of the other *Fortune* Global

500 companies has widened.

The average profit of companies from the Chinese mainland and Hong Kong on the list is ＄3.9 billion, lower than the global average of ＄5.8 billion and US firms' ＄8 billion. The COVID-19 pandemic and conflicts around the world have changed the global economy, and the global industrial chain has started to restructure, Wang said. "These external factors have affected the development of Chinese companies to some extent," he added.

（https://language.chinadaily.com.cn/a/202308/04/WS64ccc00fa31035260b81a5fd.html）

Passage 2 海尔集团

Warm-up Words & Expressions

解决方案服务商 provider of solutions	工业互联网平台 industrial internet platform
物联网生态品牌 IoT ecosystem brand	"独角兽"企业 unicorn enterprises
最具价值全球品牌 Most Valuable Global Brands	"瞪羚"企业 gazelle enterprises
	"小巨人"企业 small giant enterprises
欧睿国际全球大型家电品牌 Euromonitor's Global Major Appliances Brand	实体经济 real economy
海尔智家 Haier Smart Home	智慧住居和产业互联网 smart living and industrial internet
智慧家庭场景品牌 smart home scenario brand	数字化转型 digital transformation

🎧 **Listen to Passage 2 and interpret it from Chinese into English.**

海尔集团创立于1984年，是全球领先的美好生活和数字化转型解决方案服务商。

我们始终以用户为中心，在全球设立了10个研发中心、71个研究院、35个工业园、138个制造中心和23万个销售网络，连续5年作为全球唯一物联网生态品牌蝉联"BrandZ最具价值全球品牌100强"，连续14年稳居"欧睿国际全球大型家电品牌零售量"第一名。

集团旗下有4家上市公司，子公司海尔智家为《财富》世界500强公司和《财富》全球最受赞赏公司。我们拥有海尔、卡萨帝、Leader、GE Appliances、Fisher & Paykel、AQUA、Candy等全球化高端品牌和全球首个智慧家庭场景品牌三翼鸟，构建了引领全球的世界级工业互联网平台卡奥斯COSMOPlat和物联网大健康产业生态盈康一生，旗下创业加速平台海创汇已孵化加速7家"独角兽"企业、107家"瞪羚"企业和124家专精特新"小巨人"企业。

海尔作为实体经济的代表，持续聚焦实业，布局智慧住居和产业互联网两大主赛道，建设高端品牌、场景品牌与生态品牌，以科技创新为全球用户定制智慧生活，助推企业实现数字化转型，助力经济社会高质量发展、可持续发展。

2023年9月20日，世界品牌实验室在"亚洲品牌大会"上发布了2023年《亚洲品牌500强》排行榜，海尔连续18年上榜，蝉联第四。该榜单主要对亚洲品牌影响力进行测评，基本指标包括市场占有率、品牌忠诚度和亚洲领导力。

（https://www.haier.com/press-events/news/20230426_209045.shtml?spm＝net.home_pc.hg2020_home_live_20240306.5）

Passage 3 Walmart

Warm-up Words & Expressions

the logo of Walmart 沃尔玛的商标
Rogers 罗杰斯镇
Arkansas 阿肯色州
Sam Walton 山姆·沃尔顿
visionary leadership 远见卓识的领导

leverage 利用
President and CEO David Cheesewright 总裁兼首席执行官大卫·奇怀特
paycheck 付薪水的支票，薪水

🎧 **Listen to Passage 3 and interpret it from English into Chinese.**

Almost everyone knows Walmart. When people are watching TV, they see the logo of Walmart. When people drive to buy daily food and groceries, they go to Walmart. People know that it is a brand and a supermarket. Do they know what makes Walmart so successful?

Since the first Walmart store opened in 1962 in Rogers, Arkansas, we've been dedicated to making a difference in the lives of our customers. Our business is the result of Sam Walton's visionary leadership, along with generations of associates focused on helping customers and communities save money and live better. This rich heritage defines who we are and what we do today.

From our humble beginnings as a small discount retailer in Rogers, Arkansas, Walmart has opened thousands of stores in the U.S. and expanded internationally. Through innovation, we're creating a seamless experience to let customers shop anytime and anywhere online, through mobile devices and in stores. We are creating opportunities and bringing value to customers and communities around the globe.

Walmart helps people around the world save money and live better—anytime and anywhere—in retail stores, online and through their mobile devices. Each week, more than 245 million customers and members visit our nearly 11,000 stores under 65 banners in 28 countries and e-commerce websites in 11 countries. With fiscal year 2015 net sales of $482.2 billion, Walmart employs 2.2 million associates worldwide.

Walmart became an international company in 1991, and we operate in 27 countries outside the United States. With more than 6,200 stores internationally, we leverage our global resources to meet local needs. Walmart International is currently the fastest growing part of our business and is led by President and CEO David Cheesewright.

Save money. Live better. These are the words we live by at Walmart. Our "every day low cost" strategy helps people save money, stretch their paychecks, and provide a better life for their families. But the work we do to help people live better goes far beyond our store walls. It extends into our communities and around the world and affects the lives of people we will never meet.

We believe we have an opportunity and a responsibility to make a difference on the big issues that matter to us all. Issues like preserving the environment, fighting hunger, empowering women and providing access to healthy, affordable food. Walmart is driving meaningful change in a way that no other company can. And we're committed to using our size and scale to help the world live better.

Passage 4 腾讯集团

Warm-up Words & Expressions

科技向善 use technology for good
便捷的出行 access transportation
互动娱乐体验 interactive entertainment experience
云计算 cloud computing
香港联合交易所 Stock Exchange of Hong Kong
社会责任 social responsibility
可持续发展 sustainable development
开放协同 be inclusive and collaborative
双通道职业发展路径 grow vertically or horizontally in one's career
职级体系 ranking system
互联互通 interconnected

🎧 **Listen to Passage 4 and interpret it from Chinese into English.**

公司简介

腾讯是一家世界领先的互联网科技公司，用创新的产品和服务提升全球各地人们的生活品质。腾讯成立于1998年，总部位于中国深圳。公司一直秉承科技向善的宗旨。我们的通信和社交服务连接全球逾10亿人，帮助他们与亲友联系，畅享便捷的出行、支付和娱乐生活。

腾讯发行多款风靡全球的电子游戏及其他优质数字内容，为全球用户带来丰富的互动娱乐体验。腾讯还提供云计算、广告、金融科技等一系列企业服务，支持合作伙伴实现数字化转型，促进业务发展。腾讯在2004年于香港联合交易所上市。

愿景及使命

一切以用户价值为依归，将社会责任融入产品及服务之中；推动科技创新与文化传承，助力各行各业升级，促进社会的可持续发展。

价值观

正直：坚守底线，以德为先，坦诚公正不唯上。

进取：无功便是过，勇于突破有担当。

协作：开放协同，持续进化。

创造：超越创新，探索未来。

人才发展

人才是腾讯最宝贵的财富。我们一直高度重视员工的发展，不仅为员工设计专业和管理的双通道职业发展路径，让员工的能力得到更聚焦、更清晰的发展，也同时让每个人的成长贡献能够通过职级体系得到及时明确的体现。

办公环境

作为腾讯全球新总部，腾讯滨海大厦于2017年10月正式启用。这是一座集数字化、智能化于一体的智慧大厦。这座"互联互通"的大厦，象征着互联网将各个角落互相连通，更体现了腾讯是一家专注连接人和人、人和服务，以及未来人和设备的互联网高科技企业。除此以外，我们在北京、上海、成都、广州等多个城市以及美国、韩国等多个海外国家均建立了分支机构,并为当地员工打造了舒适、创新,体现腾讯文化特色的办公环境。

(https://www.tencent.com/zh-cn/about.html#about-con-1)

Section 3　Interpreting Assessment

Passage 1　An Introduction to Ford

Warm-up Words & Expressions

the Ford Motor Company 福特汽车公司
automotive 汽车的
automobile 汽车
come into being 形成,产生
assembly line 装配线
flagship 旗舰

🎧 Listen to Passage 1 and interpret it from English into Chinese.

评价项目	评价标准	原始赋分	学生得分
内容准确	忠实于原文,知识点准确,用词得当,句式合理。	30分	
内容完整	完整传达原文的内容和含义,没有漏译。	20分	
语言标准	语音语调标准,符合目标语言的地道表达方式,能够传达出原文的语气和情感。	20分	
表达流利	口译流畅自然,无重译、停顿或修正现象。	20分	
职业素养	听力反应敏捷,仪态大方,临场反应能力强。	10分	
合计		100分	
被评人			
评价人			
教师评价			

Passage 2　吉利控股集团

Warm-up Words & Expressions

吉利控股集团 Geely Holding Group
智能电动出行 smart electric mobility
上下游产业链 upstream and downstream industrial chains
汽车产业电动化和智能化转型 the electrification and intelligent transformation of the automotive industry
共享出行 shared mobility
车联网 vehicle networks
智能驾驶 autonomous driving
前沿技术 cutting-edge technology

🎧 Listen to Passage 2 and interpret it from Chinese into English.

评价项目	评价标准	原始赋分	学生得分
内容准确	忠实于原文，知识点准确，用词得当，句式合理。	30分	
内容完整	完整传达原文的内容和含义，没有漏译。	20分	
语言标准	语音语调标准，符合目标语言的地道表达方式，能够传达出原文的语气和情感。	20分	
表达流利	口译流畅自然，无重译、停顿或修正现象。	20分	
职业素养	听力反应敏捷，仪态大方，临场反应能力强。	10分	
合计		100分	
被评人			
评价人			
教师评价			

Unit 6 Product Presentation

Learning Objectives
- Master the frequently used phrases, expressions and patterns of product presentation
- Acquire cultural background knowledge about product presentation
- Discover ways to enhance the interpreting skills and performance in the context of product presentation

Ideological and Political Objectives
- Strengthen the cultivation of thinking ability and comprehensive analytical skills in the process of interpretation
- Deepen the comprehension of China's strategy for leveraging scientific and technological advancements
- Arouse the inspiration for independent research and development
- Stimulate the cultural self-confidence

Section 1   Interpreting Preparation

Key Concepts

1. Independent research and development 自主研发

Independent research and development can be defined as the process in which enterprises or individuals independently carry out research and development activities based on market demand or their own needs through their own technology, talent, and funding resources, in order to obtain innovative results and core technologies, and achieve their own development and competitive advantages.

2. China Council for the Promotion of International Trade 中国国际贸易促进委员会

Founded in 1952, China Council for the Promotion of International Trade (CCPIT) is a national foreign trade and investment promotion agency. The CCPIT will establish wide connections with relevant international organizations, trade & investment promotion agencies, commercial associations and business circle, to organize various forms of communication and cooperation. It is committed to enhancing services for companies and making positive contributions to development of bilateral and multilateral trade relationships, promotion of world economic prosperity and improvement of the well-being of all mankind.

3. Hehe Culture 和合文化

Hehe Culture is part of traditional Chinese culture. President Xi Jinping once summarized Hehe Culture quite concisely in his work *Zhejiang, China: A New Vision for Development*: "Our ancestors created an incomparable culture, a quintessential part of which is the Hehe culture. The first 'He' of Hehe indicates harmony, peace, and balance. The second 'He' indicates convergence, unity, and cooperation. Such inclusiveness is reflected in the traditional thinking of 'valuing harmony and esteeming balance', 'being understanding and open-minded', 'embracing the world through virtue', and 'living in harmony without uniformity'. This is a cultural ideal that our people seek. Harmony between nature and society and between the individual and the group is the ideal of our people and the basis of our cohesiveness and creativity."

4. Made in China 2025 中国制造 2025

"Made in China 2025" is a forward-looking initiative designed to build on China's current level of industrialization and enhance the quality of products and equipment made in China. The initiative was officially launched on May 8, 2015 by China's State Council as the country's first 10-year plan of action for transforming China's manufacturing. It aims to put China on a new path to industrialization, with a greater emphasis on innovation, with expanded use of new-generation information technology, intelligent manufacturing, consolidation of the industrial base, integration of industrial processes and systems, and with a robust multilayer talent development structure.

☞ Sight Interpreting

Passage 1 Foreign Companies up Investment in China's Manufacturing Sector

Warm-up Words & Expressions

wholly owned battery system plant 全资控股的电池系统工厂
initial annual capacity 初始年产能
high-voltage battery systems 高压电池系统
refrigeration industry 制冷行业
Ministry of Commerce 商务部
comprehensive industrial ecosystem 全面的产业生态系统
innovation vitality 创新活力
friendly business environment 友好的营商环境
Belt and Road Forum for International Cooperation "一带一路"国际合作高峰论坛
China Council for the Promotion of International Trade 中国国际贸易促进委员会

Read passage 1 and interpret it from English into Chinese.

Volkswagen (Anhui) Components Co., Ltd., Volkswagen Group's first wholly owned battery system plant in China, started production on November 21 in Hefei, the capital of East China's Anhui Province. With a total investment of over 140 million euros, the plant has an initial annual capacity of 150,000 to 180,000 high-voltage battery systems. Volkswagen Group is among the foreign companies that are increasing investments in China's manufacturing sector as the country continues to promote high-quality development of manufacturing and high-standard opening-up.

In May, refrigeration industry giant Danfoss inaugurated its global refrigeration research and development and testing center in Tianjin. In the same month, BMW Group's joint venture in China, BMW Brilliance Automotive Ltd., began the construction of a new battery production plant in Liaoning's capital Shenyang.

A total of 41,947 new foreign-invested companies were established in China during the first 10 months of 2023, data from the Ministry of Commerce showed. Specifically, the actual use of foreign investment in manufacturing rose 1.9 percent year-on-year to 283.44 billion yuan during this period, with that in high-tech manufacturing logging an increase of 9.5 percent.

China's strong appeal to foreign-funded manufacturing projects can be attributed to several key factors, including its comprehensive industrial ecosystem, huge and open market, strong R&D and innovation vitality, and friendly business environment.

At the third Belt and Road Forum for International Cooperation in October, China said it would remove all restrictions on foreign investment access in the manufacturing sector. According to a recent survey conducted by the China Council for the Promotion of International Trade, for three consecutive quarters, the surveyed foreign enterprises identified "technological innovation and R&D" as the greatest development opportunity in the Chinese market.

(https://language.chinadaily.com.cn/a/202312/04/WS656d9bc4a31090682a5f15c0.html)

Passage 2 华为 Mate X

Warm-up Words & Expressions

世界移动大会 Mobile World Congress	广角镜头 wide-angle lens
折叠手机 foldable smartphone	长焦镜头 telephoto lens
专利铰链 patented hinge	两块电池 dual batteries
处理器 processor	超级快充 Super Charge
芯片组 chipset	噱头 gimmick
启动和运行无线网络 get wireless networks up and running	被压抑的需求 pent-up demand
	爆发出热烈掌声 burst into warm applause

Read Passage 2 and interpret it from Chinese into English.

华为在 2019 世界移动通信大会中正式发布了旗下首款折叠屏手机华为 Mate X，该款手机是三星折叠手机的强劲对手。三星折叠手机 Galaxy Fold 发布不到一周，就遇上了对手，华为这款手机更薄、屏幕更大、折叠更平滑。

华为消费者业务 CEO 余承东在台上展示了新款华为 Mate X，并表示："我们为您呈现未来的设计和科技。"不同于像翻书一样由内翻开的三星折叠手机 Galaxy Fold，华为折叠手机是鹰翼式外折。这一别致的功能设计让华为手机更加轻薄。

据介绍，华为这款折叠机机身单边厚度为 5.4 mm，折叠后为 11 mm。华为的折叠屏是由外向内翻折的，据华为介绍，这是靠包含了 100 多个零件的专利铰链设计实现的。

华为Mate X搭载华为最强的5G多模终端芯片——麒麟980处理器和巴龙5000芯片组，最快可实现3秒下载一部1G的视频。Mate X是华为首款5G智能手机。华为表示，与其他推出5G设备的公司相比，它具有优势，因为它提供了启动和运行无线网络所需的全套设备。

这部手机包含了3款摄像头——40MP（mega pixel，百万像素）主摄像头、16MP的广角镜头和8MP的长焦镜头，还有一个LED闪光灯和一个开关键。Mate X的拍照系统将前后摄像头合一，还提供镜像拍照功能，让你在拍照时看到照片预览。

该设备内置两块电池，容量高达4500 mAh，同时支持华为最新的55W超级快充，堪称业内充电最快的手机。充电30分钟，就能达到85%的电量。

无论这款新手机有多创新，技术有多先进，要让一定数量级的用户体验到折叠手机和5G科技，仍然需要相当长的时间。

你也许会觉得华为Mate X这类折叠手机只是噱头，但你只要看看飞机上那些拿着手机看电影的人，就会明白，人们被压抑了许久的对平板大小的手机屏幕的需求有多大。

华为新品发布引来大量围观人群。粉丝们在活动开始前就在场外排着长队等候，那些没能入场的人就在外面看大屏幕，人群中时不时爆发出热烈掌声。Mate X明确地让我们看到华为已成为科技创新的引领者。这款新设备丝毫不逊于三星最新发布的Galaxy Fold。

（https://mp.weixin.qq.com/s/3V7ZlkJPsqkHPvGLvbDEfw）

☞ Memory Practice

🎧 **Listen to the following paragraphs carefully without taking notes and then retell the main ideas in the source language based on your memory.**

1. What is the main idea of Paragraph 1?
2. What is the main idea of Paragraph 2?

Section 2 Interpreting Practice

Passage 1 Sweet and Sour Lemon Melon

Warm-up Words & Expressions

aroma 香味	Yubari melon 夕张蜜瓜
reminiscent 回味；与……相似的	Hokkaido 北海道
horticulture 园艺	rave about 称赞
Suntory Flowers 三得利花卉园艺公司	HBC（Hokkaido Broadcasting Co., Ltd.）
blend 杂交	News《北海道放送》
rind 外皮	square-shaped watermelon 方形西瓜
stripes and striations 条纹	Ruby Roman 罗马红宝石
flesh 果肉	iconic 经典的
texture 口感	

🎧 **Listen to Passage 1 and interpret it from English into Chinese.**

The lemon melon is a newly developed type of melon that combines the sweetness and aroma of the melon with a slight sourness reminiscent of the lemon. Japanese horticulture company Suntory Flowers reportedly spent five years developing the lemon melon, breeding it from a type of melon originally imported from overseas.

The final product, which is blended with actual lemons, is juicy and sweet like a melon but slightly sour like a lemon, making the perfect fruit enjoy on a hot summer day. The lemon melon has the usual round shape of a melon, but its rind lacks the characteristic stripes and striations of a melon, and has white flesh. The texture is comparable to pears, but it softens as it ripens and ends up like Yubari melons.

There are currently only five farmers in Hokkaido growing lemon melons, and they are expected to grow about 3,800 of them this year. Lemon melons have already hit Japanese supermarket shelves, selling for around 3,220 yen a piece. Those lucky enough to have tried it can't stop raving about its delicious taste. "It has a faint sourness like a lemon, but the strong sweetness of a melon. It's delicious," a reporter from *HBC News* said. "It has a good balance of sweet and sour. It would be the perfect fruit for a hot day," another person said.

The lemon melon is the latest addition to Japan's popular luxury fruit market, which includes edible wonders like the world's most expensive watermelon, square-shaped watermelons, Ruby Roman, the world's most expensive grapes, and white jewels, Japan's iconic white strawberries.

（https://baijiahao.baidu.com/s?id=1773085146265209684&wfr=spider&for=pc）

Passage 2　奥运背包

Warm-up Words & Expressions

媒体中心 media center	保温杯 insulated cup
伊朗记者 Iranian journalist	窗花 paper-cut window grille
报道体育赛事 cover sports competition	中国结 Chinese knot
摄影记者 photography journalist	冬残奥会 Winter Paralympics
缩影 microcosm	闭环管理 closed-loop management
国货 domestic goods	试运行 trial run
艺术体操运动员 rhythmic gymnast	

🎧 **Listen to Passage 2 and interpret it from Chinese into English.**

有人发现，一些外国记者在北京2022年冬奥会媒体中心工作时，随身携带着2008年北京夏季奥运会的背包。

一名伊朗记者称，他每次报道体育赛事时，都会带着2008年北京奥运会的背包。这位记者说："对于摄影记者来说，背包是一件非常重要的物品，这个包质量很好，设计也很人性化。"

小小的背包，成为"中国制造"的缩影。大家纷纷评论：国货就是强。除了提供给媒体工作者的媒体包外，2008年夏季奥运会颁发的金牌也是质量过硬。俄罗斯艺术体操运动员达里娅·什库里欣娜的公寓被烧毁,大火过后,什库里欣娜发现她在2008年奥运会上获得的金镶玉金牌仍然完好无损。

在2022年冬奥会上,来自世界各地的媒体工作者将收到一份全新的媒体包,其中包括一个保温杯、窗花或中国结等文化纪念品以及其他礼物。

距离冬奥会还有不到一个月的时间,北京2022年冬奥会和冬残奥会的媒体中心正式启动了闭环管理试运行。在1月4日至1月22日试运行期间,该中心将接待来自世界各地的1700多名记者、摄影师和电视广播工作人员。

(https://language.chinadaily.com.cn/a/202201/12/WS61de1a06a310cdd39bc80734.html)

Passage 3　iPhone 15 Series Instructions

Warm-up Words & Expressions

rounded corner 圆角	说明
curved design 曲线设计	warranty 保修
standard rectangle 标准矩形	network configuration 网络设置
diagonally 对角的	limited recharge cycles 充电周期次数有限
stand 支架	battery life 电池续航时间
splash, water, and dust resistant 防溅、抗水、防尘	select carriers 特定运营商
	roadside assistance 道路援助
under controlled laboratory conditions 受控实验室条件下	activation 激活
	detect a severe car crash 检测到严重车祸
normal wear 日常磨损	cellular connection 蜂窝网络连接
user guide 用户手册	Wi-Fi calling 无线局域网通话功能
cleaning and drying instructions 清洁和干燥	

🎧 **Listen to Passage 3 and interpret it from English into Chinese.**

The display has rounded corners that follow a beautiful curved design, and these corners are within a standard rectangle. When measured as a standard rectangular shape, the screen is 6.12 inches or 6.69 inches diagonally. Actual viewable area is less.

Stand sold separately.

iPhone 15 and iPhone 15 Plus are splash, water, and dust resistant and were tested under controlled laboratory conditions. Splash, water, and dust resistance are not permanent conditions. Resistance might decrease as a result of normal wear. Do not attempt to charge a wet iPhone, refer to the user guide for cleaning and drying instructions. Liquid damage not covered under warranty.

All battery claims depend on network configuration and many other factors, actual results will vary. Battery has limited recharge cycles and may eventually need to be replaced. Battery life and charge cycles vary by use and settings.

5G is available in select markets and through select carriers. Speeds vary based on site conditions and carriers.

Roadside assistance and emergency SOS via satellite are included for free for two years with the activation of any iPhone 15 model. Connection and response times vary based on location, site conditions, and other factors.

iPhone 15 and iPhone 15 Pro can detect a severe car crash and call for help. It requires a cellular connection or Wi-Fi calling. Fees are determined by the roadside assistance provider, and can vary based on your location and the type of assistance provided.

(http://www.apple.com)

Passage 4 淄博烧烤

Warm-up Words & Expressions

双选会 job fair	新闻发布会 news conference
走红 go viral	指定酒店 designated hotel
肉串 skewer	烧烤节 barbecue festival
小葱 scallion	食品安全 food safety
创下纪录 set a record	公交专线 bus line
商务局 commerce bureau	

🎧 **Listen to Passage 4 and interpret it from Chinese into English.**

长期以来，山东省淄博市一直在努力宣传其独特的烧烤串、蔬菜、海鲜和其他美食，希望创造"打卡地"，直到二月之前，都收效甚微。直到一些大学生来淄博参加双选会，尝试了淄博烧烤，并拍摄了"撸串"视频发布到社交媒体上，事情发生了变化，淄博烧烤开始走红。于是，来自全国各地的年轻人开始涌入淄博吃烧烤。

淄博烧烤主打"半自助"模式——上桌的肉串只烤到七八成熟，后续火候由食客自己掌握。而桌上的小饼、小葱、调料的搭配，使得"小饼卷一切"更像北京传统烤鸭的吃法。

来自山东交通职业学院的学生许佳悦从潍坊来到淄博品尝烧烤。她说："我们可以自己用炉子烤肉，更有参与感，而且保证了串串有温度，味道也更好。"

自3月4日以来，淄博火车站的到达人数创下纪录，3月4日更是达到27 065人，创近3年以来最高纪录。火车站工作人员说，来自周围城市的大学生占很大一部分。

一家烧烤店的老板说，在过去的两周里，餐馆外面每天都排着长队。多家餐馆的老板表示，在过去的一周，尤其是周末，他们每天卖出1万多串烤串。很多客人吃饱了就在周围游览淄博的景点。

淄博市商务局局长殷启迪在新闻发布会表示，"淄博烧烤迅速走红并非偶然"，这座曾经的传统工业城市一直在努力将其发展成为一个对年轻人友好的城市。他补充说，淄博为18岁至35岁的外来游客在指定酒店提供打折房间。当地统计数据显示，几家为年轻人提供此类服务的酒店都已预订一空。

殷局长还表示，淄博还将举办烧烤节庆祝活动。市场监督部门和公共安全部门将通力合作确保食品安全和定价合理。淄博市公共交通有限公司则推出21条公交定制专线，为往返旅客提供交通服务。

(https://www.ximalaya.com/audio/639489734)

Section 3　Interpreting Assessment

Passage 1　Product Introduction

Warm-up Words & Expressions

network marketing 网络营销
health industry 保健产业
ISO-certified manufacturing facility 经过ISO认证的生产设备
Dennington Street 丹宁顿街
involve zero human contact 无人接触
the Forbes Magazine 福布斯杂志
Asia-Pacific 亚太地区
elite product 优秀的产品
aside from 除……外
flagship product 旗舰产品

plum 李子、理想之物
testimonial 证书；褒奖
obesity 肥胖
synthetic 人造的
ingredient 成分
antioxidant 抗氧化剂
vanguard 先锋，先驱
fat-blocker 阻隔脂肪
probiotic 益生菌
multiplication 增加

🎧 **Listen to Passage 1 and interpret it from English into Chinese.**

评价项目	评价标准	原始赋分	学生得分
内容准确	忠实于原文，知识点准确，用词得当，句式合理。	30分	
内容完整	完整传达原文的内容和含义，没有漏译。	20分	
语言标准	语音语调标准，符合目标语言的地道表达方式，能够传达出原文的语气和情感。	20分	
表达流利	口译流畅自然，无重译、停顿或修正现象。	20分	
职业素养	听力反应敏捷，仪态大方，临场反应能力强。	10分	
合计		100分	
被评人			
评价人			
教师评价			

Passage 2　Metapad 的推广

Warm-up Words & Expressions

北京创天下科技有限公司 Beijing Heaven Creation Technology Co., Ltd.
总部 headquarter

分公司 branch office
办事处 office
营业额 turnover

系统集成商 system integrator　　　　　展示 demonstrate
多点触屏 multi-touch screen　　　　　一体机 all-in-one computer

🎧 **Listen to Passage 2 and interpret it from Chinese into English.**

评价项目	评价标准	原始赋分	学生得分
内容准确	忠实于原文，知识点准确，用词得当，句式合理。	30分	
内容完整	完整传达原文的内容和含义，没有漏译。	20分	
语言标准	语音语调标准，符合目标语言的地道表达方式，能够传达出原义的语气和情感。	20分	
表达流利	口译流畅自然，无重译、停顿或修正现象。	20分	
职业素养	听力反应敏捷，仪态大方，临场反应能力强。	10分	
合计		100分	
被评人			
评价人			
教师评价			

Unit 7 Business Strategies

Learning Objectives

- Master the frequently used phrases, expressions and patterns of business strategies
- Be able to interpret speeches on business strategies
- Improve the interpretation skills and performance on the speech of business strategies

Ideological and Political Objectives

- Draw the attention towards Chinese traditional brands and arouse the patriotic feelings
- Understand the background of Belt and Road Initiative and Maritime Silk Road
- Strengthen the knowledge about environmental protection

Section 1 Interpreting Preparation

👉 Key Concepts

1. Belt and Road Initiative "一带一路"

The Belt and Road Initiative (BRI) —China's proposal to cooperate with other countries in building a Silk Road Economic Belt and a 21st Century Maritime Silk Road—was unveiled by President Xi Jinping during his visits to Central and Southeast Asia in September and October 2013. It is a strategic initiative launched by the central leadership and a major measure in China's all-round opening-up in the current era. It also serves as an important platform for building a community with a shared future for humanity.

2. 21st Century Maritime Silk Road 21世纪海上丝绸之路

Formed during the Qin and Han Dynasties (221 BC – AD 220), the Maritime Silk Road has always played an important role in economic and cultural exchanges between East and West. And Southeast Asia has always been a nexus of this interaction. On the occasion of the 10th Anniversary of the China-ASEAN (Association of Southeast Asian Nations) Strategic Partnership, President Xi Jinping proposed jointly building a 21st Century Maritime Silk Road in his speech to the Indonesian parliament on October 3, 2013. The initiative aims to boost China-ASEAN maritime cooperation and forge closer ties in a community with a shared future. It calls for joint efforts across the region and beyond. Starting with the launch of individual projects that are expected to help spur a wider range of cooperative activities, it envisions a network of interconnected markets linking the ASEAN, South Asia, West Asia, North Africa, and Europe, and a strategic partnership for the South China Sea and the Pacific and Indian oceans.

3. Traditional domestic brands 传统国货品牌

A growing number of Chinese enterprises have been listed in the fortune magazine. Traditional Chinese medicine brand Tong Ren Tang, alcohol brand Kweichow Moutai and Bank of China were named to the first three spots.

Some popular brands even provide products or services to consumers with a history of more than 60 years in Chinese mainland. China's top 10 brands for historical and cultural heritage this year, which based on several criteria, including brand history, value and cultural heritage, can be seen in the list below. Tong Ren Tang, a traditional Chinese medicine brand; Kweichow Moutai, a liquor brand; Zhonghua, a cigarette brand; Wuliangye, a liquor brand; Yiyuanqing, a vinegar brand; Chenliji, a traditional Chinese medicine brand; Bee&flower, a shampoo brand; Yumeijing, a cosmetic brand; and so on.

4. Green transformation 绿色转型

President Xi Jinping urged the Asia-Pacific region to promote green transition, follow the principle of common but differentiated responsibilities and deliver on what was agreed upon in the *Paris Agreement* on climate change and at the 15th Meeting of the Conference of the Parties to the *Convention on Biological Diversity*.

A sound eco-environment is the most basic public good that benefits all. China has formulated an Action Plan for Carbon Dioxide Peaking Before 2030, and moved faster to put in place a "1 + N" policy framework. Here, "1" stands for the guiding principle and top-level design for carbon peak and carbon neutrality, and "N" refers to implementation plans for key areas and industries, including the action for green energy transition, the action for peaking carbon dioxide emissions in the industrial sector, the action for promoting green and low-carbon transportation, and the action for promoting circular economy for decarbonization purposes.

☞ Sight Interpreting

Passage 1 BMW's Strategy for Electric Models

Warm-up Words & Expressions

pure electric model 纯电动车车型	carbon emission 碳排放量
mass-produced motorcycle 量产纯电动摩托车	life cycle 生命周期
Chinese debut 中国首发	climate neutrality 气候中和
presale 预售	electric vehicle ecosystem 电动车生态系统
concept vehicle 概念车	maintenance 维修
large-scale 大规模	installation service 安装服务
green transition 绿色转型	public charging pile 公共充电桩
full-value chain 全价值链	

Read Passage 1 and interpret it from English into Chinese.

BMW Group has launched five pure electric models in the Chinese market by this time. They are the BMW i7, the iX, the i4, the China-made iX3 as well as the all-new i3.

In the first half of the year, BMW Motorrad's second mass-produced motorcycle in the all-new BMW CE 04 made its Chinese debut and started a presales campaign. The first Mini-brand pure electric concept vehicle Aceman made its Asian debut in Shanghai in September. By 2023, the number of BMW Group's pure electric models will increase to 11. By 2025, BMW Group is expected to deliver its 2 millionth electric vehicle worldwide and will launch its Neue Klasse model. Half of the group's sales will be EVs (electric vehicles) by 2030.

The Lydia Plant, a large-scale plant extension opened this year in BMW's Shenyang production base, is an example of the BMW iFACTORY strategy, following the principles of "Lean, Green and Digital". Through the green transition of its full-value chain, BMW Group plans to reduce the average carbon emissions of the whole life cycle by at least 40 percent by 2030 and achieve climate neutrality by 2050.

While accelerating its electrification transformation, BMW also focuses on building an electric vehicle ecosystem. By the end of October, there are around 600 dealer shops with BMW i certification, giving the brand a huge advantage of EV maintenance network services.

BMW continues to optimize its charging products and installation services, expand its public charging network, improve the service quality and accelerate the innovation of digital functions.

There are more than 460,000 public charging piles of BMW available in China by September, including 250,000 fast charging piles covering more than 320 cities nationwide.

(https://mp.weixin.qq.com/s?__biz=MzU1NTcxODQ0OQ==&mid=2247768192&idx=1&sn=944d19fe2bdf4d04dc8b7b2015b7e638&chksm=fbde9adecca913c896d40afa1db11594202891f912e06ba64ca65cb38b2d35c7cc3364aae4f5&mpshare=1&scene=23&srcid=1004JessGMpl0JhYfzsQQfct&sharer_shareinfo=07164d1a3507fdcb966f6a0fa479f653&sharer_shareinfo_first=07164d1a3507fdcb966f6a0fa479f653#rd)

Passage 2　海尔集团创新年会演讲（节选）

Warm-up Words & Expressions

智慧家庭 Smart Home	集体所有制 collective ownership
核心能力平台 core competence platform	股份 equity
场景 scenario	创客合伙人 entrepreneurship partner
发展 evolve	上市公司 listed company
指数级增长 exponential growth	共享资源 pool resources
利用 leverage	原创技术 original technology
濒临倒闭 on the verge of shutdown	创业加速平台 entrepreneurial accelerator platform
坚持创业创新精神 uphold entrepreneurship and innovation	

Unit 7 Business Strategies

Read Passage 2 and interpret it from Chinese into English.

智慧家庭产业版图

以海尔智家为载体，聚焦打造三翼鸟体验云和智家大脑两大核心能力平台，并加快智慧厨房、智慧空气、智慧用水和全屋智能四大场景的创新发展，实现生态收入的指数级增长。同时，与有屋科技、日日顺供应链等板块实现互联互通，无缝对接，利用数字化为用户设计智慧家、建设智慧家、服务智慧家，打造全流程的最佳用户体验。

机制创新，激发活力

泰山不让土壤，故能成其大；河海不择细流，故能就其深。海尔从濒临倒闭的集体小厂能发展到今天，靠的是坚持创业创新精神，坚持以人的价值最大化为宗旨。

海尔的创客制是在不改变企业集体所有制产权性质的基础上，为激发全员创客创新活力而设计的创新机制，它实现了两个颠覆：一是即使没有股份，也可通过经营权的分享，获得收益。二是即使拥有股份，不创造增值，也没机会获得资本利得。数据显示，2021年，通过创客份额或股权获得收益的创客合伙人，范围扩大至14 681人；跟投创业公司、上市公司的人数较上一年增加81%，在共同富裕的道路上作出了有益的探索。

科技为要，自立自强

开放的创新体系优势。目前海尔已经在全球建立了"10 + N"创新中心，覆盖五大洲、20余个国家和地区，连接了超过20万专家，凝聚全球共享资源，实现了开放式创新。

从原创技术到形成产业链的成果转化优势。近10年内，海尔创造了170余项对行业有重大影响的原创技术，全部创新成果均快速转化至产业链，并给用户带来了全新的体验。

科技与创业孵化相结合的融合创新优势。海尔海创汇建立的创业加速平台，把科技创新与创业孵化贯通，目前已经孵化出5家上市公司、90家"瞪羚"企业、38家专精特新"小巨人"企业，形成了"科技助力创业，创业加速科创"的融合创新的新模式。

(https://www.haier.com/press-events/news/20220117_174923.shtml)

Memory Practice

Listen to the following paragraphs carefully without taking notes and then retell the main ideas in the source language based on your memory.

1. What is the main idea of Paragraph 1?
2. What is the main idea of Paragraph 2?

Section 2 Interpreting Practice

Passage 1 New Policy for Private Enterprises

Warm-up Words & Expressions

bolster 促进
full play to the significant role 充分发挥重要作用
hail 赞扬
shore up 提振
beef up 提高

advance Chinese modernization 推进中国式现代化
stabilize economic growth 稳定经济
tackle prominent problems 解决突出问题
consolidate the economic recovery trend 巩固经济复苏趋势
Political Bureau 政治局
Communist Party of China Central Committee 中共中央
roll out 发布
spur private investment 刺激民营企业投资
State Council 国务院
market entry barriers 市场准入壁垒
National Development and Reform Commission 国家发展改革委
tax cuts 减税
real estate investment trust products 不动产投资信托基金
cyber security company 网络安全公司

🎧 Listen to Passage 1 and interpret it from English into Chinese.

China's latest push to bolster the growth of its private sector will greatly boost the confidence of entrepreneurs and give full play to the significant role of private enterprises in creating job opportunities and reviving economic recovery amid downward pressures, experts and company executives said.

They hailed the policy measures that were announced recently to encourage private investment and stimulate the private economy, and highlighted that these steps will significantly shore up market confidence. They said the measures will also motivate private enterprises to beef up their innovation capabilities and achieve breakthroughs in crucial technologies, thus promoting industrial upgrading.

The private sector serves as a vital force in advancing Chinese modernization and plays a key role in stabilizing economic growth, expanding employment and boosting technological innovation. The country has sent a clear signal that it is committed to promoting the healthy and sustained development of the private economy. China's enhanced supportive measures, which have been introduced to tackle prominent problems facing private enterprises and to improve the business environment, are key to boosting confidence and stabilizing the expectations of private enterprises and entrepreneurs, which will further consolidate the economic recovery trend.

On July 24, a meeting of the Political Bureau of the Communist Party of China (CPC) Central Committee, which set the policy tone for the second half of the year, emphasized efforts to "effectively optimize the development environment for private enterprises". More policies should be formulated and rolled out to spur private investment, while the authorities will establish and improve regular communication and exchange mechanisms with enterprises, the meeting said.

The leadership meeting came after the CPC Central Committee and the State Council, the country's Cabinet, issued a top-level guideline on July 19, detailing 31 measures such as facilitating private enterprises' access to funding, reducing market entry barriers, promoting fair competition and supporting development of platform companies to generate jobs and spur consumption. On August 1, the National Development and Reform Commission (NDRC), the country's top economic planner, along with a group of ministries, rolled out 28 detailed measures including tax cuts and removal of red tape to bolster the private economy.

Private enterprises will be encouraged to participate in major national projects that are profitable and mature, issue real estate investment trust products for infrastructure projects and lead technological programs in key areas, the NDRC said.

Zhou Hongyi, the founder of Chinese cyber security company 360 Security Group, said the recent policy development has affirmed the significant role of private enterprises in driving technological innovation and stabilizing employment, and it will bring new historic opportunities for the high-quality development of the private economy.

(https://language.chinadaily.com.cn/a/202308/17/WS64ddd0eca31035260b81cbb8.html)

Passage 2 茅台风味拿铁

Warm-up Words & Expressions

咖啡连锁品牌 coffee chain	加冰的拿铁 iced latte
成为热门 become a hit	白酒香味 aroma of the Baijiu
53 度贵州茅台酒 volume of 53 degrees Kweichow Moutai	头晕 dizzy
	未成年人 underage people
社交媒体 social media	酒精过敏 allergic to alcohol

🎧 **Listen to Passage 2 and interpret it from Chinese into English.**

周一，贵州茅台与国产咖啡连锁品牌瑞幸联合推出的酱香拿铁正式开卖，很快成为热门。据介绍，酱香拿铁含 53 度贵州茅台酒，酒精度数低于 0.5%，很快成为国内社交媒体的热门话题。美酒和咖啡的组合深深吸引了周一精神不振的打工人。大家纷纷下单，导致北京很多门店中午之前就出现了爆单售罄的情况。

位于北京惠新东桥附近的瑞幸门店的张姓店员表示，周一上午都是以酱香拿铁订单为主。她说："明显大家更喜欢加冰的拿铁，以至于店里的冰很快就用完了"。

人们纷纷在朋友圈和微博分享消费后的感受。很多人说能闻到很浓的白酒香味，有的人喝的时候有种酒心巧克力的感觉，但是没有"上头"的感觉。但也有消费者表示，喝完有点头晕。喝了含酒的咖啡能不能开车，也成了大家热议的话题。瑞幸提示未成年人、孕妇、驾驶人员和酒精过敏者不建议饮用此款产品。北京市交管局法制科的一位工作人员建议，消费者喝完含酒精饮品后不要再开车。

茅台正在寻求可以贴近年轻消费者的方式。与瑞幸联名推出"酱香拿铁"，作为传统高端白酒品牌的茅台既实现了大众化，又连接到了年轻人。茅台最近参与了一系列的市场营销活动，包括茅台冰淇淋和其他有创新的产品。

(https://mp.weixin.qq.com/s?__biz=MzU1NTcxODQ0OQ==&mid=2247828075&idx=1&sn=ab70249119e10a575b1ec8c9cc089f8a&chksm=fbdf8035cca80923ee451f02a5af1ebe081bab2a8ca7c6f6d64576327f5680400e8f2da7e1f6&mpshare=1&scene=23&srcid=1004yfnRUNdwdUYnORKxrgtT&sharer_shareinfo=8d4f73a138d3c5001e6a0a7daf72144c&sharer_shareinfo_first=8d4f73a138d3c5001e6a0a7daf72144c#rd)

Passage 3 Pioneering the Path to the Future (Excerpt)

Warm-up Words & Expressions

premium automaker 豪华汽车公司
Jaguar Land Rover 捷豹路虎
tap into the Chinese market 深耕中国市场
autonomous, connected, electrified and sharing future
　自动化、互联化、电动化与共享化
plug-in hybrid electric vehicle 插电式混合动力车型
premium all-electric Coupé-Style SUV 豪华纯电轿跑SUV

Asia debut 亚洲首秀
new energy path 新能源路径
mobility strategy 开放性战略
innovative local company 本土创新企业
realization of sustainable and long-term development 实现长期可持续发展
joint venture 合资企业
unique British heritage 独特的英伦传统

🎧 **Listen to Passage 3 and interpret it from English into Chinese.**

A premium automaker from the United Kingdom, Jaguar Land Rover is evolving into a technology company as part of its new pioneering path, committed to a cleaner, safer and smarter future. With its global vision, the British automaker is looking to tap into the Chinese market as a comprehensive source of global resources, including research and development, innovation, procurement, human resources development and more.

Unlike traditional automakers that will not be able to escape the inevitable transformation toward an autonomous, connected, electrified and sharing future, Jaguar Land Rover is riding on the wave of this growing trend and leveraging these opportunities to make their mark on China's innovation landscape.

The company's latest plug-in hybrid electric vehicle, the Range Rover Sport P400e, and the Jaguar I-PACE, a premium all-electric Coupé-Style SUV, which is about to make its Asia debut, are extraordinary showcases of the new energy path that Jaguar Land Rover is on, and how the automaker is championing premium electric vehicles.

Taking center stage at the Jaguar Land Rover Night will be Jaguar Land Rover's announcement of its future mobility strategies as they embrace cooperation and inclusiveness. Jaguar Land Rover will be working alongside innovative local companies to drive the transformation of the auto industry and new technologies, in pursuit of mutual development and success.

Since entering China back in 2010, Jaguar Land Rover has cooperated with local partners to reinforce its advantages in products and brands, devoting itself to the realization of sustainable and long-term development in China. Surging ahead of other joint ventures, the British automaker has set a new benchmark for the pace of localization in China, deepening its roots to produce five local models in three years.

This premium Coupé-Style SUV aims to attract a younger audience and embodies the automaker's deeply ingrained roots in China. The Jaguar E-PACE shows Jaguar Land Rover's devotion to meeting the needs of Chinese consumers, marking a milestone in the automaker's history in China.

Jaguar Land Rover Night might seem like a simple presentation of the automaker's corporate strategy, brand highlights and product plan. But the reality is that the event will be a pivotal display of Jaguar Land Rover's unique British heritage and innovative breakthrough technologies. Not to be missed, Chinese customers will be able to glimpse Jaguar Land Rover's blueprint for the future as the company pioneers the way to a new era of travel.

(https://mp.weixin.qq.com/s?__biz=MzU1NTcxODQ0OQ==&mid=2247541757&idx=2&sn=daf7f72b2d9c4082a3cfdb5ceac39933&chksm = fbd261a3cca5e8b5c0f6334616d5b2557172a41f6fa02eb9aab80b94edbd15b0f67f3e1548db&mpshare=1&scene=23&srcid=1004MjANgEzgK98QDQhKeUxr&sharer_ shareinfo =406afdcf56c3a5cfed2fb01089b181fb&sharer_ shareinfo_ first =406afdcf56c3a5cfed2fb01089b181fb#rd)

Passage 4 国货品牌的线上销售战略

Warm-up Words & Expressions

争议 controversy	创下历史纪录 attract a record
直播 livestreaming	洗涤剂 detergent
淡出 fade out	活力 28 Super 28
洗发水 shampoo	网民们 netizens
79 元产品套装 79-yuan set	抗日战争 the War of Resistance Against Japanese Aggression
第三方平台 third-party platform	
暴增 soar	快车道 fast lane

🎧 **Listen to Passage 4 and interpret it from Chinese into English.**

因为一场关于"商品的质量和人们是否努力"的有争议的直播活动，一些传统国货品牌最近收获了"泼天富贵"。由于不善于进行宣传、营销，一些国产品牌淡出了大众的视野。而如今，它们又一次站在了大众面前，让人们看到了国货品牌对质量的坚守和对消费者的初心。

9月9日在李佳琦的淘宝直播间，有网友吐槽国有品牌"79元眉笔套装"价格太贵，却遭李佳琦一番怒怼："这么多年了工资涨没涨，有没有认真工作？"之后，国产品牌开始备受瞩目。

在此番言论引发大家不满后，成立于1985年的洗发水品牌蜂花率先凭借"79元产品套装"活动，获得了首批大量关注。第三方平台数据显示，蜂花官方旗舰店抖音平台的粉丝数量在9月11日后开始暴增，单场直播销售额超2500万元。而9月15日，其单日粉丝暴增55.9万创下历史纪录。

同时，很多其他老牌国货品牌也开始在社交媒体促销，向消费者展示自己的价值。成立于1950年的洗涤剂品牌活力28尤其受关注，靠三位对直播带货几乎一无所知的大叔主播"圈粉"无数。活力28抖音平台的店铺周三才首次开播，面对镜头，三位在工厂工作的大叔茫然不知所措，还是网民们自发在评论区开启教学模式，一步步教大叔们操作，领着大叔们完成了直播。第二天,活力 28 衣物清洁抖音旗舰店当日涨粉 161.8 万,并卖空了库存。

很多老国货品牌在网民的一声声"原来儿时流行的这个品牌还在""原来这个品牌在抗日战争中捐过钱物"中销量猛涨。而就在周一"九•一八事变"92 周年纪念日当天,蜂花、活力 28 等众多知名国货品牌停止直播一天,提醒国人勿忘国耻,珍惜当下的幸福生活。

这一次,很多国货终于走上了互联网营销的快车道,而大众的善意、鼓励更成为他们重回消费市场的动力。大家都希望国货能越做越好,而不是昙花一现的情怀狂欢。

(https://mp.weixin.qq.com/s?__biz=MzU1NTcxODQ0OQ==&mid=2247830448&idx=1&sn =53c52ae8ff386c725a87ac87b527a667&chksm=fbdf89eecca800f81d5a18c2aa39e6f2188cb 438b7 eb37adbedacd8f88fdf2ab15824798af50&mpshare=1&scene=23&srcid=1004RmNL88LgLjmVw EwaLlTJ&sharer_shareinfo=bfaf20ee09c68c1ce9c417be0634e725&sharer_shareinfo_first=bfaf20 ee09c68c1ce9c417be0634e725#rd)

Section 3　Interpreting Assessment

Passage 1　China, US Commerce Authorities to Establish New Working Group

Warm-up Words & Expressions

commerce authority 商务部
Gina Raimondo 吉娜•雷蒙多
deputy 副职
bureau-level government official 司局级政府官员
deputy ministerial level meeting 副部级会议
export control information exchange mechanism 出口管制信息交流机制
tariff measures 关税
semiconductor policies 半导体政策
discriminatory subsidies 歧视性补贴
sanctions on Chinese companies 制裁中国企业
unilateral and protectionist measures 单边、保护主义措施

🎧 Listen to Passage 1 and interpret it from English into Chinese.

评价项目	评价标准	原始赋分	学生得分
内容准确	忠实于原文,知识点准确,用词得当,句式合理。	30 分	
内容完整	完整传达原文的内容和含义,没有漏译。	20 分	
语言标准	语音语调标准,符合目标语言的地道表达方式,能够传达出原文的语气和情感。	20 分	
表达流利	口译流畅自然,无重译、停顿或修正现象。	20 分	
职业素养	听力反应敏捷,仪态大方,临场反应能力强。	10 分	
合计		100 分	

续表

评价项目	评价标准	原始赋分	学生得分
被评人			
评价人			
教师评价			

Passage 2　微观战略

Warm-up Words & Expressions

移动应用 mobile apps　　　　　　　灵活的 agile
取代 take over the position of　　　业务活动 business campaign
处于十字路口 stand at the cross-road　虚拟环境 virtual condition
实施 deploy　　　　　　　　　　　优势 edge
洞见 insight　　　　　　　　　　　集合概念 aggregate
可视化 visualization

🎧 **Listen to Passage 2 and interpret it from Chinese into English.**

评价项目	评价标准	原始赋分	学生得分
内容准确	忠实于原文，知识点准确，用词得当，句式合理。	30分	
内容完整	完整传达原文的内容和含义，没有漏译。	20分	
语言标准	语音语调标准，符合目标语言的地道表达方式，能够传达出原文的语气和情感。	20分	
表达流利	口译流畅自然，无重译、停顿或修正现象。	20分	
职业素养	听力反应敏捷，仪态大方，临场反应能力强。	10分	
合计		100分	
被评人			
评价人			
教师评价			

Project 3
Business Talks

Unit 8　Business Conference

Learning Objectives
- Know social etiquette and taboos in business conferences
- Master useful expressions commonly used in business conferences
- Be able to briefly interpret in business conferences

Ideological and Political Objectives
- Understand importance of international communication capacity
- Facilitate a better understanding towards national policy of economic development
- Improve confidence in China's path, guiding theories, political system and culture
- Foster an open-minded and adventurous spirit

Section 1　Interpreting Preparation

Key Concepts

1. International communication capacity 国际传播能力

President Xi Jinping has called on China Foreign Languages Publishing Administration to improve its international communication capacity to better introduce China to the world in the new era. Media groups should build up their capacity in international communication, amplify their voices on the international stage, tell stories about China well, optimize strategic planning and build flagship media groups with strong global influence. We will improve our ability to engage in international communication so as to tell China's stories well, make the voice of China heard, and present a true, multidimensional, and panoramic view of China to the world.

2. High-quality development 高质量发展

China has issued an outline to improve the overall quality of its economy amid efforts to promote high-quality development. The country aims to boost its strength in quality and steadily increase the influence of Chinese brands by 2025. Implementing the new development philosophy and promoting high-quality development is a profound change for the overall modernization drive. China will realize high-quality development in which innovation is the primary driving force; coordination is an endogenous feature; go-green is a prevailing mode; openness is the only path; and sharing is the fundamental goal.

3. Digital economy 数字经济

The digital economy refers to a series of economic activities in which data resources are used as key production factors, modern information networks are used as important carriers, and the effective use of information and communication technologies is used as an important driving force for efficiency enhancement and the optimization of economic structure. Developing a digital economy is a strategic choice for grasping the new opportunities in the new round of revolution in science and technology and industrial transformation, as it can help foster a new development paradigm, a modern economic system, and new national competitive strengths.

4. Circular development 循环发展

Circular development is a model of economic development that aims to build a circular system for industry, agriculture, and tertiary industry, which integrates production and living systems, thus forming an intensive growth model featuring a circle of resource-product-waste-recycled resource. Pursuing circular development is a major strategy for China's economic and social development. It's an effective way to promote green development and build an eco-civilization. The action plan for circular development stated that circular development will follow green transformation as the leading goal, which will be propelled by innovation, backed by institutional improvement, and supported by coordination. The major goals of circular development are to introduce a green, circular and low-carbon industrial system, an urban circular development system, a strategic supply system of resources, and new ways of life for the people.

Sight Interpreting

Passage 1　Euro-Asia Economic Forum Highlights Cooperation and Development

Warm-up Words & Expressions

Euro-Asia Economic Forum 欧亚经济论坛	cultural and tourism development 文化旅游发展
pursue future development 追求未来发展	economic and trade expo 经贸博览会
parallel sessions 平行会议	international import exhibition area 国际进口展区
policy coordination 政策协调	economic cooperation mechanism 经济合作机制
financial cooperation 金融合作	
economic and trade exchanges 经贸交流	
technological innovation 科技创新	
ecological conservation 生态保护	

Read Passage 1 and interpret it from English into Chinese.

The 2023 Euro-Asia Economic Forum, with the theme of creating opportunities for cooperation and pursuing future development, opened on Friday in Xi'an, the capital of northwest China's Shaanxi Province.

Politicians, business people and scholars from 51 countries and regions are attending the three-day forum. This year's edition features 13 parallel sessions on topics including policy coordination, financial cooperation, economic and trade exchanges, technological innovation, ecological conservation, and cultural and tourism development.

An economic and trade expo also opened on the sidelines of the forum. It consists of five areas, including an international import exhibition area and a theme area featuring five Central Asian countries.

The Euro-Asia Economic Forum, an important economic cooperation mechanism under the framework of the Shanghai Cooperation Organization, has been held every two years since its inception in 2005.

(https://english.news.cn/20230922/931e11a1924443e3bd87950084f7031e/c.html)

Passage 2 寻找商业伙伴的途径

Warm-up Words & Expressions

潜在客户 potential client	获得潜在客户 get potential client
贸易刊物 trade publications	现有客户 current client
市场调查 market survey	推荐，介绍 referral
网络论坛 networking forum	熟人 contact
专业知识 know-how	滚滚而来 roll in

Read Passage 2 and interpret it from Chinese into English.

毋庸置疑，在商业世界里，没有客户就没有生意。因此，寻找潜在客户并与其建立业务关系是所有公司的关键步骤。寻找潜在客户的方法有很多。最常见的方法有：利用互联网、商会报告、贸易刊物、市场调查和网络论坛；加入专业贸易组织；利用专业知识寻找 B2B（business to business，指进行电子商务交易的供需双方均为企业）线索；在贸易展会上宣传自己的公司；以及通过本地广告发掘潜在客户。其中，上网是发现和接触潜在客户最便捷的方式。

不过，获得潜在客户的最佳方式还是请现有客户推荐，因为现有客户了解你的公司，他们可能还认识其他可能对你提供的产品或服务感兴趣的人。定期与他们沟通，了解他们的社交网络，以便将来有可能得到他们的推荐。或者向你的熟人发送电子邮件或拨打电话，让他们知道你正在承接更多客户，并询问他们是否认识可以介绍给你的人。在建立业务关系的过程中，获得潜在客户是最难的部分，但一旦解决了这个问题，通常就会有更多的公司通过现有客户的推荐滚滚而来。

Memory Practice

Listen to the following paragraphs carefully without taking notes and then retell the main ideas in the source language based on your memory.

1. What is the main idea of Paragraph 1?
2. What is the main idea of Paragraph 2?

Section 2　Interpreting Practice

Dialogue 1　筛选供应商

Warm-up Words & Expressions

a variety of channels 各种渠道
优势和劣势 strengths and weaknesses
directory 目录、指南
Yellow Pages 黄页
trade association 贸易协会
business adviser 商业顾问
Chamber of Commerce 商会
trade press 行业媒体
auto manufacturer and distributor 汽车制造商与经销商
database 数据库

🎧 **Listen to Dialogue 1 and interpret it into the target language.**

A: 我们公司近年来扩张得很快。然而，我们很难找到更多合格的汽车零部件供应商。你能和我分享一些想法吗？

B: Generally people find suppliers through a variety of channels. It's best to build up a shortlist of possible suppliers through a combination of sources to give you a broader base to choose from.

A: 我们过去常常向朋友或业务合作伙伴寻求推荐。因为他们已经使用了一些供应商的服务，所以他们更有可能对这些供应商的优势和劣势进行诚实的评估。

B: Have you tried directories? If you're looking for a supplier in your local area, it's worth trying directories such as Yellow Pages.

A: 事实上我们的大部分供应商都分布在世界各地，所以当地的目录对我们来说行不通。

B: I see. Are you a member of a trade association? Companies from the same industry usually register as a member of the organization, and a lot of sources will be available there.

A: 的确如此。但问题是，他们也在寻找相同或相似的供应商。

B: That's a pity. Do you have business advisers? I mean business-support organizations which can point you in the direction of potential suppliers, such as the Chamber of Commerce.

A: 我们还没有这样的顾问，但是我们可能会尝试一下你提到的商会。你还有其他建议吗？

B: Nowadays, more and more exhibitions are held in one country after another. Exhibitions offer a great opportunity to talk with a number of potential suppliers in the same place at the same time.

A: 是的，展览对我们来说是寻找潜在供应商的一个重要渠道。通常我们会先在线核实展商是否与我们的业务相关且合适，然后再决定是否参加。

B: Still another channel is trade press, such as magazines featuring advertisements from potential suppliers.

A: 我们还没有尝试过贸易杂志，因为很少有人有时间坐下来阅读。人们宁愿上网搜索相关信息。

B: Then you can join auto manufacturers and distributors on the Internet. They have established the largest and most comprehensive database of commercially available auto parts. It's growing weekly and now includes more than 1,100 catalogs and 42 million commercially available records in the database.

A: 太棒了！谢谢你的信息。

Dialogue 2 Controlling Production

Warm-up Words & Expressions

customer complaint 客户投诉
loyal customer 忠实客户
羊毛地毯 wool carpet
退款或换货 refund or exchange
质量控制 quality control
采购部门 Purchasing Department

get the product off the shelf 下架产品
social media and the web 社交媒体与网络
客户体验 customer experience
discount coupon 折扣券
customer policy 客户政策

🎧 **Listen to Dialogue 2 and interpret it into the target language.**

A: I called you in because I've been hearing about too many customer complaints recently, even from some of our most loyal customers. What do you know about this?

B: 我们与一家新生产商合作的羊毛地毯出了很多问题。我们按照商店政策给予退款或换货处理。我们的员工反馈，一些客户认为我们的质量控制松懈。

A: From their point of view, they're right! It's not our fault, of course, but what are we doing about it? Has there been any follow-up on this issue?

B: 我们已经联系了采购部门，他们现在正在与生产商沟通。

A: That's not good enough! If we've had that many complaints, let's get the products off the shelves until the manufacturer cleans up their act.

B: 好的，我会和部门经理谈谈。这应该不是问题，但他们可能需要一两天的时间来补充空缺的库存。

A: Please remember, at any moment, a dissatisfied customer can share his or her opinion with the general public through social media and the web and negatively affect our business. So it's important to create an excellent experience for our customers to help develop our company's relationship with them.

B: 我明白了。我们会想出一些办法，尽我们所能确保客户有一个积极的体验并感到满意。

A: That's okay. Let's be proactive with the customers who bought those products and send them a discount coupon for their next store purchase. And let's touch base with our other recent customers to make sure that they're satisfied with our customer policies.

B: 我会立刻行动。

A: OK. Thanks.

Dialogue 3 Year-end Operation Meeting

Warm-up Words & Expressions

business efficiency 业务效率
revenue lines 收入项目

sustainable growth 可持续增长
real economy 实体经济

VAS (value added service) subscription 增值服务订阅
平均每户收入 ARPU (average revenue per-user)
minor protection program 未成年人保护计划
市场领先地位 market leadership
日活跃用户数 DAU (daily active users)
gross receipt 总收入
优化成本 optimize cost
自主研发解决方案 self-developed solution

🎧 **Listen to Dialogue 3 and interpret it into the target language.**

A: We increased our business efficiency in 2022, which benefits from new services and revenue lines. We are ready for sustainable growth.

B: 是的，我看到这份报告说，人们在微信上花费的总时间继续增加。小程序和视频号的使用时间分别同比增长了一倍和两倍。

C: Mini Program has become a leading transaction platform in China and contributing to the development of the real economy.

A: Could you present us some data about performance of Video Accounts?

B: 1.9亿用户通过视频号直播观看了2023年春晚。

A: What about Digital Content?

C: Our fee-based VAS subscriptions decreased 1% year-on-year to 234 million but video subscriptions revenue increased as we adjusted pricing.

B: 在音乐方面，我们提供了极具吸引力的会员特权，并提高了用户对各种音乐类型的参与度，从而推动了付费用户和平均每户收入值的增长。

A: This year, we conducted minor protection program, are there any influence on domestic games?

B: 未成年人花费的时间大大减少了。不过，我们依旧保持了市场领先地位，日活跃用户数在2022年第四季度恢复了同比增长。

C: Sure, it achieved record-high gross receipts during the Chinese New Year holiday in 2023.

A: Is there any progress on the aspect of cloud and other business services?

B: 我们进一步减少了亏损的活动，优化了成本，同时专注于利润率更高的自主研发解决方案。

A: I'm glad to hear that. Let's take a five-minute break. Later, we will go on talking about other business units.

Passage 评估员工

Warm-up Words & Expressions

绩效评估系统 performance appraisal system
工作绩效 job performance
公司目标 organizational goal
雇佣决策 employment decision
加薪 pay raise
职位描述 job description
管理层的期望 management's expectation
叙述形式 narrative form
同行评估和自我评估 peer and self-evaluations
职业发展 career development
继续教育 continuing education

🎧 Listen to the following passage and interpret it from Chinese into English.

大多数公司都有一个正式的绩效评估系统，定期对员工的工作绩效进行评定，通常是每年一次。一个良好的绩效评估系统可以为公司带来很大的好处。它通过让员工了解公司对他们的期望，有助于引导员工的行为朝着公司的目标发展，同时为制定雇佣决策（如加薪、晋升和解雇）提供信息。为了评估员工的绩效，需要遵循以下步骤。

首先，查阅员工的官方职位描述。使公司目标与工作目标保持一致。注意任何差异，并找到消除差异的方法。

第二，向员工传达管理层的期望。管理层与员工之间必须对工作期望、待完成工作的性质以及评估工作的标准达成共识。

第三，向员工提供关于其绩效及其与管理层设定的期望之间关系的反馈。在对评估给出诚实意见的同时，发表建设性而非破坏性的评论。

第四，培训员工。为他们提供满足和超越管理层期望所需的资源。管理层应当在指导员工方面付出持续、一致的努力，以便在为时已晚之前改善员工的绩效。

第五，评估员工的优点和缺点。这可以通过使用叙述形式、清单、同行评估和自我评估来完成。员工需要了解公司是如何得出结论的，以便能纠正任何问题。只有这样，员工才能充分发挥自己的优势，克服自己的劣势。

Section 3　Interpreting Assessment

Passage 1　The "5G Business Success" Summit

Warm-up Words & Expressions

multidimensional value realization 多维价值变现
certainty effect 确定性效应
ToC/ToH/ToB 面向个人/家庭/企业用户的技术
revenue growth 收入增长
business model 商业模式
risk-based 基于风险的
ROI (return on investment) 投资回报率
ARPU 平均每户收入
social value 社会价值
appeal to 呼吁
business blueprint 商务蓝图

🎧 Listen to Passage 1 and interpret it from English into Chinese.

评价项目	评价标准	原始赋分	学生得分
内容准确	忠实于原文，知识点准确，用词得当，句式合理。	30分	
内容完整	完整传达原文的内容和含义，没有漏译。	20分	
语言标准	语音语调标准，符合目标语言的地道表达方式，能够传达出原文的语气和情感。	20分	
表达流利	口译流畅自然，无重译、停顿或修正现象。	20分	

续表

评价项目	评价标准	原始赋分	学生得分
职业素养	听力反应敏捷,仪态大方,临场反应能力强。	10分	
合计		100分	
被评人			
评价人			
教师评价			

Passage 2 李强在博鳌亚洲论坛2023年年会开幕式上的主旨演讲(节选)

Warm-up Words & Expressions

博鳌亚洲论坛 Boao Forum for Asia
年会 annual conference
团结合作 solidarity and cooperation
变乱交织 turmoil and transformation
前所未有的挑战 unprecedented challenges
人类命运共同体 a community with a shared future for mankind
全球发展倡议 Global Development Initiative (GDI)
全球安全倡议 Global Security Initiative (GSI)
全球文明倡议 Global Civilization Initiative (GCI)
劝和促谈 facilitate peace talks
化干戈为玉帛 de-escalate tensions
和平稳定锚 an anchor for world peace
增长动力源 a source of impetus for global growth
合作新高地 a new pacesetter for international cooperation

🎧 **Listen to Passage 2 and interpret it from Chinese into English.**

评价项目	评价标准	原始赋分	学生得分
内容准确	忠实于原文,知识点准确,用词得当,句式合理。	30分	
内容完整	完整传达原文的内容和含义,没有漏译。	20分	
语言标准	语音语调标准,符合目标语言的地道表达方式,能够传达出原文的语气和情感。	20分	
表达流利	口译流畅自然,无重译、停顿或修正现象。	20分	
职业素养	听力反应敏捷,仪态大方,临场反应能力强。	10分	
合计		100分	
被评人			
评价人			
教师评价			

Unit 9 Marketing and Promotion

Learning Objectives

- Understand business analysis models
- Master useful expressions commonly used in marketing and promotion
- Improve the interpreting skills on topics of marketing and promotion

Ideological and Political Objectives

- Understand significance of strategic emerging industry and its opportunity
- Understand fairness and justice of socialist market economy in competition
- Cultivate awareness of market competition
- Foster an innovative and proactive spirit for career development

Section 1 Interpreting Preparation

☞ Key Concepts

1. Strategic emerging industries 战略性新兴产业

Strategic emerging industries are those that have considerable market potential, can drive the economy and create more jobs, and that have strong overall performance. They include energy conservation and environmental protection, new-generation information technology, high-end equipment manufacturing, integrated circuits, the Internet of Things, advanced manufacturing, new energy, new-generation mobile communications, and big data.

To adapt to changes in industrial competition, China will move faster to develop these industries, creating an innovative value chain featuring "core technology, strategic products, and engineering and large-scaled applications", extend the space for industrial development, and seek out new advantages in market competition.

2. Social fairness and justice 社会公平与正义

Fairness and justice are inherent requirements of socialism with Chinese characteristics. Based on the concerted efforts of its entire people and its economic and social development, China must step up efforts to develop institutions that are vital to ensuring social fairness and justice. It must also establish in due course a system guaranteeing social fairness that features, among other things, equal rights, equal opportunities and fair rules for all, and foster a fair social environment and ensure people's equal right to participation in governance and development.

3. The new normal of China's economy 中国经济新常态

The new normal of China's economy is characterized by a shift from high growth rates to medium-high growth rates; an on-going process of optimizing and upgrading the economic structure, and narrowing the urban-rural gap, with higher personal income as a share of GDP, and an increasing number of people benefiting from economic development; and a transition from growth driven by input and investment to one driven by innovation. This new normal would likely lead to, among others, a sizable increase in real output despite slower growth; more stable growth with a more diversified array of growth drivers; an increasingly optimized and upgraded economic structure, and more predictable development prospects; and a further revitalized market as the result of the on-going move to streamline government and delegate authorities.

4. Four-pronged Comprehensive Strategy "四个全面"战略布局

The new version of the Four-pronged Comprehensive Strategy consists of comprehensively building a modern socialist country, comprehensively expanding in-depth reform, comprehensively promoting law-based governance, and comprehensively enforcing strict Party discipline. This is a major part of the strategic thought on governance produced by the CPC Central Committee with President Xi Jinping at the core. It is a Marxist point of view based on an integration of Marxism with China's realities.

This Four-pronged Comprehensive Strategy was formulated to help solve the most pressing problems and issues currently facing the country. It caters to the needs of China's development reality.

☞ Sight Interpreting

Passage 1 PEST Analysis of New Energy Industry

Warm-up Words & Expressions

favorable policy 优惠政策	automobile consumption 汽车消费
subsidy policy 补贴政策	vehicle emission 汽车尾气排放
vehicle purchase tax exemption 免征车辆购置税	continuous innovation 持续创新
double points policy 双倍积分政策	pure electric real-time four-wheel drive technology 纯电动实时四驱技术
industrial pollution level 工业污染水平	IGBT (insulated gate bipolar transistor) industry chain IGBT 产业链
production safety requirement 生产安全要求	technology accumulation 技术积累
employee rights protection 员工权益保护	key indicator 关键指标
disposable income 可支配收入	

Read Passage 1 and interpret it from English into Chinese.

Dear leaders and colleagues,

Good morning. Today we gather together to discuss marketing strategy for next three years, here I would like to talk about macro environment for new energy industry initially from political, economic, social and technological perspectives.

In recent years, China has introduced favorable policies for new energy companies. For example, the Chinese government's subsidy policy encourages car owners to choose different prices and types of vehicles. In addition, the vehicle purchase tax exemption for new energy vehicles and the new energy double points policy also express China's determination to vigorously develop the new energy industry. However, with the growing popularity of the new energy industry, China has begun to adjust its regulations on industrial pollution levels, production safety requirements, and employee rights protection.

China's GDP has reached 532.167 billion yuan in the first half of 2021, up 12.7% year-on-year, showing an overall trend of steady growth. The annual value of China's GDP and the value of the increase can show that China's economy is running well. In addition, as the largest developing country, citizens' living standards are improving day by day, and their disposable income has increased significantly. This will lead more and more people to seek a higher level of economic consumption, and automobile consumption is among them. This positive development brings a good economic environment for the development of automobile enterprises. It is worth noting that by the end of June 2021, China had 6.03 million new energy vehicles, accounting for about 50% of global new energy vehicle ownership. This value clearly shows how hot the new energy industry is in China.

Pollution of the natural environment has become increasingly serious. As the world's largest producer and seller of cars, the air pollution caused by vehicle emissions has become widely known. In this context, China has started to tackle the problem of environmental pollution by reducing harmful emissions and calling on the public to enjoy the least environmentally damaging travel options. New energy vehicles are becoming the first choice for Chinese citizens as they require much less energy than ordinary fuel cars and can optimize the environment and save energy.

As early entrants to the new energy market in China, Chinese firms like BYD have slowly mastered several core technologies of electric vehicles through their own continuous innovation. For example, the self-developed pure electric real-time four-wheel drive technology of BYD is winning formula in terms of electric vehicle power. Some Chinese car manufacturers with a complete IGBT industry chain and mass production, have been researching and developing in this area for more than 10 years, with rich experience and technology accumulation, and the key indicators have reached the world's leading level. This strong technological R&D capability has become the driving force and foundation for continuous development.

(https://www.researchgate.net/publication/357609788_Analysis_of_BYD's_Business_Model_and_Future_Development_Prospects)

Passage 2　SWOT 分析

Warm-up Words & Expressions

产品种类繁多 a massive collection of products
有竞争力的价格 competitive price
个性化移动应用程序 personalized mobile app
用户界面友好 user-friendly interface
送货耗时 time-consuming delivery
缺少仓库 unavailability of warehouse
模糊的起源历史 vague origin history
时尚产业崛起 rise of the fashion industry
虚拟大使 virtual ambassador
社交网络 social network
社交媒体营销 social media marketing
营销策略 marketing strategy
数据处理不当 mishandled data
消费者喜好的转变 shift in consumer taste
激烈的竞争 fierce competition

Read Passage 2 and interpret it from Chinese into English.

接下来，我将基于 SWOT 分析模型，详细谈谈 SHEIN 这家公司，了解它的优势和劣势，并识别其面临的机遇和威胁。

1. 优势

产品种类繁多。无论消费者想买什么，他们都喜欢选择，因为这能给他们带来精神上的满足。

有竞争力的价格。竞争是整个商业行业的重要组成部分，而推动竞争的主要因素就是产品价格。保持销售产品的价格竞争力是公司的重要优势之一。

个性化移动应用程序。这一代的个性化移动应用程序是一大亮点。一个只显示产品而且用户界面友好的应用程序会让消费者更愿意在那里购买商品。此外，个性化应用程序还能在某种程度上体现公司的稳定性。

2. 劣势

送货耗时。有时，客户订购的货物需要立即交付，而交付产品的时间超过了预期会对公司造成巨大损失。

缺少仓库。SHEIN 的供应链缺少仓库很可能是 SHEIN 的一个严重弱点。合适的仓库会使得整个交货过程变得快速可靠，因为客户在每一步都能获得相关信息。

模糊的起源历史。有时，这对企业来说是一个严重的缺陷，尤其是当客户需要他们的产品具有长期质量保证时。

3. 机遇

时尚产业崛起。新的流行趋势是购买各种时尚产品，无论是服装、珠宝还是其他线上售卖产品。因此，在这种趋势下，提供优质服务的网站受欢迎程度也相当高。一切都取决于市场营销和消费者满意度。因此，SHEIN 可以抓住这个机会，在市场上拓展业务。

虚拟大使。SHEIN 非常重视虚拟营销，其与知名的社会影响者合作，这些人可以增加消费者对某些产品的需求，从而为公司带来好的交易。因此，SHEIN 需要选择合适的人，让他们成为整个业务的代言人。

社交网络。通过不同的社交网络进行营销有助于最大限度地接触世界各地的消费者。社交网络提供了进入最偏远地区的途径。因此，社交媒体营销可以成为一种重要的 SHEIN

营销策略，为公司在竞争激烈的市场中发展壮大提供机会。

  4．威胁

  数据处理不当。数据泄露是一个反复出现的问题。而且，这是一个非常令人担忧的问题。SHEIN 的整个业务都是以计算机为基础的。因此，这可能对公司构成相当大的威胁。

  消费者喜好的转变。我们无法预测客户在特定时期的需求。因此，像这样的企业需要时刻保持警惕，随时准备对产品进行更新换代。

  激烈的竞争。随着电子商务的普及，竞争也更加激烈。因此，要在如此众多的企业中脱颖而出可谓难上加难。

  (https://www.edrawmax.com/article/shein-swot-analysis.html#SnippetTab)

☞ Memory Practice

🎧 **Listen to the following paragraphs carefully without taking notes and then retell the main ideas in the source language based on your memory.**

1. What is the main idea of Paragraph 1?
2. What is the main idea of Paragraph 2?

Section 2　Interpreting Practice

Dialogue　Discussing Product Strategy of Gree

Warm-up Words & Expressions

空调公司 air conditioning company	质量管理体系 quality management system
适销对路的产品 marketable product	产品质量 product quality
品牌形象 brand image	总裁十二条禁令 12 Injunctions by President
打造精品战略 Making Superior Product Strategy	零缺陷工程 Zero Defection Project

🎧 **Listen to the following dialogue and interpret it into the target language.**

A: 你知道格力已经发展成为世界上最大的空调公司了吗？

B: Really? How did Gree achieve that?

A: 是的，1991 年格力电器成立时，只是一家年产不到 2 万台窗式空调的小厂。

B: That's a humble beginning. How did Gree manage to grow rapidly?

A: 格力用一系列适销对路的产品抓住了市场机遇，开始树立品牌形象，为今后的发展打下了良好的基础。

B: And then what happened?

A: 1994 年至 1996 年，格力通过实施"打造精品战略"，建立质量管理体系，来着力提高产品质量。格力还推出了"总裁十二条禁令"，推进"零缺陷工程"，以提高产品质量。

B: That sounds like a solid commitment to quality.

A: 是的，从那时起，格力就在研发、生产、运输等各个环节强调产品质量。格力的优质空调也带来了良好的销售机会。

B: It's amazing how much Gree has grown in just over 20 years.

Passage 1 如何制定营销战略

Warm-up Words & Expressions

市场调研 market research　　　　　品牌代码 brand code
目标市场 target market　　　　　　独特资产 distinctive asset
目标细分市场 target segment market　视觉风格 visual style
目标受众 target consumer　　　　　战略目标 strategic objective
定位 positioning　　　　　　　　　基准 benchmark
联想 association　　　　　　　　　SMART 标准 SMART criteria

Listen to Passage 1 and interpret it from Chinese into English.

诚挚地欢迎各位在百忙之中抽出时间参加今天的培训项目，前面的课程我们提到了营销战略的重要意义，接下来我们将详细阐述如何通过五个步骤制定成功的营销战略。

1. 准备好市场调研数据

以数据而非假设为基础制定营销战略至关重要。你可能不会在没有市场调研的情况下开发产品并向市场投放——至少你不应该这样做。市场调研是市场营销的重要组成部分，也是一个独立的话题。请记住，即使是一个廉价、快速和不完美的市场调研，也比没有调研要好。

2. 确定目标市场

第二步是决定你将瞄准哪些细分市场。或者你可以忽略哪些细分市场，因为决定不做什么往往是更重要的选择。目标细分市场指的是你决定追逐的特定细分市场。目标受众是指与你的营销传播产生共鸣的所有人，无论他们是否购买产品。

3. 以正确的定位吸引目标市场

定位是指目标市场应如何看待你的品牌。它是预期的品牌形象，由人们对品牌和产品的联想构成。定位可以让你与竞争对手区分开来。定位的力量在于通过所有营销渠道持续传达一些联想。如果做不到这一点，市场就会替你完成定位工作。这很少会与你所期望的品牌形象相一致。

4. 选择几个品牌代码，使其与众不同

品牌代码被称为独特资产，是你在传播中持续使用的任何东西。你可以将其视为定位的助手。最常见的品牌代码是你的徽标和视觉风格，但对于大多数品牌而言也仅此而已。要想在目标受众心目中脱颖而出、独树一帜，光靠这些还远远不够。你的最终目标应该是，即使不展示任何徽标，目标受众也能认出你的品牌。

5. 制定未来一年的战略目标

你需要明确的营销目标来指导你的营销工作，并提供评估基准。这就是你现在要做的战略工作。你的营销目标应符合广泛使用的 SMART 标准：具体、可衡量、可实现、相关、及时。

这部分内容各位是否有疑问,如果没有,我们就进入到小组讨论了。
(https://ahrefs.com/blog/marketing-strategy/)

Passage 2 Advertising Strategy

Warm-up Words & Expressions

advertising strategy 广告策略
create awareness 创造认知
build primary demand 建立基本需求
brand preference 品牌偏好
advertising campaign 广告活动

target group 目标群体
effective assessment of product 对产品的有效评估
outdoor advertising 户外广告
marketing strategy 营销策略

🎧 Listen to Passage 2 and interpret it from English into Chinese

Advertising strategy is an advertising plan developed by enterprises to create awareness among the customers about the product or service and motivate them to purchase the same. An advertising strategy encompasses two components: information and persuasion. The information part includes informing customers about product features and benefits, price changes, and is crucial for building primary demand. Creating persuasion in advertising strategy is important to build brand preference or change customers' perceptions especially in competitive markets.

In any advertising campaign, initially awareness is created among the customers about the product and then campaign is taken in the direction to arouse interest among the target audience so that in follow they make a purchase. An effective advertising strategy should be in consideration of these factors such as characteristics of the target group, understanding the environment, market definition and effective assessment of product. Communication media is of paramount importance when it comes to formulate an advertising strategy. After the audience is segmented and targeted proper assessment of media channels should be done.

The major channels used by enterprises in implementing their advertising strategy are video (television), audio (radio), print media (newspapers, magazines, flyers), Internet (social media, direct mails) and outdoor advertising. Advertising strategy is important marketing strategy adopted by companies.

Passage 3 定价策略(节选)

Warm-up Words & Expressions

整车质保 whole vehicle warranty
基础保养 basic maintenance
降价 price cut
起售价 starting price
福利反馈 welfare feedback
累计交付量 cumulative delivery

价格调整 price adjustment
加速普及 accelerate popularity
战略产品规划 strategic product planning
用户需求 user demand
全球规模的客户 global-scale customer

🎧 **Listen to Passage 3 and interpret it from Chinese into English.**

自 2023 年 1 月 17 日 14 时起，小鹏汽车启动 G3i、P5 和 P7 的新春价格体系。同时，小鹏汽车还表示，在公告发布前一年内订购了上述系列的首任车主，整车质保延长到 10 年或 20 万公里，并赠送 4 年基础保养。在新价格体系中，小鹏汽车 G3i、P5 和 P7 的售价分别为 14.89 万，15.69 万和 20.99 万。

此前，特斯拉宣布 Model 3 与 Model Y 双双降价，最高降幅为 4.8 万元。Model 3 起售价降至 22.99 万元，降价 3.6 万元；Model Y 起售价降至 25.99 万元，降价 2.9 万元。不过，对于特斯拉突发大降价，不少刚提车的老车主深感不满。

"相比于特斯拉无任何反应，小鹏给近 1 年的用户都提供了福利反馈。""老用户感受到了温暖，至少有一点点补偿。"在小鹏汽车官宣新价格体系的评论区，网友纷纷表态。

小鹏汽车 2022 年累计交付量为 120 757 台，启动新价格体系的 G3i、P5 和 P7 三款车型在这一年交付量超过 10 万台。业内认为，小鹏汽车新的定价属于正常的价格调整，符合它的价格策略。小鹏汽车希望通过此轮价格调整，在技术领先的同时，追求规模经济，让智能化加速普及。未来，小鹏汽车将聚焦于公司的战略产品规划跟研发，以用户需求为导向，以期获取更长期的、全球规模的客户。

(https://www.tfcaijing.com/index.php/article/page/766968724744436469784536363359466b4c2f6f51773d3d)

Section 3　Interpreting Assessment

Passage 1　Market Performance of China's Foldable Smartphone

Warm-up Words & Expressions

foldable smartphone 可折叠智能手机　　niche market 细分市场
remarkable growth 显著增长　　an upward trend 上升趋势
market share 市场份额　　become receptive to 对……接受

🎧 **Listen to Passage 1 and interpret it from English into Chinese.**

评价项目	评价标准	原始赋分	学生得分
内容准确	忠实于原文，知识点准确，用词得当，句式合理。	30 分	
内容完整	完整传达原文的内容和含义，没有漏译。	20 分	
语言标准	语音语调标准，符合目标语言的地道表达方式，能够传达出原文的语气和情感。	20 分	
表达流利	口译流畅自然，无重译、停顿或修正现象。	20 分	
职业素养	听力反应敏捷，仪态大方，临场反应能力强。	10 分	
合计		100 分	
被评人			

续表

评价项目	评价标准	原始赋分	学生得分
评价人			
教师评价			

Passage 2　提升客户满意度

Warm-up Words & Expressions

客户服务 customer service
跟进并改进 follow up and improve
更换产品 exchange a product
特殊服务 special service
公司的最佳利益 company's best interest
采取纠正措施 initiate a corrective action

帮助业务发展与繁荣 help business grow and prosper
用不诚实的方式 in a dishonest manner
业务损失 loss of business
诉讼 lawsuit

🎧 Listen to Passage 2 and interpret it from Chinese into English.

评价项目	评价标准	原始赋分	学生得分
内容准确	忠实于原文，知识点准确，用词得当，句式合理。	30分	
内容完整	完整传达原文的内容和含义，没有漏译。	20分	
语言标准	语音语调标准，符合目标语言的地道表达方式，能够传达出原文的语气和情感。	20分	
表达流利	口译流畅自然，无重译、停顿或修正现象。	20分	
职业素养	听力反应敏捷，仪态大方，临场反应能力强。	10分	
合计		100分	
被评人			
评价人			
教师评价			

Unit 10 Business Negotiation

Learning Objectives

- Know some common trade terms and payment terms
- Master useful expressions widely used in business negotiations
- Be able to interpret concisely in business negotiations

Ideological and Political Objectives

- Facilitate a better understanding about new forms and models of foreign trade
- Cultivate a positive attitude towards new industrial transformation
- Comprehend the business ethics involved in forming partnerships
- Foster an awareness of win-win cooperation in business negotiation

Section 1 Interpreting Preparation

Key Concepts

1. New forms and models of foreign trade 外贸新业态新模式

New forms and models of foreign trade are the innovative practice of foreign trade entering a new stage of development and implementing the new development concept, which are main force in the development of China's foreign trade, as well as the important trend in the development of international trade. In recent years, China has seen rapid development in its new forms and models of foreign trade, with cross-border e-commerce experiencing particularly rapid growth. Accelerating the development of new forms and models of foreign trade is conducive to promoting the high-quality development of trade, fostering new advantages in international economic cooperation and competition, and playing an important role in serving the construction of a new development pattern.

2. Global partnerships 全球伙伴关系

China has actively developed global partnerships and expanded the convergence of interests with other countries. China will promote coordination and cooperation with other major countries and work to build a framework for major-country relations featuring overall stability and balanced development. China will deepen relations with its neighbors in accordance with the principle of amity, sincerity, mutual benefit, and inclusiveness and the policy of forging friendship and partnership with its neighbors. China will, guided by the principle of upholding justice while pursuing shared interests and the principle of sincerity, real results, affinity, and good faith, work to strengthen solidarity and cooperation with other developing countries.

3. Regional comprehensive economic partnership 区域全面经济伙伴关系

After eight years of negotiations, 15 Asia-Pacific countries signed the Regional Comprehensive Economic Partnership (RCEP) on November 15, the world's biggest trade pact. The agreement involves all 10 member countries of the Association of Southeast Asian Nations and five of its major trading partners—China, Japan, the Republic of Korea, Australia and New Zealand. China stands ready to conclude high-standard free trade agreements with more countries in the world.

4. Upholding justice while pursuing shared interests 树立正确义利观

Upholding justice reflects Chinese values. China hopes to see common prosperity spread across the world, and in particular, accelerated development in developing countries. The pursuit of shared interests should be aligned with the need to search for mutual benefit, rather than being turned into a zero-sum game. China has the obligation to provide assistance to poor countries within the limits of its own resources. It is sometimes necessary to work for justice at the expense of self-interest, and fulfill this obligation despite an unfavorable calculus in financial terms. A healthy approach to the relationship between upholding justice and pursuing shared interests is a principled approach that values friendship, adheres to moral standards, refuses to succumb to the temptations of greed, encourages to seek gains only when the justice is not adversely affected, and embraces a readiness to sacrifice self-interest for justice when need arises.

Sight Interpreting

Passage 1 Maintain Business Relations

Warm-up Words & Expressions

cultivate 培养
cost-effective 经济有效的
initiate 开始

notation 注释，记号
commit to 承诺
cordial 热诚的，诚恳的

Read Passage 1 and interpret it from English into Chinese.

Maintaining relationships of all types is important, but maintaining business relationships may have the most significant financial impact, as these relationships often equal to financial gain. By some estimates, the cost of keeping an existing customer is as low as one-tenth of the cost of acquiring a new one. So cultivating strong business relationships offers a cost-effective way to do business. Here are some tips that can help you do that.

Lay the foundation early. Identify potential clients or partners early. Express your interest, meet with them, and learn about their goals and objectives. Then, if that firm moves into your market, you're at the top of their list. Why? Because you've already established contact and initiated a business relationship. People like to work with people they know.

Keep notes. You likely have a method of jotting down contact information from your business contacts, but this vital how-to-get-in-touch info isn't the only thing you should note. It is wise to also write down notations about the individual's interests or your relationship with him.

Maintain contact. Avoid allowing months or even years to slip by between contacts. While you don't want to take up your business acquaintance's time with unnecessary phone calls just to chat, a quick call to follow up on the last piece of business you completed together is wise.

Respond to requests rapidly. Make communication a top priority. If those with whom you have a business relationship feel like they are constantly kept waiting when they try to get in touch with you, they will likely become frustrated. If at all possible, try to make a same-day contact return policy and commit to not leaving the office until you have returned your calls or emails to ensure that this communication doesn't fall by the wayside.

Remain cordial at all times. While there is a difference between a business contact and a friend, you should aim to treat these individuals in a friendly manner at all times. By doing so, you can build a relationship that could prove advantageous for your business. To ensure that you maintain your cordial relationship, avoid contacting business contacts when you are angry or upset.

Passage 2 处理客户投诉

Warm-up Words & Expressions

赔偿 compensation
合同规定 contract stipulation
索赔 claim
违约 breach the contract
保险公司 insurance company
运输公司 shipping company
理赔 settlement

友好的 amicable
现实的态度 realistic attitude
相关证明 relevant certificate
直接损失 direct loss
低价 lower price
更换有缺陷的商品 replace faulty goods

Read Passage 2 and interpret it from Chinese into English

在国际贸易中，如果一方未能按合同履约，给另一方造成损失，那么后者可要求前者赔偿。这必须在特定时限内根据合同规定进行。根据造成损失的原因，负责赔偿的一方会有所不同。如果卖方违约，买方应根据合同规定向卖方索赔。如果买方违约，则由买方负责赔偿损失，卖方应提出索赔。如果损失发生在运输途中，则由保险公司或运输公司承担责任。遭受损失的一方应向保险公司或船运公司索赔。

关于索赔和理赔，有关各方都应本着友好、务实和现实的态度。对有关案件应进行深入调查，以确定真正的原因是什么以及哪一方应承担责任。损失金额和赔偿方式应以调查结果为依据。证据应完整、清晰，调查机构应有权出具相关证明。否则，相关方可能会拒绝索赔。

如果索赔合理，可以通过以下方式解决：退款并赔偿其他直接损失或费用、低价出售商品或更换有缺陷的商品。

Memory Practice

🎧 **Listen to the following paragraphs carefully without taking notes and then retell the main ideas in the source language based on your memory.**

1. What is the main idea of Paragraph 1?
2. What is the main idea of Paragraph 2?

Section 2　Interpreting Practice

Dialogue 1　Payment Term Negotiation

Warm-up Words & Expressions

付款条件 terms of payment　　　　　货币市场 monetary market
装运单据 shipping document　　　　　不稳定 unstable
不可撤销信用证 irrevocable letter of credit　　contract 合同
deposit 押金　　　　　　　　　　　signature 签名
balance 余额

🎧 **Listen to Dialogue 1 and interpret it into the target language.**

A: 史密斯先生，除了付款条件外，我们已经解决了与这笔交易有关的所有问题。

B: Ms. Zhang, could you accept open account?

A: 恐怕不行。电汇付款可以，我们目前也接受长期客户凭装运单据以不可撤销信用证付款。

B: To tell you the truth, a letter of credit (L/C) would increase the cost of my import. When I open a letter of credit with a bank, I have to pay a deposit. That'll tie up my money and increase my cost.

A: 请咨询您的银行，看他们是否会将所需押金降至最低。

B: Well, to meet you halfway, what do you say if 50% by L/C and the balance by open account 30 days?

A: 非常抱歉。由于总金额太大，而目前世界货币市场相当不稳定，我们不能接受信用证以外的任何付款方式。

B: OK, I have no alternative but to accept your terms of payment.

A: 那么，我们在所有要点上都达成了一致。

B: Yes, we're glad the deal has come off nicely and hope there will be more to come. When can the contract be ready for signature?

A: 我这周就能准备好。

B: The earlier the better. I'm leaving next Monday.

A: 本周五上午 10 点怎么样？我会把合同副本送到你住的酒店让你过目。

B: OK, that suits me fine.

Dialogue 2 协商价格

Warm-up Words & Expressions

new product promotion 新产品推广
报价 quotation
预测需求 forecast

佣金 commission
货运代理 freight forwarder
大幅削减 slash

🎧 **Listen to Dialogue 2 and interpret it into the target language.**

A: This is Mike speaking. What can I do for you?

B: 上周我们在展会上见过。您看到了我们展出的新系列作品，很感兴趣。

A: Yeah, we are pretty interested in new indoor series.

B: 我们很高兴听到这个消息。您对哪些产品型号特别感兴趣？

A: Let me check your electronic catalogue. I prefer to know HIL series first. Could you please give your lowest quotation based on CIF (cost insurance and freight) Malaysia?

B: 谢谢您的询问。您能告诉我们您需要多少件吗？

A: It's hard to say as we're not sure if your products are popular among the market, we would like to start with a trial order about 500 pieces. Could you give me a competitive price for new product promotion?

第二天

B: 您昨天是否收到了以马来西亚到岸价为基础的报价？

A: Yes, but it's pity to tell you that your price is much higher than others'.

B: 我们的报价基于数量，我可以了解下你们对这个系列的预测需求吗？

A: If both your product and price are competitive, we predict that there would be a large purchasing amount, almost 20,000 pieces for each month.

B: 一般来说，我们的报价与采购量保持一致，如果是长期深入合作，未来我们可以考虑支付佣金。

A: It sounds good. But the aid is too slow to be helpful.

B: 在这条航线上我们的货代缺少价格竞争力，如果贵公司有货代，按照广州离岸价报价如何？

A: That's a good idea. Please update price based on FOB (free on board) Guangzhou.

B: 预计运费将大幅削减，我通过电子邮件给您发送正式报价。

A: Fantastic. I'll be waiting for your reply.

B: 保持联系。

Dialogue 3 Choosing Freight Forwarder

Warm-up Words & Expressions

international market 国际市场　　　　　　国内市场 domestic market

货车队 truck fleet
运输服务 transport service
外包 outsource
海运 ocean shipping
承运商 carrier
报关 customs clearance
工资和福利 salary and benefits
开销 overhead

🎧 **Listen to Dialogue 3 and interpret it into the target language.**

A: With the expansion of our business into international market, we will export products overseas next year. So, Tracey, I'd like to hear your opinion about transportation and related activities.

B: 我们一直专注于国内市场，因此，使用我们自己的货车队和运输服务，合理而且价格实惠。不过，如果我们将货物运往海外，最好还是依靠专业的货运代理。

A: Why? Can't we arrange transport to other countries?

B: 事实上，由于出口涉及复杂的程序，在决定是否外包运输需求时，我们需要考虑很多因素。

A: What factors do you mean?

B: 运输需求的规模或复杂程度；我们是否具备自行安排运输的专业知识或经验；我们是否有时间管理运输过程。此外，还有海运成本、与承运商的关系等。

A: Is it possible to train our own team?

B: 一方面，履行某些职责（如报关）需要证书，而培训本身远远不够。另一方面，如果要雇用全职员工，公司就必须支付工资和福利，而且一个团队所需的开销也会增加。

A: So it seems apparent that you prefer freight forwarders.

B: 根据我们的估算，在最初的几个月里，我们每周都要协调几批货物，之后会更多，所以外包运输服务会更经济。

A: In that case, we should now start to find some reliable freight forwarders, so as to be ready for our export.

B: 好的，先生！我们现在就开始行动，并随时向您汇报进展情况。

Dialogue 4　包装与转运

Warm-up Words & Expressions

包装要求 packing requirement
bubble wrap 气泡膜
foam carton 泡沫纸箱
regular plastic 普通塑料
额外费用 additional expense
fragile 易碎的
handle with care 小心轻放
keep dry 保持干燥
prompt delivery 及时交付
port of shipment 装运港
转运 transship
修改 amend

🎧 **Listen to Dialogue 4 and interpret it into the target language.**

A: 我知道你们对订单有一些特殊的包装要求。

B: Yes, we do. First of all, we would like the boards to be wrapped in some type of bubble wrap.

A: 好的，这是我们所有木板的标准包装。

B: Can you also package boards in foam cartons instead of the regular plastic?

A: 没问题，但需要支付一点额外费用。

B: How much will it be exactly?

A: 让我确认下，大约2%的额外开支。

B: Well, that's acceptable. Because we want to make sure that we use really strong boxes, and that the boards are very secure inside.

A: 我们会注意的。还有其他要求吗？

B: Yes. Mark on the cartons "Fragile, handle with care" and "Keep dry".

A: 这也是惯例。

B: I know that this is a lot of trouble, but in the past, we've had a lot of problems with shipping.

A: 我完全理解。现在多费点事，多花点钱，就能保证有高质量的成品。

两周后

B: We urgently need this batch of goods, it has just occurred to me that another possibility to ensure a prompt delivery.

A: 具体是什么？能够详细描述下吗？

B: How about making Hong Kong the port of shipment instead of Seattle?

A: 恐怕我们不能同意。您订购的货物是在西雅图生产的。我们想指出的是，我们接受的所有订单都是从纽约或西雅图发货的，而不是香港。

B: It's like this. There are only a few ships sailing every month from Seattle to Yokohama, while sailings from Hong Kong are quite frequent. If shipment is effected from Hong Kong, we will receive the goods much earlier.

A: 我明白了。你们想让货物从西雅图经香港转运到横滨。是这样吗？

B: Yes, exactly, because I want these goods on our market at the earliest possible date.

A: 您的想法挺好的，那么信用证应该修改为"允许转运；从西雅图经香港运往横滨"。您的意思是这样吗？

B: Yes, exactly. Thanks for your cooperation.

Section 3　Interpreting Assessment

Dialogue 1　建立新的业务关系

Warm-up Words & Expressions

合资企业 joint venture　　　　　mutual benefit 互惠互利
电动滑板车 electric scooter　　　共同的愿望 common desire
具体行程 specific schedule

Unit 10　Business Negotiation

🎧 Listen to Dialogue 1 and interpret it into the target language.

评价项目	评价标准	原始赋分	学生得分
内容准确	忠实于原文，知识点准确，用词得当，句式合理。	30 分	
内容完整	完整传达原文的内容和含义，没有漏译。	20 分	
语言标准	语音语调标准，符合目标语言的地道表达方式，能够传达出原文的语气和情感。	20 分	
表达流利	口译流畅自然，无重译、停顿或修正现象。	20 分	
职业素养	听力反应敏捷，仪态大方，临场反应能力强。	10 分	
合计		100 分	
被评人			
评价人			
教师评价			

Dialogue 2　订单协商

Warm-up Words & Expressions

cubicle desk unit 隔间办公桌　　　　保险 insurance
warehouse 仓库　　　　　　　　　　交货日期 delivery date
陈列室 showroom　　　　　　　　　distribution hub 配送中心
estimate 估价　　　　　　　　　　　partial shipment 部分货物
商品 merchandise　　　　　　　　　运输途中 in transit
包装 packaging

🎧 Listen to Dialogue 2 and interpret it into the target language.

评价项目	评价标准	原始赋分	学生得分
内容准确	忠实于原文，知识点准确，用词得当，句式合理。	30 分	
内容完整	完整传达原文的内容和含义，没有漏译。	20 分	
语言标准	语音语调标准，符合目标语言的地道表达方式，能够传达出原文的语气和情感。	20 分	
表达流利	口译流畅自然，无重译、停顿或修正现象。	20 分	
职业素养	听力反应敏捷，仪态大方，临场反应能力强。	10 分	
合计		100 分	
被评人			
评价人			
教师评价			

Project 4
Business Cooperation

Unit 11 Investment Invitation

Learning Objectives

- Identify and comprehend key economic terms and phrases that appear in the interpreting process
- Learn about economic cooperation mentioned in the article, including China-ASEAN cooperation, the Belt and Road Initiative, and the dynamics of cooperation and competition in the global economy
- Utilize economic data and trends in the article to gain insights into the current state of the global economy, as well as the factors influencing international investment and trade

Ideological and Political Objectives

- Emphasize the importance of international cooperation, mutual benefit, and trust in fostering global economic growth and stability
- Promote the commitment to openness and economic resilience
- Highlight the value of cultural exchange, cultural diplomacy, and the celebration of multiculturalism in building harmonious international relations
- Showcase the positive impact of international events on strengthening economic ties, reducing poverty, and promoting inclusive growth
- Advocate for policies and actions that prioritize domestic manufacturing, supply chain resilience, and national competitiveness

Section 1 Interpreting Preparation

☞ Key Concepts

1. China International Import Expo (CIIE) 中国国际进口博览会（进博会）

In May 2017, Chinese President Xi Jinping announced at the Belt and Road Forum for International Cooperation that China will hold China International Import Expo (CIIE) starting from 2018. It is a significant move for the Chinese government to hold CIIE to give firm support to trade liberalization and economic globalization and actively open the Chinese market to the world. It facilitates countries and regions all over the world to strengthen economic cooperation and trade, and to promote global trade and world economic growth in order to make the world economy more open.

2. Maori war dance 毛利战舞

This refers to the traditional dance form of the Maori people in New Zealand, which includes movements, percussion, chants, and vocalizations.

3. China-ASEAN Expo (CAEXPO) 中国—东盟博览会（东博会）

The China-ASEAN Expo (CAEXPO) is an international economic and trade event jointly confirmed by the leaders of China and ASEAN. It was proposed by the Chinese side at the 7th ASEAN-China Summit in October 2003 that the CAEXPO be annually held in Nanning, Guangxi, China from the year 2004 onwards. The proposal gained positive feedback from the heads of state/government of the 10 ASEAN countries, and was written into the Chairman's Statement released afterwards. The 1st CAEXPO was successfully concluded in Nanning in November 2004, since then Nanning has become the permanent host city of the CAEXPO.

4. China International Fair for Trade in Services (CIFTIS) 中国国际服务贸易交易会（服贸会）

The China Beijing International Fair for Trade in Services, or Beijing Fair for short, was co-hosted by the Ministry of Commerce and the People's Government of Beijing Municipality in 2012 with the approval of the CPC Central Committee and the State Council, in an effort to boost the international competitiveness of China's service industry and trade in services, and give full play to the role of the two areas in accelerating the transformation of the economic development model. It was renamed the China International Fair for Trade in Services in 2019, and its abbreviation Beijing Fair was changed to CIFTIS in 2020. After that, CIFTIS is on track to be upgraded as the Chinese economy moves into a new phase of growth.

☞ Sight Interpreting

Passage 1 Nation Going All Out to be Investment Magnet

Warm-up Words & Expressions

remain an investment hotspot 保持投资热点
lower market entry threshold 降低市场准入门槛
Chinese modernization, driven by highquality development 高质量发展全面推进中国式现代化
amplify 放大
spillover effect 溢出效应
market-oriented, law-based and internationalized 市场化、法治化、国际化

Read Passage 1 and interpret it from English into Chinese.

China will strengthen efforts to remain an investment hotspot by lowering market entry thresholds, creating a better business environment and improving foreign investment utilization levels, officials said.

Chinese modernization, driven by high-quality development, will provide foreign investors with a broader market space and more opportunities for collaboration, said Commerce Minister Wang Wentao on November 5 on the sidelines of the ongoing sixth China International Import Expo in

Shanghai. "China's fundamentals, including its super large market scale, complete industrial supporting facilities and an upward economic trend, will not change, and such comprehensive strengths are still prominent," Wang, who gave a speech at the "Invest in China Year" summit and Shanghai city promotion event in Shanghai, said.

The event aims to amplify the spillover effect of the CIIE, showcase the achievements made by the Ministry of Commerce's "Invest in China Year", and demonstrate investment opportunities in Shanghai. "We will continue to create a first-class business environment that is market-oriented, law-based and internationalized, and work hand in hand with everybody to create an open and prosperous future," said Gong Zheng, mayor of Shanghai. As of end-September, Shanghai was home to 940 multinational corporations' regional headquarters and 551 foreign-funded research and development centers, Gong said.

Markus Steilemann, CEO of Covestro, said China is one of Covestro's largest markets, contributing to one-fifth of the group's total sales revenue last year. Steilemann said the company's total investment in China surpassed 3.9 billion euros as of the end of 2022, and that its investment will continue.

Themed "Working Together for a Bright Future of Openness and Prosperity", the summit, jointly held by the Ministry of Commerce and the Shanghai Municipal People's Government, looked to better enable CIIE to play a bigger role in investment promotion and showcase China's investment opportunities.

(https://language.chinadaily.com.cn/a/202311/07/WS6549e6e4a31090682a5ece5b.html)

Passage 2　新西兰小企业进入中国大市场，进博会"真的"不虚此行(节选)

Warm-up Words & Expressions

新西兰小企业 New Zealand small business	毛利战舞 Maori war dance
进入中国大市场 enter the large Chinese market	传统舞蹈形式 traditional dance form
	团体舞蹈 group dance
新发展格局 new development paradigm	新西兰总理希普金斯 New Zealand Prime Minister Chris Hipkins
高水平开放 high-level opening-up	
国际公共产品 international public product	中央广场舞台 central square stage
经贸往来 economic and trade exchanges	在展馆内进行表演 perform inside the exhibition hall
文化交流 cultural exchanges	
新西兰联合品牌馆 New Zealand joint brand pavilion	交易的是商品和服务 goods and services are traded
展台 exhibition space	交流的是文化和理念 culture and ideas are exchanged
旅游资源和教育资源 tourism resources and educational resources	独具魅力的新西兰 charm of New Zealand

Read Passage 2 and interpret it from Chinese into English.

过去十年，"一带一路"成为深受欢迎的国际公共产品和国际合作平台。作为中国构建新发展格局的窗口、推动高水平开放的平台、全球共享的国际公共产品，进博会与"一带一路"相得益彰、共促发展。

在这条路上，不只有经贸往来，也有文化交流。

中国是新西兰旅游最重要的市场之一，第五届进博会上，新西兰联合品牌馆共有400平方米的展台，除了企业外，商会还特别邀请了新西兰旅游局和新西兰教育局前来参展，展示新西兰的旅游资源和教育资源。

今年，除了旅游资源外，毛利战舞也将借由进博会的开放窗口再次向世界展示其所代表的当地特色文化。

毛利战舞，又称新西兰毛利战舞，泛指新西兰毛利人的传统舞蹈形式，是一种通过动作、拍打配以叫嚷和哼声来表演的团体舞蹈。今年6月25日，新西兰总理希普金斯率团抵达北京，在希普金斯的访华代表团成员中，就有来自今年新西兰全国毛利战舞比赛冠军部落的代表。本届进博会上，毛利战舞将登上"四叶草"中央广场舞台，同时也将在展馆内进行表演。

交易的是商品和服务，交流的是文化和理念。"希望通过进博会大舞台，最具新西兰文化特色的毛利战舞能大放异彩，让中国、让世界看到独具魅力的新西兰。"李瑞秦说。

（https://www.investsh.org.cn/cn/investsh/ywjqs/20230919113444479442987）

Memory Practice

Listen to the following paragraphs carefully without taking notes and then retell the main ideas in the source language based on your memory.

1. What is the main idea of Paragraph 1?
2. What is the main idea of Paragraph 2?

Section 2 Interpreting Practice

Passage 1 The Path to Growth: Three Priorities for Action（Excerpt）

Warm-up Words & Expressions

- slowdown 放缓
- labor market 劳动力市场
- consumer spending 消费支出
- advanced economy 发达经济体
- uplift 提振
- emerging economy 新兴经济体
- steeper climb 更加陡峭的攀升
- higher interest rate 更高的利率
- low-income country 低收入国家
- borrowing cost 借贷成本
- per-capita income growth 人均收入增长
- poverty and hunger 贫困和饥饿
- monetary and fiscal policy actions 货币和财政政策行动
- geopolitical tensions 地缘政治紧张
- inflation 通货膨胀
- robust recovery 强劲复苏
- vulnerable people and countries 弱势群体和国家

Listen to Passage 1 and interpret it from English into Chinese.

The slowdown has continued this year. Despite surprisingly resilient labor markets and consumer spending in most advanced economies, and the uplift from China's reopening, we expect the world economy to grow less than 3 percent in 2023.

As you will see in our *World Economic Outlook* next week, growth remains weak by historical comparison—both in the near and medium term. There are also stark differences between country groups.

Some momentum comes from emerging economies—Asia especially is a bright spot. India and China are expected to account for half of global growth in 2023. But others face a steeper climb. Economic activity is slowing in the United States and the Euro Area, where higher interest rates weigh on demand. About 90 percent of advanced economies are projected to see a decline in their growth rate this year.

For low-income countries, higher borrowing costs come at a time of weakening demand for their exports. And we see their per-capita income growth staying below that of emerging economies. That is a severe blow, making it even harder for low-income nations to catch up.

Poverty and hunger could further increase, a dangerous trend that was started by the Covid crisis.

Strong and coordinated monetary and fiscal policy actions over the past years prevented a much worse outcome. But with rising geopolitical tensions and still-high inflation, a robust recovery remains elusive. This harms the prospects of everyone, especially for the most vulnerable people and countries.

(https://www.imf.org/en/News/Articles/2023/04/06/sp040623-SM23-CurtainRaiser)

Passage 2　李强在第二十届中国—东盟博览会和中国—东盟商务与投资峰会开幕式上的致辞（节选）

Warm-up Words & Expressions

绿城 Green City
中国—东盟博览会和中国—东盟商务与投资峰会 CAEXPO and CABIS
20 年历程 over the course of 20 years
面向和平与繁荣的战略伙伴关系 strategic partnership for peace and prosperity
海上丝绸之路 Maritime Silk Road
命运共同体 community with a shared future
经贸合作 economic and trade cooperation
中国—东盟关系 China-ASEAN relations
亚太区域合作 cooperation in the Asia-Pacific
圆满成功 full success

Listen to Passage 2 and interpret it from Chinese into English.

尊敬的各国领导人，

各位嘉宾，

女士们，先生们，朋友们：

大家上午好！很高兴与大家相聚在美丽的"绿城"南宁，出席第二十届中国—东盟博览会和中国—东盟商务与投资峰会。10 天前在雅加达，在座的许多朋友参加了第 26 次中国—东盟领导人会议,今天,大家又相会在南宁,这充分说明了中国和东盟交流的热度、合作的深度。首先我谨代表中国政府,对本次博览会和峰会的召开表示热烈祝贺,对出席会议的各国领导人和嘉宾表示诚挚欢迎!

中国—东盟博览会和商务与投资峰会已经走过了20年历程,一路见证了双方关系的不断发展。20年前,中国作为对话伙伴国家率先加入《东南亚友好合作条约》,与东盟建立起面向和平与繁荣的战略伙伴关系。10年前,习近平主席在印尼国会发表重要演讲,提出愿同东盟国家共建21世纪海上丝绸之路,携手共建更为紧密的中国—东盟命运共同体,得到东盟各国积极响应,开启了双方友好合作的新篇章。2年前,在中国—东盟建立对话关系30周年纪念峰会上,习近平主席提出共建和平、安宁、繁荣、美丽、友好"五大家园",与东盟各国领导人一起擘画了未来合作发展的崭新蓝图。这些年来,我们坚持团结自强,坚定不移走和平发展道路,在变乱交织的世界中牢牢守护了地区的和平与安宁,共同创造了经济腾飞的奇迹,地区经济总量占全球比重从2002年的6.1%上升到去年的21.5%,20多亿人民的生活水平显著提高;我们坚持合作共赢,推动互联互通取得突破性进展,持续推进区域经济一体化和经贸合作,在全球经济乏力的背景下实现了贸易投资逆势攀升,中国与东盟贸易额20年间增长了16.8倍,双方已连续3年互为最大贸易伙伴,累计双向投资总额超过了3800亿美元;我们坚持胸怀天下,共同应对各种全球性挑战,在减贫、应对气候变化、环境保护、能源转型等领域不断打造新的合作亮点。中国—东盟关系已经成为亚太区域合作中最为成功和最具活力的典范,成为推动构建人类命运共同体的生动例证。

抚今追昔,我们理应为取得的成就感到自豪,也深感走过的历程极为不易和艰辛。展望未来,我们既满怀信心和憧憬,也有一些隐忧和焦虑。动荡不安的世界,纷繁复杂的形势,有许多难题和挑战需要我们共同应对。置身当今时代的大背景,面对百年未有之大变局,我们既要审时度势、顺势而为,更要善于把握那千变万化中的"不变"、万象丛生中的"本质"和贯穿事物发展变化始终的"主线"。当下中国与东盟关系的良好局面来之不易,凝结着各方的共同努力。我认为,这当中有其本质的内核和贯穿始终的主线,这就是习近平主席精辟概括的"亲、诚、惠、容"四个字。这四个字既是中国周边外交方针的基本取向,也是睦邻友好的相处之道,更是我们共创美好未来的重要法宝。我们要在践行"亲、诚、惠、容"这四个字上下更大功夫,努力营造有利于发展繁荣、和平安宁的良好环境,并使各国自身的发展更好地惠及周边国家、造福地区人民。

……

女士们、先生们、朋友们!

经过20年的共同努力,中国—东盟博览会、商务与投资峰会已经成长为推进区域一体化的重要平台,取得了丰硕成果。站在新的起点上,我们要继续建设好、运用好这一平台,进一步加强交流、增进感情,创造商机、共享成果,携手共建更为紧密的命运共同体,共同开创更加繁荣美好的明天。

最后,预祝会议取得圆满成功!

谢谢大家!

(https://www.gov.cn/yaowen/liebiao/202309/content_6904599.htm)

Passage 3 Speech at the High-Level Conference on Investment in Central America

Warm-up Words & Expressions

Central America 中美洲
obstacles to investment 投资的障碍
policies to remove those obstacles 消除障碍的政策
exchanges of goods, capital, and ideas 货物、资本和思想的交换
manage globalization 管理全球化
maximize its benefits 最大化利益
minimize its costs and risks 最小化成本和风险

foreign direct investment (FDI) 外商直接投资
technology, knowledge, and managerial expertise 技术、知识和管理专业知识
vertical integration 垂直一体化
development of supply chains 供应链的发展
macroeconomic stability 宏观经济稳定
financial sector risks 金融市场风险

🎧 **Listen to Passage 3 and interpret it from English into Chinese.**

Thank you very much. It is a great pleasure to participate in this conference. I hope it will be the first of many on this important subject. I want to begin by thanking President Arias again for his inspiring speech last night and the government of Costa Rica for hosting this conference. I would also like to give a special welcome to our guests from the private sector, whose presence is essential to the success of the conference. I look forward to hearing your views later this morning.

We are here to talk about investment in Central America—obstacles to investment and policies to remove those obstacles—and I'll say something about these in a few minutes. But it's useful to step back and ask why investment is important, and what it can do for countries and for people.

We live in a world of globalization. The pace of technological change is staggering. The extent and speed with which innovations in one country cross borders through exchanges of goods, capital, and ideas is unprecedented. We cannot stop this process. President Arias wisely said in a speech in New York last December that the dilemma that developing nations face is that "if we cannot export more and more goods, we will end up exporting more and more people". Nor should we want to stop globalization: it carries with it the prospect of improving the lives of people in all countries. What we should try to do is to manage globalization and make it work for citizens. The task for governments and for institutions like the International Monetary Fund is to try to maximize its benefits and minimize its costs and risks.

Chief among the opportunities that globalization gives rise to is the prospect of higher growth and higher living standards. And by encouraging foreign direct investment, Central America can gain access to technology, knowledge, and managerial expertise from abroad, and trigger vertical integration and the development of supply chains. One important goal should be to make the region as a whole attractive to investors. Foreign companies are more likely to invest in Costa Rica, although the country has a population of less than 5 million, if doing so will give them a foothold in Central America, which has a population of over 25 million.

...

For all countries in the region, maintaining macroeconomic stability is clearly an important part of the growth and investment equation. Most countries in Central America are doing well. Average growth was over five percent last year, which is above the level of recent years. Inflation is in single digits in most countries in the region. And Central American countries have achieved these results notwithstanding a significant deterioration in the terms of trade. Nevertheless, there are some caution flags. Real primary spending increased by over 9 percent on average in Central America in 2006, and current expenditure accounted for most of this rise. Capital investment remains relatively low in the region. More needs to be done to reduce financial sector risks, especially from off-shore centers. And Central America remains vulnerable to external shocks, especially a downturn in the United States, given the high share of the region's exports that go to the United States.

(https://www.imf.og/en/News/Articles/2015/09/28/04/53/sp020207)

Passage 4 1—8月我国对外直接投资持续增长

Warm-up Words & Expressions

对外直接投资 outbound direct investment
"一带一路" Belt and Road Initiative (BRI)
非金融类直接投资 non-financial direct investment
对外承包工程 foreign contracted project
营业额 turnover
储能企业 energy storage company
绿色能源 green energy
中欧经贸高层对话 China-EU High-Level Economic and Trade Dialogue
中共中央政治局委员 member of the Political Bureau of the CPC Central Committee
国务院副总理 Vice Premier of the State Council
中欧经贸高层对话中方牵头人 Chinese leader of the China-EU High-Level Economic and Trade Dialogue
欧盟委员会执行副主席 Executive Vice President of the European Commission
以合作代替对抗 replace confrontation with cooperation
防范和化解风险 prevent and resolve risk
传统消费高峰期 traditional peak period of consumption

🎧 **Listen to Passage 4 and interpret it from Chinese into English.**

商务部于周四表示，今年前8个月，中国对外直接投资持续增长，特别是对"一带一路"共建国家的直接投资。

商务部表示，今年1—8月，我国对外非金融类直接投资5856.1亿元人民币，同比增长18.8%。其中，我国企业在"一带一路"共建国家非金融类直接投资1403.7亿元人民币，同比增长22.5%。

前8个月，我国对外承包工程完成营业额6486.2亿元人民币，同比增长6.1%；新签合同额8633.4亿元人民币，同比增长2%。其中，我国企业在"一带一路"共建国家承包工程完成营业额5295.2亿元人民币，同比增长4.8%；新签合同额7253.5亿元人民币，同比增长 5.6%。

本月早些时候，隶属于中国家电制造商美的集团旗下的全球性储能企业深圳科陆电子有限公司宣布在美国成立公司，以加强其在北美市场的业务，巩固其在全球的行业地位。

"美的集团对绿色能源领域充满信心，我们将利用储能领域的专业知识，深耕绿色能源市场。在美国成立新公司将使我们能够进一步进入包括北美市场在内的全球市场。"美的集团副总裁伏拥军表示。

商务部周四时于在北京举行的新闻发布会上宣布，第 10 次中欧经贸高层对话将于 9 月 25 日在北京举行，中共中央政治局委员、国务院副总理、中欧经贸高层对话中方牵头人何立峰与欧盟委员会执行副主席、中欧经贸高层对话欧方牵头人东布罗夫斯基斯将共同主持对话。

周四，中国政府欧洲事务特别代表吴红波在中国与全球化智库主办的论坛上致辞时指出，中欧之间拥有巨大的合作潜力。

吴红波表示："我们已经确定了几个有前景的合作领域，包括绿色经济、数字化、人工智能和高端制造。"

他说："欧盟是开放经济的坚定倡导者和绿色发展的坚定支持者，公平合理的国际竞争应成为其绿色发展和转型的催化剂。"

吴红波补充说，以合作代替对抗，中欧双方可以增强防范和化解风险的能力，为全球经济发展作出贡献。

此外，随着中国传统消费高峰期中秋节和国庆节即将到来，商务部正在组织一系列活动促进国内消费。

商务部将推动出台一批支持汽车后市场发展的举措，进一步推动我国消费加速复苏。

(http://cn.chinadaily.com.cn/a/202309/22/WS650d49aba310936092f23249.html?ivk_sa=1023197a)

Section 3　Interpreting Assessment

Passage 1　News on China-ASEAN Cooperation Forum

Warm-up Words & Expressions

high-quality development 高质量发展
emerging industry 新兴产业
facilitate the flow of various resources 促进各种资源的流动
integration in the field 领域内的深层融合
exchanges and cooperation 交流与合作
industrial transformation 产业转型
innovation vitality 创新活力
new energy vehicles 新能源汽车
digital economy 数字经济
efficient flow 高效流动
openness and inclusiveness 开放包容
integrated development model 协同发展模式
minister-level dialogue 部长级对话
emerging industries face many barriers 新兴产业面临许多障碍

🎧 Listen to Passage 1 and interpret it from English into Chinese.

评价项目	评价标准	原始赋分	学生得分
内容准确	忠实于原文，知识点准确，用词得当，句式合理。	30 分	
内容完整	完整传达原文的内容和含义，没有漏译。	20 分	
语言标准	语音语调标准，符合目标语言的地道表达方式，能够传达出原文的语气和情感。	20 分	
表达流利	口译流畅自然，无重译、停顿或修正现象。	20 分	
职业素养	听力反应敏捷，仪态大方，临场反应能力强。	10 分	
合计		100 分	
被评人			
评价人			
教师评价			

Passage 2 2023 年中国国际服务贸易交易会全球服务贸易峰会新闻

Warm-up Words & Expressions

国际经贸合作 international economic and trade cooperation
数字化 digitalization
智能化 intelligence
绿色化 greening
高质量发展 high-quality development
包容发展 inclusive development
联动融通 connectivity and integration
发展动能 drivers for development
自由贸易区 free trade zone
投资负面清单 negative list for investment
电信 telecommunication
自由贸易试验区 pilot free trade zone
自由贸易港 free trade port
互利共赢 mutual benefit
数字贸易改革创新 reform and innovation in digital trade
知识密集型服务 knowledge-intensive service
多边贸易体制 multilateral trading regime

🎧 Listen to Passage 2 and interpret it from Chinese into English.

评价项目	评价标准	原始赋分	学生得分
内容准确	忠实于原文，知识点准确，用词得当，句式合理。	30 分	
内容完整	完整传达原文的内容和含义，没有漏译。	20 分	
语言标准	语音语调标准，符合目标语言的地道表达方式，能够传达出原文的语气和情感。	20 分	
表达流利	口译流畅自然，无重译、停顿或修正现象。	20 分	
职业素养	听力反应敏捷，仪态大方，临场反应能力强。	10 分	

续表

评价项目	评价标准	原始赋分	学生得分
合计		100 分	
被评人			
评价人			
教师评价			

Unit 12　Business Management

Learning Objectives

- Gain knowledge about Huawei's historical approach to information and digital transformation and learn about Huawei's latest strategic initiative, the All Intelligence Strategy
- Develop the skills necessary to handle content from various domains by interpreting passages related to technology, business, sustainability, and more
- Explore how data-driven decision-making is integral to improving products and providing personalized user experiences in Google

Ideological and Political Objectives

- Foster an awareness of political structures and systems, both in domestic and international contexts, in order to understand how these systems influence the world
- Emphasize the importance of global technological collaboration and partnerships
- Highlight commitment to sustainability, especially in areas of education, environmental protection, healthcare, and balanced development, in line with political goals of global well-being and equality
- Understand cybersecurity and privacy protection
- Promote the idea of global citizenship, emphasizing that individuals can play a role in shaping political and ideological discourse on a global scale

Section 1　Interpreting Preparation

☞ Key Concepts

1. All Intelligence Strategy 全面智能化战略

The "All Intelligence Strategy" proposed by Huawei aims to accelerate the intelligent transformation of various industries. It emphasizes the connectivity of all objects, the modeling of all applications, and the calculability of all decisions.

2. AI ecosystem 人工智能生态系统

This term refers to the interconnected network of hardware, software, data, and services that support AI applications and development.

3. Digital transformation 数字化转型

Digital transformation involves leveraging digital technologies to fundamentally change business operations and strategies. It often includes the adoption of digital tools, processes, and data analytics to improve efficiency and competitiveness.

4. Sustainable development 可持续发展

Sustainable development is a concept that advocates for meeting the needs of the present without compromising the ability of future generations to meet their own needs. It often includes considerations for environmental, economic, and social factors.

5. Corporate social responsibility (CSR) 企业社会责任

CSR is the idea that businesses have a responsibility to positively impact society and the environment beyond their financial interests. It may involve initiatives related to community welfare, social charity, and environmental protection.

6. Cybersecurity 网络安全

Cybersecurity focuses on protecting computer systems, networks, and data from theft, damage, or unauthorized access in the digital realm.

☞ Sight Interpreting

Passage 1 How Do Companies Manage Employees Working From Home? (Excerpt)

Warm-up Words & Expressions

fingerprint technician 指纹鉴定师
computer-monitoring program 电脑监控软件
virtual face time 虚拟面谈
computer security-monitoring program 电脑安全监控软件
sensitive data 敏感数据
personal information 私人信息
violate employees' privacy 侵犯员工的隐私

productivity 工作效率
prevent leaks 防止泄露
sales specialist 销售专员
monitoring program 监控软件
top Facebook users 使用 Facebook 最多的人
be chained to their jobs 被绑定在工作上
run errands 处理杂务

Read Passage 1 and interpret it from English into Chinese.

Amy Johnson works from her home in Dixon, Illinois, talking with clients and filing reports for her job as a fingerprint technician. In one way, though, she might as well be sitting at a desk next to her boss in Chicago.

Using a computer-monitoring program, Timothy Daniels, vice president of operations for Accurate Biometrics, can track whether Ms. Johnson and other employees are working—or slacking off. Once a week, he looks at summaries of "what websites they're using, and for how long". He says, "It enables us to keep a watchful eye without being over-invasive."

Ms. Johnson knows her computer is monitored. "But it doesn't bother me," she says, "I'm not doing anything I shouldn't be doing."

Working from home used to be a welcome break from the stress and interruptions of the office.

And let's be honest, it also offered the flexibility of squeezing in some errands or a nap between conference calls.

These days, working from home is more like being in the office, with bosses developing new ways to make sure employees are on task. Some track projects and schedule meetings on shared calendars. Others require "virtual face time" via email, instant messaging or calls. And some, like Accurate Biometrics, monitor computer use of employees, both at home and in the office.

Gartner Inc., a Stamford, Conn., technology-research company, predicts use of computer security-monitoring programs will rise to 60% of employers by 2015, from fewer than 10% now. The systems are used mainly to secure sensitive data and comply with government rules, but they also generate lots of personal information on employees' online behavior. To avoid violating employees' privacy, employers should tell employees they're being monitored and track only business-related activities, attorneys say.

The security program Mr. Daniels uses, InterGuard by Awareness Technologies in Los Angeles, is used by financial-services, healthcare and other employers to track productivity, prevent leaks and comply with security regulations. Like most monitoring programs, it also allows Mr. Daniels to see whether all his employees, including 16 office workers and 24 who work from home, are using their computer time in productive ways. Employees know the program is in place.

Such programs can help bosses spot people who need help, as well as those who are wasting time, says Elena Proskumina, a sales specialist for NesterSoft, a Woodbridge, Ontario, maker of a monitoring program called WorkTime. "One popular report among WorkTime clients is 'top Facebook users'," she says.

Employers say the idea isn't to keep people chained to their jobs for eight hours straight. They realize that people working from home may take breaks to run errands or handle other non-work tasks.

(https://www.kekenet.com/read/201207/191689.shtml)

Passage 2 华为提出全面智能化战略,加速千行万业的智能化转型

Warm-up Words & Expressions

信息化和数字化 informatization and digitization
客户需求 customer demand
技术创新 technological innovation
All IP 战略 All IP strategy
All Cloud 战略 All Cloud strategy
连接无处不在 ubiquitous connectivity
数字化转型升级 digital transformation and upgrading
智能化时代 the age of intelligence

历史性的战略机遇 historic strategic opportunity
All Intelligence 战略 All Intelligence strategy
千行万业 thousands of industries
算力底座 base of arithmetic power
百模千态 a hundred models and a thousand modes
软硬芯边端云 soft and hard core edge-end cloud

百花齐放 blossoming	产业合作伙伴 industrial partners
硬件开放 hardware openness	生态联盟 ecological alliance
软件开源 software open source	人才联盟 talent alliance

Read Passage 2 and interpret it from Chinese into English.

华为在信息化和数字化的浪潮中，十年一个台阶，基于客户需求和技术创新的双轮驱动，先后提出了 All IP 战略、All Cloud 战略，促进了联接无处不在的，加速了数字化转型升级。面向智能化时代，为了抓住 AI 这一历史性的战略机遇，华为提出 All Intelligence 战略。

All Intelligence 战略的目标是加速千行万业的智能化转型，让所有对象可连接，让所有应用模型化，让所有决策可计算。

华为副董事长、轮值董事长、CFO 孟晚舟表示："在全面智能化战略的指引下，华为将持续打造坚实的算力底座，使能百模千态，赋能千行万业。"

首先，华为致力于打造中国坚实的算力底座，为世界构建第二选择。孟晚舟表示："我们将持续提升'软硬芯边端云'的融合能力，做厚'黑土地'，满足各行各业多样性的 AI 算力需求。"

其次，华为将通过算力底座、AI 平台、开发工具的开放，支持大模型在智能化时代的"百花齐放"，努力做好"百花园"的"黑土地"。孟晚舟表示："我们支持每个组织使用自己的数据训练出自己的大模型，让每个行业用自己的专业知识发展出自己的行业大模型。"

"数十年来，我们深入通信与计算的理论本质，在数学与算法、化学与材料科学、物理与工程技术、标准与专利等领域，持续投入，不断探索，构建起根技术优势。"面向智能化未来，孟晚舟表示，华为将持续深耕根技术，坚持硬件开放、软件开源，与产业合作伙伴一道发展产业和生态联盟、人才联盟，构筑繁荣的算力生态。

（https://www.huawei.com/cn/news/2023/9/huawei-all-intelligence）

☞ Memory Practice

🎧 **Listen to the following paragraphs carefully without taking notes and then retell the main ideas in the source language based on your memory.**

1. What is the main idea of Paragraph 1?
2. What is the main idea of Paragraph 2?

Section 2　Interpreting Practice

Passage 1　New Policies Encourage Foreign Firms to Expand Operation

Warm-up Words & Expressions

the slowdown in global economic recovery 全球经济复苏放缓

cross-border investment 跨境投资

China's high-quality opening-up 中国高质

量对外开放
market-driven, legally structured and globally integrated 市场驱动、法治化和全球一体化
statement on further optimizing the foreign investment environment and increasing efforts to attract foreign investment 关于进一步优化外商投资环境，加大吸引外商投资力度的意见
equal treatment of foreign-invested enterprises and domestic enterprises 对内外资企业一视同仁

🎧 **Listen to Passage 1 and interpret it from English into Chinese.**

Given the slowdown in global economic recovery and the decline in cross-border investments, government officials and multinational corporation executives said these policy measures will promote China's high-quality opening-up by using the advantages of the country's huge and lucrative market, optimize the attraction and utilization of foreign investment, and establish a business environment that is market-driven, legally structured and globally integrated.

Aimed at improving the environment for foreign investment and attracting more global capital, the State Council, China's Cabinet, issued a statement on further optimizing the foreign investment environment and increasing efforts to attract foreign investment on Sunday. The government's commitment to enhancing the environment for foreign investment includes six key areas, such as ensuring the effective utilization of foreign investment and guaranteeing equal treatment of foreign-invested enterprises and domestic enterprises.

Addressing a news conference in Beijing, Chen Chunjiang, Assistant Minister of Commerce, said these policies will support the operations of foreign companies in China, guide their development and deliver timely services. "The Ministry of Commerce will strengthen guidance and coordination with relevant government branches on policy promotion, create a more optimized investment environment for foreign investors, and effectively boost their confidence," Chen said. Further steps will be taken to enforce the requirement of treating domestic and foreign-funded enterprises equally in government procurement activities, said Fu Jinling, head of the Economic Construction Department of the Ministry of Finance.

Amid a slowing global economic growth, foreign direct investment in China amounted to 703.65 billion yuan in the first half of 2023, a decline of 2.7 percent year-on-year, data from the Ministry of Commerce showed. While China's FDI growth faces challenges, the robust requirement for high-quality goods and services within its super-sized market continues to provide good prospects for global investors, said Wang Xiaohong, Deputy Head of the Information Department at the Beijing-based China Center for International Economic Exchanges.

(https://language.chinadaily.com.cn/a/202308/15/WS64db3d42a31035260b81c496.html)

Passage 2 华为投资控股有限公司 2022 年可持续发展报告（节选）

Warm-up Words & Expressions

全球合作伙伴 global partner
技术创新 technological innovation
科技守护自然、自然守卫者 Tech4 Nature, Nature Guardians

生物多样性保护效率 biodiversity conservation efforts
无障碍体验 accessibility features
手机 OS 和 UI 适老化评级结果 smartphone OS/UI elderly-friendliness ratings
金融普惠服务 financial inclusion service
网络安全认证证书 cyber security certificate
业务连续性管理体系 business continuity management system

全球化、多元化的供应战略 globalized and diversified supply strategies
合作共赢、共同发展 mutual development and shared success
安全、可靠、有竞争力的健康产业链 secure, reliable, competitive, and healthy industry value chain
数字世界的美好生活 a better life in the future digital world

🎧 **Listen to Passage 2 and interpret it from Chinese into English.**

华为 TECH4ALL 数字包容倡议围绕公平优质教育、保护脆弱环境、促进健康福祉、推进均衡发展四大领域，携手全球合作伙伴持续推进技术创新，以实际行动为世界带来更多美好的改变。2022 年，华为 TECH4ALL 教育项目已在全球 600 多所学校落地，逾 22 万名师生、待业青年及老年人从中受益。科技守护自然、自然守卫者等环保项目积极探索用 ICT 技术保护森林、湿地和海洋，已覆盖全球 46 个自然保护地，有效提升了生物多样性保护效率，促进自然资源可持续管理。华为终端持续优化无障碍体验，让更多人感受到科技的温度，在中国电信研究院发布的 2022 年手机 OS 和 UI 适老化评级结果中，HarmonyOS 2.0 荣获唯一的五星评级，并获得"适老先锋"称号。华为 Mobile Money 解决方案为 20 多个国家、4 亿多人口提供了金融普惠服务，让偏远地区的人们也有机会使用移动钱包、移动支付等数字业务，促进当地社区数字经济发展。华为努力通过数字技术，助力世界更平等、可持续地发展。

华为将网络安全和隐私保护作为公司的最高纲领，通过打造安全可信的产品、解决方案和服务，帮助客户消减风险，提升网络韧性。2022 年，华为共获得 30 余张网络安全认证证书，包括 CC EAL4+ 认证、ISO 19790 和 ISO 27034 认证等，表明华为的产品安全能力达到了国际公认的最佳实践的标准。2022 年华为对全球 300 多起重大事件和突发灾害进行了专项保障和及时处理，积极践行华为一直奉行的宗旨：在当地，服务当地。此外，为保障供应连续性和对客户的及时交付，华为建立了成熟的业务连续性管理体系，坚定不移地拥抱全球化、多元化的供应战略，奉行"合作共赢、共同发展"的理念，携手全球合作伙伴，共创安全、可靠、有竞争力的健康产业链，共同守护数字世界的美好生活。

(https://www-file.huawei.com/-/media/corp2020/pdf/sustainability/sustainability-report-2022-cn.pdf)

Passage 3 Google's Innovative Business Management Strategies

Warm-up Words & Expressions

technology giant 科技巨头
competitive edge 竞争优势
culture of innovation 创新文化

data-driven decision-making 数据驱动决策
market trend 市场趋势
strategic acquisition 战略性收购

market presence 市场份额
user-centric 用户至上
business strategy 商业战略
user experience 用户体验
brand loyalty 品牌忠诚度
global expansion 全球扩张

environmental responsibility 环境责任
renewable energy 可再生能源
carbon neutrality 碳中和
carbon footprint 碳足迹
corporate responsibility 企业责任

🎧 **Listen to Passage 3 and interpret it from English into Chinese.**

In the ever-evolving tech landscape, Google stands as an iconic example of successful business management. With its meteoric rise from a simple search engine to a global technology giant, Google has showcased innovative strategies that have helped it maintain its competitive edge. In this article, we will explore some of the key aspects of Google's business management that have contributed to its remarkable success.

1. A culture of innovation

Google's commitment to innovation is deeply ingrained in its corporate culture. Google encourages its employees to spend a portion of their work hours on personal projects, fostering creativity and entrepreneurial spirit. This approach has led to the development of groundbreaking products such as Gmail, Google Maps, and more. Google's relentless pursuit of innovation keeps it at the forefront of technological advancements.

2. Data-driven decision-making

Data is the lifeblood of Google's operations. Google collects and analyzes vast amounts of data to gain insights into user behavior and market trends. This data-driven approach enables Google to make informed decisions, refine its products, and deliver personalized experiences to its users. The meticulous analysis of data also plays a pivotal role in Google's advertising business, making it one of the leaders in online advertising.

3. Strategic acquisitions

Google has a history of strategic acquisitions that have expanded its product portfolio and market presence. Notable acquisitions include YouTube, Android, and Nest Labs. These acquisitions have not only added valuable assets but have also allowed Google to diversify its offerings and remain relevant in a rapidly changing tech landscape.

4. User-centric focus

Google's commitment to delivering user-centric products and services has been a cornerstone of its business strategy. By prioritizing the user experience and providing free, high-quality services, such as Google Search, Google Drive, and Android OS, Google has built a massive user base and maintained user trust. This user-centric approach has translated into strong brand loyalty.

5. Global expansion

Google has pursued an aggressive global expansion strategy, making its products and services accessible worldwide. Its commitment to providing services in multiple languages and adapting to local markets has contributed to its global success. Google's presence in various countries allows it to tap into diverse talent pools and user demographics.

6. Environmental responsibility

In recent years, Google has demonstrated a commitment to environmental sustainability. The company has set ambitious goals to operate on 100% renewable energy and achieve carbon neutrality. Google's investments in clean energy projects and its focus on reducing its carbon footprint align with growing global concerns about climate change and corporate responsibility.

Conclusion

Google's journey from a small startup to a tech behemoth has been shaped by innovative business management strategies. Its culture of innovation, data-driven decision-making, strategic acquisitions, user-centric focus, global expansion, and commitment to environmental responsibility have propelled it to the forefront of the tech industry. As Google continues to evolve, its ability to adapt and innovate will likely remain central to its enduring success in the competitive world of technology.

Passage 4 格力介绍

Warm-up Words & Expressions

核心技术 core technology
改变世界的产品 product that change the world
打造自身的品牌 build one's own brand
忧患意识 sense of crisis
进取精神 enterprising spirit
自主发展 independent development
国家重点实验室 national key laboratory
国家工程技术研究中心 national engineering technology research center
国家级工业设计中心 national industrial design center
国家认定企业技术中心 national certified enterprise technology center
机器人工程技术研发中心 robot engineering technology research and development center
按需投入 invest on demand
研发投入 R&D investment
知识产权局排行榜 National Intellectual Property Administration ranking
"国际领先"技术 "internationally leading" technology

🎧 **Listen to Passage 4 and interpret it from Chinese into English.**

一家企业想要掌握话语权，必须先掌握核心技术，能够创造出改变世界的产品的企业，才能真正打造自身的品牌。

一家没有创新的企业是一家没有灵魂的企业，一家没有核心技术的企业是没有脊梁的企业，一个没有脊梁的人永远站不起来。

——董明珠

格力电器始终保持忧患意识和进取精神，认识到只有真正掌握核心科技，才能真正掌握企业的命运，才能实现企业的自主发展。格力电器至2019年建有15个研究院，共有96个研究所、929个实验室、2个院士工作站（电机与控制、建筑节能），拥有国家重点实验室、国家工程技术研究中心、国家级工业设计中心、国家认定企业技术中心、机器人工程技术研发中心各1个，同时成为国家通报咨询中心研究评议基地。

公司提出研发经费"按需投入、不设上限",仅 2018 年研发投入就达到 72.68 亿元。经过长期沉淀积累,在 2018 年国家知识产权局排行榜中,格力电器排名全国第六、家电行业第一。至 2019 年共拥有 28 项"国际领先"技术,获得国家科技进步奖 2 项、国家技术发明奖 2 项、中国专利奖金奖 4 项。

(https://gree.com/about/business)

Section 3 Interpreting Assessment

Passage 1 Effective Communication in Business Management

Warm-up Words & Expressions

effective communication 有效沟通
business management 商业管理
performance metrics 绩效指标
share information 分享信息
role clarity 角色明确
foster collaboration 促进协作
communication channel 沟通渠道
collaboration culture 协作文化
positive work culture 积极的工作文化
job satisfaction 工作满意度
turnover rate 离职率
address challenges 解决挑战
timely communication 及时的沟通

🎧 **Listen to Passage 1 and interpret it from English into Chinese.**

评价项目	评价标准	原始赋分	学生得分
内容准确	忠实于原文,知识点准确,用词得当,句式合理。	30 分	
内容完整	完整传达原文的内容和含义,没有漏译。	20 分	
语言标准	语音语调标准,符合目标语言的地道表达方式,能够传达出原文的语气和情感。	20 分	
表达流利	口译流畅自然,无重译、停顿或修正现象。	20 分	
职业素养	听力反应敏捷,仪态大方,临场反应能力强。	10 分	
合计		100 分	
被评人			
评价人			
教师评价			

Passage 2 京东集团

Warm-up Words & Expressions

正道成功 success through integrity/success through the right path
合法方式 legitimate/legal means
诚信经营 integrity in business
客户为先 customer first
新标杆 new benchmark

企业社会责任 corporate social responsibility
高质量就业 high-quality employment
乡村振兴 rural revitalization
供给侧结构性改革 supply-side structural reform
物流基础设施 logistics infrastructure
供应链整合能力 supply chain integration
实体经济数字化转型 digital transformation of the real economy
产业和消费双升级 double upgrade of industry and consumption
员工子女救助基金 employee children's assistance fund
数智化社会供应链 digitalized social supply chain
技术服务能力 technical service capability

🎧 **Listen to Passage 2 and interpret it from Chinese into English.**

评价项目	评价标准	原始赋分	学生得分
内容准确	忠实于原文，知识点准确，用词得当，句式合理。	30分	
内容完整	完整传达原文的内容和含义，没有漏译。	20分	
语言标准	语音语调标准，符合目标语言的地道表达方式，能够传达出原文的语气和情感。	20分	
表达流利	口译流畅自然，无重译、停顿或修正现象。	20分	
职业素养	听力反应敏捷，仪态大方，临场反应能力强。	10分	
合计		100分	
被评人			
评价人			
教师评价			

Unit 13　Business Exhibition

Learning Objectives

- Gain insight into China's long-term commitment to the fundamental national policy of opening-up to the outside world. Learn about China's strategy of pursuing mutually beneficial openness and its dedication to economic globalization
- Understand the role of international investment and trade fairs in fostering investment, business relationships, and global economic cooperation
- Develop an understanding of the context and key elements of international business, trade, technology, and economic collaboration

Ideological and Political Objectives

- Emphasize the importance of international cooperation and openness, highlight China's active participation in global economic collaboration
- Highlight the Belt and Road initiative and China's contributions to global development, along with its vision of making greater efforts for a common global future
- Convey China's commitment to principles of peace, development, cooperation, and mutual benefit, as well as its dedication to maintaining international order and promoting global development
- Call for unity and cooperation among countries in the face of global challenges, aiming to jointly create a better future and demonstrating China's support for multilateralism and global governance

Section 1　Interpreting Preparation

🢒 Key Concepts

1. Digital economy 数字经济

The digital economy refers to the economic activities driven by digital technologies and the Internet. It encompasses various sectors and industries that leverage digital tools and platforms to conduct business, exchange information, and create value.

2. Market expansion strategy 市场拓张策略

A market expansion strategy outlines how a company plans to enter and grow within new markets.

Participating in exhibitions can be part of a broader strategy for reaching international markets.

3. AI governance 人工智能管理

AI governance encompasses policies, guidelines, and ethical frameworks that govern the development, deployment, and use of artificial intelligence (AI) technologies. In the context of business exhibitions, AI governance may relate to ensuring ethical and responsible use of AI-driven tools and applications in exhibition.

4. Business exhibition 商务会展

A business exhibition, such as CES (Consumer Electronics Show), is a large-scale event where companies from various industries showcase their products, services, and innovations to targeted audiences, including potential customers, partners, investors, and the media planning and execution.

5. G20 Summit G20 峰会

The G20 Summit is an annual international meeting of leaders from the world's major economies to discuss and coordinate global economic policies, financial stability, and other important issues. It serves as a platform for international cooperation and decision-making.

6. International Consumer Electronics Show (ICES) 国际消费电子展览会

ICES is one of the world's largest and most influential consumer electronics trade shows. It's an annual event where businesses, particularly those in the tech and consumer electronics industries, showcase their latest products and innovations. Exhibitors at ICES aim to increase their global visibility, optimize market share, and seek international opportunities.

☞ Sight Interpreting

Passage 1 Speech by Minister Josephine Teo at Future Economy Conference & Exhibition (Excerpt)

Warm-up Words & Expressions

digitally transition 数字化转型	digital utility 数字化实用工具
digital economy 数字经济	SingPass 新加坡电子身份验证系统
vibrant environment 充满活力的环境	PayNow 即时支付系统
talent pipeline 人才储备	InvoiceNow 电子发票系统
open and innovative 开放和创新	Singapore Trade Data Exchange (SGTraDex)
5G standalone networks 5G 独立网络	新加坡贸易数据交流平台
Future Communications Research & Development Program (FCP) 未来通信研发计划	small and medium enterprises (SMEs) 中小型企业

Read Passage 1 and interpret it from English into Chinese.

We are committed to helping our companies digitally transition and maximize new opportunities within the digital economy on three counts.

One, as we enter a new phase of recovery, we will ensure a vibrant environment where firms can thrive in the digital economy.

Two, we will sustain the growth of the digital economy through a robust talent pipeline.

Three, we will remain open and innovative, partnering with all of you to co-create a digital future for all.

Let me share more about our plans in each of those areas.

Over the years, we have laid the foundations for a thriving digital economy. Beginning with the first National IT Plan in 1986, we have made strong and sustained investments to connect people and businesses digitally.

Singapore has in place an advanced, secure and resilient digital infrastructure, which is critical to enable the digital economy. In telecommunications, we are among the world's first in rolling out 5G standalone networks.

We had set a target that by 2025, we will achieve nationwide outdoor 5G coverage. Based on my very recent discussions with our telcos, this target is very likely to be achieved ahead of time.

In any case, we are already setting our sights on the next bound, committing $70 million into the Future Communications Research & Development Program (FCP), to conduct cutting-edge communications and connectivity research, including 6G, standards of which have not been written, and therefore an open field for us to participate actively in to shape the future.

Riding on our investments in physical infrastructure, we have also developed a set of digital utilities—services that enable businesses and citizens to transact easily and safely across the economy. Some of these utilities, such as SingPass, PayNow and InvoiceNow, facilitate day-to-day transactions, creating significant network benefits across the nation.

Others, like the Singapore Trade Data Exchange (SGTraDex), help particular sectors, such as maritime, tackle a fragmented business landscape through data sharing, which will drive efficiencies across our supply chain ecosystem.

Our support also extends to individual firms, especially small and medium enterprises (SMEs) which form the vast majority of businesses in Singapore. Recognizing that different sectors each have unique needs, in 2017, we launched the Industry Digital Plans to provide guidance on the digital tools and training that SMEs in each sector would need. In the same year, we also launched the SMEs Go Digital program, to provide access to digital solutions at each stage of a firm's growth. Since then, more than 80,000 businesses have benefited from SMEs Go Digital, supported by 20 Industry Digital Plans.

Industry insights have been instructive in shaping government support. For this, I would like to thank Singapore Business Federation (SBF) for your strong partnership in engaging the industry when we developed the Better Data Driven Business (BDDB) program.

We look forward to working with all of you to build a vibrant digital economy that is connected, secure and resilient. I wish everyone the best in their digital journey, and a very fruitful discussion today. Thank you.

(https://www.mci.gov.sg/media-centre/speeches/minister-josephine-teo-at-future-economy-conference-and-exhibition/)

Passage 2 后疫情时代的中国企业：出海，走出去，寻找更多商机！（节选）

Warm-up Words & Expressions

小微企业 small and micro enterprises	消费电子产品制造商 consumer electronics manufacturer
出海 go overseas	展位 booth
后疫情时代 post-pandemic era	北美营销本部 North America marketing division
商机 business opportunity	总经理 general manager
全球知名度 global visibility	液晶显示器品牌 LCD display brand
海外市场份额 overseas market share	QLED 智能屏 QLED smart screen
海外合作伙伴 overseas partner	Mini LED 智能屏 mini LED smart screen
拉斯维加斯 Las Vegas	
会展中心 convention center	

Read Passage 2 and interpret it from Chinese into English.

中国企业，无论是大牌企业、独角兽初创公司还是小微企业，在今年的消费类电子产品展销会（CES）上都有一个共同的目标，那就是：出海，走出去，在后疫情时代寻找更多的商机。

为实现这一目标，他们将最好的产品带到拉斯维加斯，希望借此增加全球知名度，优化海外市场份额，与海外合作伙伴一起发展壮大。

在拉斯维加斯会展中心，中国知名消费电子产品制造商 TCL 在中央厅包下了面积足足 1650 平方米的展位，毗邻索尼、LG、三星和松下等竞争对手，非常显眼。TCL 陈列的各类拳头展品琳琅满目，包括超大屏幕 Mini LED QLED 电视系列、音箱、智能手机和增强现实演示厅等。

TCL 实业北美营销本部总经理张文海表示，只有与全球最强的对手竞争，并在竞争最激烈的市场中生存下来，企业才能发展壮大。

据 TCL 统计，2022 年前三季度，TCL 智慧屏全球销量达到 1662 万台。目前，TCL 已是全球和北美地区第二大液晶显示器品牌，并在全球重点市场保持领先地位。TCL 高端 QLED 智能屏和 Mini LED 智能屏销量全球领先。

张文海说，北美，尤其是美国，一直是 TCL 最重要、最大的市场。他说道："我们以用户为中心，十分重视消费者体验。一直以来，我们始终坚持为客户提供最好的产品和售后服务。"

在美国，TCL 与谷歌、Roku 和杜比等高科技企业一直保持着密切的合作关系。在全球范围，TCL 在 Mini LED、QLED 电视、AR/VR、5G、人工智能和云计算等技术领域积极投入，与全球领先企业合作。

作为中国制造企业国际化的先行者，TCL 历经二十余年，如今从国际化走向全球化。张文海说："我们是这一过程的见证者和受益者之一。"

（https://mp.weixin.qq.com/s/itb0E6SVyUGyhANRp5ggiA）

📖 Memory Practice

🎧 **Listen to the following paragraphs carefully without taking notes and then retell the main ideas in the source language based on your memory.**

1. What is the main idea of Paragraph 1?
2. What is the main idea of Paragraph 2?

Section 2　Interpreting Practice

Passage 1　News on CIFIT

Warm-up Words & Expressions

China International Fair for Investment and Trade (CIFIT) 中国国际投资贸易洽谈会	opportunity for overseas investment 海外投资机会
high-level opening-up 高水平对外开放	infrastructure 基础设施
guest country of honor 主宾国	market accessibility 市场准入
business ecosystem 商业生态系统	growth potential 增长潜力
collaboration potential 合作潜力	United Nations Industrial Development Organization (UNIDO) 联合国工业发展组织
global business connections 全球商业关系	

🎧 **Listen to Passage 1 and interpret it from English into Chinese.**

As one of the most influential investment events in the world, the China International Fair for Investment and Trade (CIFIT) strives to create an important platform for high-level opening-up. Representatives from overseas and international institutions have expressed that participating in the exhibition is of great significance and that the CIFIT is a very dynamic platform that can promote investment and business relations.

Qatar can be called "an old friend" of CIFIT. As a guest country of honor this year, Qatar will spotlight the strengths and competitiveness of its business ecosystem and showcase innovation, expertise and collaboration potential.

According to a high-ranking official from Qatar, CIFIT stands as an event of high repute in Asia, renowned for providing a vibrant platform to cultivate global business connections, exchange views and expertise, and promote opportunities for overseas investment.

This year, Qatar's focus remains on fostering meaningful partnerships, driving economic growth and fostering enduring international connections.

Qatar's advanced infrastructure, market accessibility, growth potential and commitment to safety are fundamental factors that draw investors and businesses to Qatar.

Fatou Haidara, deputy to the director-general of United Nations Industrial Development

Organization (UNIDO), said that as a co-organizer, UNIDO actively participates in various activities at CIFIT each year, including its exhibitions, discussions, and forums.

"We are pleased that many of our reports such as the *African Investment Report*, *Ethiopian Industrial Upgrading Report* and *2018 BRICS + Countries E-commerce Development Research Report* have been released at CIFIT, enhancing the investment attractiveness of developing countries."

Haidara said: "This year, we are carrying out over 600 projects, with a total value of just under \$630 million. For instance, UNIDO has assisted Ethiopia in developing its agro-industrial parks, creating jobs for more than 100,000 people drawn from local communities to date."

(https://mp.weixin.qq.com/s/faDWmJEywE3JQVzBI8aOOA)

Passage 2 习近平在第五届中国国际进口博览会开幕式上的致辞

Warm-up Words & Expressions

国家元首 head of state
政府首脑 head of government
国际组织负责人 head of international organization
代表团团长 head of delegation
第五届中国国际进口博览会 the Fifth China International Import Expo (CIIE)
新发展格局 new development paradigm
百年未有之大变局 unprecedented changes in a century
经济复苏 economic recovery
经济全球化 economic globalization
基本国策 fundamental national policy
互利共赢 mutually beneficial
开放战略 open strategy
丝路电商 Silk Road e-commerce
自由贸易试验区 free trade pilot zone
海南自由贸易港 Hainan Free Trade Port
经济政策协调 economic policy coordination
数字经济伙伴关系协定 *Digital Economy Partnership Agreement* (DEPA)
高标准自由贸易区 high-standard free trade area
人类命运共同体 a community with a shared future for mankind
多边主义 multilateralism

🎧 **Listen to Passage 2 and interpret it from Chinese into English.**

尊敬的各位国家元首、政府首脑，
尊敬的各位国际组织负责人，
尊敬的各代表团团长，
各位来宾，

女士们，先生们，朋友们：

大家好！我谨代表中国政府和中国人民，并以我个人名义，向出席第五届中国国际进口博览会的各位嘉宾，表示热烈的欢迎和诚挚的问候！

5年前，我宣布举办进博会，就是要扩大开放，让中国大市场成为世界大机遇。现在，进博会已经成为中国构建新发展格局的窗口、推动高水平开放的平台、全球共享的国际公共产品。

开放是人类文明进步的重要动力，是世界繁荣发展的必由之路。当前，世界百年未有之大变局加速演进，世界经济复苏动力不足。我们要以开放纾发展之困、以开放汇合作之力、以开放聚创新之势、以开放谋共享之福，推动经济全球化不断向前，增强各国发展动能，让发展成果更多更公平惠及各国人民。

女士们、先生们、朋友们！

中国共产党第二十次全国代表大会强调，中国坚持对外开放的基本国策，坚定奉行互利共赢的开放战略，坚持经济全球化正确方向，增强国内国际两个市场两种资源联动效应，不断以中国新发展为世界提供新机遇，推动建设开放型世界经济。

——中国将推动各国各方共享中国大市场机遇，加快建设强大国内市场，推动货物贸易优化升级，创新服务贸易发展机制，扩大优质产品进口，创建"丝路电商"合作先行区，建设国家服务贸易创新发展示范区，推动贸易创新发展，推进高质量共建"一带一路"。

——中国将推动各国各方共享制度型开放机遇，稳步扩大规则、规制、管理、标准等制度型开放，实施好新版《鼓励外商投资产业目录》，深化国家服务业扩大开放综合示范区建设；实施自由贸易试验区提升战略，加快建设海南自由贸易港，发挥好改革开放综合试验平台作用。

——中国将推动各国各方共享深化国际合作机遇，全面深入参与世界贸易组织改革谈判，推动贸易和投资自由化便利化，促进国际宏观经济政策协调，共同培育全球发展新动能，积极推进加入《全面与进步跨太平洋伙伴关系协定》和《数字经济伙伴关系协定》，扩大面向全球的高标准自由贸易区网络，坚定支持和帮助广大发展中国家加快发展，推动构建人类命运共同体。

女士们、先生们、朋友们！

"山重水复疑无路，柳暗花明又一村。"路就在脚下，光明就在前方。中国愿同各国一道，践行真正的多边主义，凝聚更多开放共识，共同克服全球经济发展面临的困难和挑战，让开放为全球发展带来新的光明前程！

谢谢大家。

（https://www.mfa.gov.cn/web/ziliao_674904/zyjh_674906/202211/t20221104_10800671.shtml）

Passage 3　Minister Wang Wentao Attends and Addresses Invest in China Year Summit and Shanghai City Promotion

Warm-up Words & Expressions

the Invest in China Year 投资中国年
Secretary of the CPC Shanghai Municipal Committee 上海市委书记
Chief Executive of the Hong Kong Special Administrative Region 香港特别行政区行政长官
Fortune Global 500 companies 世界500强企业
utilization of foreign investment 利用外资
Ministry of Commerce of the People's Republic of China (MOFCOM) 中华人民共和国商务部
CPC Central Committee 党中央
the State Council 国务院
optimize the business environment 优化营商环境

Listen to Passage 3 and interpret it from English into Chinese.

On November 5, the Invest in China Year Summit and Shanghai City Promotion was held in Shanghai. Chen Jining, Secretary of the CPC Shanghai Municipal Committee, Wang Wentao, Minister of Commerce of China, and John KC Lee, Chief Executive of the Hong Kong Special Administrative Region attended the event and delivered speeches. Gong Zheng, Mayor of Shanghai, attended the event and promoted Shanghai City. Rebeca Grynspan, Secretary-General of the United Nations Conference on Trade and Development, Pamela Coke-Hamilton, Executive Director of the International Trade Center, and some CEOs of *Fortune* Global 500 companies attended and addressed the event. Ling Ji, Vice Minister of Commerce and Deputy China International Trade Representative, presided over the meeting.

Wang Wentao said that the Chinese government attaches great importance to the utilization of foreign investment. President Xi Jinping has stressed on many occasions that we need to intensify efforts to attract and utilize FDI. Since the beginning of this year, Ministry of Commerce of the People's Republic of China (MOFCOM) has actively held the Invest in China Year activities to attract investment, advance high-level opening-up, promote exchanges and enhance cooperation. In the eight months since the launch of the Invest in China Year initiative, MOFCOM has held nearly 20 major events, and more than 500 supporting investment promotion activities at or above the provincial level have been organized around the country, with positive results being achieved.

Wang Wentao stressed that MOFCOM will continue to follow the decisions and plans of the CPC Central Committee and the State Council, further relax access to foreign investment, promote institutional opening-up, improve service levels, and optimize the business environment. MOFCOM will continue to build the brand of Invest in China, and bring FDI utilization to the next level so that China will remain an attractive destination for foreign investment.

More than 300 people from 18 provincial-level people's governments, local commercial departments, and representatives of multinational companies and foreign business associations attended the meeting.

(http://english.mofcom.gov.cn/article/newsrelease/significantnews/202311/20231103453160.shtml)

Passage 4 李强在二十国集团领导人第十八次峰会第一阶段会议上的讲话（节选）

Warm-up Words & Expressions

宏观经济政策协调 macroeconomic policy coordination
国际经济金融体系 international economic and financial system
数字经济 digital economy
二十国集团"绿色发展协议" G20 "Green Development Pact"
绿色低碳发展 green and low-carbon development
海洋生态环境 marine ecological environment
要团结不要分裂 solidarity over division
要合作不要对抗 cooperation over confrontation
要包容不要排斥 inclusiveness over exclusion
中国国际进口博览会 China International Import Expo
互利共赢的合作机遇 the opportunity of mutually beneficial cooperation

🎧 **Listen to Passage 4 and interpret it from Chinese into English.**

我们要切实加强宏观经济政策协调，维护国际经济金融体系安全，推动数字经济创新发展，为世界经济增长传递信心、提供动力，做推动全球经济复苏的伙伴；我们要坚定推进经济全球化，支持多边贸易体制，坚决反对人为将经贸问题政治化，共同维护全球产业链供应链稳定畅通，做推动全球开放合作的伙伴；我们要共同守护地球绿色家园，秉持共同但有区别的责任原则，实施好二十国集团"绿色发展协议"，促进绿色低碳发展，保护海洋生态环境，做推动全球可持续发展的伙伴。归结起来就是，我们要团结不要分裂，要合作不要对抗，要包容不要排斥。惟其如此，全球发展之路才能越走越宽广，人类未来才能越来越美好。

长期以来，中国始终倡导和平、发展、合作、共赢，坚持做世界和平的建设者、全球发展的贡献者、国际秩序的维护者。我们将坚定不移深化改革、扩大开放，坚定不移推动高质量发展，坚定不移推进中国式现代化。今年以来，中国经济整体回升向好，高质量发展扎实推进。中国发展前景光明，必将为全球经济复苏和可持续发展注入更多新动能。我们将于今年10月举办第三届"一带一路"国际合作高峰论坛，11月举办第六届中国国际进口博览会，欢迎各方积极参与，分享互利共赢的合作机遇。我们愿同各方一道，为人类共同的地球、共同的家园、共同的未来，付出更大努力、作出更大贡献！

（http://www.catl.org.cn/2023-09/12/content_115707279.html）

Section 3 Interpreting Assessment

Passage 1 Lenovo Group Further Invests in Cutting-edge Technology

Warm-up Words & Expressions

cutting-edge technology 尖端技术	original innovation 原始创新
technological prowess 技术实力	computing power 算力
technological revolution 科技革命	new computing 新计算
industrial transformation 产业变革	computing architecture 计算架构
technological innovation 科技创新	application-oriented chip design 面向应用的芯片设计
economic upgrading 经济升级	
digital and intelligent transition 数字化和智能化转型	end-to-end cloud collaboration 端到端的云协作
large computing 大计算	IPOs (Initial Public Offerings) 首次公开招股
AI platform 人工智能平台	unicorns 独角兽企业

🎧 **Listen to Passage 1 and interpret it from English into Chinese.**

评价项目	评价标准	原始赋分	学生得分
内容准确	忠实于原文，知识点准确，用词得当，句式合理。	30 分	
内容完整	完整传达原文的内容和含义，没有漏译。	20 分	
语言标准	语音语调标准，符合目标语言的地道表达方式，能够传达出原文的语气和情感。	20 分	
表达流利	口译流畅自然，无重译、停顿或修正现象。	20 分	
职业素养	听力反应敏捷，仪态大方，临场反应能力强。	10 分	
合计		100 分	
被评人			
评价人			
教师评价			

Passage 2 广交会新闻

Warm-up Words & Expressions

对外开放 opening-up	疫情防控平稳转段 smooth transition of epidemic prevention and control
对外贸易 foreign trade	
企业开拓国际市场 enterprises expand into international markets	线下展 offline exhibition
	常态化运营线上平台 online operation will run throughout the year
重要贡献 significant contribution	

Warm-up Words & Expressions

新题材 new theme
线上展 display online
新产品 new product
高端化、智能化、定制化、品牌化 high-end, intelligent, customized, branded

新面孔 new face
涌现 emerge
丰富业态 enrich business formats
高质量发展 high-quality development

🎧 **Listen to Passage 2 and interpret it from Chinese into English.**

评价项目	评价标准	原始赋分	学生得分
内容准确	忠实于原文,知识点准确,用词得当,句式合理。	30 分	
内容完整	完整传达原文的内容和含义,没有漏译。	20 分	
语言标准	语音语调标准,符合目标语言的地道表达方式,能够传达出原文的语气和情感。	20 分	
表达流利	口译流畅自然,无重译、停顿或修正现象。	20 分	
职业素养	听力反应敏捷,仪态大方,临场反应能力强。	10 分	
合计		100 分	
被评人			
评价人			
教师评价			

参考答案及译文

Unit 1　Interpreting Skills（口译技巧）

Section 1　Memory Training（记忆训练）

Practical Training（实战操练）

▶ **Passage Retelling（文章复述）**

Passage 1【参考译文】

Greater Bay Area: A Springboard for Greater Opportunities
Keynote Speech by Commissioner Liu Guangyuan at
the 4th Guangdong-Hong Kong-Macao Greater Bay Area Conference（Excerpt）

The Honorable Vice-Chairman Leung Chun-ying,

Publisher and Editor-in-chief Zhou Shuchun,

Deputy Secretary-General Eva Cheng,

Distinguished guests,

　　Ladies and gentlemen,

　　Good morning! I'm very honored to attend the Fourth Guangdong-Hong Kong-Macao Greater Bay (GBA) Area Conference. Let me begin by extending warm congratulations on the conference on behalf of the Commissioner's Office of the Ministry of Foreign Affairs in the HKSAR.

　　The GBA is a new window of China's high-level opening-up. China is fostering a new development paradigm featuring "dual circulations", with domestic circulation as the mainstay, domestic and international circulations reinforcing each other, and is committed to building a more market-oriented, law-based and world-class business environment. The GBA, as one of the most open and dynamic region in China, is an "innovation pilot zone" for China to build a new pattern of opening-up. With the steady progress of major cooperation platforms such as Qianhai, Hengqin and Nansha, and more opening-up measures in trade, finance, science and technology, the GBA has shown to the world that China will not change its resolve to open wider at a high standard; China will not change its determination to share development opportunities with the world; and China will not change its commitment to an economic globalization that is more open, inclusive, balanced and beneficial for all.

　　The GBA is a new benchmark in the successful practice of "one country, two systems". In the development of the GBA, one fundamental principle has been firmly followed—that is sticking to the very basis of "one country", well leveraging the benefits of "two systems" and acting in strict accordance with the Constitution and the Basic Law. For Hong Kong and Macao, "one country, two systems" is their biggest advantage, and the GBA is their best stage. The Central Government attaches high importance to the long-term prosperity and stability of Hong Kong and Macao as well as the well-being of the people, and has adopted a series of policies to support the two SARs (special administrative region) and their cooperation with Guangdong Province. The purpose is to harness the strengths of Hong Kong and Macao and respond to the needs of the country. When Hong Kong and Macao further integrate into the overall national development, they could unlock new growth potential and make new achievements, thus unleashing huge dividends of integrated development and contribute to enduring success of "one country, two systems".

The GBA is a new platform for win-win cooperation between China and the world. The GBA will set up high-standard trade and investment rules, and forge new strengths in international cooperation and competition. Countries around the world are welcome to take part in the region, deepen cooperation, and achieve win-win. At present, the international trade volume in the GBA has topped 14 trillion RMB, and its FDI (foreign direct investment) has reached 103.7 billion US dollars. It is home to dozens of *Fortune* Global 500 headquarters and a growing number of talents both at home and abroad, gradually turning into a global top-tier bay area and a world-class city cluster. The GBA has also been recognized as a fertile ground for foreign investment and business in China, a driver for win-win cooperation between China and the world, and a catalyst for global economic balance and sustainable growth.

Finally, I wish this conference a resounding success!

Thank you!

Passage 2 【参考译文】

普林斯顿大学校长2023年开学演讲（节选）

今天，我很高兴在此迎接普林斯顿大学2027届的学生，并庆祝新学年的开始。

大学生活的奇迹之一在于，每年秋天当我们的教室、运动场、食堂和校园里无数的其他空间都焕发着勃勃生机，我们欢迎社区新成员的加入时所感到的激动之情。我很高兴你们在这里！

我意识到，如果新年伊始让人感到振奋和开心，那么它也会让人感到困惑和不安。通常所有这些情绪都是同时发生的，而这种兴奋与不安交织的心情可能会在普林斯顿的学习生涯中持续下去。

事实上，当我与普林斯顿的校友们谈论他们的教育时，他们最常使用的词是"转变"。我想说我也会如此形容自己在普林斯顿大学的本科生涯，安东尼·罗梅罗也是这么评价他在这里的时光的。我希望这也能成为你们的真实写照。

转变是一件美妙的事情，它的要求也很高。它会带来烦恼和快乐、挫折和幸福。没关系，其实这是接受良好教育的一部分经历。

世界上最伟大的小说家之一托妮·莫里森教授曾在普林斯顿大学写道："每一扇门、每一棵树和每一个转角处都回荡着笑声、忠诚和爱的低语、喜悦、悲伤和胜利的泪水。"

我非常喜欢这段话，部分原因是它提到学习和成长并不容易，对任何人来说都不容易。当我们挑战自我时，当我们成长和改变时，当我们深切关心在学术和课外活动方面付出的努力以及我们的社区时——正如我们应该且必须关心的那样——不可避免地会有胜利和悲伤，不仅有欢笑，也会有泪水。

Section 2　Note-taking Skills（记录技巧）

Practical Training（实战操练）

Note-taking Training（记录练习）

Passage 1 【参考译文】

中拉民营经济合作论坛在广东东莞举行

5月24日，中拉民营经济合作论坛在广东东莞举行。论坛公布的数据显示，2022年广东省与拉美和加勒比国家共同体（拉共体）的贸易额同比增长9.5%，超655亿美元。

2022年，中国同拉美和加勒比地区的贸易总额达4857亿美元，同比增长7.7%。

在广大民营企业的积极参与下，近年来广东不断加强与拉美和加勒比国家的友好交往和经贸合作与交流，与拉共体缔结友城18对，有11个拉美国家在广州（广东省省会）设立总领事馆。

根据广东省政府数据，2022年，广东省民营经济增加值达6.98万亿元，民营经济进出口总额达4.87万亿元。

广东将继续坚定不移推进高水平对外开放，构建市场化、法治化、国际化的营商环境，深化同拉美和加勒比国家的民营经济合作。

Passage 2【参考译文】

Canton Fair Offers Boon to Exporters

At a booth inside the Pazhou International Convention and Exhibition Center in Guangzhou, capital of Guangdong Province, Xu Yajie, a sales manager, has been busy all day introducing colorful ceramic products to buyers from the United Arab Emirates.

As an employee of Guangdong Sitong Group Co., Ltd., Xu said, "A higher number of overseas buyers, especially those from countries and regions involved in the Belt and Road Initiative, have visited the booth with interest in innovative products."

Guangdong Sitong is a ceramic company based in Chaozhou, Guangdong. It is among 9,674 companies showcasing their latest innovative products and services during the second phase of the 134th China Import and Export Fair, also known as the Canton Fair.

The event opened on Monday with an exhibition area of 515,000 square meters, displaying products and services in building materials, furniture, home decorations, gifts and household goods.

Guangdong Sitong, which exports to more than 90 markets worldwide, displayed tailor-made ceramic products during the event, Xu said.

"Thanks to preliminary preparations, especially in terms of increased investment in the design and research of new products, buyers from overseas markets like the Middle East, Europe and the United States, have shown greater intention for orders," Xu added.

Improvements in design and technology over the years have made the company's ceramic products offer more added value in the global market, especially in Germany, the Middle East and Central Asia, she said.

"We have seen an increased number of buyers from Germany, which has stricter market standards in design and technology for ceramic products. This has illustrated our products' competitiveness in overseas markets."

As of Wednesday, some 150,000 overseas buyers from 214 countries and regions have attended the event, an increase of more than 50 percent compared with the same phase of the last session of the fair, according to event organizers.

Talent Group, a high-end candle and aromatherapy producer based in Dalian, Liaoning Province, is displaying its latest innovative candle and aromatherapy series during the fair.

Its Restore series is mainly made of shea butter, a low-carbon material for candle and aroma products, which makes them more competitive in the international market, said Wang Lixin, Talent's chairman.

"Utilizing low-carbon global resources and incorporating traditional Chinese culture in design has greatly boosted our products' value in the global market. They are widely acclaimed by overseas buyers during the exhibition, especially those from developed markets," Wang said.

Section 3 Syntactic Linearity（顺句驱动）

Practical Training（实战操练）

Setence Interpreting（句子口译）

【参考译文】
1. 我很吃惊，他竟这样说话。
2. 政府的关键作用在于促进社会的人力开发，并使穷人获得必要的劳动技能。
3. 他们一直忙个不停，从早上8点干到现在。
4. 他们要把准备工作做完，然后再考虑其他建议。
5. 我国将在京都会议召开之前递交自己的报告。

Section 4 Skills for Sight Interpreting（视译技巧）

Practical Training（实战操练）

Sentence Interpreting（句子口译）

【参考译文】
1. To meet the needs of people in all countries for a better life is the mission of the Belt and Road Initiative.
2. Many people in the West know that compared with people in other countries, the Chinese are the least concerned about religion.
3. In Chinese culture, the tiger is a symbol of courage and power./Chinese culture sees the tiger as a symbol of courage and power.
4. In 2022, the number of college graduates is expected to reach 10.76 million./In 2022, there are 10.76 million college graduates./10.76 million college students are expected to graduate in 2022.
5. In 2021, Beijing achieved a GDP growth rate of 8.5%./In 2021, Beijing's GDP grew by 8.5%.
6. Jo 和她的朋友 Laurie 吵架了，但最后和好了。
7. 对于在中国的西方人来说，建立有效的管理者团队意味着吸引当地的管理人才。
8. 那男孩肩上扛着枪，假装自己是名战士。
9. 《天路历程》是一则寓言故事，讲述了人类灵魂所受到的诱惑与所取得的胜利。
10. 美国人在北美自由贸易区是否对美国有利这一问题上仍然存在分歧。

Passage Interpreting（文章口译）

Passage 1 【参考译文】

Openness Crucial for APEC Economies (Excerpt)

The Asia-Pacific Economic Cooperation Ministerial Meeting focused on topics such as supporting the multilateral trade system, regional economic integration, supply chain cooperation, digital economy and promoting inclusivity and sustainable trade and investment, the Ministry of Commerce said in an online statement on November 11.

Wang called for holding a high-level officials' meeting again before the World Trade Organization's 13th Ministerial Conference (MC13) to build consensus. With an open attitude, APEC should push for the goals set forth in joint statements and initiatives, such as investment facilitation, and integrate them into a multilateral framework, he added.

China's foreign trade with other APEC economies amounted to $3.74 trillion in 2022, representing 59.7 percent of the country's total import and export value. Among China's top 10 trading partners, eight of them are APEC economies, said the Ministry of Commerce.

China is the largest trading partner of 13 APEC economies. A total of 15 APEC economies have signed free trade agreements with China.

Foreign direct investment from other APEC economies utilized by China accounted for 86.6 percent of the country's total FDI in 2022, while 5 APEC economies were listed among the top 10 sources of foreign investment, the Ministry of Commerce added.

Wang said APEC should uphold the central role of the Free Trade Area of the Asia-Pacific (FTAAP). The *Regional Comprehensive Economic Partnership Agreement* and the *Comprehensive and Progressive Agreement for Trans-Pacific Partnership* are the two possible paths for the FTAAP that have been jointly determined by APEC leaders. It is essential to adhere to openness, inclusiveness and continuously advance the expansion process to benefit more economies.

Wang said that development should be prioritized, taking full account of the interests of developing economies. China is willing to enhance practical cooperation in the digital economy and green growth with more APEC economies.

As the International Monetary Fund has upwardly revised its growth projection for the Chinese economy in 2023, raising it from 5 percent to 5.4 percent, Wang said China will further expand high-standard opening-up, share development opportunities of its vast market with other APEC economies and the world, and jointly promote high-quality development and prosperity.

Echoing that sentiment, Robert Yap, executive chairman of YCH Group, a Singapore-based logistics conglomerate, said the company will provide more supply chain solutions in the Asia-Pacific region to become a vital connecting point for China's regional trade and supply chains.

YCH Group announced two strategic partnerships with Chinese firms during the sixth China International Import Expo in Shanghai earlier in November.

"These collaborative endeavors transcend traditional business ventures, offering innovative solutions to surmount the operational challenges of international business expansion while providing substantial benefits to Chinese companies seeking market expansion into member countries of the Association of Southeast Asian Nations," Yap said.

Passage 2【参考译文】

耶鲁大学2027届学生开学典礼致辞（节选）

大家上午好！

我很荣幸能够欢迎新生和你们的家人来到学校，并宣布你们的本科生涯正式启航。我很高兴这一天终于到来了，你们来到这里，让我非常欣喜。

你们能成为耶鲁一员的原因显而易见。你们的学术造诣、领导才能和出色的驱动力让你们脱颖而出，坐在了这片几百年来优秀学子都坐过的草地上。此外，你们在各个方面的多样性也反映出耶鲁致力于营造一个包容性的教育环境的承诺。

现在，当你们准备踏入耶鲁校园并留下自己的独特足迹时，让我告诉你们一个我对校友们多年来的观察结果。你们的很多前辈都感叹，在愉快的开学典礼之后，时间会过得飞快，一转眼就要进行毕业典礼了。

这个残酷的事实在耶鲁的非官方校歌《美好校园年华》中也有体现。歌词把你们在校的时光形容为"最短暂、最欢快的光阴""快速地""从指间流走"。毕业时唱这首歌是耶鲁最重要的传统之一。

所以，请你们好好享受这个非凡之地，珍惜那些吸引你选择耶鲁的特质。

Section 5　Figures Interpreting（数字口译）

Practical Training（实战操练）

Sentence Interpreting（句子口译）

【参考译文】

1. In 2023, in the first quarter of the year, Guangdong's general trade volume of imports and exports reached 1.06 trillion yuan, up by 3.8%, accounting for 57.5% of the total value of Guangdong's imports and exports trade.

2. The comprehensive recovery of cross-border logistics has promoted the development of bonded business. In the first quarter, the imports and exports of Guangdong bonded logistics reached 315.64 billion yuan, increased by 14.8%.

3. Guangdong's imports and exports to countries jointly building the Belt and Road increased by 10.9%, registering for 29.4% of the total value of imports and exports; imports and exports to other RCEP member countries increased by 2.8%.

4. 2007年总进口量预计比2006年增加6.5%，而出口量预计会下降4%。净进口量预计在2007年会增加大约8.6%，随后在2008年会下降1.4%。

5. 根据12月1日地下储存设施的报告，天然气储存量达到了历史最高纪录，为35.45万亿立方英尺，这比2002年至2006年5年的平均水平32.54万亿立方英尺要高8.9%。

6. 1978年，中国只生产了14.9万辆汽车。汽车年产量在1992年达到100万辆，在2000年达到200万辆，在2004年达到500万辆，在2008年超过900万辆。

Passage Interpreting（文章口译）

Passage 1【参考译文】

Profits of China's industrial firms extended gains for a third consecutive month in October, pointing to further signs of a stabilizing economy. Data from the National Bureau of Statistics (NBS) showed on November 27 that industrial enterprises with annual revenue of at least 20 million yuan each saw their total profits increase 2.7 percent year-on-year in October after a notable 11.9 percent rise in September.

Yu Weining, a statistician at the NBS, attributed the continued recovery in industrial profits to the steady rebound in industrial production and improved corporate profitability with a series of macro policies taking effect gradually. For the January-October period, industrial enterprises with annual revenue of at least 20 million yuan each saw their total profits fell 7.8 percent year-on-year to 6.12 trillion yuan, narrowing from the 9 percent drop in the first nine months, the bureau said.

Notably, profits of raw materials manufacturing firms surged 22.9 percent in October amid continued recovery in downstream demand. Profits of consumer goods manufacturing enterprises increased by 2.2 percent in October with policies on expanding demand and boosting consumption taking effect gradually, witnessing profits rise for a third consecutive month. During the January-October period, profits of equipment manufacturing enterprises rose by 1.1 percent on a yearly basis, NBS data showed.

Passage 2【参考译文】

海关总署12月7日发布的数据显示，2023年前11个月，我国货物贸易进出口总值37.96万亿元，同比基本持平。其中，出口21.6万亿元，同比增长0.3%，进口16.36万亿元，同比下降0.5%。贸易顺差5.24万亿元，同比扩大2.8%。据海关总署统计，11月中国进出口总值达3.7万亿元，同比增长1.2%。前11个月，我国出口机电产品12.66万亿元，增长2.8%，占出口总值的58.6%。

Unit 2　Protocol Routine（迎来送往）

Section 1　Interpreting Preparation（口译准备）

Sight Interpreting（视译）

Passage 1【参考译文】

欢迎中国代表团的致辞

女士们、先生们：

　　大家晚上好！

　　热烈欢迎来自中国的贵宾。我谨代表西蒙葡萄园对大家的到来表示衷心的感谢。

　　很高兴有这个机会向尊敬的中国代表团展示我们美丽且卓越的葡萄园，与大家一起探讨潜在的商业合作渠道。中国代表团的这次到访标志着我们在强化两国关系上迈出了里程碑式的一步。

　　在这座美丽的葡萄园中相聚，让人不禁想起我们共同珍视的酿酒艺术精神与传承。我们的葡萄园坐落在澳大利亚知名的葡萄酒产区，历经世代辛勤耕耘和精心呵护。我们的葡萄园出品了一系列在国内外享有盛誉的优质佳酿，这是我们引以为豪的成就。

　　今晚，我们有幸与中国朋友共聚一堂。你们的到来充分体现了中国市场对澳大利亚葡萄酒日益增长的关注和需求。我们坚信，这次来访必将有力地催化双方建立长期的伙伴关系，并开启新的合作篇章。

　　我们的葡萄园见证了传统技艺与现代创新的和谐融合。我们既坚守着代代相传的悠久酿酒智慧，又积极采用前沿技术。这样的独特融合使我们能够酿造出蕴含本土风土、风味独特且香气四溢的澳大利亚葡萄酒。

　　我们相信，我们葡萄园对品质、可持续性及创新理念的执着追求将得到诸位的认可。我们相信，通过携手合作，我们可以建立一种伙伴关系，不仅能推动彼此业务的发展，更能促进两国间的文化交流与相互理解，增进友谊。

　　最后，请允许我再次向所有远道而来的贵宾表达最热烈的欢迎。愿此次访问成为我们伙伴关系的崭新起点，让我们两国关系更加紧密，创造共享成功的传奇。

　　谢谢大家。

Passage 2 【参考译文】

Remarks by H. E. Xi Jinping President of the People's Republic of China

At the Closing Ceremony of the Sixth Meeting of the China-France Business Council

Ladies and Gentlemen,

Friends,

    Both China and France are parts of the Eurasian continent, located at its east and west ends respectively. China is a typical Eastern civilization, and France showcases the Western. Our two countries do not have geopolitical conflicts, and we do not have clashes of fundamental interests. What we do have in common is we both think independently, both are fascinated by our splendid cultures, and we are engaged in result-oriented cooperation based on many shared interests. Our experiences in the past and at present both show that there is no reason for failures in bringing out the best in China-France relations. We have now reached a new crossroads in the development of mankind and face global changes unseen in a century. Against this backdrop, China is ready to enhance all-round exchanges and cooperation with France, bring the China-France relationship to a new stage and make it even more productive.

    Looking to the future, we will work with France to enrich the economic and trade dimensions of the China-France comprehensive strategic partnership. As one of the earliest participants in China's reform and opening up, France has contributed to China's modernization drive and benefited from it. Deeper friendship calls for frequent exchanges and closer cooperation. We always view France as a priority and trustworthy partner of cooperation. We are committed to expanding our business relations in both width and depth by opening up new areas, creating new models and fostering new growth areas. China will continue to make full use of the "French farm to Chinese dining table" whole-chain rapid coordination mechanism, and bring more cheese, ham, wine and other quality agricultural products from France to the dining tables of Chinese families. China has decided to extend visa exemption entry for citizens from 12 countries including France on short-term visits to China until the end of 2025, a step that will further boost people-to-people exchanges.

    Looking to the future, we will work with France to deepen China-Europe mutually beneficial cooperation. China and Europe are two major forces in building a multipolar world, two big markets that promote globalization, and two great civilizations that advocate cultural diversity. China-Europe relations are crucial for peace, stability and prosperity of the world. The two sides should always define China-Europe relations as a comprehensive strategic partnership, continue to enhance political mutual trust, remove various distractions, and jointly oppose attempts to turn business relations into political, ideological or security issues. We hope that Europe will work together with us to increase understanding through dialogue, resolve differences through cooperation, and defuse risks with enhanced mutual trust. We should turn China and Europe into each other's key partners for business cooperation, priority partners for cooperation in science and technology, and trustworthy partners for cooperation in industrial and supply chains. China will, on its own initiative, further open up the service sector including telecommunication and medical services, and open its market wider to create more opportunities for companies of France, Europe and beyond.

(https://english.news.cn/20240507/0c86bf580fe7420d8fbac0a6298e68c6/c.html)

Memory Practice（记忆训练）

Paragraph 1

Greeting someone is a simple way to say "Hello". It's easier for people from the same community to greet each other compared to those from different backgrounds. Selecting the appropriate greeting is important when initiating a conversation. English has formal and informal greetings. Formal greetings are used in business meetings and formal functions. "Good morning" "Good afternoon" and "Good evening" are commonly used. "How do you do?" is a formal greeting. "How are you doing?" is another form. Informal greetings are more numerous and used in everyday situations. "Hi" is a common informal greeting. "Hiya" is a friendly variation, often used in the UK. "Hey" is a casual greeting used among friends or in relaxed settings.

Paragraph 2

外事送别礼仪流程：

1. 确定送别规格。在确定送别规格的时候，主要根据来访者的身份、访问的性质和目的确定，同时还要注意遵循惯例，综合平衡。一般按照国际惯例的对等原则，主要迎送人员应与来宾的身份相当。

2. 安排交通工具。了解来访宾客的离程时间以后，要尽早预订机票、车票或者是船票，安排送行人员和送行车辆。

3. 赠送礼品。赠送的礼品要有纪念意义、物美价廉，不能送过于贵重的礼品，这样会有行贿的嫌疑，会使对方内心不安。

4. 为宾客送行。根据车次、航班时间，及时与负责行李的部门、人员确定提取行李的时间，并通报客人递交行李的时间，到达车站、机场后要安排好客人等候休息，办理好有关手续后将有关票证、证件等交还给客人。

Section 2　Interpreting Practice（口译实训）

Dialogue 1【参考译文】

机场接机

A: Excuse me, are you Mr. Brown from New Zealand?

B: 是的，我是夏天进出口公司的托尼·布朗。如果我没猜错的话，您就是李先生吧。

A: Yes, I am Li Ming, the Marketing Manager of Guangzhou Natural Beauty Cosmetics Co., Ltd. It's a pleasure to meet you. Welcome to Guangzhou, Mr. Brown!

B: 很高兴认识您，谢谢您来机场接我。

A: My pleasure. How is your flight?

B: 一路都很好。顺便问一下，我们在哪取行李？

A: This way, please.

B: 非常感谢。

A: You must be tired after such a long journey.

B: 的确有点累。我没法快速倒时差，但明早就好了。

A: OK, we've got all the luggage. I'll drive you to the hotel. It is situated next to the lake, offering a picturesque view. It's only 30 minutes' drive from the airport. I'm sure you'll like it.

B: 太好了，我喜欢景色优美的酒店。

A: We've prepared some snacks for you in your room, hoping they'll give you an energy boost.

B: 你们考虑得真周到！谢谢！

A: My pleasure. We will host a reception dinner in your honor at 7:00 tomorrow evening. By the way, are there any tourist attractions you'd like to visit? I'll be glad to show you around.

B: 看情况吧。如果一切顺利的话,我想留出一天时间来观光。我对粤菜和广东文化非常感兴趣,很想去一些必去景点,希望能更深入地了解广州。

A: No problem. I'll make some arrangements for this tour. Guangzhou is indeed rich in cultural heritage and many scenic spots worth exploring.

B: 非常感谢,我很期待。

A: You're welcome. I hope you'll enjoy your stay here. See you tomorrow.

B: 明天见。

Dialogue 2【参考译文】

酒店办理入住

A: Good afternoon! Welcome to New Century Hotel. What can I do for you?

B: 您好!我想办理入住。

A: Yes, sir. May I have your name, please? Did you make a reservation?

B: 我叫托尼·布朗。我想应该有人为我订了房间。

A: Just a moment, please. I'll check it out for you right away. Sorry to keep you waiting, sir. But we don't have your reservation record here. Excuse me, what is the date of your reservation?

B: 我预订了今天到周五的房间,总共4晚。

A: I see. Let me take a closer look... It turns out that our reservation system has recently been upgraded, and there may be some minor problems. We are really sorry for the inconvenience.

B: 没关系,这种事时有发生。

A: Please rest assured that we still have vacancies. I'll take a look, um, there's still a double room and a deluxe suite not checked in. Which one do you want?

B: 非常感谢。我更喜欢双人间。我可以住多久?除了常规房费外还有额外费用吗?

A: You can stay till Friday, the room rate will remain at the original price, and we will provide free breakfast as an apology.

B: 您真是太好了!我之前还有点担心会没有房间呢。

A: You're welcome. This is what we should do. I hope you will enjoy your stay in New Century Hotel. Please contact me directly if you need anything.

B: 好的,非常感谢您的帮助!

Dialogue 3【参考译文】

讨论行程

A: Mr. Brown, have you been to Guangzhou before?

B: 没有。这是我第一次来广州,但是我听过很多有关广州的故事。广州是一个有着丰富历史和文化的大都市,也是中国最重要的经济和交通运输中心之一。我非常期待探索这座城市。

A: That's great. Mr. Brown, I've arranged a trip for you in Guangzhou for these days. Please let me know if there are any changes.

B: 好的。你能先简单介绍一下日程安排吗?

A: My pleasure. Nothing is arranged for this afternoon, so you can have a good rest to overcome the jet-lag. At 5:30 p.m., you'll be having dinner with our general manager at Guangzhou Restaurant.

B: 太好了,这样我就有时间休息了,可以缓解一下旅途的劳累。明天有什么安排?

A: From 9:00 to 11:00 tomorrow morning, we have arranged a tour of our production plant and laboratory. This will give you a more comprehensive understanding of our product quality and production process. Luncheon will be served at the Hilton Hotel at 12 o'clock. In the afternoon, we will hold a business meeting to discuss the details of cooperation and marketing strategies. In the evening, we will taste local delicacy together.

B: 太棒了。我衷心期待能够有机会参观贵公司的生产设施，并安排一场商务会谈。这样的实地考察与深入交流将有助于我全面而深入地了解贵公司的运营实力和产品特性。

A: I'm glad you are interested in our factory. The day after tomorrow morning, we will have breakfast in Tao Tao Ju, a historic Chinese time-honored brand in Guangdong. After that, we will visit some retailers and beauty salons in Guangzhou to feel the marketing and popularity of our products. In the afternoon, we will meet with the marketing team to discuss the marketing strategies. In the evening, we will take you to enjoy a Cantonese opera show to appreciate the charm of Guangzhou culture.

B: 听起来很不错。很期待看到你们的营销活动，听听你们营销团队的意见。这次文化体验之旅无疑将为我提供一个深度接触与沉浸于广州丰富文化遗产的独特良机。

A: On the last day, we will hold a wrap-up meeting to determine the details of cooperation. After that, a farewell luncheon will be held to celebrate our cooperation. Your flight is at 10 a.m. the day after the meeting. I will pick you up from the hotel at 8 a.m. and take you to Guangzhou Baiyun International Airport. Do you think these arrangements are OK?

B: 看来这几天将会非常高效和充实。李先生，谢谢你为我安排如此周到且详尽的行程规划。对于未来合作的可能性，我感到无比振奋。

A: You're welcome, Mr. Brown. This is what I should do. I'm looking forward to working with you!

Dialogue 4【参考译文】

机场送机

A: Mr. Brown, our visit is coming to an end. Thank you for coming. This collaboration has been tremendously beneficial. We're very pleased to establish a strategic partnership with your company.

B: 李先生，衷心感谢贵公司的盛情接待，此次商务访问可谓收获颇丰。贵公司的产品质量与服务水平给我留下了深刻的印象。

A: I hope that through this visit to our factory and laboratories, you now have a more intuitive understanding of our product quality and R&D (research and development) capabilities. In the future, we can pursue cooperation across multiple regions.

B: 是的，贵公司的先进生产设备和强大的研发能力让我印象深刻。我相信我们可以在多个领域建立强有力的合作伙伴关系。这次的商务会谈富有成果，意义重大。

A: Guangzhou is a city with a long history. You are very welcome to visit again in the future, to continue exploring the cultural charms of this city.

B: 广州是一座历史悠久、文化底蕴深厚、充满活力的城市。不论是游览名胜古迹还是品味地道美食，都令我难以忘怀。随着对广州了解的深入，愈发激起我对这座城市探索的热情。还有很多地方我都想去走走。

A: Yes, I sincerely wish our cooperative journey smooth sailing. You are welcome back to Guangzhou any time.

B: 谢谢。希望我们的合作关系能持续蓬勃发展。我期待再次参观广州和贵公司！

A: We've arrived at the airport terminal. Which airline are you flying with?

B: 南方航空。

A: China Southern flights depart from Terminal 1. Please go straight ahead, through the doors in front, then turn right. You'll see the check-in counters there.

B: 感谢您陪我度过这个充实而美好的下午。虽然这是一次短途旅行,但非常富有成果。再次感谢您的帮助。我会将这次经历珍藏在心中。保持联系。

A: Sure! I'll look forward to your next visit to Guangzhou.

B: 我一定会来的。

A: Goodbye and have a nice fight!

Section 3 Interpreting Assessment（口译测评）

Passage 1 【原文】

A Speech by Her Majesty the Queen Delivered via Video Message to the COP26 Evening Reception（Excerpt）

I am delighted to welcome you all to the 26th United Nations Climate Change Conference. And it is perhaps fitting that you have come together in Glasgow, once a heartland of the industrial revolution, but now a place to address climate change.

This is a duty I am especially happy to discharge, as the impact of the environment on human progress was a subject close to the heart of my dear late husband, Prince Philip, the Duke of Edinburgh.

Indeed, I have drawn great comfort and inspiration from the relentless enthusiasm of people of all ages—especially the young—in calling for everyone to play their part.

In the coming days, the world has the chance to join in the shared objective of creating a safer, stabler future for our people and for the planet on which we depend.

None of us underestimates the challenges ahead, but history has shown that when nations come together in common cause, there is always room for hope. Working side by side, we have the ability to solve the most insurmountable problems and to triumph over the greatest of adversities.

For more than seventy years, I have been lucky to meet and to know many of the world's great leaders. And I have perhaps come to understand a little about what made them special.

It has sometimes been observed that what leaders do for their people today is government and politics. But what they do for the people of tomorrow—that is statesmanship.

I, for one, hope that this conference will be one of those rare occasions where everyone will have the chance to rise above the politics of the moment, and achieve true statesmanship.

It is the hope of many that the legacy of this summit—written in history books yet to be printed—will describe you as the leaders who did not pass up the opportunity; and that you answered the call of those future generations.

That you left this conference as a community of nations with a determination, a desire, and a plan, to address the impact of climate change; and to recognize that the time for words has now moved to the time for action.

Of course, the benefits of such actions will not be there to enjoy for all of us here today—we none of us will live forever. But we are doing this not for ourselves but for our children and our children's children, and those who will follow in their footsteps.

And so, I wish you every good fortune in this significant endeavor.

（https://www.royal.uk/queen%E2%80%99s-speech-cop26-evening-reception）

Passage 1 【参考译文】

英国女王在第 26 届联合国气候变化大会欢迎晚宴上的致辞（节选）

非常荣幸在此欢迎大家参加第 26 届联合国气候变化大会。大家相聚于格拉斯哥是再合适不过了，因为这里曾是工业革命的中心，现在又成为解决气候变化问题的地方。

我非常乐意履行这一职责，因为环境对人类进步的影响也曾是我亲爱的亡夫、爱丁堡公爵菲利普王子最关心的话题。

事实上，各个年龄段的人，尤其是年轻人，不断呼吁每个人发挥自己的作用，我从中得到了极大的慰藉和启发。

在接下来的日子里，世界还有机会加入这个共同的目标，这个目标将为人类和我们赖以生存的地球创造一个更安全、更稳定的未来。

我们没有低估未来的挑战，但历史表明，当各国为了共同的事业团结在一起时，希望总是存在的。通过携手努力，我们能够解决无法克服的问题，战胜巨大的困境。

七十多年来，我有幸认识了世界上许多伟大的领导人，我或许已经了解了一些使他们与众不同的原因。

有时人们会觉得，领导人为其今天的人民所做之事体现在政府工作和政治活动，但他们为未来的人民所做之事才体现了真正的政治家精神。

此次会议是个难得的机会，我希望每个人都有机会超越当前政治，实现真正的政治家精神。

许多人希望此次峰会的遗产能载入史册，把各位书写成没有错过机会，并响应了后人的号召的领导人。

带着你们在这次会议留下的决心、愿望和计划，以一个国际共同体去应对气候变化的影响，并认识到，已经到了从言语转变至行动的时候了。

当然，并非在座的所有人都能享受到这些行动的回报，我们无法永生。但我们这样做不是为了自己，而是为了我们的子孙后代，以及那些将效仿他们的人。

祝各位在这项伟大的事业中一切顺利。

Passage 2 【原文】

驻欧盟使团团长傅聪大使在庆祝中华人民共和国
成立七十四周年国庆招待会上的致辞（节选）

尊敬的各位使节，

女士们、先生们、朋友们，

大家晚上好！

很高兴与各位新老朋友齐聚一堂，共同庆祝中华人民共和国 74 周年华诞。我谨代表中国驻欧盟使团向大家表示热烈欢迎，向长期致力于中欧友好合作的各界人士表示衷心感谢！

74 年来，在中国共产党领导下，中国发生了历史性变化，解决了绝对贫困问题，建成世界上最大规模的教育、社会保障以及医疗卫生体系，创造了经济快速发展和社会长期稳定的两大奇迹。今年是中国改革开放 45 周年。改革开放不仅深刻影响了中国，也给世界各国带来巨大机遇。今天中国人民正满怀信心，迈上以中国式现代化全面推进中华民族伟大复兴的新征程！

今年是全面贯彻落实中共二十大精神的开局之年，也是疫后复苏的关键之年。这一年，中国高质量发展迈出更加坚实步伐，绿色发展成为中国经济的新亮点。上半年中国国内生产总值同比增长 5.5%，处在世界主要经济体前列，展现出巨大韧性和发展潜力。中国经济韧性强、潜力大、活力足，长期向好的基本面不会改变。展望未来，中国发展前景光明，必将为全球经济复苏和可持续发展注入更多新动能、带来更多新机遇。

当今世界变乱交织，人类社会面临诸多挑战，在此形势下，习近平主席提出全球发展倡

167

议、全球安全倡议、全球文明倡议，为解决发展赤字、破解安全困境、加强文明互鉴给出了中国答案。

今年是中国欧盟建交48周年，也是中欧建立全面战略伙伴关系20周年。自去年12月到任以来，我有幸结识各届欧方朋友，见证了疫情后中欧关系向前向上发展的积极势头。一年来，习近平主席、李强总理多次同米歇尔主席、冯德莱恩主席举行会晤，为中欧关系提供战略引领。中欧环境与气候、经贸、数字领域高层对话顺利重启。

同时，我也感受到中欧关系面临的阻力和困难。我想强调，防风险和合作不是对立的，相互依存和不安全也不是简单画等号的。不合作才是最大的风险，不发展才是最大的不安全。作为世界两大力量、两大市场、两大文明，中欧关系关乎全球稳定和亚欧大陆繁荣。我们应求同存异，聚同化异，坚持开放合作，丰富人文交流，始终以中欧关系的稳定性应对国际形势的不确定性，共促人类发展繁荣。

在座各位为推进中欧友好、增进双方人民相近相知作出了积极贡献。希望大家继续做中欧友好合作的建设者和维护者，共同推动中欧关系稳步向前。

值此中华人民共和国成立七十四周年之际，祝愿祖国繁荣昌盛、中欧友谊行稳致远、各位朋友幸福安康！

谢谢大家！

（https://www.fmprc.gov.cn/web/wjdt_674879/zwbd_674895/202309/t20230926_11150287.shtml）

Passage 2【参考译文】

Speech by Ambassador Fu Cong at the Reception Celebrating the 74th Anniversary of the Founding of the People's Republic of China（Excerpt）

Your Excellencies,

Ladies and Gentlemen,

Dear Friends,

Good evening!

It is my great pleasure to get together with all of you tonight to celebrate the 74th anniversary of the founding of the People's Republic of China. On behalf of the Chinese Mission to the European Union, I would like to express my warm welcome to all of you and extend my sincere thanks to people from various sectors who have long been committed to China-EU friendship and cooperation.

In the past 74 years, China has witnessed historic changes under the leadership of the Communist Party of China (CPC). We have eliminated absolute poverty, built the world's largest education, social security and healthcare systems, and achieved rapid economic growth and long-term social stability. 45 years ago, China launched reform and opening-up, a policy that has not only changed China profoundly, but also created huge opportunities to the rest of the world. Today, we are confidently embarking on a new journey to promote the great rejuvenation of the country through a Chinese path to modernization.

The year 2023, which marks the beginning of full implementation of the guiding principles adopted at the 20th CPC National Congress, is also a crucial year as we emerge from the COVID-19 pandemic. We have made solid progress in high-quality development with green development as its key and distinctive feature. In the first half of this year, China's gross domestic product (GDP) grew by 5.5 percent year on year, one of the highest among major economies. This demonstrates the strong resilience, tremendous potential and great vitality of the Chinese economy. The fundamentals sustaining China's long-term growth remain unchanged. Looking ahead, China's development enjoys bright prospects, and will inject more and fresh impetus to the global recovery and sustainable development, and bring more new opportunities.

Today, in a world of turmoil and transformation, humanity is faced with unprecedented challenges. In this context, President Xi Jinping put forward the Global Development Initiative, the Global Security Initiative and the Global Civilization Initiative, providing Chinese perspectives for addressing the global development deficit, meeting global security challenges, and strengthening exchanges among civilizations.

This year marks the 48th anniversary of the establishment of diplomatic relations between China and the EU, as well as the 20th anniversary of the comprehensive strategic partnership. Since I arrived here last December, I've had the opportunity to meet many European friends and witnessed the positive momentum of China-EU relations. President Xi Jinping and Premier Li Qiang met with President Michel and President von der Leyen on several occasions, providing strategic leadership for this important relationship. High-level dialogues on environment and climate, economy and trade, and digital cooperation have been resumed.

I am also aware of the difficulties facing China-EU relations. I would like to emphasize that risk prevention and cooperation are not mutually exclusive, and interdependence should not be simply equated with insecurity. As a matter of fact, it is the lack of cooperation that brings the biggest risk, and it is the lack of development that constitutes the biggest insecurity. As two major forces, markets and civilizations, China and the EU have a big role to play in preserving global stability and prosperity of the Eurasian continent, and the world at large. To promote development and prosperity in this uncertain world, it's important that we seek common ground while reserving differences, integrate commonalities and resolve differences, adhere to openness and cooperation, and increase people-to-people exchanges to ensure a stable and robust China-EU relationship.

Many of you have contributed to China-EU friendship and mutual understanding between the two peoples. I want to thank you for your contribution, and hope you could continue to do so in the future. Let us work together to promote the steady development of China-EU relations.

On the occasion of the 74th anniversary of the founding of the People's Republic of China, I would like to propose a toast to the prosperity of the motherland, to the strength of the China-EU friendship, and to the happiness and good health of all of you!

Thank you!

(http://eu.china-mission.gov.cn/eng/mh/202309/t20230926_11150390.htm)

Unit 3　Ceremonial Address（礼仪致辞）

Section 1　Interpreting Preparation（口译准备）

Sight Interpreting（视译）

Passage 1【参考译文】

查尔斯三世在欢迎南非共和国总统国宴上的致辞（节选）

拉马福萨总统先生：

　　我和妻子倍感荣幸，在白金汉宫欢迎您的莅临。

　　南非和英联邦一样，一直是我生活中的一部分。我母亲经常回忆她在1947年访问南非的经历，那是我出生的前一年，在她21岁生日那天，她在开普敦庄严宣誓，将毕生致力于服务英联邦的人民。

这是我和妻子第一次主持国事访问，您的光临使我们深感荣耀。

南非人民坚定地传承那些为建立民主作出卓越贡献的先辈们的遗志，这种精神令人深受鼓舞。作为领导人，作为联合国、二十国集团以及英联邦的合作伙伴，我们肩负着创造机遇、推动繁荣与保障安全的重任，以支持贵国实现这些目标。总统先生，我了解到您正通过"领养学校基金会"积极践行这一理念，而英国也愿通过我们的志奋领奖学金项目，助力南非学子在全英各地大学深造学习。

只有通过我们两国几代人的共同努力，才能应对当前时代最为严峻的挑战。例如，在科学和创新方面的合作对于保护人民的健康、应对未来流行病的准备至关重要。尤为紧要的是，我们必须探寻并落实切实有效的解决方案，直面气候变化及生物多样性丧失这两大现实威胁。为此，我感到自豪的是，英、法、德、美和欧盟与南非建立了持久的合作关系，共同支持贵国实现公正能源转型，实现可持续、绿色和经济活力的未来。各方携手努力，确保今年12月在加拿大蒙特利尔达成全球生物多样性框架这一雄心勃勃的目标，这便是我们现代合作关系典范的具体体现。

总统先生，您的来访为我们提供了一个宝贵的契机，让我们共同擘画前进的道路，投资彼此的潜力，并肩作战，携手面对世界难题，共同追求平等、正义与公平的美好未来。

值此辞旧迎新之际，全世界都在向伟大的南非前大主教德斯蒙德·图图致敬，他的一生和精神遗产令人敬佩。他曾经的至理名言"我的人性与你的人性紧密相连，唯有并肩，方能成为完整的人类"时常回响在我的心头。我相信这句话对我们所有人都是一堂重要的人生课，也是指引英南两国合作关系的一条重要纽带。

女士们，先生们，在我们矢志继续这一伟大征程之际，请诸位起身，共同举杯，为拉马福萨总统阁下，为南非人民，献上最诚挚的敬意！

Passage 2【参考译文】

Address by H. E. Li Qiang, Premier of the State Council of the People's Republic of China, at the Opening Plenary of the Annual Meeting of the New Champions 2023 (Excerpt)

Ladies and Gentlemen,

Friends,

As a responsible major country, China has all along stood firmly on the right side of history and on the side of human progress. Holding high the banner of peace, development and win-win cooperation, China is committed to building world peace, promoting global development and upholding the international order. Most notably, since the 18th National Congress of the Communist Party of China, we have focused on promoting high-quality development, realized the goal of building a moderately prosperous society in all respects as planned, ended absolute poverty in China once and for all, and embarked on a new journey toward building a modern socialist country in all respects. Today, the Chinese economy is deeply integrated into the world economy. China has developed itself by embracing globalization, and grown into a most staunch force for globalization.

Over the past decade, China has been an important source of impetus for the steady growth of the world economy. In the past ten years, the Chinese economy grew at 6.2 percent on average annually. Its share in global economic output increased from 11.3 percent in 2012 to about 18 percent. China's trade in goods ranked the top in the world for six years in a row. On average, China's contribution to global growth was over 30 percent, making the country the biggest engine driving this growth. In the first year of the COVID-19 pandemic, China was the only major economy that registered a positive growth. In the past three years, China achieved an average annual growth of 4.5 percent, about 2.5 percentage points higher than the world average, and was among the best performers of the world's major economies. As it pursues interconnected development with other countries, China has honored its WTO accession commitments by opening up its market to the rest of the world and sharing its development opportunities with all, making itself a major trading partner of over 140 countries and regions. China's development has improved the lives of the Chinese people, and provided people in other countries with a large amount of quality yet inexpensive products. China has served as an important anchor and source of impetus for free trade and stable growth in the world.

(https://www.chinadaily.com.cn/a/202306/29/WS649cbfc9a310bf8a75d6c2e3.html)

Memory Practice（记忆训练）

Paragraph 1

This World Environment Day is a call to beat plastic pollution.

Every year, over 400 million tons of plastic is produced worldwide—one third of which is used just once.

Every day, the equivalent of over 2,000 garbage trucks full of plastic is dumped into our oceans, rivers, and lakes.

The consequences are catastrophic.

Microplastics find their way into the food we eat, the water we drink, and the air we breathe.

Plastic is made from fossil fuels—the more plastic we produce, the more fossil fuel we burn, and the worse we make the climate crisis.

But we have solutions.

Last year, the global community began negotiating a legally binding agreement to end plastic pollution.

This is a promising first step, but we need all hands-on deck.

A new report by the UN Environment Programme shows that we can reduce plastic pollution by 80 percent by 2040—if we act now to reuse, recycle, reorient, and diversify away from plastics.

We must work as one—governments, companies, and consumers alike—to break our addiction to plastics, champion zero waste, and build a truly circular economy.

Together, let us shape a cleaner, healthier, and more sustainable future for all.

(https://minusma.unmissions.org/en/message-world-environment-day-5-june-2023)

Paragraph 2

习近平主席强调，中国的发展将为各国带来更多新的机遇。中国将始终高举和平、发展、合作、共赢旗帜，坚定不移推进高水平对外开放，以高质量发展实现中国式现代化，进而惠及世界各国人民。南亚是中国近邻，我们欢迎南亚国家继续搭乘中国发展的快车，分享中国发展的红利。中国和南亚是拥有超过30亿人口的庞大市场，经济总量约占全球五分之一，蕴含着巨大合作潜力和广阔发展空间。我们愿同南亚各国一道，把握历史机遇，加强团结协作，培育发展新动能，构建发展共同体，为地区的长治久安、稳定繁荣不断作出新的贡献。

(https://www.mfa.gov.cn/web/ziliao_674904/zyjh_674906/202308/t20230817_11127940.shtml)

Section 2　Interpreting Practice（口译实训）

Passage 1【参考译文】

一次技术会议的主题演讲

大家早上好。很荣幸出席此次世界科技大会，与诸位共同探讨人工智能的最新发展趋势和创新实践。

我们正处在一个人工智能蓬勃发展的时代。很难相信人工智能在过去几年里发展得有多快。人工智能从主要局限于学术研究迅速转变为日常生活中无所不在的应用。人工智能内嵌在我们的智能手机中，为我们的社交媒体提供动力，帮助我们进行网购等。

近期最为引人注目的进展当属自然语言处理与计算机视觉技术的突破。像Siri和Alexa这样的人工智能助手已经能够理解并响应用户的语音指令。聊天机器人也能与人类进行越来越自然的文字对话。人工智能算法也能够详细描述照片和视频中的内容。

在计算机视觉方面，人工智能支持面部识别等新功能，在安防和照片分类方面有许多应用。自动驾驶汽车公司使用人工智能来解析复杂的环境信息。尽管这一技术尚处于初级阶段，但无疑将深刻改变未来的交通格局。

人工智能在医疗保健和金融服务等特定行业也取得了长足进步。在医疗保健领域，人工智能用于分析医学图像以支持诊断，甚至还能提出治疗方案。人工智能聊天机器人正在成为虚拟医疗助手。在金融领域，人工智能算法用于管理投资、检测欺诈、实现个性化银行业务。

当然，面对新技术的应用，我们必须确保对人工智能的运用遵循道德原则且负责任。人工智能存在潜在的风险和偏差，必须防患于未然。但如果利用得当，人工智能将极大地造福人类。

展望未来，一些极具吸引力的人工智能功能已在孕育之中。例如，深度学习算法将在自然语言理解和生成领域实现更深的突破。我们可能很快就会有能真正像人类一样交谈并成为得力助手的人工智能。在计算机视觉方面，算法正朝着对图像和视频进行常识推理的方向发展。迁移学习技术将使人工智能系统能够快速适应新任务和新环境。

今天与会的公司及研究人员正处于这些令人激动人心的创新的前沿。我热切期待大会后续的日程安排，渴望了解各位正在推动的卓越工作。人工智能的未来一片光明，通过负责任的合作，我们完全有能力构建一个人工智能赋能的世界，让其更好地服务于人类生活。谢谢大家！

Passage 2【参考译文】

A Message from the Principal Wang Shuguo of Xi'an Jiaotong University to Graduates of the Class of 2023 (Excerpt)

Today, I want to touch on three key points.

First, the sense of duty. People cannot live fully without a deep sense of duty. What is our deepest duty? It is the duty to our country. I have discussed this before, but why do I bring it up again now? Because the duty to our country is the foundation that supports a fulfilling life. Without this sense of duty, it is hard for any individual to achieve great things, to smoothly navigate life's journey, or to find direction and purpose. Without this duty, you will lose souls and feel lost.

Second, perseverance. In the speeches by graduates, they shared the difficulties that they faced in their studies. The one who left civilian life for the military has been deeply tempered. All of them endured profound training beyond normal limits, but they persisted. What empowered them? Perseverance. Without perseverance, one cannot endure for the long haul or accomplish great things. Perseverance is essential to living life without regrets.

Progress requires perseverance through difficulties and challenges. Life inevitably involves struggles, and perhaps the value of life lies in constantly facing new problems and creating new solutions. As you enter society, you will likely encounter unforeseen obstacles. You should face them bravely, tackle them head-on, and solve them sincerely.

Third, reform and innovation. The world is changing rapidly, with new technologies beyond imagination. The society, knowledge, and systems are reconstructing in ways we could not foresee. This era embraces possibility and provides unlimited opportunity to display your talents. You come of age at an exciting time of infinite potential. But you must seize the opportunity on the new track and boldly step into the future.

Our school anthem speaks of "the light of the world". This inspires me deeply. I hope you always keep our country in mind, carry your perseverance and your spirit of reform and innovation through life. They are your spiritual wealth, a light buried in your heart, illuminating your path. With them, you can become pillars of our nation, stand tall in the world, and truly be the light of the world.

I sincerely wish the best for you, my students!

Passage 3【参考译文】

老员工退休告别致辞

大家晚上好，今天我们齐聚一堂，怀着既感慨又喜悦的心情，共同庆祝我们挚爱的朋友和同事玛丽的荣休时刻。

玛丽，在过去的30载光阴里，你无疑是我们公司取得辉煌成就不可或缺的核心力量。你的满腔热情、无私奉献与深厚的专业素养，对每一位团队成员都产生了无法估量的影响。

我还记得你在1992年加入公司的那一刻。即使是一名青涩的毕业生，你也展现出了超群的才能和沉稳干练的气质。随着岁月的沉淀，凭借卓越的职业操守和领导风范，你迅速脱颖而出，晋升至公司的高层位置。

玛丽，在你的引领下，我们成功攻克了一系列最具挑战性且至关重要的项目。你不仅带领我们开辟了新的市场疆域，还帮助公司在瞬息万变的行业中保持与时俱进。一次又一次，你激励着团队不断超越自我，创造出超出预期的成绩。你的专业技术底蕴和高瞻远瞩的战略思维，无疑是我们公司一笔无比宝贵的财富。

除了对公司业务的贡献之外，你的善良和热情也深深打动了我们。作为新员工的导师，你悉心指导，耐心培养；作为朋友，你始终关心他人，乐于倾听并鼓舞着每一位同事。在此，我想代表所有人说：能与你共事，实为一件幸事。

虽然在你退休后，我们将无比怀念你在办公室的日子，但我们更由衷地为你即将拥有更多时间陪伴家人，踏上旅行的新征程，追寻新冒险而感到欣喜。你为公司付出的心血已足够多，现在该好好享受属于你自己的美好时光了。

衷心祝愿你在人生的新篇章中万事顺遂。感谢你为我们团队所做的一切。你永远是我们团队的一分子。我们爱你！

恭喜你，退休快乐！

Passage 4【参考译文】

A Speech at a Dinner Party

Distinguished guests, ladies and gentlemen,

It is a tremendous honor to join you tonight in welcoming the delegation from our esteemed partners, the Facial Cosmetics Sales Company of Australia. On behalf of Guangzhou Natural Beauty Cosmetics Co., Ltd., I extend our warmest welcome to our friends from Australia. What a joy it is to unite with companions from afar!

Over the years, the Facial Cosmetics Sales Company has made invaluable contributions promoting our products in the Australian market. I speak for all employees in expressing heartfelt gratitude for your long-term support and partnership. Your recognition and advocacy of our brand empowered us to gain a foothold in Australia and earn the favor of Australian consumers.

I recall five years ago when you first decided to introduce our skincare products. To ensure a smooth launch, our teams engaged in thoughtful discussions and meticulous preparation, jointly formulating localization strategies. The end result was universal acclaim from Australian consumers, with sales volumes continuing to rise. This affirms the tremendous fruits of pragmatic cooperation between Chinese and Australian enterprises.

Looking ahead, I am confident that we will continue collaborating to deliver more quality products that aid the economic and social development of both countries. On behalf of Guangzhou Natural Beauty Cosmetics Co., Ltd. leadership, I offer warm wishes to our Australian friends for a happy new year and prosperity.

Finally, I invite everyone to raise a glass in tribute to the cherished friendship and cooperation between China and Australia!

Section 3　Interpreting Assessment（口译测评）

Passage 1　【原文】

UN Secretary-General's Message to the Opening of the United Nations World Data Forum

Excellencies, distinguished guests, ladies and gentlemen,

Welcome to the fourth United Nations World Data Forum.

My thanks to the Government of the People's Republic of China for hosting this important event.

My friends,

Today in the 21st century, data represents what oil represented in the 20th century—a driver of development and progress.

This forum highlights the great value of timely, open and high-quality data.

From the daily decisions that governments make. To the investments that support economies, jobs and health and education systems. To our ability to make progress towards the Sustainable Development Goals, and build the peaceful and prosperous future that every person deserves. Data and statistics make all this easier.

Three years ago, we launched the United Nations Data Strategy to build more data expertise across the UN System, and create more innovative ecosystems that unlock the full potential of data for the betterment of people and planet alike.

The strategy also sparked inspiring initiatives like Data4Now and Citizen Generated Data to allow people and communities to gather and take control of the data affecting their daily lives.

But we must continue pressing forward.

Progress on the Sustainable Development Goals has stalled—even reversed—as we reach the halfway point of the 2030 Agenda.

This forum is a key opportunity to turbocharge the transformative power of data and accelerate progress at this critical moment.

Throughout, we need to continue working to ensure that companies and states alike respect our right to privacy and to own the personal data that we generate.

Data—when used responsibly—is the bedrock of a sustainable future.

Let's find new ways to harness and apply this vital resource and shape a better tomorrow for all people.

（https://www.un.org/sg/en/content/sg/statement/2023-04-24/secretary-generals-video-message-the-opening-of-the-united-nations-world-data-forum）

Passage 1【参考译文】

联合国秘书长在联合国世界数据论坛开幕式上的致辞

尊敬的各国使节、尊敬的来宾、女士们、先生们：

欢迎参加第四届联合国世界数据论坛。

感谢中华人民共和国政府主办这次重要活动。

朋友们，

在21世纪的今天，数据代表着石油在20世纪所代表的东西——发展和进步的驱动力。

本次论坛凸显及时、开放和优质数据的巨大价值。

从政府的日常决策到对支持经济、就业、卫生和教育系统的投资，再到我们有能力在实现可持续发展目标方面取得进展和建设每个人都应得到的和平与繁荣的未来，数据和统计使这一切变得更加容易。

三年前，我们启动了联合国数据战略，以便在整个联合国系统建立更多的数据专业知识，并创建更多创新性的生态系统，以释放数据的全部潜力，造福于人类和地球。

数据战略还引发了"为现在服务的数据"和"公民产生的数据"等鼓舞人心的倡议，使人们和社区能够收集和控制影响其日常生活的数据。

但我们必须继续努力向前。

当我们进展到《2030年可持续发展议程》的一半时，可持续发展目标的进展已经停滞，甚至逆转。

本次论坛是一个重要机遇，可在这一关键时刻推动数据变革并加速进展。

在整个过程中，我们需要继续努力，确保公司和国家都尊重我们的隐私权及我们有权拥有自己生成的个人数据。

负责任地使用数据是可持续未来的基石。

让我们找到新的方法来控制和应用这一重要资源，为所有人创造更加美好的明天。

（https://www.unwdf2023.org.cn/content/content_8520491.html）

Passage 2【原文】

李强在二十国集团领导人第十八次峰会第一阶段会议上的讲话（节选）

尊敬的莫迪总理，

各位同事：

很高兴出席二十国集团新德里峰会。感谢莫迪总理和印度政府为峰会召开作出的周到安排，热烈欢迎非洲联盟加入二十国集团。

本次峰会的主题是"一个地球、一个家园、一个未来"，这个主题意义重大，与习近平主席提出的构建人类命运共同体理念高度契合。大家应该都有这样的同感，就是当"地球村"这个概念在世界各地被普遍使用时，不仅意味着经济科技的发展压缩了时空距离，更意味着地球上国与国之间、人与人之间的关系变得更为紧密，就像同一个村庄里的村民，人类越来越成为一个命运共同体。特别是最近几年，在百年变局和世纪疫情交织叠加的影响下，我们身处的世界发生了很大变化。这些变化带给我们最重要的启示，就是人类命运休戚与共，在重大危机和共同挑战面前，谁都不能独善其身，唯有团结合作才是人间正道。

在人类共同生活的"地球村"里，不论是大国小国，不论身处何方，我们在谋求自身利益的同时，都应当以全局的视野，多作一些对人类前途命运的思考。也正是基于这样的考量，习近平主席提出了全球发展倡议、全球安全倡议、全球文明倡议。我们呼吁，各国应当相互尊重、求同存异、和平共处，携手应对全球挑战，共同创造美好未来。特别是在世界经济复苏和可持续发展面临巨大挑战的当下，二十国集团成员更应当坚守团结合作的初心，为了人类的共同未来和福祉，扛起和平与发展的时代责任。

（https://www.fmprc.gov.cn/zyxw/202309/t20230910_11140648.shtml）

Passage 2【参考译文】

Remarks by Chinese Premier Li Qiang at Session Ⅰ of the 18th G20 Summit (Excerpt)

Your Excellency Prime Minister Narendra Modi,

Colleagues,

It is my great pleasure to attend the G20 New Delhi Summit. I wish to thank Prime Minister Modi and the Indian government for the thoughtful arrangements made for the summit, and warmly welcome the African Union into the G20!

The theme of this summit "One Earth, One Family, One Future" is of high significance, and encapsulates a similar vision with President Xi Jinping's proposal of building a community with a shared future for mankind. We may all have this feeling: when "global village" becomes a commonplace notion worldwide, it is not just about reduced time and space brought by economic growth and technological advances, but more importantly the ever-closer ties between countries and individuals on this planet. It is like we are villagers living in the same village, and humanity is in a community with a shared future. In particular, under the compounded impacts of unprecedented global transformation and a once-in-a-century pandemic, much has changed in our world in recent years. The most important thing these changes tell us is that humanity is bound by a common stake. No one can stay unaffected in the event of major crises and common challenges, and solidarity and cooperation is the only right way forward.

In this "global village" where we all live, all countries, regardless of size or location, should take a broader view and do more thinking about the future of humanity while pursuing one's own interests. It is with such consideration in mind that President Xi Jinping put forward the Global Development Initiative, the Global Security Initiative and the Global Civilization Initiative. We call on all countries to respect each other, seek common ground while reserving differences, live together in peace, and work jointly to meet global challenges and create a better future. In particular, given the huge challenges confronting the global recovery and sustainable development, it is all the more important for G20 members to stick to solidarity and cooperation, and live up to our responsibility for peace and development, in the interest of humanity's shared future and well-being.

(http://en.people.cn/n3/2023/0910/c90000-20069916.html)

Unit 4　Business Travel（商务旅游）

Section 1　Interpreting Preparation（口译准备）

Sight Interpreting（视译）

Passage 1【参考译文】

"红色旅游"在 Z 世代中越来越受欢迎（节选）

橘子洲位于湖南长沙市中心，也是青年时期的毛泽东广泛开展革命活动的地方。位于洲头的毛泽东青年艺术雕塑，是全国最具吸引力和影响力的红色景点之一。如今，橘子洲已经成为展示长沙形象的重要窗口，也是热门的旅游打卡地。

由于独特的地理位置和丰富的历史背景，长沙成为许多年轻人首选的"红色旅游"目的地和打卡地。顾名思义，红色旅游不仅涵盖了对历史的回顾以进行爱国主义教育，还融入了休闲游览元素。这两者的结合赋予了红色旅游独特的魅力。

无论是拥有千年学术历史的岳麓山，还是毛泽东青年时代吟诗作赋的橘子洲，抑或是见证海上丝绸之路传奇的铜官窑遗址，独特的湖湘文化为这些景点提供了坚实的基础，使文化与旅游在这里得以深度融合，为长沙构建出丰富多元的旅游资源，显著提升了城市知名度。

红色旅游正在逐步成为一种常态化的旅游体验。携程网数据显示，2022 年上半年，88% 的游客预订了当地或附近红色景点的门票。年轻人喜欢那些将红色旅游与当代流行文化和创意产品结合的景区，以更时尚的方式铭记历史、抒发爱国情怀。

对于出生于 20 世纪 60 年代和 70 年代的人来说，探访红色景点是一种荣誉的象征，能唤醒他们对青春岁月的记忆。但对更多年轻人而言，"红色旅游"是他们学习历史、开阔视野、塑造生活方式的一种方式。最新发布的《2021 年 Z 世代红色旅游消费偏好调查报告》显示，13～27 岁的 Z 世代已经成为红色旅游的主要参与群体，他们更偏爱历史遗迹、革命纪念品和博物馆、革命老区深度游和表演艺术等红色旅游项目。

不仅如此，中国的历史文化和红色旅游也引起了外国朋友的浓厚兴趣。当两名来自俄罗斯的交换生出现在橘子洲时，他们很快成为焦点。他们表示，在中国生活的三年时间里，对中国历史文化充满了好奇。疫情得到缓解后，他们向中国朋友询问哪里最能代表中国历史和文化，得到的回答就是长沙。

Passage 2【参考译文】

Capital of Gourmet Food

According to research, Guangzhou has been known as the Capital of Gourmet Food for 2,000 years. As one of the eight major cuisines in China, Cantonese cuisine features vastly diverse ingredients and exquisite production, emphasizing the color, fragrance, taste, shape and freshness of food. Cantonese dishes are of light taste, and change seasonally to highlight freshness and nutrition. In areas around Beijing Road, Shangxiajiu Pedestrian Street and Xiguan Food Street, well-known snacks, dim sum and flavored food are everywhere. Soup, tea and late-night snacks are also part of Guangzhou's food culture.

The city is home to a large number of time-honored Cantonese restaurants, Chaozhou cuisine restaurants, bustling tea houses and restaurants serving other Chinese cuisines, such as Hunan restaurants, Sichuan restaurants, hot pot restaurants, Shandong restaurants and Huaiyang restaurants. There are also many good places to go for Western cuisines, such as Western restaurants, coffee shops, and Western fast food restaurants. Additionally, a lot of affordable small restaurants, food stalls, traditional snack bars which serve special dishes, hot pots, barbecues and snacks also thrive in the city.

Located in the south subtropical zone, Guangzhou has fresh fruits on the market all year round, and earns the reputation of the "Hometown of Fruits". It is blessed with over 200 kinds of fruits, among which lychee, banana, papaya and pineapple are known as the "Four Famous Fruits in Lingnan". In addition, other fruits such as mango, starfruit, pomegranate, longan, white olive, black olive, wampee, bayberry, jackfruit, Sanhua plum and watermelon are also well-received.

Memory Practice（记忆训练）

Paragraph 1

Whereas travel was once a luxury, it is now regarded as a necessity. More people are traveling for business, pleasure, education, health, sports, and family than ever before. In 2017, there were 1.2 billion international travelers, and it is estimated that there will be 1.8 billion by 2030. This means more demand for accommodation, transport, restaurants, and all the services that provide for travelers' needs.

Low-cost carriers have enabled lower-income and middle-income consumers, larger families, and groups to travel. These travelers are more diverse than ever before and may not be interested in standard hotel rooms.

The lower search costs have made it easier to find niche products and have facilitated discovery of relatively unknown products. It has also meant that a platform can be more effective in promoting specific listings to target markets. The lower cost of verifying identity and reputation has supported transactions between strangers who do not have a public reputation.

(https://documents1.worldbank.org/curated/en/161471537537641836/Tourism-and-the-Sharing-Economy-Policy-Potential-of-Sustainable-Peer-to-Peer-Accommodation.pdf)

Paragraph 2

淇澳社区位于广东珠海东北部、珠江口内西侧的淇澳岛，东与香港、深圳隔海相望，南面水域与万山群岛相连，社区面积约23.8平方千米，现有居民540多户，户籍人口约2200人，流动人口约1100人。淇澳岛人文历史悠久，拥有苏兆征故居陈列馆、白石街抗英遗址、中华白海豚基地、国内连片面积最大的"淇澳红树林自然保护区"、珠江三角洲最完整的新石器时代末期渔猎文化遗址——"沙丘遗址"等人文景点。

这里曾发生过抵抗英国鸦片商贩武装入侵事件，保存有炮台遗址和"白石街"。1833年10月，英国鸦片贩子向村内开炮，愤怒的村民聚集在村天后宫前，用火炮还击，鸦片船队以失败告终，战后英国人赔偿白银3000两，淇澳村民用赔款修缮被炮火损坏的天后宫，铺筑"白石街"，以铭其事。1994年，白石街、天后宫和古炮台被核定公布为珠海市文物保护单位，2010年被核定公布为广东省第六批文物保护单位。

淇澳社区着力发展壮大集体经济，挖掘释放生态红利，设立淇澳岛生态保护补偿与政府扶持专项资金，累计投入5000多万元建设海岸观光带、南芒湾滨海公园和淇澳红树林自然保护区,营建"生态海岛+美丽岸线",大力发展"生态+旅游"产业。充分利用苏兆征故居陈列馆党史党性教育基地红色资源,发展"红色+旅游"产业,每年超过15万人次到此接受革命传统教育。

(https://www.gdzz.gov.cn/hsc/content/post_13124.html)

Section 2　Interpreting Practice（口译实训）

Dialogue 1【参考译文】

Business Travel in Guangzhou

A：您好,张小姐。我很高兴能到广州出差。

B：Welcome to Guangzhou, Mr. Smith.

A：谢谢。我很期待接下来的会议,也期待在出差期间多看看广州。我以前没来过广州。能跟我详细讲讲这个城市吗?

B：I'm very glad to hear that you are looking forward to your trip to Guangzhou. Guangzhou, a city with a long history, is also the frontier city of China's reform and opening-up, and its economy is developing very rapidly. There are many must-see attractions here, such as the night tour of the Pearl River, enjoying the spectacular night view along the banks of the Pearl River and feeling the prosperity and charm of the city. Chimelong Safari Park, you can see many rare animals, such as panda, white tiger, macaw, etc. Sun Yat-sen Memorial Hall, a memorial building to commemorate Dr. Sun Yat-sen, the forerunner of China's democratic revolution. There are many places where you can try authentic Guangzhou cuisine. I will help you arrange your itinerary and let you feel the charm of this city.

A：听起来很不错!晚上乘坐游船欣赏城市夜景、游览长隆野生动物园、参观中山纪念堂,以及品尝地道粤菜,这些都让我心驰神往。非常感谢您愿意花时间带我四处看看。这将使我的旅行更加愉快。

B：I'm glad to be your tour guide and enjoy the beauty of Guangzhou. I believe that through this tour, you will have a deeper understanding of Guangzhou and will also guide our cooperation to develop. I look forward to spending a few wonderful days with you!

A：我也是。再次感谢您,张小姐!有您当导游,这将是一次既难忘又硕果累累的旅行。

Dialogue 2【参考译文】

Business Travel After the Pandemic

A：Ms. Anna, the COVID-19 pandemic has had a great impact on the global economy, and many enterprises are reducing their business travel budgets. As the business manager at British Airways, do you agree with this?

B：是的,自新冠疫情暴发以来,全球众多企业纷纷缩减了商务旅行预算。在过去的两年里,我们确实感受到了企业差旅需求的减少。

A：What efforts has British Airways made to cope with this situation? Has the company's operation and prospects been greatly affected?

B：面对这一挑战,我们已经采取了一系列应对措施,包括优化飞行路线、缩小飞机尺寸、降低运营成本等。毋庸置疑,这段时期对我们航空行业而言是极具考验的。但我们相信,随着疫苗的推广和经济的复苏,商务旅行的需求将会稳步回升。

A：What other efforts has the company made to retain customers and business volume?

B: 我们始终将旅客的需求放在首位。为了继续提供优质服务，我们推出更灵活的机票政策，提供免费改签服务。

A: We have noticed that although enterprises are reducing their business travel expenses, many necessary business exchanges and expansion will continue. What trend do you think the business travel market will show after the pandemic?

B: 没错，面对面的会议与活动仍具有不可替代的价值。随着疫情的结束，我认为商务旅行将会不断恢复，但不会完全回到疫情之前的水平。一些线上合作仍将普遍存在。灵活性将是关键，公司将视情况进行线上或线下交流。我们航空公司旨在提供可定制的旅行解决方案，以满足这种不断发展的企业需求。

A: Thank you very much for accepting our interview, Ms. Anna!

B: 不客气。

Passage 1 【参考译文】

拥抱智能旅游 顺应行业趋势（节选）

虽然传统旅游业是许多经济体的支柱，但智能旅游业是后疫情时代的发展趋势。新冠疫情为我们提供了重新思考未来旅游业的机会，我们需要转变传统旅游，使其顺应行业趋势以确保其在未来的危机中具有恢复力。

2020年，疫情导致国际旅游业收入下降了60%，影响了数百万份工作，尤其是妇女和非正规经济部门的工作。全球GDP也遭受了重大打击。我们可能得通过采用智能旅游和智能目的地战略来开辟国际旅游前进的道路。

智能旅游是传统旅游和电子旅游的演变，涉及技术驱动的创新和信息、通信技术及物联网的广泛应用。包括智能售票、智能安全服务、虚拟现实旅游和机器人城市向导。

如果大规模旅行再次受到限制，增强现实或虚拟现实可能会为游客提供另一种难忘和独特的旅游体验。对这些数字技术的投资可能会对这些城市的经济发展产生溢出效应。增强现实使信息能够通过界面叠加到现实世界中，集成物理和虚拟对象以增强体验。增强现实已经在游客景点中得到应用，如博物馆、美术馆、主题公园和联合国教科文组织认定的世界遗产。例如，希腊奥林匹亚的 Archeoguide 采用增强现实技术来数字化重建希腊遗产遗址。

数字技术还可以促进人力资本发展，将主导传统旅游业的低技能工作升级为高端工作。技术发展可以增强旅游目的地的创新能力和竞争力，打造更具恢复力和可持续性的未来。

重要的是，为旅游业数字化进行设计和调整可以确保旅游目的地的可持续性和恢复力。智能解决方案和技术，如物联网、人工智能、大数据、增强现实和区块链技术，使城市能更好地应对灾害和风险，并减轻旅游业的风险。例如，通过免费 Wi-Fi 和大数据，社交网络平台可以提供受灾害、疾病和风险影响的地区的最新信息，向有关部门指出如何调配资源，并向游客标明应避开的地方。

Passage 2 【参考译文】

"Natural Studio" Boosts the Boom of Overseas Chinese Cultural Tourism Industry

The hit TV drama *The Knockout*, or *Kuangbiao* in Chinese, has sparked huge interest in many of its main filming locations in Jiangmen, Guangdong Province.

As a famous hometown of overseas Chinese, Jiangmen not only retains ancient Western-style buildings, but also has a strong urban living atmosphere. It shows unique characteristics of different eras, and is known as a "natural studio", attracting many films and TV dramas to be shot here.

Changdi Historical and Cultural Block was one of the filming locations where *Kuangbiao* was filmed.

As a result of the drama's popularity, tourists swarmed in the block every day, and everyone flocked to take photos to tick off (or "daka" in Chinese), which was really lively.

A few hundred meters away from Xuding Street, Qimingli, which was built by overseas Chinese in 1914, has recently become more lively. On the basis of traditional Lingnan residential style, the buildings in Qimingli have a large number of Western elements such as columns and arches. The overall structure is light, elegant and simple, full of romantic atmosphere of Western culture, and has the characteristics of overseas Chinese villages.

In Qimingli, we can see a house plate in front of each house, the address of the building and the house number are engraved on the upper part of the house plate. The passage engraved on the bottom of the house plate gives a detailed introduction to the history of the building and the origin of the owner.

In Qimingli, in addition to overseas Chinese cultural exhibition projects such as Overseas Chinese Postal Relics Museum and Jiangmen Museum of Intangible Souvenir, many coffee shops transformed from overseas Chinese houses also attracted many tourists to stop. Jiangmen, as a famous hometown of overseas Chinese, the coffee culture brought back from overseas by the ancestors of Wuyi has also been integrated into local daily life.

According to the data from the tourism platform, thanks to the popularity of film and TV dramas and tourism boom over the Spring Festival holiday, the number of tourists and tourism revenue in Jiangmen during the Spring Festival holiday reached a year-on-year increase of 34.48% and 29.47%, the number of consumers in related scenic spots increased by nearly five times compared to the previous month, and search popularity of Jiangmen reached a month-on-month increase of nearly 130%.

In the future, the Publicity Department of CPC Jiangmen Municipal Committee will endow the city with the mission of building an important cultural exchange platform for overseas Chinese in accordance with the *Outline Development Plan for the Guangdong-Hong Kong-Macao Greater Bay Area*. We are committed to the tapping, integration and flexible use of overseas Chinese cultural resources, and strive to make Jiangmen an Internet-famous site, as well as a root-seeking place for overseas Chinese and a gathering place for film industry.

Section 3　Interpreting Assessment（口译测评）

Passage 1【原文】

Chinese Cities to See Tourism Peak in New Year's Day Holiday

China's major railway ticket booking platform 12306 showed that, as of 15:00 on December 17, tickets for a number of trains are sold out, including those departing from Beijing to Wuhan, Nanjing to Hefei, Hangzhou, Chengdu to Chongqing, and Xi'an, as train tickets officially went on sale on December 16, the first day available to book trains for the 2024 New Year's Day holiday, *China Securities Journal* reported on December 19.

Data from Chinese travel agency Tongcheng Travel showed on the first day of the New Year's Day holiday (December 30), tickets for short-distance travel in urban areas such as Beijing to Tianjin, Shanghai to Nanjing, Shenzhen to Guangzhou, and Chongqing to Chengdu are in high demand. The travel demand is mainly to visit relatives.

According to research institute of Tongcheng Travel, travelers who are visiting relatives and ice-snow tourism will heat up destinations such as Harbin, Shenyang, Urumqi and Hulunbuir in Inner Mongolia autonomous region in Northeast and Northwest China, as well as Zhangjiakou in North China.

In terms of hotel booking, home stays and hotel rooms for New Year's Eve are popular choices for tourists. As of now, orders for 2024 New Year holiday home stays in popular cities on Tujia, a home stay online platform, increased nearly four times year-on-year. Data from travel portal Qunar also showed hotel rooms bookings in Harbin, Nanjing, Wuhan, Shanghai and Beijing from December 31 to January 1, especially those in luxury hotels, have higher bookings. Tickets for Universal Beijing Resort, Disneyland in Shanghai and Hong Kong, Chimelong Ocean Kingdom in Zhuhai Guangdong province and Harbin Ice and Snow World are rapidly booking out in advance.

In addition, Tongcheng Travel's data also showed that the popularity of domestic islands travel on its platform for the New Year's Day holiday increased by 72 percent year-on-year, and the popularity of Southeast Asian islands travel increased by three times year-on-year.

(https://language.chinadaily.com.cn/a/202312/20/WS6582adc7a31040ac301a8b8f.html)

Passage 1 【参考译文】

元旦假期全国多地将迎来出游高峰

据《中国证券报》12月19日报道，自12月16日起，2024年元旦假期的火车票正式开售。中国铁路大型售票平台12306的数据显示，截至12月17日15时，从北京出发前往武汉、南京出发前往合肥、杭州，以及成都出发前往重庆、西安等城市的多趟列车车次便已显示"售罄"。

国内旅行机构同程旅行的数据显示，元旦假期首日（12月30日），核心城市群的短途线路车票较为紧俏，比较热门的线路主要有：北京至天津、上海至南京、深圳至广州、重庆至成都等，出行需求主要以探亲为主。

同程旅行的研究部门认为，元旦假期探亲与旅游客流叠加，同时受冬季冰雪旅游热的带动，预计哈尔滨、沈阳、乌鲁木齐、呼伦贝尔以及张家口等冰雪游目的地人气将大幅上升。

从酒店预订情况来看，特色民宿和跨年夜酒店是游客的热门选择。截至目前，途家民宿平台上热门城市2024年元旦假期民宿的订单同比增长近4倍。旅游门户网去哪儿的数据显示，哈尔滨、南京、武汉、上海和北京的跨年夜（12月31日—1月1日）酒店，特别是豪华型酒店，预订量较高。北京环球影城、上海迪士尼乐园、香港迪士尼乐园、珠海长隆海洋王国、哈尔滨冰雪大世界等景区的门票提前迅速售罄。

同城旅行的数据还显示，平台上元旦假期国内海岛游的热度同比上升72%，东南亚海岛游的热度同比上升了3倍。

Passage 2 【原文】

寻味顺德（节选）

在顺德人眼中，烧猪的意义，已经超出了美食的范畴，它暗含着对先祖的感恩敬畏，以及对家族延续的祈愿。

岭南地区自古远离动乱纷争。人们依血脉亲缘，形成稳定的宗族聚落。祠堂是家族的中心，也是每一个族人的精神归属。如今在顺德，大小祠堂有300多座，它们依旧是村落中最古老威严的建筑。

88岁的陈光鉴，每年清明节都要从香港回到老家沙滘。熟悉的滋味，唤醒老人的童年记忆。陈光鉴从做工开始，在香港打拼半个多世纪，一步步建立自己的企业。半生辛劳换来殷实家业，他坚信这是祖先的庇佑。

清明节这天，两万名来自世界各地的陈氏后裔，一起祭拜先人。人们咬食甘蔗，在先人面前展现强劲的牙口，在追念故人时，也展望美好生活。

在珠三角地区，祭祖是一年中最隆重的家族聚会。宗族历史，先人事迹，都在族谱的记载和老人们的讲述中被传颂。

一场大型宴会正在紧张筹备。烧猪由族人集资购买，繁多的烧猪显示着家族的兴旺。祠堂中几千人围桌而坐，在清明期间的顺德，在每个村落都能见到。传统乡村的长幼尊卑、乡里亲情，在这一刻，凝聚在宗族宴席的餐桌上。

精心处理过的头菜，为即将离乡的人们画上清明的句号。对于顺德人，它不仅是一道美食、一种味道，更是儿时的记忆、尘封的故乡。

（https://tv.cctv.com/2016/05/02/VIDE06CSxIcN6EYc4JXHJ1kw160502.shtml?spm = C55924 871139.PT8hUEEDkoTi.0.0）

Passage 2 【参考译文】

A Bite of Shunde (Excerpt)

For people from Shunde, the roasted pig is more than just food. It represents the appreciation and revere towards ancestors, and the wish for the continuation of the family.

Lingnan has always been a sanctuary from wars and conflicts since ancient times. People formed stable family settlement, according to bloodlines. The ancestral hall is the center of the family. It is also the spiritual harbour of everyone in the family. There are over 300 ancestral halls in Shunde today. They still remain the most ancient and dignified buildings in the villages.

Chen Guangjian, who is 88 years old, comes back from Hong Kong to his hometown Shajiao every year during Qingming Festival. The familiar flavours bring back his childhood memories. Chen Guangjian started off as a labor, struggled for half a century in Hong Kong, and gradually builds up his own enterprise. Decades of hard work earned him an enterprise. He believes this is because of the blessing of ancestors.

On the day of Qingming Festival, 20,000 descendants of Chen come from all over the world, to worship their ancestors.

Biting the sugarcane, shows the ancestors your powerful bite. They look forward to a bright future while honoring the past families.

In the region of Pearl River estuary, worshipping ancestors is the most important family event. Family history and ancestors' achievements get preserved in the family pedigree and the elder one's tales.

The preparation of a big banquet is underway. The family members pooled the money to buy the roasted pigs. The number of pigs shows the prosperity of the family. Thousands of people sit around the tables in the ancestral hall. You can see this scenery in every village in Shunde, during Qingming festival. Respecting the elderly and the amicable ambiance of the traditional Chinese village, are best interpreted by this moment at the family banquet.

The cured mustard writes an end note for the people who will leave the hometown. For people from Shunde, it's not just food, but a taste, the memories from childhood, and the distant hometown.

Unit 5 Enterprise Introduction（企业介绍）

Section 1 Interpreting Preparation（口译准备）

☞ Sight Interpreting（视译）

Passage 1【参考译文】

阿里云

电商巨头阿里巴巴集团旗下子公司阿里云将在未来三年将2000亿元人民币投入到云基础设施上，以满足新冠疫情暴发后国内对数字服务需求的增长。该公司在二月份宣布，阿里云第四季度的收益相比前一年同期增长了62%。

新冠疫情使人们对数字服务产生了额外需求，数字服务通常依靠云计算服务和数据中心来实现。阿里云是中国最大的云计算服务供应商，但在国际上要排在亚马逊和微软之后。阿里巴巴的投资将主要用在操作系统和芯片研发上，同时也会用在数据中心网络上，这些技术将会在数据中心网络中运用。

从今年年初开始，阿里巴巴的技术利用率显著提高。为了降低新冠病毒传播风险，很多公司要求员工在家办公，因此全国的公司都更加依赖像钉钉这样的工具。钉钉是阿里巴巴的企业通信应用程序。在学校受疫情影响停课以后，钉钉也提供网上学习平台。

同时，阿里巴巴帮助中国政府推行健康通行证系统，这个数字检疫方法根据用户的健康状况和出行史把用户分为红、黄、绿三个等级。

周一，阿里云智能总裁张建锋在声明中说："新冠疫情给各行业的整体经济造成了附加压力，但也引导我们更多地投入到数字经济中。"阿里巴巴在过去两年提高了对云计算的投入，把它视为发展的主动力。阿里巴巴首席执行官张勇此前在接受美国消费者新闻与商业频道采访时说云计算会成为这家电商巨头的"主要业务"。

Passage 2【参考译文】

About Huawei

Who is Huawei

Founded in 1987, Huawei is a leading global provider of information and communications technology (ICT) infrastructure and intelligent terminal. We have 207,000 employees and operate in over 170 countries and regions, serving more than three billion people around the world. We are committed to bringing digital to every person, home and organization for a fully connected, intelligent world.

Research & Innovation

Scientific exploration and technological innovation drive civilization and society forward. Huawei understands the importance of research and innovation and how openness is critical for both. We are ready and willing to work with academia and industry to explore the frontiers of science and technology, push innovation forward, create value for industry and society as a whole, and build a better intelligent world.

Huawei's total R&D (research and development) investment over the last decade now exceeds CNY 977.3 billion. In 2022, our total R&D spending was CNY 161.5 billion, representing 25.1% of total revenue. At the end of 2022, more than 114,000 employees, or 55.4% of our workforce, worked in

R&D department. By the end of 2022, Huawei held a total of over 120,000 active patents.

Milestones

We entered into a golden age of 5G applications with industry producing over 20,000 use cases. Huawei created the GUIDE business blueprint and "Lighting up the 5.5G Era" initiative to support this boom in applications. We developed more than 100 scenario-based solutions and multiple business units (BU) to focus on specific industries, including the Mine BU, Smart Road, Waterway & Port BU, Government Public Services Digitalization BU, Electric Power Digitalization BU, Digital Finance BU, and Aviation & Rail BU. We launched Harmony OS 3, significantly expanding Super Device capabilities. Huawei Cloud was deployed in 29 regions around the world, and is becoming the preferred choice of customers in industries such as finance and manufacturing to migrate to the cloud.

Huawei's TECH4ALL education projects benefited over 600 schools and more than 220,000 people, including students, teachers, and youths. Huawei joined ITU's (International Telecommunication Union) Partner2Connect digital alliance, promising to help 120 million people in remote areas across more than 80 countries connect to the digital society by 2025.

Quality Policy

Always keep in mind that quality is the foundation of Huawei's survival, and the reason for the customer to choose Huawei.

We communicate customers' requirements and expectations to the entire value chain of Huawei accurately, to build quality together.

We respect rules and processes and do things right the first time.

We fulfill potential of employees around the globe for continuous improvement.

We work with customers to balance opportunities and risks, quickly responding to their needs and achieving sustainable growth.

We undertake to provide customers quality-assured products, services, and solutions and consistently enable customers to experience our commitment in creating value for each of them.

Memory Practice（记忆训练）

Paragraph1

Apple Inc. is an American multinational corporation headquartered in Cupertino, California, that designs, develops, and sells consumer electronics, computer software, online services, and personal computers. Its best-known hardware products are the Mac line of computers, the iPod media player, the iPhone smartphone, and the iPad tablet computer. Its online services include iCloud, iTunes Store, and App Store. Apple's consumer software includes the OS X and iOS operating systems, the iTunes media browser, the Safari web browser, and the iLife and iWork creativity and productivity suites.

(https://wenku.baidu.com/view/c031be1a3a68011ca300a6c30c2259010202f378.html?fr=income2-doc-search&_wkts_=1713254134669&wkQuery=Apple%2BInc.%2Bis%2Ban%2BAmerican%2Bmultinationa)

Paragraph 2

特斯拉CEO马斯克最近在Twitter上发消息解释了公司标志的意义。从表面上看，特斯拉标志只是一个简单的"T"字，它代表了公司产品。实际上还有另一层意思，"T"还象征着电力发动机的横截面。马斯克说，"T"字标志的主体代表着从发动机转子伸出的一根杆子，而上面的第二根线条代表着定子。特斯拉标志呈圆形，顶部向外突出，看起来和电力发动机的横截面差不多。不同发动机的架构有时会有很大的差异，所以标志只能进行简单的解释。

（https://www.ciplawyer.cn/whcycycy/130120.jhtml?prid=172）

Section 2　Interpreting Practice（口译实训）

Passage 1【参考译文】

世界 500 强榜单

2023 年 8 号 2 日，《财富》世界 500 强企业榜单公布，中国企业今年上榜数超过了美国。业内专家表示，该榜单显示出中国在新能源等新兴领域在全球舞台上日益增长的实力。

中国（含台湾地区）共有 142 家企业上榜，这是中国企业连续第五年在数量上位居榜首。美国和日本分别以 136 家和 41 家的数量紧随其后。

世界最大的电动汽车电池制造商宁德时代首次上榜，排名第 292 位。另一家中国新能源汽车制造商比亚迪，与 2022 年相比上升了 12 位，排名第 212 位。共计 9 家中国汽车制造商上榜，其中大多数都是凭借新能源汽车技术排名上升。

北京社科院高级研究员王鹏表示，多家中国企业上榜表明，中国在新能源领域的国际影响力日益增强。近年来，中国在新能源汽车相关技术和产品方面势头强劲。

王鹏称，许多中国新能源汽车公司在新能源领域的技术突破已经走在了全球前列。他表示，鉴于中国的巨大市场，未来几年，新能源领域的中国企业有望在全球舞台上占有更多份额。中国汽车工业协会的数据显示，2022 年中国新能源汽车销量约为 689 万辆，同比增长超 93%。

市场咨询机构 SNE 研究中心在 2022 年发布的一份报告显示，按使用量计算，全球前 10 大新能源汽车电池制造商中，中国企业占了 6 家。然而，商务部国际贸易经济合作研究院前高级研究员王志乐在一份报告中表示，今年许多中国领军企业的排名有所下降，且他们的平均利润与其他世界 500 强企业之间的差距有所扩大。

内地和中国香港上榜企业的平均利润为 39 亿美元，低于全球平均的 58 亿美元和美国企业的 80 亿美元。王志乐表示，新冠疫情和全球冲突改变了全球经济，全球产业链开始重组。他补充道："这些外部因素在一定程度上影响了中国企业的发展。"

Passage 2【参考译文】

Haier Group

Founded in 1984, Haier Group is the world's leading provider of solutions for better living and digital transformation.

Users have always been in the center of our businesses, we have built 10 R&D (research and development) centers, 71 research institutes, 35 industrial parks, 138 manufacturing centers and a sales network of 230,000 nodes around the world. We are the world's only IoT ecosystem brand that has been ranked in the Kantar BrandZ Top 100 Most Valuable Global Brands for 5 consecutive years. We also retain the top position in Euromonitor's Global Major Appliances Brand for 14 consecutive years.

The Group has four listed companies, and our subsidiary Haier Smart Home is named among the *Fortune* Global 500 companies and Fortune Most Admired Companies. We have several global high-end brands, including Haier, Casarte, Leader, GE Appliances, Fisher & Paykel, AQUA and Candy, and have the world's first smart home scenario brand, SAN YI NIAO. We have built the world-leading industrial internet platform COSMOPlat and the IoT health industry ecosystem INCAIER. Our entrepreneurial acceleration platform HCH has incubated 7 unicorn enterprises, 107 gazelle enterprises and 124 specialized and sophisticated small giant enterprises.

Being an iconic company in the real economy, Haier Group always focuses on the industries. We build a landscape of two pillars, smart living and industrial internet. We build high-end brands, scenario brands and ecosystem brands. We are committed to use technological innovation to deliver customized smart living for global users and to realize successful digital transformation for corporate clients, and to endeavor for high-quality and sustainable economic and social development.

On September 20, 2023, the World Brand Laboratory released the "2023 The Top 500 Asian Brands List" at the Asian Brand Conference. Haier has been ranked on the list for 18 consecutive years, ranking fourth in a row. This list mainly evaluates the influence of Asian brands, with basic indicators including market share, brand loyalty, and Asian leadership.

Passage 3 【参考译文】

沃尔玛

几乎每个人都知道沃尔玛。人们看电视能看见沃尔玛的商标，开车购买食品和日用品也会去沃尔玛。人们知道沃尔玛是一个品牌超市，但是人们知道沃尔玛成功的原因吗？

自1962年第一家沃尔玛店在阿肯色州的罗杰斯镇开业以来，我们一直致力于为顾客的生活创造不凡。我们的事业是山姆·沃尔顿富有远见卓识的领导，以及一代又一代同仁竭诚帮助客户和社区节省费用和提高生活品质的结果。这个丰富的文化遗产定义了我们的身份以及我们如今的营业方向。

沃尔玛最初只是阿肯色州罗杰斯镇的一家不起眼的折扣零售商，现在沃尔玛在美国开了数以千计的商店，同时也在全球扩张。通过创新，我们正在打造一种无缝体验，能让客户通过移动设备在商店随时随地在线购物。我们正为世界各地的客户和社区创造机会，带来价值。

沃尔玛可以帮助世界各地的人们节省金钱，生活得更好——他们可以随时随地在线或使用移动设备在零售商店购物。我们在28个国家设有65家旗舰店，旗下有近11 000家门店，并在11个国家设有电子商务网站，每周光顾的客户或会员超过2.45亿人。2015财政年净销售额为4822亿美元。目前沃尔玛在全球范围内雇佣的员工达到220万人。

沃尔玛于1991年成为一家国际公司，除了美国之外，我们在27个国家都有业务经营。我们在全球拥有超过6200家门店，可以利用全球的资源来满足各地的需求。目前沃尔玛国际是公司业务增长最快的，由总裁兼首席执行官大卫·奇怀特领导。

"节省开销，生活更加美好"，这是我们沃尔玛人信守的承诺。我们的"每天低成本"战略帮助人们省钱，延长薪水的使用时间，为人们的家人提供更好的生活。但是为了让人们生活得更好，我们所做的已经远远超出店内服务。它延伸到人们的社区，延伸到世界各地，影响着人们的生活，尽管我们从未相见。

我们相信，我们有机会，有责任在对关系到我们所有人的重大问题上发挥作用。这些问题包括环境保护、战胜饥饿、妇女权益保障、卫生平价的食品供应。沃尔玛正在推动有意义的变革。在某种程度上说，这是其他任何公司都不能做到的。我们决心尽自己所能，让全世界的人们生活得更好。

Passage 4 【参考译文】

Tencent

Company profile

Tencent is a world-leading internet and technology company that develops innovative products and services to improve the quality of life of people around the world. Founded in 1998 with its headquarter in Shenzhen, China, Tencent's guiding principle is to use technology for good. Our communication and social services connect more than one billion people around the world, helping them to keep in touch with friends and family, access transportation, pay for daily necessities, and even be entertained.

Tencent also publishes some of the world's most popular video games and other high-quality digital content, enriching interactive entertainment experiences for people around the globe. Tencent also offers a range of services such as cloud computing, advertising, FinTech, and other enterprise services to support our clients' digital transformation and business growth. Tencent has been listed on the Stock Exchange of Hong Kong since 2004.

Vision & Mission

User value is our guiding principle, we strive to incorporate social responsibility into our products and services; promote technology innovation and cultural vitality, to help industries digitally upgrade and to collaborate for the sustainable development of society.

Culture values

Integrity: uphold principles, ethics, openness and fairness.

Proactivity: pursue positive contributions, volunteer for responsibility and push for breakthroughs.

Collaboration: be inclusive and collaborative, strive to progress and evolve.

Creativity: push for breakthrough innovations, explore the possibilities of the future.

Talent development

Employees are Tencent's most valuable asset. We place great importance on staff training and development, offering opportunities for our staff to grow vertically or horizontally in their career. This approach allows employees to develop their capabilities in a more focused and clear manner, and be recognized for their contributions clearly and timely through our ranking system.

Our office

Opened in October 2017, Tencent's Binhai Building is a fully digital and intelligent structure, and also serves as Tencent's new global headquarter. The design of the interconnected building symbolizes the connectivity that brings together all remote corners of the Internet, and also visualizes the connection of people and people, people and services, and people and devices in the future. We have also set up branch offices in China, namely Beijing, Shanghai, Chengdu, and Guangzhou, and overseas including United States and South Korea, to provide a comfortable and innovative office environment for local employees to immerse themselves in Tencent's culture.

Section 3　Interpreting Assessment（口译测评）

Passage 1【原文】

An Introduction to Ford

Hello, everyone. Today, I'd like to say something about the history of the Ford Motor Company. The Ford Motor Company is one of the world's largest automotive companies, established by Henry Ford in 1903.

In 1908, the Model T, the world's first automobile for the common man, came into being. Thus began the world's automotive revolution. 1913 saw another world's first for Ford Motor Company—the assembly line. This innovation helped the sales of the flagship Model T reach astonishing 15 million units, a record that resulted in Henry Ford being acclaimed worldwide as "the man who put wheels on the world".

Today, as the world's leading automotive company, what gives us a sense of pride is still that we maintain Henry Ford's founding principles: "Consumers are the focus of everything we do. Our work must be done with our consumers in mind, providing better products and services than our competitors."

In 2004, the Ford Motor Company generated net income of US＄3.5 billion, serving 327,000 customers in over 200 countries and regions in six continents.

In 1913 the first Model T was exported to China, a first step along the road to Ford Motor Company's entry into the country. In 1924, Dr. Sun Yat-sen wrote to Henry Ford, inviting him to build and develop an automotive industry for China. In 1978, the Ford Motor Company's CEO Henry Ford Ⅱ met Mr. Deng Xiaoping and expressed his desire to cooperate extensively in moving the industry ahead.

Passage 1 【参考译文】

福特公司简介

大家好，今天我们来谈一谈福特汽车公司的发展史。福特汽车公司是世界上最大的汽车企业之一。由亨利·福特先生于1903年所创立。

1908年福特汽车公司生产出世界上第一辆属于普通百姓的汽车——T型车，世界汽车工业革命就此开始。1913年，福特汽车公司又开发出世界上第一条装配线，这一创举使旗舰款T型车的销售量达到了1500万辆的惊人数字，这一纪录使亨利·福特被誉为"给世界装上轮子"的人。

今天福特汽车公司仍然是世界一流的汽车企业，令我们感到自豪的是，我们仍然坚守着亨利·福特的创业理念："消费者是我们一切工作的中心所在。我们在工作中必须时刻想着我们的消费者，提供比竞争对手更好的产品和服务。"

2004年，福特汽车公司为全球200多个国家和地区的327 000名消费者提供服务，创造了35亿美元的纯利润。

1913年，第一辆T型车销往中国，福特汽车公司迈出了开发中国市场的第一步。1924年孙中山先生致信亨利·福特，请他帮助中国建立和发展汽车工业。1978年福特汽车公司的董事长亨利·福特二世得到了邓小平先生的会见，表达了他愿意与中国广泛合作，促进中国汽车工业发展的愿望。

Passage 2 【原文】

吉利控股集团

浙江吉利控股集团（以下简称"吉利控股"）始建于1986年，1997年进入汽车行业，一直专注实业、技术创新和人才培养，不断打基础、练内功，坚定不移地推动企业转型升级和可持续发展。现资产总值超5100亿元，员工总数超过12万人，连续十二年进入《财富》世界500强（2023年排名第225位），是全球汽车品牌组合价值排名前十中唯一的中国汽车集团。

吉利控股致力于成为具有全球竞争力和影响力的智能电动出行和能源服务科技公司，业务涵盖汽车及上下游产业链、智能出行服务、绿色运力、数字科技等。

吉利控股总部设在杭州，旗下吉利、领克、极氪、几何、沃尔沃、极星、路特斯、伦敦电动汽车、远程新能源商用车、雷达新能源汽车、曹操出行、礼帽出行等围绕各自品牌定位，积极参与市场竞争。吉利控股以汽车产业电动化和智能化转型为核心，在新能源科技、共享出行、车联网、智能驾驶、车载芯片等前沿技术领域，打造科技护城河，做强科技生态圈。

吉利控股在中国上海、杭州、宁波，瑞典哥德堡，英国考文垂，美国加州，德国法兰克福等地建有造型设计和工程研发中心，研发、设计人员超过2万人，拥有国内外创新专利超1.4

万项。其在中国、美国、英国、瑞典、比利时、马来西亚建有世界一流的现代化整车和动力总成制造工厂,拥有各类销售网点超过4000家,产品销售及服务网络遍布世界各地。

(https://zgh.com/overview/)

Passage 2 【参考译文】

Geely Holding Group

Zhejiang Geely Holding Group ("Geely Holding") was founded in 1986. In 1997, Geely Holding entered the automotive industry and has since focused our core business on the development and production of automobiles. Geely has continued to grow with a focus on continuous technological innovation, talent development, and strengthening core competitiveness, all the while staying committed to promoting transformation, upgrading and sustainable development. Since 2012, Geely Holding has ranked among the *Fortune* Global 500 for twelve consecutive years (ranked 225th in 2023) with assets totaling over 510 billion RMB, and more than 120,000 global employees. Geely Holding ranked among Brand Finance's Top 10 Most Valuable Auto Portfolio Brands 2022—the only Chinese auto group on the list.

Geely Holding is committed to becoming a globally competitive and influential smart electric mobility technology enterprise and energy service provider, engaged in automotive, upstream and downstream industrial chains, intelligent travel services, green transportation capacity, digital technology, etc.

Headquartered in Hangzhou, Geely Holding today owns and manages a number of brands: Geely Auto, Lynk & Co, ZEEKR, Geometry, Volvo Cars, Polestar, Lotus, London Electric Vehicle Company, Farizon Auto, RADAR AUTO, Cao Cao Mobility, Li Mao Mobility and other brands. They are around the brand positioning and actively participate in market competition. With the electrification and intelligent transformation of the automotive industry as the core, Geely Holding has also been developing cutting-edge technologies in new energy, shared mobility, vehicle networks, autonomous driving, on-board chips, building a science and technology moat and strengthen the science and technology ecosystem.

Geely Holding has established R&D and design centers globally in Shanghai, Hangzhou, Ningbo, Gothenburg, Coventry, California, Frankfurt, etc., with more than 20,000 R&D and design personnel and more than 14,000 innovation patents. Geely Holding operates world-class vehicle and powertrain manufacturing plants in China, U.S., U.K., Sweden, Belgium, and Malaysia, meanwhile owning a worldwide sales and service network comprised of more than 4,000 branches.

Unit 6　Product Presentation(产品介绍)

Section 1　Interpreting Preparation(口译准备)

☞ Sight Interpreting(视译)

Passage 1 【参考译文】

更多外资企业投资"中国制造"

大众汽车集团在华首家全资控股的电池系统工厂——大众汽车(安徽)零部件有限公司于11月21日在华东安徽合肥投产。该工程总投资超过1.4亿欧元,初始年产能为150 000~

180 000个高压电池系统。随着中国继续推动制造业高质量发展和高水平对外开放,大众汽车集团成为众多扩大对中国制造业投资的外国公司之一。

5月,制冷行业巨头丹佛斯在天津成立了丹佛斯全球制冷研发测试中心。同月,宝马集团在中国的合资企业华晨宝马汽车有限公司开始在辽宁沈阳建设新的电池生产厂。

商务部数据显示,2023年前10个月,全国新设立外商投资企业41 947家。制造业实际使用外资金额达到2834.4亿元,同比增长1.9%,其中高技术制造业增速达到9.5%。

中国制造业领域吸引外资的积极因素包括全面的产业生态系统、庞大开放的市场、强大的研发和创新活力以及友好的营商环境。

在10月举行的第三届"一带一路"国际合作高峰论坛上,中国表示将全面取消制造业领域外资准入限制措施。中国国际贸易促进委员会最近一项调查显示,受访外资企业连续三个季度认为"技术创新与研发"是中国市场最大的发展机遇。

Passage 2 【参考译文】

Huawei Mate X

Huawei has launched its foray into foldable smartphones, with the Huawei Mate X officially unveiled at Mobile World Congress 2019 as a competitor to Samsung's Galaxy Fold. Samsung's Galaxy Fold announcement isn't even a week old yet, and we already have a competitor that is thinner, has a bigger screen, and folds flatter.

The company's CEO of consumer business, Richard Yu, unveiled the new Huawei Mate X, on stage, saying: "We bring you the future of design, the future of technology." Unlike the Samsung folding phone, the Galaxy Fold, which opens inwards, like a book, the Huawei phone opens outwards. Given this different functionality, Huawei has managed to make this device incredibly thin.

When open, the Huawei Mate X is 5.4 mm thick, and when closed, it's only 11 mm. The foldable screen of the Huawei Mate X is folded around the outside of the device, with the help of a patented hinge with over 100 components, the company said.

The phone will run on Huawei's Kirin 980 processor and Balong 5,000 chipset, which supports 5G. The company said the super-fast chipset will allow users to download a 1 gigabyte movie in just 3 seconds. The Mate X is Huawei's first 5G-enabled smartphone. Huawei said it has an advantage over other companies launching 5G devices because it provides the full-range of equipment needed to get wireless networks up and running.

The Mate X houses three cameras—a 40 MP main camera, a 16 MP wide angle lens, and an 8 MP telephoto lens—and an LED flash, and a power button. It features a camera system that can play the role of both front and rear cameras. It also offers mirror shooting that lets you see the picture while you take it.

To power the phone, the device has dual batteries which make up 4,500 mAh. It also features Huawei's new Super Charge 55W to make this device the fastest charging phone in the industry. You should be able to get 85 percent power off a mere 30-minute of charging.

No matter how innovative and technology advanced the new device is, it will take a lot more time for a critical mass of consumers to experience the benefits of foldable phones and 5G technology.

You might dismiss foldable phones like the new Huawei Mate X as just a gimmick. But all you have to do is look at all the people on airplanes who choose to watch movies holding up their phones to realize there's pent-up demand for tablet-size viewing on a phone.

The Huawei launch drew huge crowds. Fans queued outside the venue hours before the kickoff and those who couldn't get in watched the event outside on a big screen. At times, they burst into warm applause. The Mate X clearly shows that Huawei is a technology innovation leader. The new device has nothing to envy to Samsung's latest Galaxy Fold announcement.

☞ Memory Practice（记忆训练）

Paragraph 1

Living Heritage: Chinese Silk

Delicate and soft to the touch. Silk has threaded its way throughout China's history. One cannot be certain of its origin, but the humble ancient Chinese people credited their own wisdom to Leizu, wife of the Yellow Emperor, who is the legendary ancestor of Chinese people, as the inventor of sericulture.

In the Western Han Dynasty, with diplomat and explorer Zhang Qian opening up the routes to the Western regions, silk graced countries in Central Asia, later extending its reach to other parts of Eurasia and beyond. Fittingly, its name marked China's major international trade routes, the ancient Silk Road and Maritime Silk Road.

In the hands of Chinese artists, the thinnest threads can weave pictures of immense possibilities, and the softest material can traverse thousands of years. As one of the many marvels of ancient China, silk is not merely a type of textile. It is a cultural icon, and an embodiment of elegance and grace.

（https://mp.weixin.qq.com/s?__biz = MzAwOTkyMTA5OA = = &mid = 2247535141&idx = 1&sn = 00ddda98facfa8752d38fca7bb2960f9&chksm = 9b5a3d00ac2db416438f32aec5e1095ca425378e1a2d07c41106942bca60e989978fb5169a8e&scene = 27）

Paragraph 2

近日，由福布斯中国、中国电子商会主办，保定市人民政府联合主办的"首届福布斯中国客户服务企业100颁奖典礼暨数智化服务产业发展论坛"在河北省保定市成功举办。在本次颁奖典礼上，联想凭借智能化服务创新应用、强大的服务布局、贴心专业的服务态度，一举获得2022年"福布斯中国客户服务企业100"大奖！这也再次证明了联想在市场与行业间所享有的良好服务口碑。2022年"福布斯中国客户服务企业100"奖项，是首个对全国范围客户服务企业进行排名的权威评选。该评选通过对企业的服务能力、客服运营能力、客户满意度、品牌影响力等指标的评估，在20个行业领域内共选出100家企业，打造衡量企业客服水平的标杆。

（https://www.sohu.com/a/729156501_120008919）

Section 2　Interpreting Practice（口译实训）

Passage 1 【参考译文】

酸酸甜甜的"柠檬西瓜"

柠檬西瓜是新开发的西瓜品种，兼具西瓜的香甜和与柠檬相似的微酸口感。日本三得利花卉园艺公司据称花了五年时间用一种进口西瓜的种子培育出了柠檬西瓜。

和柠檬杂交后培育出的成品瓜，既像西瓜般多汁甘甜，又有柠檬般的微酸，非常适合在炎热的夏日食用。柠檬西瓜和普通西瓜一样是圆形，但是外皮没有西瓜的标志性条纹，果肉呈白色。柠檬西瓜的口感和梨类似，但是熟透后会更软，比较接近夕张蜜瓜。

目前北海道只有5个农民在种植柠檬西瓜，他们今年预计会种出大约3800个柠檬西瓜。柠檬西瓜已经在日本超市上架销售，一块瓜的价格大概为3220日元。有幸尝过柠檬西瓜的人对这种美味的瓜赞不绝口。《北海道放送》的记者称："有柠檬的微酸，又和西瓜一样很甜，太好吃了。"另一个人表示:"甜和酸的比例恰到好处,堪称热天消暑的完美水果。"

柠檬西瓜是日本备受欢迎的奢侈水果市场上的最新产品,日本曾经推出的珍奇水果包括世界上最昂贵的西瓜——方形西瓜、世界上最昂贵的葡萄——罗马红宝石葡萄,还有日本经典的白色草莓——白宝石草莓。

Passage 2 【参考译文】

Beijing Olympic Backpacks

Foreign reporters have been seen carrying around backpacks from the 2008 Summer Olympics as they work inside the media center for the Beijing 2022 Winter Olympic Games.

An Iranian journalist said he would carry the bag from Beijing 2008 every time he covered sports competitions. "A backpack is a very important item for a photography journalist, and this bag is of high quality and its design is user-friendly," said the journalist.

A small backpack has become the microcosm of "Made in China", and people have commented that domestic goods are strong. Apart from the bags supplied to media workers, the gold medals awarded during the 2008 Summer Olympics also demonstrated a high level of quality. After a fire destroyed the apartment of Russian rhythmic gymnast Daria Shkurikhina, she found that the gold medal she had earned from the 2008 Summer Olympics, which was inlaid with jade, remained undamaged.

For the 2022 Winter Olympic Games, media workers from around the world will receive a new media package that contains items such as an insulated cup and cultural souvenirs depicting paper-cut window grilles or Chinese knots, among other gifts.

With the Games less than one month to go, the media center for the 2022 Beijing Winter Olympics and Winter Paralympics has officially launched a trial of its closed-loop management. During the trial run from January 4 to January 22, the center will host over 1,700 journalists, photographers, and broadcasting staff from around the world.

Passage 3 【参考译文】

iPhone 15 系列手机使用说明

显示屏采用曲线优美的圆角设计,四个圆角位于一个标准矩形内。按照标准矩形测量时,屏幕的对角线长度是 6.12 英寸或 6.69 英寸。实际可视区域较小。

手机支架需单独购买。

iPhone 15 和 iPhone 15 Plus 可防溅、抗水、防尘,在受控实验室条件下进行了测试。防溅、抗水、防尘功能并非永久有效,防护性能可能会因日常磨损而下降。请勿为处于潮湿状态的 iPhone 充电,请参阅用户手册了解清洁和干燥说明。由浸入液体而导致的损坏不在保修范围之内。

所有电池性能信息取决于网络设置和许多其他因素,实际结果可能有所不同。电池充电周期次数有限,最终可能需要更换。电池续航时间和充电周期次数依使用和设置情况的不同而可能有所差异。

5G 功能适用于特定国家或地区的特定运营商。速度基于现场状况和不同运营商而可能有所差异。

激活任何一款 iPhone 15 系列手机在两年内可以通过卫星请求免费道路援助或者紧急 SOS 援助。网络连接和援助时间可能基于求助方位、现场状况和其他因素而有所差异。

iPhone 15 和 iPhone 15 Pro 系列机型可检测到严重车祸并拨打求救电话,需要使用蜂窝网络连接或无线局域网通话功能。费用由援助方决定,可能根据求助的方位和援助类型而有所差异。

Passage 4 【参考译文】

Zibo's Barbecue

The city Zibo in Shandong Province has long sought to publicize its unique take on roasted skewers of meat, veggies, seafood and assorted other foodstuffs, hoping that it would become a must-try "brand" of the city.

Until late February this year, the publicity of Zibo barbecue had achieved limited success. That is, until some college students attending a job fair in the city went to try the barbecue and took videos of themselves enjoying the food and posted them onto social media. Zibo's special barbecue has gone viral. As a result, youths from across the country have started to pour into Zibo to try its now famous barbecue.

What makes barbecue special in Zibo is that the skewers are 70~80 percent cooked before being brought to the table, where diners can finish off the cooking at their own little stove of hot coals. On top of that, diners have pancakes, scallions and other dressings at the table so they are able to assemble their own barbecue-filled package a bit like how traditional Peking duck is prepared.

Xu Jiayue, a student from Shandong Transport Vocational College, came to Zibo from neighboring city Weifang to try the barbecue for herself. "The stoves allow us to cook the meat, which gives us a feeling of participation, and it allows us to eat the meat at a perfect temperature, which ensures a good taste and flavor," she said.

Zibo has had record numbers of arrivals at its train station since March 4. A total of 27,065 visitors arrived on March 4, setting a record for daily passengers arriving at the railway station in the past three years. College students from neighboring cities accounted for a large proportion of the passengers, officials from the train station said.

One barbecue restaurant owner said that there were long lines outside the restaurant every day for the past two weeks. Several owners of restaurants said they were selling more than 10,000 skewers of meat, chicken wings or vegetables a day during the past week, especially on the weekends. Once the hungry diners have had their fill of barbecue, many of them have been setting out to visit Zibo's other attractions while they're in the area.

"Zibo barbecue going viral is not accidental," Yin Qidi, head of the city's commerce bureau, said at a news conference held to address the barbecue craze. The once traditional industrial city has been putting a lot of effort into developing the city into a young people friendly one, Yin said, adding that the city offers rooms with extra discounts in designated hotels to outside visitors between the ages of 18 and 35. Local statistics showed several hotels offering such services for young people were fully booked.

To capitalize on its recent fame, the city plans to hold a barbecue festival, Yin said. Authorities including the market supervision and public security have joined in to ensure food safety and reasonable pricing in the "barbecue sector", and the city's public transportation company has opened 21 bus lines especially for transporting people to barbecue restaurants.

Section 3 Interpreting Assessment（口译测评）

Passage 1 【原文】

Product Introduction

Dear customers,

Good morning! Now I am presenting to you three major things about our company: the product, the company's locations and the packages that we offer.

Now let's start with the company. The company's name is BWL, which stands for Best Work Lifestyle. BWL is a 20-year old company founded in New Zealand. And we have enjoyed 20 whole years of experience in network marketing and health industry. We have our own ISO-certified manufacturing facilities, located in Dennington Street. Our certified manufacturing facilities guarantee that all the manufacturing and all the packaging methods that we have involve zero human contact. With that, we can guarantee that all our products are safe and of good quality.

If you can see on the map, we already have offices in 12 countries. Once the Forbes Magazine mentioned that there are 200 billion-dollar companies in Asia-Pacific. And according to them, our company is one of them. So venturing into our business equals to venturing into a billion dollar company.

Our products are divided into two categories. We have "Outward Harmony" and "Inner Harmony". "Outward Harmony" focuses on beauty, especially beautiful skin. These are all our products. The first is "Dr. Secret". Dr. Secret is an elite product for the skin. If you can see, here are pictures of our customers who use the Dr. Secret products.

Aside from "Outward Harmony", we have the "Inner Harmony" series. "Inner Harmony" focuses on health. The product that you are seeing here on the screen is our flagship product. It is called the "plum". I am sure that you have already heard pretty testimonials about plums. Plums are highly beneficial to those who suffer from low sugar level, obesity, and digestions problems. The plums that we are selling are natural fruits. There are even seeds in them. This is how natural and authentic our products are. They are not synthetic, rather, they are real fruits grown in orchards by farmers. You can have a taste of them. In fact, you can actually eat them.

Our products have four major ingredients. Number one is "plum"—the fruit—itself. This fruit is rich in vitamin C, fiber, and minerals. Aside from that, we have "Ingredient D". "Ingredient D" is a great antioxidant which contains anti-cancer substances. And the next one is "Green Vanguard". It is also an antioxidant. However, this functions as fat-burner and fat-blocker. Last but not least, we have our probiotics which help with digestion of our stomachs and the multiplication of the good bacteria inside our bodies.

Passage 1 【参考译文】

产品介绍

各位顾客，早上好！

现在我主要从三个方面给大家介绍本公司：公司的产品，公司所在地，以及我们提供的套装产品。

现在，首先介绍我们公司。本公司的名称是 BWL，代表了 Best Work Lifestyle。BWL 成立于新西兰，有 20 年的历史。我们在网络销售、保健产业领域有整整 20 年的经验。在丹宁顿大街，我们拥有经过 IOS 认证的生产设备。这些经过认证的生产设备能够保证整个生产过程及包装方式均无人接触。这样，我们就能够确保所有的产品都符合安全优质的标准。

你在地图上可以看到，我们在 12 个国家都设有办事处。福布斯杂志曾报道，在亚太地区有 200 家"十亿美元"资产的公司。根据这一报道，我们公司是其中之一。所以与我们合作就等同于与一家十亿美元资产的公司合作。

我们的产品分为两类。一种是"外在和谐美"，另外一种是"内在和谐美"。"外在和谐美"专注于美容,尤其是皮肤护理。这些都是我们的护肤产品。第一款是"秘密医生"。"秘密医生"是皮肤护理产品中的佼佼者。请看,这些是我们使用过"秘密医生"的客户的照片。

除了"外在和谐美",我们还有"内在和谐美"产品系列。"内在和谐美"专注于健康。在屏幕上您能看到的产品是我们的旗舰产品。名字叫"李子"。我确定您听过不少对"李子"的夸奖。李子对那些有低血糖、肥胖症以及消化问题的人有很大的好处。我们售卖的李子都是天然的水果,里面甚至还有种子。这能看出我们产品多么天然正宗。它们都不是人工合成物,而是农民在地里种植的真正的水果。你可以尝一尝,还可以把它们吃下去。

我们的产品有四种主要成分。第一种就是"李子",它本身就是水果。这种水果富含维生素C、纤维素和矿物质。除此之外,我们也有"D成分",这是蕴含抗癌物质的抗氧化剂。另外一种是"绿色先锋",它也是一种抗氧化剂。不过,它能起到燃烧脂肪和阻隔脂肪的作用。最后是益生菌,它可以帮助胃部消化,增加我们体内有益细菌的数量。

Passage 2【原文】

Metapad 的推广

女士们,先生们:

大家上午好!

首先,请允许我为大家介绍我们的公司。我们公司名叫北京创天下科技有限公司,创建于1998年,总部位于北京。我们在上海、广州、成都、重庆、杭州、昆明、乌鲁木齐、济南、武汉以及西安等城市设有分公司或办事处。员工超过170人,年营业额超过5亿元。

我们公司是国内主要的企业级IT产品和服务供货商,专注于为客户提供企业级IT产品和专业服务,并协同应用软件开发商和系统集成商,为客户提供全面的IT解决方案。

今天我要给大家重点推荐的是我们公司自主研发和生产的电子产品——55英寸多点触摸屏计算机——Metapad,以及这款产品如何能更好地帮助您展现电子软件、应用程序以及营销和销售平台。

使用我们生产的Metapad,您将能够轻易地把应用程序演示出来,甚至还可以让您的观众互动。借助多点触屏,您能够随意找出希望展示的任何内容。Metapad是多功能一体机,容易安装,管理和使用。

您有没有试过在您的产品展销活动中通过视频与您的客户进行通话呢?选择Metapad,选择一种全新的体验。

谢谢大家!

Passage 2【参考译文】

Promotion for Metapad

Ladies and gentlemen,

Good morning!

First of all, please allow me to introduce our company. Our company is called Beijing Heaven Creation Technology Co., Ltd. (BHCTL). It was founded in 1998, with its headquarter located in Beijing. We have our branch offices and offices in Shanghai, Guangzhou, Chengdu, Chongqing, Hangzhou, Kunming, Urumqi, Jinan, Wuhan, Xi'an etc. Our company has more than 170 employees, and the annual turnover amounts to more than 500 million yuan.

BHCTL is one of the major suppliers of IT products and services. We focus on providing IT products and professional services for enterprises, and we cooperate with application software developers as well as system integrators to supply them with comprehensive IT solutions.

Today, I am here to show you our company's self-developed and self-manufactured electronic product—our 55 inch multi-touch screen computer—Metapad, and how it can help you better show off your software, apps, and platforms that you market and sell.

With Metapad, you can easily show off your apps, and even let your audience interact. With this multi-touch screen, you can easily pull up whatever you would like to demonstrate. Metapad, an all-in-one computer, is easy to set up, manage, and use.

Have you ever had a video conference with someone in your sales exhibition to talk to your customers? Choose Metapad, choose a whole new experience.

Thank you.

Unit 7　Business Strategies（商务策略）

Section 1　Interpreting Preparation（口译准备）

Sight Interpreting（视译）

Passage 1【参考译文】

宝马电动车转型战略

截至目前，宝马集团在中国市场已推出了 5 款纯电动车车型，包括创新纯电动 BMW i7、创新 BMW iX、创新 BMW i4 和国产的新 BMW iX3 和全新 BMW i3。

今年上半年，宝马摩托车第二款量产纯电动摩托车——全新 BMW CE 04 完成了中国首发并已开启预售。MINI 品牌首款纯电动都市跨界概念车——MINI Concept Aceman 也已于 9 月在上海完成亚洲首秀。2023 年，宝马在中国的纯电动车车型将增加至 11 款。到 2025 年，宝马集团预计在全球交付第 200 万辆纯电动车，并将在同年推出 BMW"新世代"车型，至 2030 年预计宝马集团 50% 的销量来自于纯电动车车型。

今年在沈阳生产基地开业的华晨宝马大规模升级项目，即里达工厂，是 BMW iFACTORY 生产战略的典范，具有"精益、绿色、数字化"三大核心特征。通过全价值链的绿色转型，宝马集团计划于 2030 年将单车全生命周期平均碳排放量较 2019 年降低至少 40%，最迟到 2050 年完全实现气候中和。

加速品牌向电动化转型的同时，宝马同样聚焦于构筑电动车生态系统。截至 10 月底，BMW i 品牌认证的经销商店已达到 600 家，宝马的电动车维修服务网络有着极大优势。

与此同时，BMW 不断优化充电墙盒产品及安装服务，扩展公共充电网络，提升服务质量并加快数字化功能的创新。

在充电网络建设方面，截至今年 9 月，BMW 公共充电网络在全国已接入超过 46 万个公共充电桩，其中包含 25 万个快充桩，覆盖全国 320 多个城市。

Passage 2【参考译文】

A Speech at the Annual Innovation Conference of Haier Group (Excerpt)
Smart Home

Built on Haier Smart Home, two core competence platforms, namely, SAN YI NIAO Experience Cloud and Smart Home Brain, will be prioritized in future development. Besides, four scenarios, including smart kitchen, smart air supply, smart water supply and whole-house intelligence, will evolve

197

at faster pace, for realizing exponential growth of ecosystem revenue. In addition, Haier will further promote connectivity and seamless integration with Eoroom and RRS Supply Chain, and leverage digital technology to deliver smart home solution featuring design, implement and services, thus delivering a better user experience throughout the whole process.

Institutional innovation and inspiring dynamism

Embracing soil makes Mount Tai a vast mountain; the ceaseless inflow of rivers makes the ocean deep. Evolving from a small factory on the verge of shutdown, Haier's current success is attributable to its effort of upholding entrepreneurship and innovation and seeking utmost value of people.

On the premise that the collective ownership remains unchanged, the system is an ingenious system designed for motivating vigor and vitality of all in innovation and entrepreneurship. It features two radical movements: one, an entrepreneurship partner may earn from sharing right of management even though he/she has no equity therein; and two, an entrepreneurship partner with equity therein is not entitled to income from capital investment if making no contribution to appreciation. Data shows that Haier's entrepreneurship partners earning via share or equity distribution rose to 14,681 in 2021, and Haier saw an increase of 81% in the number of co-investors in startups and listed companies from a year earlier. Indeed, Haier did make valuable exploration in the journey of seeking common prosperity.

Scientific and technological self-reliance

Strength in open innovation system. Right now, Haier has pooled resources from over 20 states/regions across five continents and gathered over 200,000 experts for open innovation via "10 + N" innovation centers worldwide.

Strength in transformation from original technology to formation of industrial chain. In the recent decade, Haier originated around 170 original technologies making a great difference on the industry, all of which have been commercialized in the industry chain and brought users new experience.

Strength in integrative innovation of technology and business incubation. Haier's HCH entrepreneurial accelerator platform is a business incubator blended with scientific and technological innovation, arising out of which are 5 listed companies, 90 "gazelle" companies, and 38 "small giant" enterprises. In a word, it sets up a new pattern of integrative innovation that characterize "Technology promotes entrepreneurship, while entrepreneurship accelerates technology innovation".

☞ Memory Practice（记忆训练）

Paragraph 1

China has made considerable progress in terms of facilitating high-quality development in the Belt and Road Initiative (BRI) over the past decade, with over three-quarters of the countries and major international organizations joining the initiative, according to the country's top economic regulator.

The BRI has become a popular platform offering international public goods, playing a positive role in promoting health, green and digital construction of the Silk Road and fostering new growth points for the world economy.

The initiative has contributed to the prosperity of the world economy. For instance, China and countries involved in the BRI have built economic and trade cooperation zones, creating more than 400,000 jobs for local people. Under the framework of the BRI, China and countries involved in the BRI have built a wide range of infrastructure projects and projects key to local people's livelihood such as hospitals and schools, which not only promote economic growth and generate jobs but also improve the local people's livelihood.

(https://language.chinadaily.com.cn/a/202306/28/WS649bcf6aa310bf8a75d6c1b7.html)

Paragraph 2

海上丝绸之路，是古代中国与外国交通贸易和文化交往的海上通道，也称"海上陶瓷之路"和"海上香料之路"。海上丝路萌芽于商周，发展于春秋战国，形成于秦汉，兴于唐宋，转变于明清，是已知最为古老的海上航线。中国海上丝路分为东海航线和南海航线两条线路，其中主要以南海为中心。南海航线，又称南海丝绸之路，起点主要是广州和泉州。南海丝路从中国经中南半岛和南海诸国，穿过印度洋，进入红海，抵达东非和欧洲，途经100多个国家和地区，成为中国与外国贸易往来和文化交流的海上大通道，并推动了沿线各国的共同发展。

中国境内海上丝绸之路主要由广州、泉州、宁波三个主港和其他支线港组成。2017年04月20日，国家文物局正式确定广州为海上丝绸之路申遗牵头城市，联合南京、宁波、江门、阳江、北海、福州、漳州、莆田、丽水等城市进行海上丝绸之路保护和申遗工作。

(https://baike.baidu.com/item/海上丝绸之路/439948?fr=ge_ala)

Section 2　Interpreting Practice（口译实训）

Passage 1【参考译文】

民营企业新政策

专家和企业高管表示，中国促进民营企业发展的最新政策将会大大增强民营企业家的信心，充分发挥民营企业创造就业机会的重要作用，在经济下行压力较大的背景下推动经济复苏。

他们赞扬新近公布的鼓励民营投资和刺激民营经济的政策措施，并强调这些举措将会显著提振市场信心。他们指出，这些措施还能激励民营企业提高创新能力，实现关键技术的突破，从而推动产业升级。

民营企业是推进中国式现代化的重要力量，在稳经济、扩就业和推动技术创新方面发挥着重要作用。国家已经发出明确信号，将致力于推动民营企业的健康可持续发展。中国推出更有力的扶持政策是为了解决民营企业面临的突出问题，改善营商环境，对于民营企业增强信心、稳定预期十分关键，并将进一步巩固经济复苏趋势。

中共中央政治局于7月24日召开会议，部署下半年经济工作。会议强调"切实优化民营企业发展环境"。会议指出，应制定和推出更多刺激民营企业投资的政策，与此同时应建立健全与企业的常态化沟通交流机制。

此前，中共中央、国务院于7月19日发布了关于促进民营经济发展壮大的指导意见，提出了31条具体措施，包括完善融资支持政策制度、破除市场准入壁垒、落实公平竞争政策制度、支持平台企业发挥在扩大就业和刺激消费方面的作用。8月1日，国家发展改革委等多个部门发布了28条促进民营经济发展的举措，包括减税和优化涉企服务。

国家发展改革委指出，将鼓励民营企业参与具有一定收益水平、条件相对成熟的国家重大工程，支持民间投资项目参与基础设施领域不动产投资信托基金试点，支持民营企业参与重大科技攻关。

中国网络安全公司360集团的创始人周鸿祎表示，最近制定的政策肯定了民营企业在推动技术创新和稳定就业方面的重要作用，并将为民营经济的高质量发展带来新的历史机遇。

Passage 2 【参考译文】

Moutai-flavored Latte

In collaboration with Kweichow Moutai, domestic coffee chain Luckin Coffee introduced a Moutai-flavored latte on Monday, and it quickly became a hit. The latte, containing less than 0.5 percent alcohol by volume of 53 degrees Kweichow Moutai, soon became one of the most discussed topics on Chinese social media, with many people curious about the combination of the traditional Chinese white liquor (Baijiu), and coffee. Before midday, some Luckin branches in Beijing quickly sold out of their Moutai-flavored latte.

An employee surnamed Zhang, who works at a Luckin branch near Huixingdong Bridge in Beijing, said the special latte made up most of the orders at her shop on Monday morning. "It seems that people prefer iced latte, so we quickly used up the ice at the branch," She said.

People then started to share their reactions after trying the latte on social media. Most people agreed that the aroma of the Baijiu is very strong. And while some people said they can taste the flavor of the liquor but not the actual alcohol, others said that they clearly felt dizzy after drinking the coffee. Meanwhile, people also raised the question about if they are allowed to drive after drinking Moutai-flavored latte. Luckin stated that underage people, pregnant women, drivers and those who are allergic to alcohol are advised not to order the drink. An officer with the Beijing Traffic Administration Bureau also asked people not to drive no matter how much alcohol is actually in the latte.

Moutai has been looking for ways to be more accessible and pull in a new generation of users. By working with Luckin Coffee, Moutai has made its brand younger and has generated more opportunities to develop its extended product portfolio for younger consumers in the future. Moutai has been engaged in an array of marketing campaigns recently, including Moutai ice cream and other creative products.

Passage 3 【参考译文】

未来之路 捷足先登（节选）

作为英伦豪华汽车公司，捷豹路虎积极向科技公司转型，打造清洁、安全、智能的未来出行。在研发、创新、采购、人力资源等领域，其将继续深耕中国市场，从而推动全球汽车产业发展。

在全球汽车产业向自动化、互联化、电动化与共享化不断变革的今天，捷豹路虎紧握机遇，让创新发生在中国。

新款路虎揽胜运动版插电式混合动力车型 P400e 的推出以及即将进行亚洲首秀的捷豹首款豪华纯电轿跑 SUV I-PACE，不仅有力印证了捷豹路虎在新能源路径上的积极布局，更将引领电动豪华汽车新风尚。

与此同时，捷豹路虎坚持合作共赢、兼容并蓄的理念，将于捷豹路虎之夜活动当晚宣布构建面向未来出行的开放性战略举措，与本土创新企业携手推动新业态、新模式、新技术，实现共赢发展。

自 2010 年正式进入中国以来，捷豹路虎与本土伙伴精诚合作，加强品牌与产品优势，致力于实现在中国市场的长期、可持续发展。其深耕中国市场，创造了"三年五款车型"下线的国产化新速度，领先于其他合资企业，成为行业新标杆。

国产车型豪华轿跑 SUV 捷豹 E-PACE 主要面向年轻消费群体，是捷豹路虎长期以来重视中国消费者需求、扎根中国市场的重要历史见证。

捷豹路虎之夜不仅是在华首次企业战略、品牌魅力、产品布局的集中呈现，更将是捷豹路虎兼具独特的英伦传统与科技创新、全面战略布局的展现。广大中国消费者将借此一览捷豹路虎面向未来、捷足先登的宏伟蓝图。

Passage 4 【参考译文】

Online Strategy of Domestic Products

Traditional Chinese brands have recently made a strong comeback thanks to a livestreaming controversy over the quality of products and whether people were working hard enough to afford them. Chinese brands that have faded out in popularity due to a lack of marketing and online presence seized the opportunity to show they could deliver value-for-money quality goods.

Domestic brands were put under the spotlight after China's top online sales host Li Jiaqi questioned whether people had worked hard enough to get a pay rise, during a livestreaming session on Taobao Live, Alibaba's livestreaming platform, on September 9. A follower had earlier commented that a Chinese cosmetic brand's eyebrow pen and two refills priced at 79 yuan is too expensive.

Bee & Flower, a shampoo brand founded in 1985 and once a household name in China, introduced a 79-yuan set of two large bottles of shampoo and a large bottle of hair conditioner, which quickly attracted people's attention. According to the third-party platform sales data, the number of followers of Bee & Flower's account on Douyin, the Chinese version of TikTok, started to soar on September 11. On September 15, it had attracted a record—559,000 followers. Sales generated during one livestreaming session exceed 25 million yuan.

Other Chinese brands also started to promote themselves on social media and asked people to give them a chance to prove themselves. People showed particular interest in Super 28, a detergent brand founded in 1950. Three humble middle-aged factory employees of the company began a livestreaming on its official Douyin account on Wednesday. The trio wanted to seize the opportunity to revive the brand, but clearly knew little about selling products on social media. Netizens had to teach them how to list products during the livestreaming sessions. The next day, their sincerity and the quality of the company's products had helped the brand's Douyin account attract more than 1.618 million followers, with all available stock sold out on that day.

Many domestic brands have seen a surge in sales as many netizens said they were surprised to see that some of the brands and products that were popular during their childhood still existed, and the parent companies had donated money and goods to help China win the War of Resistance Against Japanese Aggression. Many of the brands, including Bee & Flower and Super 28, announced that they would not offer livestreams on the 92nd anniversary of the September 18 Incident that marked the start of Japan's invasion of China. They also asked people to remember history and cherish peace.

This time, many domestic products have finally embarked on the fast lane of internet marketing, and the goodwill and encouragement of the public have become the driving force for them to return to the consumer market. Everyone hopes that domestic products can become better and better, rather than a fleeting emotional frenzy.

Section 3　Interpreting Assessment（口译测评）

Passage 1 【原文】

China, US Commerce Authorities to Establish New Working Group

China and the United States will establish a new communication channel between their commerce authorities, according to a statement released by China's Ministry Commerce. During his meeting with US Commerce Secretary Gina Raimondo on Monday in Beijing, Chinese Commerce Minister Wang Wentao and his US counterpart agreed to form a working group. This group will comprise deputy ministerial and bureau-level government officials from both countries alongside business representatives, to seek solutions to specific commercial issues, said the statement.

The working group will hold deputy ministerial level meetings twice a year. Wang and Raimondo have agreed to maintain regular communication and to meet at least once annually. Both sides have initiated an export control information exchange mechanism, serving as a means to interpret their respective export control systems and enhance communication. They will exchange information related to export control in accordance with their respective laws.

The Chinese commerce minister emphasized his serious concerns regarding various issues, including the US Section 301 tariff measures on China, semiconductor policies, two-way investment restrictions, discriminatory subsidies and sanctions on Chinese companies during the meeting on Monday.

In addition to stressing that broadening the concept of national security is detrimental to normal economic and trade interactions, Wang highlighted that implementing unilateral and protectionist measures goes against market rules and the principles of fair competition, ultimately harming the security and stability of global industrial and supply chains. Despite multiple assurances from the US that they don't intend to decouple from China, Wang expressed the hope that concrete actions would align with these statements.

（https://language.chinadaily.com.cn/a/202308/29/WS64ed9dd7a31035260b81ed35.html）

Passage 1 【参考译文】

中美商务部宣布建立新工作组

据中国商务部消息，中美两国商务部之间将建立新的沟通渠道。中国商务部部长王文涛和美国商务部部长吉娜·雷蒙多周一在北京会晤时同意成立一个工作组。声明称，该工作组由中美副部长级和司局级的政府官员组成，并有企业代表参加，以寻求解决具体商业问题的办法。

工作组将每年举行两次副部级会议。两位部长同意经常性沟通，每年至少见一次。双方还启动了出口管制信息交流机制，作为解释各自出口管制制度和改善沟通的机制。双方将按照各自法律，就出口管制信息进行交流。

王文涛在周一的会议上重点就美国对华301关税、半导体政策、双向投资限制、歧视性补贴、制裁中国企业等表达严正关切。

王文涛表示，泛化国家安全不利于正常经贸往来，实施单边、保护主义措施不符合市场规则和公平竞争原则，只会损害全球产业链和供应链的安全稳定。王文涛表示，美方多次表示不寻求与中方脱钩，希望美方将表态落在实处。

Passage 2 【原文】

微观战略

女士们，先生们：

请你们看看投影仪上显示的趋势，我认为现在是我们公司实实在在地再次联系我们的消费者的时候了。

在我演示数据之前，我想请你们先看看自己手上的移动设备。移动应用软件正在取代传统软件。在我们的行业里将会出现一次巨大的变革，我们也正处于谋划战略的十字路口。你看到的这些数据都将用于战略性数据和战略研究。我们把它作为解决方案中的一部分，该方案就是进一步密切联系我们的消费者。

首先，我们怎样利用这些数据？我们要创造商业价值，我们要找到利用数据的方法，并把这些数据转变为对我们的商业伙伴有意义的东西。因此，我们已经把"微观战略"应用放在公司平台上，我们要在全球范围实施这个战略方针。我们将会提供的是有关全球消费者的做法和想法，同时我们还需要创造一种更加快捷的方法，可以将这些洞见传达给我们的商业伙伴。因此，我们正在利用越来越多的资源收集信息，同时看到我们对全球发生变化的反应能力也在不断增强。

其次，我们将利用可视化这一更为快捷灵活的手段，创造有利于我们业务活动的虚拟环境。我们将集中公司全部的、最好的统计师来统计我们的消费者的喜好，并想出推销公司产品的最有效的一些办法。有了这些，我确信我们很快能知道我们和竞争者相比的优势。

最后但同样重要的是，我们如何对传统的财务报告进行革新，使其能帮助我们预测市场即将发生的变化，洞察消费者的喜好，并为我们提供能有效影响消费者购买决策的策略。请让我最后一次表明我的观点。我们把"微观战略"作为我们企业战略的开拓性策略和了解每一位消费者的基础。所谓消费者不是一个集合概念，我们不关注集合概念，相反，我们要观察每一个消费者，并且保证他们都能从我们的公司获得非凡的品牌体验。

谢谢大家，祝各位晚安！

Passage 2【参考译文】

Micro Strategy

Ladies and gentlemen,

When you look at the trend shown here on the projector, I think it is high time for us as a company to reconnect with our consumers.

Before I start showing statistics, I would like to ask you to take a minute and look at your own mobile devices. Mobile apps are taking over the position of traditional software. A tremendous change is going to happen in our business, and we are now standing at the crossroad. We must rethink our strategic planning. All these statistics you are witnessing are then used for strategic data and insights. We see that as part of the solution to get closer to our consumers.

First of all, what do we do with all these data? We want to create a business value by turning the data into something meaningful for our business partners. Therefore, we have put the use of "Micro Strategy" on top of the platform, as a strategic guideline which we will deploy worldwide. We are going to provide information about what our consumers do and think out there in the real world. And we also need to create a way of delivering those insights to our business partners. So that is why we are utilizing more and more resources to collect and gather information, and are becoming more and more capable of reacting to the changes we see taking place around the globe.

Second, we will use visualization to be more agile in creating virtual conditions that are favorable to our business campaigns. We will gather together all the best statisticians inside our corporation to calculate our consumers' interests and figure out the most effective ways to push our products. With this, I am confident that we will soon have an edge over our competitors.

Last but not least, the most important thing is how you transition from the traditional financial reporting into something which helps you to predict what is about to happen in the market place, what the consumer will like, and helps you to more precisely target consumers with regard to their purchase decisions. Let me make myself clear for one last time. We are using the "Micro Strategy" as an innovative approach to our corporate strategy and as the foundation for understanding each and every one of our consumers. We are not talking about aggregates. We will not look at aggregates; rather, we will look at a single consumer, and make sure he or she gets a great brand experience with our corporation.

Thank you, and have a good night!

Unit 8　Business Conference（商务会议）

Section 1　Interpreting Preparation（口译准备）

Sight Interpreting（视译）

Passage 1【参考译文】

欧亚经济论坛强调合作与发展

以"创合作机遇，谋未来发展"为主题的2023年欧亚经济论坛于周五在中国西北部陕西省省会西安开幕。

来自51个国家和地区的政界、商界人士和学者参加了为期3天的论坛。今年的论坛有13场平行会议，主题包括政策协调、金融合作、经贸交流、科技创新、生态保护和文化旅游发展。

论坛期间还举办了经贸博览会。博览会由5个展区组成，包括国际进口展区和中亚五国主题展区。

欧亚经济论坛是上海合作组织框架下的重要经济合作机制，自2005年创办以来每两年举办一次。

Passage 2【参考译文】

Ways to Find Business Partners

It goes without saying that in the business world, no clients, no business. Therefore, finding potential clients to establish business relations is a key step for any company. There are many ways to find potential clients. The most common methods include using the Internet, Chambers of Commerce reports, trade publications, market surveys, and networking forums; joining professional and trade organizations; using industry know-how for B2B leads; promoting your company at trade shows; and generating leads through local advertising. Among these, going online is the most convenient way to identify and reach potential clients.

The best way to get potential clients, however, is to ask your current clients for referrals because your current clients know your company and they probably know others who may be interested in the products or services you offer. Communicate with them regularly to learn about their social networks for possibilities of future referrals. Or send emails or make phone calls to your contacts to let them know that you are taking on additional clients and ask if they know someone who they could refer to you. In forming business relationships, getting your potential clients is the hardest part, but once that is settled, more companies usually roll in by means of current clients' recommendations.

Memory Practice（记忆训练）

Paragraph 1

Investment deals worth 84.48 billion yuan were reached during the 14th China-Northeast Asia Expo, which concluded Sunday in Changchun, capital of northeast China's Jilin Province. A total of 99 projects were signed during the five-day expo, setting a new record in terms of project investment scale. Themed "Joint Development of Northeast Asia in Cooperation for the Future", the expo saw the offline participation of over 20,000 merchants from 123 countries and regions.

(https://english.news.cn/20230827/b844534256634f6396af1f36136ebaf7/c.html)

Paragraph 2

第7届中国—南亚博览会将于8月16—20日在云南昆明举办。该博览会已成为中国同南亚国家经贸交流的重要平台。本届博览会主题是"团结协作，共谋发展"，由商务部和云南省人民政府共同举办，是今年中国同南亚国家重要的经贸交流活动之一。这也是自新冠疫情发生以来南博会首次全面恢复线下举行。本届南博会共设置15个展馆，展览面积达15万平方米，线上同步展示展馆内容。展馆包括南亚馆、东南亚馆、境外馆、生物医药和大健康馆、文化旅游馆、高原特色现代农业馆、数字经济馆等，规模和上届相比有所扩大。

(https://www.news.cn/2023-07/25/c_1129768048.htm)

Section 2 Interpreting Practice（口译实训）

Dialogue 1【参考译文】

Selecting Suppliers

A: Our company is expanding rapidly in recent years. However, we have trouble finding more qualified suppliers of auto parts. Do you have some ideas to share with me?

B: 一般来说，人们会通过各种渠道找到供应商。最好通过整合多种资源建立一个可能的供应商候选名单，以便有更广泛的选择基础。

A: We used to ask friends or business partners for recommendation. Since they have used the services of some suppliers, they are more likely to have an honest assessment of the strengths and weaknesses for those suppliers.

B: 你们尝试使用过目录或指南吗？如果你们在当地寻找供应商，可以尝试如黄页之类的目录。

A: In fact, most of our suppliers are located worldwide, so local directories don't work for us.

B: 我明白了。那你们是贸易协会的会员吗？同行业的公司通常会注册为该组织的会员，那里有很多资源。

A: That's true. But the problem is that they are looking for the same or similar suppliers.

B: 那真是可惜。你们有没有商业顾问？我是说那些可以指引你找到潜在供应商的商业支持组织，比如商会。

A: We don't have such advisers yet, but we may try the Chamber of Commerce as you mentioned. Do you have other suggestions?

B: 如今，越来越多的展览在不同国家举办。展览提供了一个在同一地点同时与多个潜在供应商交谈的绝佳机会。

A: Yes, exhibition is an important channel for us to find potential suppliers. And mostly we will first check online whether the exhibitors are relevant and suitable for our business before deciding to participate or not.

B: 还有一个渠道是行业媒体，比如刊登有潜在供应商广告的杂志。

A: We haven't tried magazines yet, for few people have time to sit down and do some reading. They'd rather go to the Internet to search for relevant information.

B: 那么你们可以在互联网上加入汽车制造商和经销商。他们已经建立了最大、最全面的商业汽车零部件数据库。数据库每周都在增长，目前已经包括了1100多个目录和4200万条商业记录。

A: That sounds amazing! Thank you for your information.

Dialogue 2 【参考译文】

控制生产

A: 我叫你来是因为我最近听到了太多的客户投诉，甚至包括我们一些最忠实的客户。你对此了解多少？

B: We've had a lot of problems with wool carpets from a new manufacturer. We've handled it according to the store policy of giving a refund or an exchange. Feedback from our staff indicates that some customers think quality control of our product is lax.

A: 从他们的角度来看，他们是对的！当然，这不是我们的错，但我们对此做了什么？这个问题有后续跟进吗？

B: We've contacted the staff of our Purchasing Department, and they're dealing with the manufacturer right now.

A: 这还不够！如果我们收到了那么多投诉，就应该下架这些产品，直到生产商解决问题。

B: Alright. I'll talk to the department manager about it. It shouldn't be a problem, but it'll probably take them a day or two to restock the empty space.

A: 请记住，任何时候，任何不满意的客户都可以通过社交媒体和网络向大众分享他们的看法，从而给我们的业务带来负面影响。因此，为我们的客户创造优质的体验对于帮助发展我们公司与他们之间的关系非常重要。

B: I see. We will work out some ways and do everything we can to make sure our customers have a positive experience and feel satisfied.

A: 那就好。让我们积极主动地面对购买了这些产品的客户，给他们赠送下次购物的折扣券。另外，与其他最近的客户保持联系，以确保他们对我们的客户政策感到满意。

B: I'll get on right away.

A: 好的，谢谢你。

Dialogue 3 【参考译文】

年度运营会议

A: 我们在2022年提高了业务效率，这得益于新的服务和收入项目。我们已经为可持续增长做好了准备。

B: Yeah, I saw this report that aggregate time spent on WeChat continued to increase. Time spent on mini programs and video accounts doubled and tripled year on-year respectively.

C: 小程序已经成为中国领先的交易平台，为实体经济的发展作出了贡献。

A: 能否介绍一下视频号业绩的表现数据？

B: 190 million users watched Spring Festival Gala of 2023 via live streaming on video accounts.

A: 数字内容的业绩如何呢？

C: 我们的收费增值服务订阅用户数减至2.34亿，同比减少了1%，但由于我们调整了定价，视频订阅的收入增加了。

B: For music, we offered attractive membership privileges and enhanced user engagement in various music genres, driving growth in paying users and ARPU.

A: 今年我们开展了未成年人保护计划，对国内游戏有影响吗？

B: Minor time spent was greatly reduced. However, we have sustained our market leadership, resuming year-on-year growth in DAU in the fourth quarter of 2022.

C: 是的，在2023年春节假期的总收入创下了新高。

A: 在云服务和其他商业服务方面有什么进展吗？

B: We further reduced loss-making activities and optimized costs, while focusing on self-developed solutions with healthier profit margin.

A: 我很高兴听到这个消息。我们先休息5分钟。稍后，我们将继续讨论其他部门的业务。

Passage【参考译文】

How to Assess Employee Performance

Most companies have a formal performance appraisal system in which employee job performance is rated on a regular basis, usually once a year. A good performance appraisal system can greatly benefit a company. It helps direct employees behavior toward organizational goals by letting employees know what is expected of them, and it yields information for making employment decisions, such as those regarding pay raises, promotions, and discharges. To assess employee performance, the following steps are to be followed.

First, consult the employees' official job description. Align the organizational goals with the job's objective. Note any discrepancies and find ways to bring the discrepancies back in line.

Second, communicate the management's expectations to the employees. A common understanding must exist between the management and the employees regarding the work expectations, the nature of work to be accomplished and the standards by which the work is evaluated.

Third, offer the employees feedback concerning their performance and its relationship to the expectations set forth by the management. Be constructive instead of destructive with comments while being honest about your appraisal.

The fourth step is to train the employees. Provide the required resources for them to meet and exceed the management's expectations. Constant and consistent efforts should be made by the management in coaching employees in order to modify performance before it is too late.

The fifth step is to assess the employees' strengths and weaknesses. It is done by using a narrative form, a checklist, peer and self-evaluations. The employees need to understand how the company has come to the conclusions, so that they are able to correct any problems. Only in this way can the employees give full play to their strengths and overcome their weaknesses.

Section 3　Interpreting Assessment（口译测评）

Passage 1【原文】

The "5G Business Success" Summit

On February 27, 2023, the "5G Commercial Success" Summit was held. Peng Song, the president of Huawei ICT Strategy and Marketing, delivered a keynote speech on "Multidimensional Value Realization, Accelerating 5G Commercial Success", pointing out that the current three-year development outcome of 5G is equivalent to five-year development of 4G, and the first wave of operators have already achieved commercial success and generated "certainty effects". We can continue to realize value from multiple dimensions such as ToC/ToH/ToB to make 5G business more successful.

Peng Song pointed out that on the aspect of the global user penetration rate, three-year development of 5G is comparable to five-year development of 4G, and that operators with more than 20% 5G user penetration in the first wave have generally achieved remarkable mobile business revenue growth. At the same time, as terminals, content, experiences and business models continue to be enriched, more operators and partners are being attracted to join the wave of booming 5G, which indicates that the market is shifting from risk-based to revenue-based decision making, and that 5G commercial success is accelerating towards certainty. Huawei believes that rapid 5G users and network traffic migration are the basis for commercial success, and achieving a 30% share of 5G eMBB (enhanced mobile broadband) network traffic obtained in three years can ensure ROI less than four years. If FWA (fixed wireless access) and ToB services are deployed simultaneously, it will further shorten the time of ROI.

By the end of 2022, 5G users had exceeded 1 billion; ARPU of global top 20 operators have a growth of 10%, compared to 1% growth of the global baseline. Finally, Peng Song said that 5G not only brings economic value to operators, but also contains huge social value behind it. Facing to the future, Huawei appeals to global operators and industry partners by working together to lead the future with the GUIDE business blueprint persistently and further stimulate the potential of 5G networks.

（https://www.huawei.com/cn/news/2023/2/mwc2023%205g%20business%20success）

Passage 1【参考译文】

"5G 商业成功"峰会

"5G 商业成功"峰会于2023年2月27日举办。华为ICT战略与营销总裁彭松发表"多维价值变现，加速5G商业成功"主题发言，指出当前5G发展三年的成果等于4G发展五年，第一波运营商已经取得了商业成功，并且产生"确定性效应"。面向未来，可以持续从ToC/ToH/ToB（这里分别指：面向个人/家庭/企业用户的技术）多维度进行价值变现，让5G商业更成功。

彭松指出，5G发展三年的全球用户渗透率和4G发展五年的水平相当，而且第一波5G用户渗透率超过20%的运营商普遍取得了显著的移动业务收入增长。同时，随着终端、内容、体验和商业模式的不断丰富，更多的运营商和合作伙伴加入繁荣5G的浪潮中，由此说明市场正在由基于风险决策转向基于收益决策，5G商业成功加速走向确定性。华为认为，5G用户的快速增长和流量迁移是商业成功的基础，三年实现5G eMBB流量占比达到30%，可以在四年内取得投资回报，如果同步部署FWA宽带接入和面向企业用户的ToB业务，则将会进一步缩短投资回报周期。

截至2022年年底，5G用户已超过10亿；全球top 20运营商的平均每户收入增长10%，相比全球基线增长1%。最后，彭松表示5G不仅为运营商带来了经济价值，其背后还蕴含着巨大社会价值。面向未来，华为呼吁全球运营商、产业伙伴一起，持续用GUIDE商业蓝图引领未来，进一步激发5G网络潜能。

Passage 2【原文】

李强在博鳌亚洲论坛2023年年会开幕式上的主旨演讲（节选）

各位来宾，

女士们，先生们，朋友们：

很高兴和大家相聚在美丽的海南岛，共同出席博鳌亚洲论坛2023年年会。首先，我谨代表中国政府，对年会的召开表示热烈祝贺！对各位嘉宾的到来表示诚挚欢迎！对大家长期以来给予中国发展的关心支持表示衷心感谢！

这次年会以"不确定的世界：团结合作迎挑战，开放包容促发展"为主题，契合当前形势和各方关切,具有很强的现实意义。当今世界,变乱交织,人类社会面临前所未有的挑战,不稳定、不确定、难预料成为常态。在这个充满不确定性的大变局中,人们迫切希望能有更多更强大的确定性力量,来推动世界朝着美好的未来前进。

10年前,习近平主席首次提出人类命运共同体的重要理念,此后又在包括博鳌亚洲论坛在内的诸多国际场合,深刻阐明了构建人类命运共同体的中国主张,进一步提出全球发展倡议、全球安全倡议、全球文明倡议,为全球发展与治理提供了中国方案。10年来,中国以务实行动推动构建人类命运共同体,取得一系列重大实践成果。特别是高质量共建"一带一路",带动广大发展中国家加快发展,为世界经济拓展了新空间。同时,在倡导政治解决危机,解决国际热点问题,劝和促谈、化干戈为玉帛等方面,也作出了卓有成效的努力,展现了负责任的大国担当。这些都是人类命运共同体理念的生动实践。事实证明,人类命运共同体理念,已经成为引领时代潮流和人类进步的旗帜,成为推动世界持久和平、共同繁荣确定性力量的源泉。

现在,亚洲和世界都处在历史演变的十字路口。我们要高举人类命运共同体理念的旗帜,携手构建亚洲命运共同体,打造世界的和平稳定锚、增长动力源、合作新高地,为世界和平与发展注入更多确定性,努力创造人类更加美好的未来。

(http://www.catl.org.cn/2023-04/12/content_85225119.html)

Passage 2 【参考译文】

Keynote Speech by H. E. Li Qiang Premier of the State Council of the People's Republic of China at the Opening Plenary of the Boao Forum for Asia Annual Conference 2023 (Excerpt)

Distinguished Guests,

Ladies and Gentlemen,

Friends,

It gives me great pleasure to join you in the beautiful Hainan island for the Boao Forum for Asia Annual Conference 2023. Let me begin by extending, on behalf of the Chinese government, warm congratulations on the opening of the Annual Conference, a hearty welcome to all participating guests, and sincere appreciation to you all for your longstanding care and support for China's development.

The theme of this year's Annual Conference, "An Uncertain World: Solidarity and Cooperation for Development amid Challenges", is highly relevant to our times and responsive to our shared concerns. In a world of turmoil and transformation, humanity is faced with unprecedented challenges. Instability, uncertainty and unexpected developments have become the norm. Amid the momentous shifts where uncertainty abounds, people yearn for more and stronger forces of certainty to drive the world to a brighter future.

Ten years ago, President Xi Jinping put forward the vision of building a community with a shared future for mankind. Later, he expounded China's proposition on this vision at this Forum and on many other international occasions, and went on to propose the Global Development Initiative (GDI), the Global Security Initiative (GSI) and the Global Civilization Initiative (GCI). These initiatives are China's proposals for global development and governance. Over the past ten years, China has taken concrete actions to advance the building of a community with a shared future for mankind, and achieved a series of major outcomes. The high-quality Belt and Road cooperation, in particular, has helped developing countries achieve faster development and opened up new space for the growth of the world economy. Meanwhile, China has made productive efforts as a major responsible country to champion political settlement of crises, resolve international hot-spot issues, facilitate peace talks and de-escalate tensions. These are the real steps that China has taken to build a community with a shared future for mankind. What has happened shows that the vision of a community with a shared future for mankind has become a banner that guides the trend of the times and human progress, and a source of certainty for lasting peace and shared prosperity in the world.

Asia and the entire world are at a crossroads of history. We must hold high the banner of the vision of a community with a shared future for mankind, and join hands to foster an Asian community with a shared future. We need to work together to build an anchor for world peace, a source of impetus for global growth, and a new pacesetter for international cooperation, to add certainty to world peace and development and shape a better future for humanity.

Unit 9　Marketing and Promotion（市场营销）

Section 1　Interpreting Preparation（口译准备）

Sight Interpreting（视译）

Passage 1【参考译文】

PEST 分析新能源行业

尊敬的各位领导和同事们，

上午好！今天，我们齐聚一堂，共同探讨未来三年的营销战略，在此，我想从政治、经济、社会和技术的角度，先谈谈新能源产业面临的宏观环境。

近年来，中国出台了有利于新能源企业的优惠政策。例如，中国政府的补贴政策鼓励车主选择不同价格和类型的汽车。此外，新能源汽车免征车辆购置税和新能源双倍积分政策也表达了中国大力发展新能源产业的决心。然而，随着新能源产业的日益普及，中国也开始对工业污染水平、生产安全要求和员工权益保护等方面的法规进行调整。

2021年上半年，中国国内生产总值（GDP）达到5321.67亿元，同比增长12.7%，总体呈现平稳增长态势。从中国GDP的年产值和增幅值可以看出，中国经济运行良好。此外，作为最大的发展中国家，国民生活水平日益提高，可支配收入大幅增加。这使得越来越多的人寻求更高的经济消费，汽车消费便是其中之一。这种良好的发展态势为汽车企业的发展带来了良好的经济环境。值得注意的是，截至2021年6月底，中国新能源汽车保有量为603万辆，约占全球新能源汽车保有量的50%。这一数值充分显示了中国新能源产业的火热程度。

自然环境污染日益严重。作为世界上最大的汽车产销国，汽车尾气排放造成的空气污染已广为人知。在此背景下，中国开始通过减少有害气体排放，并呼吁公众选择对环境破坏最小的出行方式来解决环境污染问题。与普通燃油汽车相比，新能源汽车所需的能源更少，既能优化环境，又能节约能源，因此逐渐成为中国民众出行的首选。

作为较早进入中国新能源市场的企业，本土企业如比亚迪通过自身的不断创新，已经慢慢掌握了电动汽车的多项核心技术，例如比亚迪自主研发的纯电动实时四驱技术是在电动汽车动力方面的制胜法宝。一些拥有完整IGBT（绝缘栅双极晶体管）产业链并实现量产的中国汽车制造商，在这一领域已经研发了十多年，有着丰富的经验和技术积累，关键指标达到了世界领先水平。这种强大的技术研发能力已成为企业持续发展的动力和基础。

Passage 2 【参考译文】

SWOT Analysis

Next I am going to talk about SHEIN based on SWOT analysis model in details to see its strengths and weaknesses, identifying its opportunities and threats faced.

1. Strengths

A massive collection of products. No matter what the consumers want to buy, they will prefer choices because that gives them mental satisfaction.

Competitive prices. Competition is a big part of the whole business industry, and the main factor that drives this competition is the product prices. Maintaining a competitive price for the products sold is one of the significant strengths on the company's part.

Personalized mobile app. Personalized mobile app in this generation is a big plus point. An app that only shows products and with a user-friendly interface can make customers prone to buy goods from there. In addition to that, personalized apps somehow depict the company's stability.

2. Weaknesses

Time-consuming delivery. Sometimes, customers order goods they need with an immediate delivery facility, and taking more than the desired time to deliver products can be a massive setback for the company.

Unavailability of warehouses. The SHEIN supply chain lacking a warehouse can be a severe weakness for the organization. The availability of proper warehouses makes the entire delivery process fast and reliable because the information is available for customers at every step.

Vague origin history. Sometimes, this can be a severe drawback for a business, especially when customers need continuous assurances about their products.

3. Opportunities

Rise of the fashion industry. The new trend is to buy every fashionable product, whether clothes or jewelry, or some other online products. So, when this is the trend, the sites providing good services stand at a high level of popularity too. Everything depends on marketing and consumer satisfaction. Thus, SHEIN can grab this opportunity and expand its business in the market.

Virtual ambassadors. SHEIN depends a whole lot on its virtual marketing. They collaborate with well-known social influencers who can increase the demand of consumers for certain products and thus bring good deals for the company. So, SHEIN needs to choose right persons to be spokespersons of the whole business.

Social networks. Marketing through different social networks helps reach a maximum number of consumers from various parts of the world. The social network provides access to the most remote areas. Thus, social media marketing can be a crucial SHEIN marketing strategy, providing an opportunity for the company to grow and sustain itself in this competitive market.

4. Threats

The mishandled data. Data breach is a recurring issue. Moreover, it is a very concerning problem. SHEIN's whole business is based on a computer. Hence, it could be a considerable threat to the company.

The shift in consumer taste. It is impossible to predict what customers want at specific periods. So, businesses like these always need to be on their toes and ready for product renewal at any time.

Fierce competitions. The competition has also exacerbated with the increase in the popularity of e-commerce. So, to stand out among so many businesses can be difficult.

Memory Practice（记忆训练）

Paragraph 1

The internet is one of humanity's great achievements. Although it facilitates economic and social development, at the same time it poses severe challenges in terms of administration and governance. The development and governance of the internet is a goal shared by all countries for the benefit of humanity, and the rule of law has proved to be essential to internet governance. It has become a global consensus to apply law-based thinking and approaches based on an understanding of the rule of law.

（https://www.chinadaily.com.cn/a/202303/17/WS6413a396a31057c47ebb4f0f.html）

Paragraph 2

2023年7月，国务院办公厅转发《关于恢复和扩大消费的措施》（以下简称《措施》）的通知。《措施》坚持有效市场和有为政府更好结合，坚持优化供给和扩大需求更好结合，坚持提质升级和创新发展更好结合。《措施》共提出6个方面、20条政策举措，希望通过优化政策和制度设计，进一步满足居民消费需求、释放消费潜力。6个方面分别为稳定大宗消费、扩大服务消费、促进农村消费、拓展新型消费、完善消费设施、优化消费环境。

（https://www.gov.cn/gongbao/2023/issue_10646/202308/content_6898891.html）

Section 2　Interpreting Practice（口译实训）

Dialogue【参考译文】

讨论格力的产品策略

A: Do you know that Gree has grown into the world's largest air conditioning company?

B: 真的吗？格力是怎么做到的？

A: Well, when Gree was established in 1991, it's just a small factory, producing less than 20,000 sets of window air conditioners annually.

B: 这是一个不起眼的开始。格力是如何迅速发展壮大的？

A: Gree captured market opportunities with a series of marketable products and started to build its brand image, which laid a good foundation for future development.

B: 后来呢？

A: From 1994 to 1996, Gree focused on improving product quality by implementing a "Making Superior Product Strategy" and establishing a quality management system. Gree also launched the "12 Injunctions by President" and promoted the "Zero Defection Project" to raise product quality.

B: 这听起来像是对质量的坚定承诺。

A: Yes, and since then, Gree has emphasized product quality in all aspects of R&D, production, and transportation. The superior air conditioners of Gree have also brought good opportunities for sales.

B: 在短短的20多年时间里，格力的发展速度令人惊叹。

Passage 1【参考译文】

How to Formulate a Marketing Strategy?

We sincerely welcome that all of you squeeze some time to participate in today's training program. In previous courses, we emphasized importance of marketing strategy, next we'll elaborate on how to formulate a successful marketing strategy in five steps.

1. Have your market research data ready

It's crucial to build your marketing strategy on data, not assumptions. You're probably not developing and launching a product into the marketplace without market research—or at least you shouldn't be. Market research is an essential part of marketing and a topic on its own. Remember that even a cheap, quick, and imperfect market research is better than no research at all.

2. Decide target market

The second step is to decide which segments of the market you'll go after. Or perhaps which segments you'll ignore as deciding what not to do is often a more important choice. Target segment market refers to a specific market segment you decide to go after. Target consumer defines everyone who resonates with your marketing communications regardless of whether they buy the products or not.

3. Appeal to your target market with proper positioning

Positioning is how your target market should perceive your brand. It's the intended brand image that consists of associations people have with your brand and products. Positioning allows you to differentiate from your competitors. The power of positioning lies in consistently conveying some associations throughout all of your marketing channels. If you fail to do this, the market will do the positioning job for you. That will seldom align with your desired brand image.

4. Choose a few brand codes to become distinctive

A brand code, known as a sort of distinctive asset, is anything that you use consistently in your communications. You can think about it as your sidekick of positioning. The most common brand code is your logo and visual style. But that's about it for most brands. It's not enough to stand out and be distinctive in the mind of your target consumer. Your ultimate goal should be that your target consumer recognizes your brand even without showing any logos.

5. Set strategic objectives for the year ahead

You need clearly defined marketing objectives to guide your marketing efforts and provide benchmarks for evaluation. That's the strategic work you have to do now. Your marketing objectives should align with the widely-used SMART criteria: specific, measurable, achievable, relevant, timely.

Do you have any questions about this part? If no, we'll move to team discussion.

Passage 2【参考译文】

广告策略

广告策略是企业制定的广告计划，旨在提高客户对产品或服务的认识，并促使他们购买。广告策略包括两个组成部分：信息和说服。信息部分包括告知客户产品的特点和优点、价格变化，这对于建立基本需求至关重要。广告策略中的说服对于建立品牌偏好或改变购买者感知非常重要，在竞争激烈的市场中尤为如此。

在任何广告活动中，首先要让客户了解产品，然后引起目标受众的兴趣，使他们购买产品。有效的广告策略需要考虑目标群体的特点、对环境的了解、市场定义以及对产品的有效评估等因素。在制定广告策略时，传播媒介至关重要。在对受众进行细分并锁定目标后，就要对媒体渠道进行适当评估。

企业实施广告策略的主要渠道包括视频（电视）、音频（广播）、印刷媒体（报纸、杂志、传单）、互联网（社交媒体、邮件）和户外广告。广告策略是企业采用的重要营销策略。

Passage 3 【参考译文】

Pricing Strategies (Excerpt)

Starting from 14:00 on January 17, 2023, XPENG Motors launched pricing system of the Chinese New Year for G3i/P5/P7. At the same time, XPENG Motors also said that for the first batch of owners who ordered above series within one year prior to the announcement, the whole vehicle warranty is extended to 10 years or 200,000 kilometers and 4 years of basic maintenance is given. In the new price system, the G3i/P5/P7 of XPENG Motors are at price of 148,900 yuan, 156,900 yuan and 209,900 yuan respectively.

Previously, Tesla announced a price cut for both Model 3 and Model Y, with a maximum reduction of 48,000 yuan. The starting price of Model 3 was reduced to 229,900 yuan with a price cut of 36,000 yuan. The starting price of Model Y was reduced to 259,900 yuan with a decrease of 29,000 yuan. However, for Tesla's sudden big price cut, many previous car owners who just picked up their cars are deeply dissatisfied. "Compared to no response from Tesla, XPENG Motors has given welfare feedback to nearly one-year users", "Old users felt the warmth, at least a little compensation", netizens said in the comment area where XPENG Motors officially announced the new price system.

The cumulative delivery of XPENG Motors is 120,757 units in 2022. The three models of G3i/P5/P7, which started the new price system, have more than 100,000 deliveries this year. The industry believes that the new pricing of XPENG Motors is a normal price adjustment, in line with its price strategy. XPENG Motors hopes that through this round of price adjustment, striving for leading technology at the same time, pursuing scale economy, as well as accelerating popularity of intelligence. In the future, XPENG Motors will focus on the company's strategic product planning as well as research and development, being orientated to user demand, with a view of acquiring more long-term, global-scale customers.

Section 3　Interpreting Assessment（口译测评）

Passage 1 【原文】

Market Performance of China's Foldable Smartphone

The foldable smartphone market has seen remarkable growth in China, with shipments jumping 173 percent year on year to reach 1.26 million units in the second quarter of 2023, according to an industry report.

In the first half of the year, the country shipped 2.27 million foldable phones, marking a 102-percent surge from the same period last year, said the global market research firm International Data Corporation (IDC).

Huawei has maintained its top position in the domestic foldable smartphone market with a market share of 43 percent in the second quarter of the year, while vivo climbed to second place, occupying a market share of 19.7 percent. OPPO secured a market share of 15.9 percent, ranking third in the second quarter, data from the IDC shows.

Since the introduction of foldable phones, the niche market has maintained rapid growth and is currently the only segment that continues to show an upward trend within the smartphone market as a whole, said the IDC.

With the gradual improvement of hinge and screen-related technologies, and the continued decrease in product prices, consumers are becoming increasingly receptive to foldable smartphones, IDC added.

(http://en.people.cn/n3/2023/0821/c90000-20061005.html)

Passage 1 【参考译文】

中国可折叠智能手机的市场表现

据一份行业报告称,可折叠智能手机市场在中国取得了显著增长,出货量同比猛增173%,2023年第二季度达到126万部。

全球市场研究公司国际数据公司(IDC)表示,今年上半年,中国的可折叠手机出货量达到227万部,比上一年同期激增102%。

今年第二季度,华为继续保持国内可折叠智能手机市场第一的位置,市场份额为43%,而vivo则攀升至第二位,市场份额为19.7%。IDC的数据显示,OPPO市场份额为15.9%,在第二季度排名第三。

IDC表示,自可折叠手机问世以来,该细分市场一直保持快速增长,是目前整个智能手机市场中唯一持续呈上升趋势的细分市场。

IDC补充说,随着铰链和屏幕相关技术的逐步完善,以及产品价格的持续下降,消费者对可折叠智能手机的接受度越来越高。

Passage 2 【原文】

提升客户满意度

亲爱的同事们:

很荣幸今天给大家分享如何提升客户满意度。

当客户为产品或服务付费时,我们假定产品能正常工作,或者收到的服务如同承诺的那样。理想情况下,客户会感到满意,不会有投诉。

如果出现问题并且客户对此提出投诉,我们应迅速回应并解决客户的问题。这通常是通过公司的客户服务活动来完成的。但同时,我们需要跟进并改进业务流程以纠正问题。

我们需要立即回应投诉并解决问题。这可能是退款、更换产品或进行某些维修。

为确保客户完全满意,一些公司将提供特殊服务或在其他产品上提供降价。这样做是为了确保客户会回头继续购买。

解决任何问题并努力确保它们不再发生符合公司的最佳利益。对于公司而言,不利用客户投诉来采取纠正措施是愚蠢的。

迅速且正确地解决客户投诉可以帮助业务发展和繁荣。忽略投诉或用不诚实的方式处理投诉可能导致业务损失甚至诉讼。

我的分享到此结束,谢谢大家聆听!

Passage 2 【参考译文】

Improving Customer Satisfaction

Dear colleagues,

I'm very pleased to share with you about how to improve customer satisfaction today.

When the customer pays for a product or service, we assume that the product will work correctly or that the service received is as promised. Ideally, the customer will be satisfied, and there will be no complaints.

If there is a problem and the customer complains about it, we should quickly answer the complaint and solve the customer's problem. This is often done through the company's customer service activity. But also, we need to follow up and improve business processes to rectify the problems.

We need to immediately answer the complaint and solve the problem. It may be to give money back, exchange a product or do some repair.

To make sure the customer is completely satisfied, some companies will provide some special service or a reduced price on another product. This is done to assure the customer will come back for more business.

It is in the company's best interest to solve any problems and try to make sure that they don't happen again. It is foolish for a company not to use customer complaints to initiate a corrective action.

Quickly and properly solving customer complaints can help businesses grow and prosper. Ignoring complaints or dealing with them in a dishonest manner can result in loss of business or even lawsuits.

That's what I want to share today, thank you for listening!

Unit 10　Business Negotiation（商务洽谈）

Section 1　Interpreting Preparation（口译准备）

Sight Interpreting（视译）

Passage 1 【参考译文】

保持业务关系

保持各种类型的关系都很重要，但保持业务关系可能对财务影响最大，因为这些关系往往等同于财务收益。据估计，保持一个现有客户的成本仅为获取一个新客户的成本的十分之一。因此，培养稳固的业务关系是一种经济有效的经营方式。以下是一些可以帮助你做到这一点的技巧。

尽早奠定基础。尽早确定潜在客户或合作伙伴。表达你的兴趣，与潜在客户会面，了解他们的目标和目的。这样，如果该公司进入你的市场，你就会成为他们的首选。为什么？因为你已经与他们建立了联系并建立了业务关系。人们喜欢与熟人合作。

记笔记。你可能已经有了记下业务联系人联系方式的方法，但你应该记下的不仅仅是这些重要的如何取得联系的信息。最好还能记下对方的兴趣爱好或你与他的关系。

保持联系。避免几个月甚至几年才联系一次。虽然你不想为了聊天而打不必要的电话占用熟人的时间，但快速打电话跟进你上一个一起完成的业务是明智之举。

迅速回应请求。将沟通作为重中之重。如果那些与你有业务关系的人在试图与你联系时感到一直在等待，他们很可能会感到沮丧。如果可能的话，尽量制定当天联系当天回复的策略，并承诺在回复完电话或电子邮件之前不离开办公室，以确保这次沟通不会不了了之。

始终保持亲切。虽然业务联系人和朋友是有区别的，但你应始终以友好的方式对待这些人。这样做可以建立一种对你业务有利的关系。为确保友好关系持续，请避免在生气或不高兴时联系业务联系人。

Passage 2 【参考译文】

Dealing with Customer Claims

In international trade, if one party fails to perform according to the contract and brings loss to another party, the latter may ask the former for compensation. This must be done within a specific time limit and based on the contract stipulation. Depending on the cause of the loss, different parties will be responsible for the claim lodged. If the seller breaches the contract, the buyer should make a claim against the seller according to the contract stipulation. If the buyer breaches the contract, the buyer will be responsible for the loss and the seller should claim money. If the loss takes place during transit, it's the insurance company or the shipping company that takes responsibility. The party who has suffered loss should file a claim against the insurance company or the shipping company.

With regard to claims and settlement, all parties concerned should have an amicable, practical and realistic attitude. The case in question should be investigated in depth to ascertain what the real cause is and which party should be responsible. The amount of loss and the method of compensation should be based on the results of the investigation. The proof should be complete and clear, and the investigation authority should be competent to issue the relevant certificates. Otherwise, the claim can be refused by the relevant party.

If a claim is justified, it can be settled in the following ways: making a refund and compensating for other direct losses or expenses, selling the goods at lower prices, or replacing the faulty goods.

Memory Practice（记忆训练）

Paragraph 1

China has released its first national five-year plan on modern logistics to accelerate building a modern logistics system and promote high-quality development.

The five-year plan on modern logistics for the 14th Five-Year Plan period (2021—2025) was released by the General Office of the State Council.

The plan stresses work to improve the resilience and safety of the industrial chain and supply chain, promote the construction of a modern logistics system, improve the quality, increase efficiency, and cut the costs of modern logistics.

(https://www.chinadaily.com.cn/a/202212/15/WS639b00d5a31057c47eba49c6.html)

Paragraph 2

2023年上半年，我国服务贸易继续保持增长态势。服务进出口总额3.14万亿元，同比增长8.5%。我国知识密集型服务进出口实现稳步增长，进出口总额1.36万亿元，同比增长12.3%，占服务进出口总额的比重达43.5%。与此同时，旅行服务明显恢复。上半年，我国旅行服务进出口6509.4亿元，同比增长65.4%。旅行服务中，出口增长52.4%，进口增长66.4%。

(https://language.chinadaily.com.cn/a/202308/04/WS64cca144a31035260b81a58d.html)

Section 2　Interpreting Practice（口译实训）

Dialogue 1【参考译文】

协商付款条件

A: Well, Mr. Smith, we've settled everything in connection with this transaction except the terms of payment.

B: 张女士，贵司能接受开放账期吗？

A: I'm afraid not. T/T (telegraphic transfer) is accessible. Currently we also accept payment by irrevocable letter of credit payable against shipping documents from our long-term partners.

B: 说实话，信用证会增加我的进口成本。当我在银行开信用证时，必须支付押金。这会占用我的资金，增加我的成本。

A: Consult your bank and see if they will reduce the required deposit to a minimum.

B: 好吧，折中考虑一下，如果50%以信用证支付，余额以开放账期30天支付，你觉得怎么样？

A: I'm very sorry. Since the total amount is so huge and the world monetary market is rather unstable at the moment, we cannot accept any terms of payment other than a letter of credit.

B: 好吧，我别无选择，只能接受你们的付款条件。

A: Well, then, we've agreed on all the major points.

B: 是的，我们很高兴交易顺利完成，希望以后会有更多的交易。合同什么时候可以签署？

A: I'll have it ready this week.

B: 越早越好。我下周一就要走了。

A: How about this Friday morning at 10 am? I'll have a copy of the contract sent to your hotel for you to look over.

B: 好的，我没问题。

Dialogue 2 【参考译文】

Price Negotiation

A: 我是迈克，我能为您做什么？

B: Last week, we met each other on the exhibition. You saw our new series products on display and took much interest in them.

A: 是的，我们对新的室内系列很感兴趣。

B: We are glad to hear that. What product models are you particularly interested in?

A: 让我看看你们的电子目录。我想先了解 HIL 系列。您可以按照马来西亚到岸价给出最低报价吗？

B: Thank you for your inquiry. May I know how many pieces you require?

A: 很难说，因为我们不确定贵公司的产品在市场上是否受欢迎，我们想先订购 500 件。您能提供一个有竞争力的价格以助力新产品推广吗？

Next Day

B: Have you received quotation based on CIF Malaysia yesterday?

A: 收到了，但很遗憾地告诉您，贵公司的价格比别人的高很多。

B: Our quotation is based on quantity. May I know your forecast for this series?

A: 如果贵公司的产品和价格有竞争力，那么我们预估订购数量很大，每个月差不多有 2 万件。

B: Generally speaking, our price is consistent with purchasing quantities. For long-term and deep cooperation, we can consider to offer you commission in the future.

A: 听起来不错。但这份支持对目前的情况来说并无帮助。

B: What about price based on FOB Guangzhou if you have a freight forwarder as we don't have competitive one on this route?

A: 这是个好主意，请按照广州离岸价更新价格。

B: Freight expense will be expected to slash. I'll send you official quotation in details by e-mail.

A: 太好了，我等待您的回复。

B: Keep in touch.

Dialogue 3 【参考译文】

选择货运代理

A: 随着我们的业务向国际市场拓展，明年我们将向海外出口产品。那么，特蕾西，我想听听你对运输和相关活动的看法。

B: Since we have been concentrating on domestic market, it's natural and more economical to use our own truck fleet and transport services. However, if we send cargo overseas, it is better to rely on the expertise of professional freight forwarders.

A: 为什么？我们不能自己安排到其他国家的运输吗？

参考答案及译文

B: In fact, as export involves complicated procedures, there are many factors to consider when deciding whether or not to outsource our transporting needs.

A: 你指的是哪些因素？

B: The scale or complexity of transport needs; whether we have the expertise or experience to arrange transport ourselves; whether we have the time to manage the process, and further, the costs for ocean shipping and relationship with carriers, so on and so forth.

A: 有可能培训我们自己的团队吗？

B: On the one hand, certificates are required in performing some duties such as customs clearance, and training itself is far from enough. On the other hand, to hire full-time employees, the company will have to pay salary and benefits, and the overhead for a team will also increase.

A: 这么看来，你显然更倾向于选择货运代理公司。

B: According to our estimate, we will have to coordinate several shipments every week during the first several months, and even more after that, so it will be more economical to outsource transport services.

A: 那么我们现在就应该开始寻找一些可靠的货运代理，为出口做好准备。

B: Yes, sir! We'll get started right now and keep you informed of the progress.

Dialogue 4 【参考译文】

Packaging and Transshipment

A: I understand that you have some special packing requirements for your order.

B: 是的。首先，我们希望木板用某种气泡膜包裹。

A: OK. That's standard for all our boards.

B: 你们能用泡沫纸箱而不是普通塑料打包这些木板吗？

A: That's no problem, but there will be a small additional expense.

B: 具体是多少钱？

A: Let me check, about 2% additional expense.

B: 嗯，可以接受。因为我们要确保使用非常结实的箱子，木板包装在里面会更安全。

A: We'll take care of that. Anything else?

B: 还有在纸箱上标明"易碎，小心轻放"和"保持干燥"。

A: That's customary as well.

B: 我知道这很麻烦，但之前我们在运输方面遇到过很多问题。

A: I understand totally. A little extra trouble and expense now will guarantee top-quality finished products.

Two weeks later

B: 我们急需这一批次的货，我刚想到另一种可以及时交货的可能。

A: What is it? Could you explain it in details?

B: 把装运港从西雅图改到香港如何？

A: I'm afraid we can't agree to that. The goods you ordered are manufactured in Seattle. We wish to point out that all orders accepted by us are shipped from New York or Seattle, rather than Hong Kong.

B: 是这样的。每个月从西雅图到横滨的船只有几艘，而从香港出发的船却很多。如果从香港发货，我们就能更早地收到货物。

219

A: I see. You want to have your goods shipped from Seattle to Yokohama via Hong Kong, where they can be transshipped. Is that the idea?

B: 是的，没错，因为我想让这些货物尽早进入我们的市场。

A: Your idea may be a good one, and then the L/C should be amended to "Transshipment allowed; shipment from Seattle to Yokohama via Hong Kong." Is that what you mean?

B: 是的，没错。谢谢您的合作。

Section 3 Interpreting Assessment（口译测评）

Dialogue 1【原文】

建立新的业务关系

A: 我是来自红星有限公司贸易部的李越。我们是一家来自中国的合资企业，主要生产电动滑板车。昨天您在广交会留了名片，所以我知道了您的名字和地址。

B: Yes, we are looking for Chinese suppliers recently. I am very pleased to receive your phone call.

A: 我们致力于设计、生产、销售电动产品多年，远销欧洲市场。希望我们的产品能满足您的需求。

B: We are one of the largest wholesalers of electric products in Singapore. We are considering to establish long-term business relationships with well-reputed companies.

A: 看来我们意见一致。我们也想找到长期合作伙伴以拓展海外市场。

B: Terrific, but I think we need to know more about your company.

A: 这也是我给您打电话的原因。我诚挚地邀请您来参观我们的工厂，看看我们公司先进的生产线和研发部门。

B: Thank you very much. I'll confirm the schedule with my boss about the exact day to visit your factory. As it's our first time to visit China, we are not very familiar with it, I hope you can help us arrange the transport and accommodation during the visit.

A: 待你们确定具体行程后，我们会去你们所在的酒店接你们，并妥善安排好当天的一切。

B: That's very kind of you. I am looking forward to establishing a good business relationship with you, and I hope we can work together successfully for mutual benefit.

A: 我想我们有共同的愿望。

Dialogue 1【参考译文】

Establish New Business Relations

A: This is Li Yue from the trading department of Red Star Co., Ltd. Our company is a joint venture from China that mainly produces electric scooters. You left your business card at the Canton Fair yesterday where I got your name and address.

B: 是的，我们最近正在寻找中国供应商。很高兴接到你的电话。

A: We have been devoting ourselves to designing, producing and selling electric products for many years, which are exported to European market. We hope our products can meet your needs.

B: 我们是新加坡最大的电动产品批发商之一。我们正在考虑与口碑良好的公司建立长期的业务关系。

A: We see eye to eye. We also want to find long-term partners to expand overseas market.

B: 太棒了，但我认为我们有必要先多了解下贵公司。

A: That's why I'm calling you. I sincerely invite you to visit our factory and see our advanced production line and R&D department.

B: 非常感谢。我先跟老板确认下行程安排，确定去贵司工厂参观的具体时间。因为这是我们第一次来中国，不是很熟悉，希望您能帮忙安排下参观期间的交通和住宿。

A: After you confirm the specific schedule, we will go to the hotel you stay to pick you up and arrange all above on that day.

B: 您真好。期待与贵司建立良好的业务关系，希望我们能合作成功，互惠互利。

A: I suppose we share a common desire.

Dialogue 2【原文】

订单协商

A: Good morning, I'm Jane from Sunny Trading Company. I'd like to place an order for your cubicle desk units.

B: 当然可以。您想订购多少张？

A: Quite a few. Do you have any desks available in the warehouse?

B: 我们有大量库存。还有一个陈列室，手头也有不少，应该不成问题。

A: Well then. I'd like to order 80 units by the end of the month. Could I get an estimate before placing an order?

B: 当然可以，我今天下班前就能给您。

A: What does the estimate include?

B: 包括商品、包装和运输费用、必要的关税、任何税费和保险费。

A: Do you ship door-to-door?

B: 当然，所有货物都是送货上门的。交货日期取决于您的所在地，但我们通常可以在14个工作日内交货。

A: Thank you for your help.

B: 这是我的荣幸。您可以在今天下午5点之前收到邮件。

……

A: Uh-huh. I checked with our distribution hub in Phoenix and they signed for a delivery this morning. But it was just a partial shipment: only 40 sets. Could you help us check the rest of order?

B: 请稍等，我在电脑上查一下，看起来订单被分成了两批，两批货的发货时间相隔了两天，第二批货物仍在运输途中。

A: Oh, I see. What about delivery time for the rest of goods? We desperately need them.

B: 我知道在周末之前把这批货送到商店对贵司来说有多重要，所以让我来处理。我会给物流公司打个电话，再次确认一下剩余的运输货物。

A: Great. Thank you.

B: 我再看看这次分批发货的原因，以后的订单，我会跟进发货明细及到货时间。

A: Terrific! I really appreciate your going the extra mile on this.

B: 不客气，一收到确切消息，我会尽快给您答复。

Dialogue 2【参考译文】

Order Negotiation

A: 上午好，我是阳光贸易公司的简，我想订购你们的隔间办公桌。

B: Certainly. How many pieces do you want to purchase?

A: 一些，你们仓库里还有库存吗？

221

B: We keep a large supply in stock. There's also a showroom with quite a few on hand. It shouldn't be a problem.

A: 那好。月底前我要 80 套。在下订单之前能给我一个估价吗?

B: Certainly, I'll have it for you by the end of the day.

A: 估价包括什么?

B: It includes merchandise, packaging and shipping, duty if required, any taxes and insurance.

A: 你们送货上门吗?

B: Certainly, all shipments are door-to-door. Delivery dates depend on your location, but we can usually deliver within 14 business days.

A: 谢谢您的帮助。

B: My pleasure. You can expect an e-mail by 5 this afternoon.

……

A: 嗯,我跟凤凰城的配送中心核实过了,他们今天早上签收了一批货。但只是部分货物,只有 40 套。您能查一下剩下的订单吗?

B: Sure, just bear with me a sec while I check on my screen. It looks like the order was divided into two shipments and they were shipped two days apart. The second shipment is still in transit.

A: 哦,我明白了。剩余货物什么时候到? 我们急需。

B: I know how important it is for you to get this order to the stores before the weekend, so let me do this. I'll call logistics company to double-check the rest of the shipment.

A: 那太好了,谢谢。

B: And I'll see what reasons might be for the separate shipment. Besides I will follow up goods delivery in details and arriving time for future orders.

A: 太好了! 我真的很感谢您在这件事上的额外付出。

B: No problem. I'll get back to you as soon as I've got confirmed message.

Unit 11　Investment Invitation（招商引资）

Section 1　Interpreting Preparation（口译准备）

Sight Interpreting（视译）

Passage 1【参考译文】

全国上下齐心协力,打造投资热土

官员称,中国将降低市场准入门槛,优化营商环境,提升利用外资水平,让中国始终成为投资的热土。

第六届中国国际进口博览会当前正在上海举行,中国商务部部长王文涛 11 月 5 日在参加相关活动时表示,中国正以高质量发展全面推进中国式现代化,必将为广大外商发展提供更广阔的市场空间和更多的合作机遇。王文涛在"投资中国年"高峰会议暨上海城市推介活动上致辞时说:"中国所拥有的超大规模市场、完备产业配套、经济向好的基本面不会改变,综合优势依然突出。"

该活动旨在放大进博会溢出效应,展示商务部"投资中国年"系列活动的举办成效和上海的投资机遇。上海市市长龚正表示,将会持续打造市场化、法治化、国际化的一流营商环境,与大家携手共科思创首席执行官施乐文表示,中国是科思创最大的市场之一,2022年中国销售额约占集团销售额的五分之一。创开放繁荣的美好未来。据龚正介绍,截至9月底,上海已有940家跨国公司的地区总部和551家外资研发中心。

科思创首席执行官施乐文表示,中国是科思创最大的市场之一,2022年中国销售额约占集团销售额的五分之一。施乐文称,截至2022年底,科思创在中国的投资总额已超过39亿欧元,并且科思创将继续在中国投资。

为了进一步发挥中国国际进口博览会在投资促进方面的积极作用,展示中国投资机遇,商务部和上海市人民政府共同举办了以"共创开放繁荣的美好未来"为主题的"投资中国年"高峰会议。

Passage 2【参考译文】

New Zealand Small Business Entering the Large Chinese Market, a Fruitful Journey

Over the past decade, the Belt and Road Initiative has become a highly popular international public good and a platform for international cooperation. As a window to China's new development paradigm, a platform for high-level opening-up, and a globally shared international public product, the China International Import Expo (CIIE) complements the Belt and Road Initiative and jointly promotes development.

On this path, there is not only economic and trade exchanges but also cultural exchanges.

China is one of New Zealand's most important tourism markets. In the 5th CIIE, the New Zealand joint brand pavilion occupies 400 square meters of exhibition space. In addition to enterprises, the chamber of commerce has also specially invited the New Zealand Tourism Bureau and the New Zealand Education Bureau to participate, showcasing New Zealand's tourism resources and educational resources.

This year, in addition to tourism resources, Maori war dance will once again take advantage of the open window of the CIIE to showcase the unique local culture it represents to the world.

Maori war dance, also known as New Zealand Maori war dance, refer to the traditional dance forms of New Zealand's Maori people, which involve coordinated movements, percussion, chanting, and vocalization in group dances. On June 25 of this year, New Zealand Prime Minister Hipkins led a delegation to Beijing, and among the members of Hipkins' delegation were representatives from the tribal champion of this year's national Maori war dance competition. At this year's CIIE, the Maori war dance will take the stage at the "Four-Leaf Clover" central square stage and will also perform inside the exhibition hall.

Goods and services are traded, while culture and ideas are exchanged. "We hope that through the grand stage of the CIIE, the Maori war dance, which embodies the unique cultural characteristics of New Zealand, can shine brightly and let China and the world see the charm of New Zealand," said Li Ruiqin.

☞ Memory Practice (记忆训练)

Paragraph 1

The 16th Pujiang Innovation Forum has raised its curtain in Shanghai, with the opening ceremony held on Sunday.

With the theme of "Open Innovation Ecosystem: Innovation for Global Connectivity", the three-day forum has attracted more than 300 guests from 32 countries and regions, nearly 40 percent of them from overseas.

Brazil is the Country of Honor, and Hubei is the Province of Honor this year. President Xi Jinping noted that today's world is going through accelerating changes unseen in a century, while scientific and technological innovation is an important force for humankind to jointly address risks and challenges and promote peace and development. He hoped the forum will make new contributions in advancing international scientific and technological cooperation and enhancing the common well-being of humankind.

(https://en. pujiangforum. cn/en/en_news_show. aspx?channel_id = 20&cateid = 328&id = 116)

Paragraph 2

习近平指出,当前,世界百年未有之大变局加速演进,新一轮科技革命和产业变革深入发展。科技创新是人类共同应对风险挑战、促进和平和发展的重要力量。中国将坚定奉行互利共赢的开放战略,不断加大高水平对外开放力度,持续以更加开放的思维和举措推进国际科技交流合作,建设具有全球竞争力的开放创新生态,同各国携手打造开放、公平、公正、非歧视的科技发展环境。希望浦江创新论坛坚持以创新为主题,启迪创新思想、传播创新理念、激励创新精神,为推进国际科技合作、增进人类共同福祉作出新的贡献。

(m.news.cn/2023 – 09/10/c_1129855112.htm)

Section 2 Interpreting Practice（口译实训）

Passage 1 【参考译文】

实现增长之路：三大优先行动事项

今年,经济放缓仍在继续。尽管大多数发达经济体的劳动力市场和消费支出出乎预料地展现出了韧性,且中国重新开放提振了经济,但我们预计2023年的全球经济增速将低于3%。

正如大家将在下周发布的《世界经济展望》中所看到的,与过去水平相比,经济增长无论从短期还是中期看都将持续疲软。不同国家组别之间也存在着明显的差异。

部分增长势头来自新兴经济体——其中,亚洲的表现尤为亮眼。预计2023年,印度和中国两国将贡献全球经济增长的一半。但其他国家面前则是危峰兀立。美国和欧元区的经济活动正在放缓,更高的利率拖累了需求。今年,预计约有90%发达经济体的经济增速将出现下滑。

对于低收入国家来说,它们在出口需求走弱之际又遭遇了借贷成本的上升。我们看到低收入国家的人均收入增长始终低于新兴经济体。这对低收入国家来说是一记沉重打击,使它们实现收入趋同的难度进一步增加。

贫困和饥饿问题可能会进一步加剧,这是由新冠疫情危机引发的另一大危险趋势。

过去几年来,各方协调出台的强有力货币和财政政策行动帮助避免了形势的进一步恶化。但随着地缘政治愈发紧张、通胀居高不下,要实现强劲的复苏仍然十分艰难。这损害了所有人的未来前景——尤其是最弱势的群体和国家。

Passage 2 【参考译文】

Remarks by Chinese Premier Li Qiang at the Opening Ceremony of the 20th China-ASEAN Expo and China-ASEAN Business and Investment Summit (Excerpt)

Leaders of the ASEAN Countries,

Distinguished Guests,

Ladies and Gentlemen,

Friends,

Good morning! It's a great pleasure to join you in the beautiful "Green City" Nanning for the 20th China-ASEAN Expo (CAEXPO) and China-ASEAN Business and Investment Summit (CABIS). Many present today attended the 26th China-ASEAN Summit in Jakarta ten days ago, and now we are meeting again in Nanning. This speaks volumes about the intensity and depth of the exchanges and cooperation between China and ASEAN. At the outset, on behalf of the Chinese government, I wish to extend warm congratulations on the opening of CAEXPO and CABIS, and a hearty welcome to the leaders and guests attending the event.

Over the course of 20 years, CAEXPO and CABIS have borne witness to the sustained growth of China-ASEAN relations. Twenty years ago, as ASEAN's dialogue partner, China was the first country to join the *Treaty of Amity and Cooperation in Southeast Asia* (TAC), and together with ASEAN established a strategic partnership for peace and prosperity. Ten years ago, President Xi Jinping delivered an important speech at the Indonesian parliament, during which he proposed that China and ASEAN countries build a 21st Century Maritime Silk Road and foster a closer China-ASEAN community with a shared future. His proposal received positive response from ASEAN countries and opened a new chapter of friendship and cooperation between the two sides. Two years ago, at the Special Summit to Commemorate the 30th Anniversary of China-ASEAN Dialogue Relations, President Xi Jinping proposed that China and ASEAN build a peaceful, safe and secure, prosperous, beautiful and amicable home, and together with leaders of ASEAN countries, mapped out a new blueprint for the future of China-ASEAN cooperation and development.

Over the years, we have upheld unity for strength. Keeping firm to the path of peaceful development, we have preserved regional peace and tranquility in a world fraught with turbulence and change, and jointly created the miracle of economic takeoff. Our combined GDP as a share of the global total surged from 6.1 percent in 2002 to 21.5 percent last year, and our two billion-plus people are significantly better off. We have upheld win-win cooperation, made breakthroughs in connectivity, and steadily advanced regional economic integration and economic and trade cooperation. Trade and investment between the two sides has grown despite a weak global economy. Our trade grew by 16.8 times over the past 20 years, and we have been each other's largest trading partners for three years running. Two-way cumulative investment has surpassed USD 380 billion. We have upheld the common good of the world, jointly tackled global challenges, and fostered a steady stream of cooperation highlights in poverty reduction, climate action, environmental protection and energy transition. The China-ASEAN relationship has grown into the most successful and vibrant model for cooperation in the Asia-Pacific, and is a vivid illustration of building a community with a shared future for mankind.

Looking back, we have every reason to be proud of these achievements, and feel keenly about the trials and tribulations along the way. Looking ahead, we are full of confidence and hope, but not without concerns and worries. We, in this turbulent and complex world, are faced with many difficult issues and challenges that require a collective response. Against the backdrop of unprecedented global transformation, we must size up the situation and adapt to the overall trend. More importantly, we need to bear in mind the essential principles that remain constant despite the myriad of changes in the world, and the overarching vision that guides us to where we are today. The sound relations between China and ASEAN we enjoy today are the hard-won result achieved through our years-long concerted efforts. In my view, the essential principle and vision that made this feat possible are the insightful proposition of amity, sincerity, mutual benefit and inclusiveness put forth by President Xi Jinping. As a fundamental guideline of China's neighborhood diplomacy, these four words represent the right approach to build friendly ties with neighbors and hold the key to our shared endeavor for a brighter future. We need to make greater efforts to practice the principles of amity, sincerity, mutual benefit and inclusiveness, foster an environment conducive to development, prosperity, peace and tranquility, and bring more benefits to neighboring countries and people in the region through our own development.

...

Ladies and Gentlemen, Friends,

Thanks to our collective efforts in the past two decades, CAEXPO and CABIS have grown into an important platform for regional integration, and produced fruitful results. From this new starting point, we must continue developing and making good use of the platform to reinforce exchanges, strengthen friendship, create more business opportunities and share greater benefits. Let us work together to build a closer community with a shared future and usher in a more prosperous and brighter future.

To conclude, I wish the event a full success.

Thank you.

Passage 3【参考译文】

中美洲投资高级会议上的讲话

非常感谢。很高兴参加这次会议。我希望这将是关于这个重要主题的众多内容中的第一段讲话。首先，我要再次感谢阿里亚斯总统昨晚鼓舞人心的讲话，感谢哥斯达黎加政府主办这次会议。我还要特别欢迎来自私营部门的嘉宾，他们的出席对于会议的成功至关重要。我期待今天上午晚些时候听到大家的意见。

我们今天在这里讨论的是中美洲的投资事宜——投资的障碍以及消除这些障碍的政策——我将在稍后谈论这些问题。但退一步说，讨论投资为什么很重要，以及它能为国家和人民做什么，是很有必要的。

我们生活在一个全球化的世界。技术变革的速度是惊人的。一个国家通过货物、资本和思想的交换实现创新成果跨境传播的程度和速度是前所未有的。我们无法阻止这个过程。阿里亚斯总统去年12月在纽约发表演讲时明智地表示，发展中国家面临的困境是"如果我们不能出口越来越多的商品，我们最终将输出越来越多的人口"。我们也不应该想要阻止全球化，它带来了改善各国人民生活的前景。我们应该努力做的是管理全球化并使其为公民服务。各国政府和国际货币基金组织等机构的任务是努力最大化其利益并最小化其成本和风险。

全球化带来的机遇中最主要的是更高的增长率和更高的生活水平。通过鼓励外商直接投资，中美洲可以获得国外的技术、知识和管理专业知识，并引发垂直一体化和供应链的发展。一个重要目标应该是使整个地区对投资者具有吸引力。如果投资人口不到500万的哥斯达黎加能帮助外国公司在拥有超过2500万人口的中美洲地区获得立足之地，那么他们更有可能在哥斯达黎加投资。

......

对于中美洲地区所有国家而言，保持宏观经济稳定显然是增长和投资等式的重要组成部分。大多数中美洲国家都表现良好。去年平均增长率超过5%，高于近年来的水平。中美洲地区大多数国家的通货膨胀率为个位数。虽然贸易条件显著恶化，但中美洲国家还是取得了这些成果。尽管如此，还是要提防很多问题。2006年，中美洲的实际基本支出平均增长了9%以上，而经常性支出占了这一增长的大部分。中美洲的资本投资仍然相对较低。需要采取更多措施来降低金融市场风险,尤其是来自离岸中心的风险。中美洲仍然容易受到外部冲击的影响,尤其受美国经济低迷影响,因为中美洲地区对美国的出口比例很高。

Passage 4 【参考译文】

China's Outbound Direct Investment Further Rises from January to August

China's outbound direct investment has continued to grow in the first eight months of this year, especially in economies involved in the Belt and Road Initiative (BRI), the Ministry of Commerce said on Thursday.

From January to August, China's outbound non-financial direct investment reached 585.61 billion yuan, up 18.8 percent year-on-year. In particular, Chinese companies' non-financial direct investment in the countries and regions involved in the BRI achieved 140.37 billion yuan, up 22.5 percent on a yearly basis, according to the Ministry of Commerce.

Meanwhile, during the eight months, turnover of China's foreign contracted projects reached 648.62 billion yuan, up 6.1 percent year-on-year. The value of China's newly signed contracts in foreign countries reached 863.34 billion yuan, a year-on-year increase of 2 percent. The turnover of China's foreign contracted projects in the economies involved in the BRI reached 529.52 billion yuan, up 4.8 percent year-on-year. The value of China's newly signed contracts in BRI economies achieved 725.35 billion yuan, up 5.6 percent year-on-year.

Shenzhen CLOU Electronics Co., Ltd., a subsidiary of Chinese home appliance maker Midea Group and a global energy storage company, announced earlier this month that it established a company in the United States to strengthen its business in the North American market and further consolidate its industry position globally.

"Midea Group has strong confidence in the green energy sector. We will leverage our expertise in energy storage to dive deep into the green energy market. The establishment of the new company in the US will enable us to further penetrate the global market, including North America," said Fu Yongjun, vice-president of Midea Group.

Additionally, the 10th China-EU High-level Economic and Trade Dialogue will be held in Beijing on September 25 and He Lifeng, member of the Political Bureau of the CPC Central Committee, Vice Premier of the State Council, and Chinese leader of the China-EU High-Level Economic and Trade Dialogue, will co-chair the meeting with Valdis Dombrovskis, Executive Vice President of the European Commission, and European leader of the China-EU High-Level Economic and Trade Dialogue, announced by the Ministry of Commerce during a news conference in Beijing on Thursday.

Speaking at a forum hosted by the Center for China and Globalization in Beijing on Thursday, Wu Hongbo, special representative of the Chinese government on European affairs, noted that both China and Europe have substantial untapped potential for cooperation.

"We have identified several promising areas for collaboration, including the green economy, digitalization, artificial intelligence and high-end manufacturing," Wu said.

"As the EU is a strong advocate of open economies and a staunch supporter of green development, fair and equitable international competition should act as a catalyst for its green development and transformation," he said.

Wu added that by replacing confrontation with cooperation, both China and the EU can enhance their ability to prevent and resolve risks while contributing to global economic development.

On another front, with the upcoming Mid-Autumn Festival and National Day holiday, a traditional peak period of consumption in China, the Ministry of Commerce is organizing a group of activities to help boost domestic spending.

The Ministry of Commerce will also help promote the introduction of a batch of policies and measures to support the aftermarket of cars to further push the accelerated consumption recovery in China.

Section 3　Interpreting Assessment（口译测评）

Passage 1 【原文】

News on China-ASEAN Cooperation Forum

China will work with the Association of Southeast Asian Nations to promote high-quality development of key segments of emerging industries and facilitate the flow of various resources to deepen integration in the field, Minister of Industry and Information Technology Jin Zhuanglong said.

China and the ASEAN are highly complementary in emerging industries and there is strong willingness for exchanges and cooperation among businesses on both sides, he said at the China-ASEAN Forum on Emerging Industries in Shenzhen, Guangdong Province, on Tuesday.

Noting that the ASEAN has enormous potential for industrial transformation and innovative development, Jin said China will work with the region to stimulate innovation vitality and promote high-quality development of key areas by focusing on sectors like new energy vehicles, digital economy and energy electronics.

The two sides will look for a batch of major projects that are highly technological, with large investment volume and can drive industrial development to create a new driving force for industrial collaboration and build a new highland for innovative development, he said.

China will strengthen cooperation with the ASEAN to facilitate the efficient flow of people, goods, capital and information between industrial parks, industries and regions to deepen integration in industrial chain, supply chain and value chain, he said.

The country will adhere to openness and inclusiveness and strive to create an integrated development model of emerging industries with China-ASEAN characteristics, he said.

The minister also highlighted the importance of high-level communication in the industrial sector between China and the ASEAN, proposing to accelerate the establishment of a minister-level dialogue and exchange mechanism to create a sound environment for the development of emerging industries.

Agus Gumiwang Kartasasmita, Indonesia's Minister of Industry, said as the ASEAN makes efforts to play a leading role in the field of electric vehicles globally, there is large potential for cooperation between the region and China.

Malaithong Kommasith, Industry and Commerce Minister of Laos, said emerging industries face many barriers like a lack of consumer awareness, insufficient financing, high costs of research and development, and unfriendly environment. "Therefore, promoting regional cooperation on emerging industries could be a strategic choice for the ASEAN and China to recover from the COVID-19 pandemic, foster economic growth and attain development in the region," he said.

（https://language.chinadaily.com.cn/a/202307/05/WS64a5180ca310bf8a75d6d663.html）

Passage 1 【参考译文】

中国—东盟合作论坛新闻

工业和信息化部部长金壮龙表示，中国将和东盟合作，推动新兴产业重点领域高质量发展，促进该领域各种资源的流动和深层次融合。

他周二在广东省深圳举行的中国—东盟新兴产业论坛上表示，中国与东盟在新兴产业方面互补性很强，双方企业交流合作意愿强烈。

金壮龙指出，东盟在探索产业转型与创新发展方面潜力巨大，中方愿与东盟合作，聚焦新能源汽车、数字经济、能源电子等新兴产业领域，激发创新活力，促进重点领域高质量发展。

金壮龙表示，双方将挖掘一批科技含量高、投资体量大、产业带动性强的重大项目，激发产业合作新动力，建设创新发展新高地。

他说，中方愿与东盟加强合作，促进人流、物流、资金流、信息流在园区间、产业间、地区间高效流动，实现产业链、供应链、价值链的更深层次融合。

他表示，中方将坚持开放包容，努力构建具有中国—东盟特色的新兴产业协同发展模式。

金壮龙还强调了中国与东盟工业领域高层交流的重要性，提出要加快建立中国—东盟工业领域部长级对话交流机制，为新兴产业的发展营造良好环境。

印尼工业部部长阿古斯表示，东盟致力于在全球电动汽车领域发挥带头作用，东盟地区和中国之间的合作潜力巨大。

老挝工业和贸易部部长贡玛西表示，新兴产业面临着许多障碍，比如缺乏消费者意识、资金不足、研发成本高、环境不友好等。贡玛西表示，因此促进地区间新兴产业的合作将是东盟和中国在新冠疫情后实现经济复苏、增长和地区发展的一个战略选择。

Passage 2【原文】

2023年中国国际服务贸易交易会全球服务贸易峰会新闻

9月2日上午，国家主席习近平在北京向2023年中国国际服务贸易交易会全球服务贸易峰会发表视频致辞。

习近平指出，当前，百年变局加速演进，世界经济复苏动力不足。服务贸易是国际贸易的重要组成部分，服务业是国际经贸合作的重要领域。全球服务贸易和服务业合作深入发展，数字化、智能化、绿色化进程不断加快，新技术、新业态、新模式层出不穷，为推动经济全球化、恢复全球经济活力、增强世界经济发展韧性注入了强大动力。

习近平强调，今年是中国改革开放45周年，中国将坚持推进高水平对外开放，以高质量发展全面推进中国式现代化，为各国开放合作提供新机遇。中国愿同各国各方一道，以服务开放推动包容发展，以服务合作促进联动融通，以服务创新培育发展动能，以服务共享创造美好未来，携手推动世界经济走上持续复苏轨道。

我们将打造更加开放包容的发展环境。扩大面向全球的高标准自由贸易区网络，积极开展服务贸易和投资负面清单谈判，扩大电信、旅游、法律、职业考试等服务领域对外开放，在国家服务业扩大开放综合示范区以及有条件的自由贸易试验区和自由贸易港，率先对接国际高标准经贸规则。放宽服务业市场准入，有序推进跨境服务贸易开放进程，提升服务贸易标准化水平，稳步扩大制度型开放。

我们将拉紧互利共赢的合作纽带。加强同各国的发展战略和合作倡议对接，深化同共建"一带一路"国家服务贸易和数字贸易合作，促进各类资源要素跨境流动便利化，培育更多经济合作增长点。

我们将强化创新驱动的发展路径。加快培育服务贸易数字化新动能，推动数据基础制度先行先试改革，促进数字贸易改革创新发展。建设全国温室气体自愿减排交易市场，支持服务业在绿色发展中发挥更大作用。推动服务贸易与现代服务业、高端制造业、现代农业融合发展，释放更多创新活力。

我们将共享中国式现代化建设成果。着力扩大国内需求，加快建设强大国内市场，主动扩大优质服务进口，鼓励扩大知识密集型服务出口，以中国大市场机遇为世界提供新的发展动力，以高质量发展为全球提供更多更好的中国服务，增强世界人民的获得感。

习近平最后强调，世界经济开放则兴，封闭则衰。让我们共同维护来之不易的自由贸易和多边贸易体制，共同分享全球服务贸易发展的历史机遇，为开创世界更加美好繁荣的未来共同努力。

（https://language.chinadaily.com.cn/a/202309/02/WS64f53f11a310d2dce4bb3c0d.html）

Passage 2 【参考译文】

News on Global Trade in Services Summit of CIFTIS 2023

President Xi Jinping addressed the Global Trade in Services Summit of the 2023 China International Fair for Trade in Services (CIFTIS) via video on September 2, 2023 in Beijing.

President Xi Jinping pointed out that the world today is confronted with accelerated changes unseen in a century and sluggish economic recovery. Trade in services is an important part of international trade, and the service industry is an important area of international economic and trade cooperation. Global trade in services and cooperation in the service industry have developed in depth, the processes of digitization, intelligence, and greening have continued to accelerate, and new technologies, new business formats, and new models have emerged one after another, which has injected strong force into promoting economic globalization, restoring the vitality of the global economy, and enhancing the resilience of world economic development.

Noting that this year marks the 45th anniversary of China's reform and opening-up, President Xi Jinping reaffirmed the country's commitment to promoting high-standard opening-up and advancing Chinese modernization on all fronts through high-quality development, thereby providing all countries with new opportunities for openness and cooperation. China will work with all countries and parties to advance inclusive development through openness, promote connectivity and integration through cooperation, foster drivers for development through innovation, and create a better future through shared services, in a bid to jointly get the world economy onto the track of sustained recovery.

China will create a more open and more inclusive development environment, which include the expansion of a globally-oriented network of high-standard free trade zones, negotiations on the negative list for trade in services and investment, and broader opening-up in services areas such as telecommunications, tourism, law and vocational examinations. The national integrated demonstration zone for greater openness in the services sector as well as eligible pilot free trade zones and free trade ports will be the first to align policies with high-standard international economic and trade rules. The country will widen access to its services sector, advance the opening-up in cross-border services trade in an orderly manner, improve the level of standardization of services trade, and steadily expand institutional opening-up.

In terms of cooperation, China will strengthen the bond of mutual benefit and win-win cooperation by enhancing synergy with development strategies and cooperation initiatives of various countries, deepening cooperation on services trade and digital trade with Belt and Road Initiative partner countries, facilitating the cross-border flow of resources and production factors and fostering more growth areas for economic cooperation.

China will also strengthen innovation-driven development, with plans to accelerate the cultivation of new drivers for the digitalization of services trade, implement pilot reforms on basic data systems, and promote the development of digital trade through reform and innovation. The country will establish a national voluntary greenhouse gas emission reduction trading market and pledged support for the services sector's role in green development. China will push forward the integrated development of services trade with modern services industries, high-end manufacturing and modern agriculture to unleash more vitality for innovation.

The country will share the outcomes of the Chinese modernization drive with the rest of the world by vigorously boosting domestic demand, accelerating the building of a robust domestic market, taking the initiative to increase the imports of quality services, and encouraging more exports of knowledge-intensive services. China will lend new impetus to global development with the opportunities generated by China's vast market, and offer more and better Chinese services to the world through high-quality development in a bid to increase the sense of gains of people around the world.

At the end of the speech, President Xi Jinping underlined the importance of openness in the world economy and the risks of seclusion. He called on all parties to uphold the hard-won free trade and multilateral trading regime, share in the historic opportunities in the development of global trade in services, and unite for an even brighter and more prosperous future for the world.

Unit 12　Business Management（经营管理）

Section 1　Interpreting Preparation（口译准备）

Sight Interpreting（视译）

Passage 1【参考译文】

员工在家办公，企业如何管理？（节选）

艾米·约翰逊是一名指纹鉴定师，她在自己位于伊利诺伊州迪克森市的家中工作，在家里与客户讨论问题、提交工作报告。当然，她其实也可以在芝加哥坐在老板身旁工作。

蒂莫西·丹尼尔斯是约翰逊所在公司 Accurate Biometrics 的运营副总裁，通过一款电脑监控软件，他可以了解到约翰逊和其他员工是在工作还是在偷懒。丹尼尔斯每周会查看记录了他们浏览什么网站、浏览网站的时间有多长的总结。他说："这可以让我们对员工保持关注又不至于会过度侵犯员工的隐私。"

约翰逊知道她的电脑受到监控，但是她说这并未让她感到不舒服，她没有做任何不应该做的事情。

在过去，在家工作是一个摆脱办公室中的压力和干扰的受欢迎的方法。而且说实话，在家工作时间灵活，我们可以挤出时间办些杂事或是在电话会议的间隙打个盹。

如今，随着管理者想出新方法来确保员工专心工作，在家工作越来越像在办公室上班了。有些公司会跟踪项目进度并在共享日程表上安排会议，有些公司则要求通过电子邮件、即时消息或者电话来进行"虚拟面谈"。另一些公司，比如 Accurate Biometrics，会监控员工的电脑使用情况，无论他们是在家工作还是在公司上班。

位于康涅狄格州斯坦福德市的技术调研公司 Gartner 预计，到 2015 年，企业的电脑安全监控软件使用量将从现在的不足 10% 升至 60%。这些软件主要用于保护敏感数据，同时也是为了遵守政府的规定,但是它们也会生成许多有关员工上网行为的私人信息。律师称,为了避免侵犯员工的隐私,企业应告知员工他们受到监控并只跟踪与工作有关的上网活动。

丹尼尔斯所使用的安全软件是洛杉矶 Awareness Technologies 公司生产的 InterGuard,它被一些金融服务和医疗企业以及其他企业用来跟踪员工的工作效率、防止信息泄露以及遵守信息安全方面的规定。与大多数监控软件相同,它可以让丹尼尔斯查看其所有员工(包括16名在办公室上班和24名在家工作的员工)是否在有效地使用电脑。员工们都知道该监控软件的存在。

位于安大略省伍德布里奇市的监控软件 Work Time 生产商 NesterSoft 的销售专员伊莲娜·普洛斯库米娜称,此类软件可以让管理者发现谁需要帮助、谁又在浪费时间。她说,该公司监控软件 WorkTime 的客户最为关注的监控信息是"使用 Facebook 最多的人"。

各企业称,监控员工并不是为了8小时连续不断把员工绑在工作上。他们也明白,在家工作的员工可能需要抽出时间来处理杂事或是处理工作之外的其他事情。

Passage 2 【参考译文】

Huawei Proposes Comprehensive Intelligent Strategy to Accelerate Intelligent Transformation of Thousands of Industries

Huawei, in the wave of informatization and digitization, has taken a step forward in ten years. Based on the dual-wheel drive of customer demand and technological innovation, Huawei has put forward its All IP strategy and All Cloud strategy, which have promoted ubiquitous connectivity and accelerated digital transformation and upgrading. Facing the age of intelligence, Huawei has proposed the All Intelligence strategy to seize the historic strategic opportunity of AI.

The goal of the All Intelligence strategy is to accelerate the intelligent transformation of thousands of industries, making all objects connected, all applications modeled, and all decisions computable.

Meng Wanzhou, Huawei's vice chairman, rotating chairman, and CFO, said, "Under the guidance of the All Intelligence strategy, Huawei will continue to build a solid base of arithmetic power to enable a hundred models and a thousand modes, and to empower thousand of industries."

First, Huawei is committed to building a solid base of arithmetic power in China, and building a second choice for the world. Meng said, "We will continue to improve the 'soft and hard core edge-end cloud' convergence ability, make thick 'black land', and meet the diverse AI arithmetic needs of various industries."

Secondly, Huawei will support the "blossoming" of large models in the era of intelligence through the opening of the arithmetic base, AI platform, and development tools, and strive to do a good job in the "black soil" of the "hundred gardens". Meng said, "We support each organization to use its own data to train its own big model, so that each industry can use its own expertise to develop its own industry big model."

"Over the past decades, we have delved into the theoretical nature of communication and computing, and have continued to invest and explore in the fields of mathematics and algorithms, chemistry and materials science, physics and engineering technology, standards and patents, to build up a root technological advantage." Facing the intelligent future, Meng said that Huawei will continue to cultivate root technology, adhere to hardware openness and software open source, and work with industrial partners to develop industrial and ecological alliances and talent alliances, and construct a prosperous arithmetic ecosystem.

Memory Practice（记忆训练）

Paragraph 1

Chinese President Xi Jinping sent a congratulatory letter to the 2023 Pujiang Innovation Forum which opened Sunday in Shanghai.

In his letter, President Xi Jinping noted that the world today is living through accelerating changes unseen in a century, and a new round of scientific and technological revolution and industrial transformation is gaining momentum. Scientific and technological innovation is an important force for humankind to jointly address risks and challenges and promote peace and development.

China will firmly pursue a mutually beneficial and win-win strategy of opening-up, continue to expand high-level opening-up, continue to promote international scientific and technological exchanges and cooperation with a more open mindset and a broader range of measures, build a globally competitive open innovation ecosystem, and work with other countries to create an open, fair, just and non-discriminatory environment for scientific and technological development, President Xi Jinping said.

（https://language.chinadaily.com.cn/a/202309/10/WS64fff6e8a310d2dce4bb54ef.html）

Paragraph 2

今年4月，腾讯宣布推出一项促进社会价值可持续创新的计划，并将腾讯公益平台与企业社会责任部升级，设立可持续社会价值事业部。公司首期投入500亿元人民币（约76.7亿美元），对包括基础科学、教育创新、乡村振兴、碳中和、FEW（food, energy and water；食物、能源与水）、公众应急、养老科技和公益数字化等领域展开探索。SSV（sustainable social value，可持续社会价值事业部）成立后，腾讯在员工当中开展了一项调查，发现他们遇到的问题中大约70%与照顾老人有关。因此，SSV建立"银发科技实验室"，专门探索以新兴技术满足老年人需求的机会。

（https://www.tencent.com/zh-cn/articles/2201184.html）

Section 2 Interpreting Practice（口译实训）

Passage 1【参考译文】

新一批稳外资政策鼓励外国公司扩大业务

政府官员和跨国公司高管表示，受全球经济复苏放缓影响，跨境投资有所下降，新出台的政策措施将利用中国庞大可获利的市场优势，促进中国高水平对外开放，优化吸引和利用外资，建立市场驱动、法治化和全球一体化的商业环境。

为了改善外商投资环境，吸引更多国际资本，国务院于周日印发了《关于进一步优化外商投资环境，加大吸引外商投资力度的意见》。政府致力于改善外商投资环境，包括确保有效利用外资、保证对内外资企业一视同仁等六个重点领域。

在国务院政策例行吹风会上，商务部部长助理陈春江表示，这些政策将支持外国公司在华经营，加大外商投资引导力度，强化外商投资促进和服务保障工作。陈春江说："商务部将加强与政府相关部门在政策促进方面的指导和协调，为外国投资者创造更加优化的投资环境，有效增强他们的信心。"财政部经济建设司司长符金陵表示，将采取进一步措施，落实在政府采购活动中对内外资企业一视同仁的要求。

商务部数据显示，在全球经济增长放缓的背景下，2023年上半年，中国吸收的外国直接投资达到7036.5亿元人民币，同比下降2.7%。中国国际经济交流中心科研信息部副部长王晓红表示,虽然中国的外国直接投资增长面临挑战,但其超大市场对高质量商品和服务的强劲需求继续为全球投资者提供良好的前景。

Passage 2【参考译文】

Huawei Investment & Holding Co., Ltd. 2022 Sustainability Report（Excerpt）

Through the TECH4ALL digital inclusion initiative, Huawei has taken concrete steps with global partners to propel technological innovation in four areas of focus: education, environment, health, and development. Huawei believes these will bring positive changes to the world. In education, TECH4ALL education programs had benefited over 600 schools and more than 220,000 people, including teachers and students, unemployed young people, and senior citizens, by the end of 2022. In environment, Huawei's environmental protection programs, such as Tech4Nature and Nature Guardians, have been deployed in 46 protected areas around the world, including forests, wetlands, and oceans. These programs use ICT to enable more efficient and sustainable biodiversity conservation efforts and natural resource management. In health, Huawei has continued optimizing the accessibility features of devices, giving a human touch to technology. In fact, Huawei HarmonyOS 2.0 was the only five-star-rated OS and was awarded the title of "aging-friendly pioneer" according to the 2022 smartphone OS/UI elderly-friendliness ratings released by the China Telecom Research Institute. In development, Huawei Mobile Money has benefited over 400 million people in more than 20 countries, advancing financial inclusion services. It gives people in remote areas access to digital banking services like mobile wallets and mobile payments, boosting the digital economy of local communities. Huawei strives to promote a more equal and sustainable development of the world through digital technology.

Huawei makes cyber security and privacy protection a top priority. Huawei continues to develop secure and trustworthy products, solutions, and services that help customers mitigate risks and improve network resilience. In 2022, Huawei obtained more than 30 internationally recognized cyber security certificates, including CC EAL4+, ISO 19790, and ISO 27034 certificates. These are a testament to the proven security of Huawei products. In 2022, Huawei supported stable communications during over 300 major events and emergencies. These are part of Huawei's long-term commitment to serving local communities. Huawei has also established a mature business continuity management system to ensure supply continuity and timely delivery to customers. Huawei will always pursues globalized and diversified supply strategies for mutual development and shared success. Together with global partners, Huawei aims to create a secure, reliable, competitive, and healthy industry value chain, fostering a better life for all in the future digital world.

Passage 3【参考译文】

谷歌创新的商业管理战略

在不断变化的科技领域,谷歌是成功商业管理的标杆之一。从一个简单的搜索引擎崛起为全球科技巨头,谷歌展示了助力其保持竞争优势的创新战略。在本文中,我们将探讨谷歌商业管理的一些关键方面,正是这些方面促成了其卓越的成功。

1. 创新文化

谷歌对创新的执着深植于其企业文化之中。谷歌鼓励员工将工作时间的一部分用于个人项目,以培养员工的创造力和创业精神。这种方法已经促使了像 Gmail、Google Maps 等开创性产品的开发。谷歌对创新的不懈追求使其始终处于技术进步的前沿。

2. 数据驱动决策

数据是谷歌运营的生命线。谷歌收集并分析大量数据以洞察用户行为和市场趋势。这种数据驱动的方法使谷歌能够做出明智的决策,完善其产品,并为用户提供个性化体验。对数据的细致分析还在谷歌的广告业务中发挥着关键作用,使其成为了在线广告领域的领导者之一。

3. 战略性收购

谷歌一直以来都在进行战略性收购,以扩大其产品组合和市场份额。值得注意的收购案例包括YouTube、Android和Nest Labs。这些收购不仅为谷歌增加了有价值的资产,还使谷歌多元化其业务,并在迅速变化的科技领域保持相关性。

4. 用户至上

谷歌致力于提供以用户为中心的产品和服务一直是其商业战略的基石。通过优先考虑用户体验并提供免费高质量的服务,例如Google搜索、Google Drive和Android操作系统,谷歌已经建立了庞大的用户群体,并保持了用户的信任。这种用户至上的方法转化为了强大的品牌忠诚度。

5. 全球扩张

谷歌采取了积极的全球扩张战略,使其产品和服务在全球范围内均可获得。谷歌致力于提供多语言服务,并适应当地市场,这为其全球成功作出了贡献。谷歌在各个国家的存在使其能够利用多样化的人才资源和用户群体。

6. 环境责任

近年来,谷歌展示出对环境可持续性的承诺。谷歌设定了雄心勃勃的目标,以100%可再生能源运营并实现碳中和。谷歌在清洁能源项目上的投资,对减少碳足迹的关注,与全球日益增长的对气候变化和企业责任的关注相一致。

结论

谷歌从一家小型初创公司到科技巨头的发展之路是创新商业管理战略的体现。谷歌的创新文化、数据驱动决策、战略性收购、用户至上、全球扩张和对环境责任的承诺,推动了其成为科技行业的领军者。随着谷歌不断发展,其适应和创新能力将很可能仍是其在竞争激烈的科技世界中保持成功的核心因素。

Passage 4 【参考译文】

Introduction to Gree

If an enterprise wants to have the right to speak, it must first master core technologies. An enterprise can truly build its own brand only when it creates products that change the world.

An enterprise without innovation is an enterprise without a soul. An enterprise without core technology is an enterprise without a backbone. A person without a backbone can never stand up.

—by Dong Mingzhu

Gree Electric always maintains a sense of crisis and enterprising spirit, recognizing that only by truly mastering core technology can an enterprise truly master its own fate and realize the independent development. Gree Electric has established 15 research institutes by 2019, with a total of 96 research offices, 929 laboratories, and 2 academician workstations (motor and control, building energy efficiency). It has a national key laboratory, a national engineering technology research center, and a national industrial design center, a national certified enterprise technology center, and a robot engineering technology research and development center. It has also become a research and evaluation base for the national notification and consultation center.

The company proposed that R&D funds should be invested on demand, with no upper limit. In 2018 alone, R&D investment reached 7.268 billion yuan. After long-term accumulation, Gree Electric ranked sixth in the country and first in the home appliance industry in the 2018 National Intellectual Property Administration rankings. As of 2019, it has a total of 28 "internationally leading" technologies, and has won 2 National Science and Technology Progress Awards, 2 National Technological Invention Awards, and 4 China Patent Gold Awards.

Section 3 Interpreting Assessment（口译测评）

Passage 1【原文】

Effective Communication in Business Management

Effective communication is the lifeblood of successful business management. It serves as the bridge that connects leaders, employees, and various stakeholders, facilitating the exchange of ideas, expectations, and information essential for achieving organizational goals. In this article, we explore the paramount importance of effective communication in the realm of business management.

Setting clear expectations

One of the fundamental aspects of effective communication in business management is the ability of leaders to set clear expectations. Managers must convey their objectives, standards, and performance metrics to their teams explicitly. When employees have a comprehensive understanding of what is expected of them, they are more likely to align their efforts with organizational goals.

Sharing information

Effective communication involves a continuous flow of information within an organization. Managers should provide regular updates on company developments, changes in strategies, and market insights. Keeping employees informed fosters a sense of inclusion and empowers them to make informed decisions in their roles.

Ensuring role clarity

In a well-structured organization, each employee should have a defined role with associated responsibilities. Through open and transparent communication, managers can ensure that employees understand their roles, how their contributions fit into the larger picture, and how their work impacts the organization's success. This clarity prevents role ambiguity and reduces friction in workflow.

Fostering collaboration

Open communication channels encourage collaboration among team members. When employees feel comfortable sharing ideas and feedback, it enhances problem-solving and innovation. Collaboration culture can lead to more efficient processes and the development of creative solutions to challenges.

Promoting a positive work culture

Transparency and open communication contribute significantly to the creation of a positive work culture. When employees perceive that their voices are heard and their opinions valued, they are more engaged and motivated. This, in turn, leads to higher job satisfaction and lower turnover rates.

Addressing challenges promptly

Effective communication also plays a critical role in addressing challenges and conflicts promptly. When issues arise, managers should be accessible to listen to concerns, mediate disputes, and find resolutions. Timely communication prevents problems from festering and becoming more significant issues.

In conclusion, effective communication is the cornerstone of successful business management. It empowers managers to set clear expectations, share information, ensure role clarity, foster collaboration, promote a positive work culture, and address challenges promptly. By prioritizing open and transparent communication, organizations can create an environment conducive to productivity, innovation, and long-term success.

Passage 1【参考译文】

企业管理中的有效沟通

有效沟通是成功的商业管理的生命线。它充当着连接领导者、员工和各方利益相关者的桥梁，促进了思想、期望和信息的交流，这对于实现组织目标至关重要。在本文中，我们将探讨在商业管理领域有效沟通的至关重要性。

明确期望

在商业管理中有效沟通的基本方面之一是领导者明确期望的能力。管理者必须明确传达他们的目标、标准和绩效指标给他们的团队。当员工全面了解对他们的期望时，员工更有可能使自己的努力与组织目标相一致。

分享信息

有效沟通包括在组织内部不断传递信息。管理者应定期提供有关公司发展、战略变化和市场见解的更新。让员工保持信息透明度有助于他们获得参与感，并使他们能够在自己的角色中做出明智的决策。

确保角色明确

在一个结构良好的组织中，每个员工都应该有明确的角色和与之对应的责任。通过开放和透明的沟通，管理者可以确保员工了解自己的角色，了解他们的贡献如何融入更大的格局，并了解他们的工作如何影响组织的成功。这种明确性可以防止角色模糊，减少工作流程中的摩擦。

促进协作

开放的沟通渠道鼓励团队成员之间的协作。当员工乐于分享想法和反馈时，有助于解决问题和创新。协作文化能够带来更高效的流程和对挑战性问题的创造性解决方案的开发。

促进积极的工作文化

透明和开放的沟通对于创造积极的工作文化有重要影响。当员工感知到他们的声音被听到并且他们的意见受到重视时，他们会更有参与感和积极性。这反过来使得工作满意度更高和离职率更低。

及时解决挑战

有效的沟通还在及时解决挑战和冲突方面发挥着关键作用。当问题出现时，管理者应该保持沟通顺畅，听取关切，调解纠纷，并寻求解决方案。及时的沟通可以防止问题恶化。

总之，有效的沟通是成功的商业管理的基石。它使管理者能够明确期望、分享信息、确保角色明确、促进协作、促进积极的工作文化并及时解决挑战。通过优先考虑开放和透明的沟通，组织可以创造出有利于生产力、创新和长期成功的环境。

Passage 2【原文】

京东集团

京东坚守"正道成功"的价值取向，坚定地践行用合法方式获得商业成功；以合规作为立身之本，让"合规即发展"的理念深深地融入企业的各项业务中。自创立之初，京东就秉持诚信经营的核心理念，坚守正品行货，成为中国备受消费者信赖的企业。京东坚定"客户为先"的服务理念，大力发展自建物流，打造极致消费体验，成为全球领先的新标杆。

与此同时，京东不忘初心，积极履行企业社会责任，在助力实体经济高质量发展、促进高质量就业、带动高质量消费、推动乡村振兴、提升社会效率、推动供给侧结构性改革等方面不断为社会作出贡献。

疫情期间，京东坚持不间断的运营，持续保障民生供应和医疗物资运输，多管齐下促进社会就业。2016年起，京东全面推进落实电商精准扶贫工作，通过品牌打造、自营直采、地方特产、众筹扶贫等模式，在全国各地贫困地区开展扶贫工作，上线贫困地区商品超过300万种。积极投身乡村振兴，京东全面启动"奔富计划"，并于2020年10月发布"三年带动农村一万亿产值成长"的目标。京东同时在全国打造多个"奔富村"，帮助数百万农户大幅增收。依托强大的物流基础设施网络和供应链整合能力，京东大幅提升了行业运营效率，降低了社会成本。通过打造高质量消费，京东以商品和服务为抓手、以技术创新为依托，带动实体经济数字化转型，促进产业和消费"双升级"，进一步助力供给侧结构性改革，推动实体经济高质量发展。京东持续促进高质量就业，不仅努力为每一位员工提供施展才干和实现梦想的舞台，还努力成为让所有员工有归属感、幸福感的企业。截至2022年底，京东体系员工总数超过55万人。京东为员工尤其是一线员工提供有竞争力的薪酬，并为员工提供"五险一金"，2022年京东物流一线员工薪酬福利支出达446亿元，近三年累计支出1065亿元。同时京东为快递员、客服在内所有员工设立百亿"住房保障基金"，为其提供购房无息贷款，并大幅扩充"员工子女救助基金"的规模，为数十万家庭提供坚实的生活保障。

二十年来，京东始终坚持"以实助实"，凭借扎实的基础设施、高效的数智化社会供应链、创新的技术服务能力，在保持自身健康发展的同时，一直努力为用户提供极致消费体验、帮助合作伙伴高质量增长、为社会创造更多价值。

（https://about.jd.com/company）

Passage 2 【参考译文】

JD Group

JD (Jing dong) adheres to the value orientation of "success through the right path" and firmly practices legal means to achieve commercial success. It takes compliance as its foundation and deeply integrates the concept of "compliance is development" into the company's various businesses. Since its inception, JD has adhered to the core concept of "integrity in business" and adhered to genuine licensed products, becoming a company trusted by consumers in China. JD adheres to the service concept of "customer first", vigorously develops self-built logistics, and creates the ultimate consumer experience, becomes a new benchmark for global leadership.

At the same time, JD remains true to its original aspirations and actively fulfills its corporate social responsibilities. It continues to contribute to society in areas such as supporting high-quality development of the real economy, promoting high-quality employment, driving high-quality consumption, promoting rural revitalization, improving social efficiency, and promoting supply-side structural reform.

During the epidemic, JD insisted on uninterrupted operations, continued to ensure the supply of people's livelihood and the transportation of medical supplies, and promoted social employment through a multi-pronged approach. Since 2016, JD has comprehensively promoted the implementation of e-commerce targeted poverty alleviation work. Through brand building, self-operated direct procurement, local specialties, crowdfunding poverty alleviation and other models, it has carried out poverty alleviation work in poverty-stricken areas across the country, and launched more than 3 million products in poverty-stricken areas. Actively participating in rural revitalization, JD has fully launched the "Benfu Plan" and announced in October 2020 the goal of "driving the growth of rural output value of RMB 1 trillion in three years". At the same time, JD has created multiple "Benfu Villages" across the country to help millions of farmers significantly increase their income. Relying on its strong logistics infrastructure network and supply chain integration capabilities, JD has significantly improved industry operating efficiency and reduced social costs. By creating high-quality consumption, JD focuses on goods and services and relies on technological innovation to drive the digital transformation of the real economy, promote the "double upgrade" of industry and consumption, further assist the supply-side structural reform, and promote high-quality development of the real economy. JD continues to promote high-quality employment. It not only strives to provide every employee with a stage to display their talents and realize their dreams, but also strives to become an enterprise that gives all employees a sense of belonging and happiness. As of the end of 2022, the total number of employees in the JD system has exceeded 550,000. JD provides competitive salaries to employees, especially front-line employees, and provides them with "five insurances and one fund". In 2022, JD Logistics' front-line employees' salary and welfare expenses has reached 44.6 billion yuan, and the cumulative expenditure in the past three years is 106.5 billion yuan. At the same time, a tens of billions of "Housing Security Fund" was established for all employees, including delivery staff and customer service staff. JD also provided employees with interest-free loans for purchasing houses, and significantly expanded the scale of the "Employee Children's Assistance Fund" to provide solid living security for hundreds of thousands of families.

Over the past twenty years, JD has always adhered to the principle of "helping the real with the real", and with its solid infrastructure, highly efficient digitalized social supply chain, and innovative technical service capabilities, JD has been striving to provide users with the ultimate consumer experience, help its partners to achieve high-quality growth, and create more value for the society, while maintaining its own healthy development.

Unit 13　Business Exhibition（商务会展）

Section 1　Interpreting Preparation（口译准备）

Sight Interpreting（视译）

Passage 1【参考译文】

约瑟芬·特奥部长在未来经济会议暨展览会上的讲话（节选）

我们致力于在三个方面帮助我们的企业进行数字化转型并最大限度地利用数字经济中的新机遇。

第一，随着我们进入复苏的新阶段，我们将确保营造一个充满活力的环境，让企业能够在数字经济中蓬勃发展。

第二，我们将通过强大的人才储备维持数字经济的增长。

第三，我们将保持开放创新，与大家携手共创数字化未来。

下面，我将就这三个方面的计划进行更详细的分享。

多年来，我们为蓬勃发展的数字经济奠定了坚实的基础。从1986年第一个国家IT计划开始，我们进行了强有力的持续投资，以数字化的方式连接人员和企业。

新加坡拥有先进、安全和有弹性的数字基础设施，这对于实现数字经济至关重要。在电信领域，我们是全球率先推出5G独立网络的国家之一。

我们设定的目标是，到2025年，实现全国室外5G覆盖。根据我最近与我们的电信公司的讨论，这个目标很可能提前实现。

无论如何，我们已经把目光投向了下一个目标，向未来通信研发计划（FCP）投入7000万美元，进行包括6G在内的尖端通信和连接研究。6G的标准尚未制定，因此这是我们可以积极参与其中，共同塑造未来的开放领域。

在对实体基础设施的投资基础上，我们还开发了一套数字化实用工具，使企业和公民能够在整个经济中轻松、安全地进行交易。其中一些实用工具，例如新加坡电子身份验证系统、即时支付系统和电子发票系统，为日常交易提供了便利，在全国范围内创造了显著的网络效益。

其他机构，例如新加坡贸易数据交流平台（SGTraDex），通过数据共享帮助海事等特定行业解决业务碎片化问题，这将提高我们整个供应链生态系统的效率。

我们的支持还延伸至个体企业，尤其是占新加坡企业绝大多数的中小型企业（SME）。认识到不同行业都有独特的需求，于是我们在2017年推出了行业数字化计划，为各行业的中小企业提供所需的数字化工具和培训指导。同年，我们还启动了中小企业数字化计划，为企业发展的每个阶段提供数字化解决方案。自此，超过80 000家企业在20个行业数字化计划的支持下受益于中小企业数字化计划。

行业见解对于形成政府支持具有指导意义。为此，我要感谢新加坡商业联合会在我们开发"以数据驱动更优质业务"计划时与行业的密切合作。

我们期待与大家合作，打造一个互联、安全、有弹性、充满活力的数字经济。我祝愿大家在数字化之旅中一切顺利，并祝愿今天的讨论富有成果。谢谢。

Passage 2 【参考译文】

Chinese Companies in the Post-pandemic Era: Going out for More Business Opportunities (Excerpt)

Chinese enterprises, no matter whether they're big names, unicorn startups or small and micro enterprises, share a common goal at this year's CES —to go overseas seeking more business opportunities in the post-pandemic era.

To fulfill that goal, they are bringing their best products to Las Vegas, hoping to increase global visibility, optimize overseas market share and grow and develop together with their overseas partners.

At the Las Vegas Convention Center, China's major consumer electronics manufacturer TCL installed its 1,650-square-meter booth adjacent to those of competitors such as Sony, LG, Samsung and Panasonic. On the CES floor display are TCL's ultra-large-screen Mini LED QLED TV lineup, sound bars, smartphones, and augmented reality demonstrations, among others.

Mark Zhang, general manager of North America marketing division, TCL Industries, said that only by competing against the strongest players worldwide and surviving in the most competitive market can a company grow.

According to TCL, global sales of TCL smart screens reached 16.62 million sets in the first three quarters of 2022. Now, TCL is a top 2 LCD display brand both worldwide and North America, and maintain top positions in key markets around the world. TCL's sales of premium QLED smart screens and

Mini LED smart screens are leading the global market.

North America, the United States in particular, has been the most important and biggest market for TCL, said Zhang. "We are user-centric and committed to only providing customers their best experiences with purchase, usage and client service," he explained.

TCL remains in close cooperation and collaboration with American high-tech giants such as Google, Roku and Dolby. On the global stages, TCL continues to work with leading players in the fields of Mini LED, QLED TVs, AR/VR, 5G, AI and cloud computing.

As a Chinese manufacturing company that went global earlier than its counterparts, TCL has transformed from internationalization to globalization after more than two decades. "We are witnesses and beneficiaries of this process," Zhang said.

Memory Practice（记忆训练）

Paragraph 1

The 2023 China Jingdezhen International Ceramic Expo opened Wednesday in the city of Jingdezhen, a world-famous "porcelain capital" in east China's Jiangxi Province. Themed "Ceramics Facilitate World Communication, Ceramic Trade Connects the World," this year's expo has an exhibition area of 130,000 square meters. Nearly 1,000 enterprises, including more than 360 from overseas, are attending the expo. Fine traditional Chinese culture has never been interrupted since ancient times. Porcelain is a Chinese treasure and an important symbol of Chinese culture. The principle of protection first and like-for-like renovation has been followed in the protection of Taoyangli Historical and Cultural Block, thus facilitating a mutually reinforcing interaction between ceramic cultural protection and the development of cultural and tourism industry.

（https://language.chinadaily.com.cn/a/202310/19/WS6531e038a31090682a5e9b7a.html）

Paragraph 2

中国义乌国际小商品（标准）博览会，简称"义博会"，创办于1995年，是经国务院批准的日用消费品类国际性展会，由商务部、浙江省人民政府等联合主办，已连续举办28届，自第26届起义博会主办单位新增国家标准化管理委员会，并更名为中国义乌国际小商品（标准）博览会，自此成为国内首个植入标准元素的国际展览会。义博会以"面向世界、服务全国"为办展宗旨，办展特色鲜明，国际化水平突出，信息功能强劲，服务体系完善，安全卫生保障到位，参展成效显著，已成为目前国内最具规模、最具影响、最有成效的日用消费品展会。

第29届义博会将于2023年10月21—24日在浙江义乌举行。本届义博会将设国际标准展位3600个，同期还将举办中外采购洽谈会等多项经贸活动。

（https://www.yiwufair.com/cpzz/about/）

Section 2 Interpreting Practice（口译实训）

Passage 1【参考译文】

中国国际投资贸易洽谈会新闻

作为全球最具影响力的投资盛会之一，中国国际投资贸易洽谈会（CIFIT，以下简称投洽会）努力打造高水平对外开放重要平台。海外、国际机构代表纷纷表示，参展意义重大，投洽会是一个很有活力，可以促进投资和商业关系的平台。

卡塔尔是投洽会的"老朋友"了，作为今年的主宾国，卡塔尔将突出其商业生态系统的优势和竞争力,展示其创新、专长和合作潜力。

卡塔尔一位高级官员介绍,投洽会在亚洲范围内颇具盛名。它搭建了一个充满活力的平台,以培育全球商业关系、促进观点和专业知识的交流,以及增加海外投资机会,并因此而闻名。

今年的投洽会,卡塔尔的关注重点仍是促进重要的合作伙伴关系、推动经济增长,以及培养持久的国际关系。卡塔尔先进的基础设施、市场准入、增长潜力和安全保证是吸引投资者和企业的根本性因素。

联合国工业发展组织(UNIDO)副总干事法图·海达拉女士说,作为联合主办方,UNIDO每年都积极参与CIFIT的各种活动,包括展览、洽谈和论坛。"我们很高兴看到我们的许多报告,像《非洲投资报告》《埃塞俄比亚工业升级报告》和《2018年金砖国家电子商务发展研究报告》在CIFIT发布。这可以提升发展中国家的投资吸引力。"

海达拉女士说:"今年,我们正在实施600多个项目,总价值接近6.3亿美元。例如,UNIDO协助埃塞俄比亚开发农业-工业园区,至今已为当地社区创造了10万多个就业岗位。"

Passage 2【参考译文】

Remarks by H. E. Xi Jinping
President of the People's Republic of China
At the Opening Ceremony of the Fifth China International Import Expo

Your Excellencies Heads of State and Government,

Your Excellencies Heads of International Organizations,

Your Excellencies Heads of Delegations,

Distinguished Guests,

Ladies and Gentlemen,

Friends,

Good evening! I would like to extend, on behalf of the Chinese government and people and also in my own name, a warm welcome and hearty greetings to all our guests attending the Fifth China International Import Expo.

Five years ago, I announced the decision to hold the CIIE for the very purpose of expanding China's opening-up and turning our enormous market into enormous opportunities for the world. Today, the CIIE has become a showcase of China's new development paradigm, a platform for high-standard opening-up, and a public good for the whole world.

Openness is a key driving force behind the progress of human civilizations and an intrinsic path toward global prosperity and development. The world today is confronted with accelerated unprecedented changes in a century as well as a sluggish economic recovery. We should commit ourselves to openness to meet development challenges, foster synergy for cooperation, build the momentum of innovation, and deliver benefits to all. We should steadily advance economic globalization, enhance every country's dynamism of growth, and provide all nations with greater and fairer access to the fruits of development.

Ladies and Gentlemen,

Friends,

As the 20th National Congress of the Communist Party of China has underscored, China remains committed to the fundamental national policy of opening-up to the outside world, pursues a mutually beneficial strategy of open strategy, and adheres to the right course of economic globalization. We will amplify the interplay between domestic and international markets and resources, strive to create new opportunities for the world with our own development, and contribute our share to building an open global economy.

——China will work with all countries and all parties to share the opportunities in its vast market. We will step up efforts to cultivate a robust domestic market, upgrade trade in goods, develop new mechanisms for trade in services, and import more quality products. We will establish pilot zones for Silk Road e-commerce cooperation and build national demonstration zones for innovation in services trade development, so as to encourage innovation in trade and promote high-quality Belt and Road cooperation.

——China will work with all countries and all parties to share the opportunities from its institutional opening-up. We will steadily expand institutional opening-up with regard to rules, regulations, management and standards, put into full effect the new *Catalogue of Encouraged Industries for Foreign Investment*, and further develop the national comprehensive demonstration zone for further opening-up in the service sector. We will implement the strategy to upgrade free trade pilot zones, accelerate the Hainan Free Trade Port development, and tap into their role as pilot platforms for comprehensive reform and opening-up.

——China will work with all countries and all parties to share the opportunities from deepened international cooperation. We will engage fully and deeply in WTO reform negotiations, promote trade and investment liberalization and facilitation, and enhance international macro-economic policy coordination, with a view to jointly fostering new drivers for global growth. We will endeavor actively to join the *Comprehensive and Progressive Agreement for Trans-Pacific Partnership* (CPTPP) and the *Digital Economy Partnership Agreement* (DEPA) to expand the globally-oriented network of high-standard free trade areas. We will firmly support other developing countries and assist them in growing faster, and promote the building of a community with a shared future for mankind.

Ladies and Gentlemen,

Friends,

"After endless mountains and rivers that leave doubt whether there is a path out, suddenly one encounters the shade of a willow, bright flowers and a lovely village." As this ancient Chinese poem indicates, the path is unfolding before us, and a brighter future beckons beyond. China is ready to work with all countries to practice true multilateralism, build more consensus for openness, jointly overcome the difficulties and challenges confronting global economic growth, and make sure that our commitment to openness will bring about broad prospects for global development.

Thank you!

Passage 3 【参考译文】
王文涛部长出席"投资中国年"高峰会议暨上海城市推介并致辞

11月5日,"投资中国年"高峰会议暨上海城市推介在上海举行,上海市委书记陈吉宁、商务部部长王文涛、香港特别行政区行政长官李家超出席并致辞。上海市市长龚正出席并作专题推介。联合国贸易和发展会议秘书长丽贝卡·格林斯潘、国际贸易中心执行主任帕梅拉·科克-汉密尔顿以及部分世界500强企业全球CEO出席并发言。商务部副部长兼国际贸易谈判副代表凌激主持会议。

王文涛表示,中国政府高度重视利用外资工作。习近平主席多次指出,要更大力度吸引和利用外资，增强对外资的吸引力。今年以来，商务部积极举办"投资中国年"招商引资活动，推动高水平开放，促进交流、增进合作。活动启动8个月以来，商务部共举办重点活动近20场，各地组织省级以上配套招商活动500余场，取得了积极成效。

王文涛强调，商务部将继续按照党中央、国务院决策部署，进一步放宽外资准入，推动制度型开放，提升服务水平，优化营商环境，持续打造"投资中国"品牌，不断提升利用外资水平，让中国始终成为投资的热土。

18个省（区、市）人民政府负责同志，各地商务主管部门负责同志，跨国公司及外国商协会代表共300余人参加了会议。

Passage 4【参考译文】

Remarks by Chinese Premier Li Qiang at Session Ⅰ of the 18th G20 Summit (Except)

We need to step up macroeconomic policy coordination, uphold the security of the international economic and financial systems, promote innovations in the digital economy and inject confidence and impetus into global growth, to be partners in promoting the world economic recovery. We need to steadfastly advance economic globalization, support the multilateral trading regime, firmly oppose the politicization of economic and trade issues, and keep global industrial and supply chains stable and smooth, to be partners in promoting open cooperation at the global level. We need to jointly protect planet Earth as our green home. We should uphold the principle of common but differentiated responsibilities, follow through on the G20 "Green Development Pact", push forward green and low-carbon development, and protect the marine ecological environment, to be partners in promoting global sustainable development. In a word, we must choose solidarity over division, cooperation over confrontation, and inclusiveness over exclusion. Only by doing so can we open up brighter prospects for global development and usher in a better future for humankind.

China has all along stood for peace, development and win-win cooperation. We are committed to being a builder of world peace, contributor to global development and defender of the international order. Going forward, we will remain firm in deepening reform, expanding opening-up, pursuing high-quality development, and advancing Chinese modernization. This year, the Chinese economy has generally been on an upward trajectory, and solid progress has been made in high-quality development. China's development enjoys bright prospects, and will inject more and fresh impetus to the global recovery and sustainable development. China will host the third Belt and Road Forum for International Cooperation in October and the Sixth China International Import Expo in November. All parties are welcome to take an active part in these events and share the opportunities of mutually beneficial cooperation. China is ready to make greater efforts together with all other parties for the good of our common planet, common home and common future!

Section 3 Interpreting Assessment（口译测评）

Passage 1【原文】

Lenovo Group Further Invests in Cutting-edge Technology

Lenovo Group is stepping up its push to invest in hard cutting-edge technologies such as robotics and chips, as part of its broader push to hone its technological prowess.

Song Chunyu, Vice President of Lenovo Group and Senior Partner of Lenovo Capital & Incubator Group, said the world is undergoing a new round of technological revolution and industrial transformation, with technological innovation as the strongest driving force for economic upgrading, all accelerating the process of digital and intelligent transition in various industries.

Amid the digital wave, technological innovation and industrial integration have brought three new investment opportunities: large computing, AI platform and original innovation, Song said.

Lenovo Capital & Incubator Group estimated that the demand for computing power in the world will continue to grow hundredfold in the next decade. Since its establishment in 2016, new computing has been a key investment direction. Currently, it has invested in new computing architectures, application-oriented chip design and end-to-end cloud collaboration, among other areas related to computing power.

In the smart chip and new computing exhibition area, as part of Lenovo's on-going innovation exhibition this week at its headquarters in Beijing, more than 10 chip enterprises invested by Lenovo showcased their latest technologies. Cambricon Technology, for instance, showcased its latest AI chip.

As of now, Lenovo Capital & Incubator Group has invested in more than 200 startups. Fifteen of them have successfully launched IPOs (Initial Public Offerings), and more than 40 have become unicorns in related fields.

(http://www.chinadaily.com.cn/a/202307/14/WS64b132f2a31035260b816886.html)

Passage 1 【参考译文】

联想集团进一步投资尖端技术

联想集团正在加大力度投资机器人和芯片等尖端技术，作为其更广泛地磨练技术实力的一部分。

联想集团副总裁、联想创投集团高级合伙人宋春雨表示，当今世界正在经历新一轮的科技革命和产业变革，科技创新成为经济升级的最强动力，加速了各行各业向数字化和智能化转型的进程。

宋说，在数字化浪潮中，技术创新和产业融合带来了大计算、人工智能平台和原始创新三大新的投资机会。

联想创投集团预计，未来十年全球对算力的需求将持续增长百倍。自2016年成立以来，新计算一直是联想创投集团的重点投资方向。目前，它已投资于新型计算架构、面向应用的芯片设计和端到端的云协作等与算力相关的领域。

在智能芯片与新计算展区，作为联想本周在北京总部持续举办的创新展的一部分，联想投资的10多家芯片企业展示了他们的最新技术。例如寒武纪科技就展示了其最新的人工智能芯片。

截至目前，联想创投集团已投资超过200家初创企业。其中15家已完成首次公开招股，40多家已成为相关领域的独角兽企业。

Passage 2 【原文】

广交会新闻

广交会是中国对外开放的重要窗口和对外贸易的重要平台，是企业开拓国际市场的重要渠道。67年来，广交会为服务国际贸易、促进内外联通、推动经济发展作出了重要贡献。党的十八大以来，习近平总书记两次向广交会致贺信，充分肯定了广交会的重要作用，为广交会的发展指明了方向。

疫情防控平稳转段后，第133届广交会首次全面恢复线下展，4月15日至5月5日分三期在广州举办，同时全年常态化运营线上平台。这是全面贯彻落实党的二十大精神开局之年举办的首届广交会，是中国取得疫情防控重大决定性胜利后举办的首届广交会，也是有史以来规模最大的一届广交会，意义重大。在全面建设社会主义现代化国家新征程上，全体外贸人主动作为、积极创新，努力让广交会这本书常写常新。

题材新。面对国际贸易新趋势和全球市场新需求，本届广交会紧贴市场热点，增设工业自动化及智能制造、新能源及智能网联汽车、智慧生活、"银发经济"等新题材，向全球充分展示中国产业升级、贸易转型和科技创新成果。这是广交会展区结构与时俱进的重要调整，有助于加强全球新兴产业交流，推动贸易创新发展。

产品新。本届广交会用"新"促转型。线上展300多万件展品中，新产品达80万件，绿色低碳产品超50万件。举办新品首发首展首秀活动约300场，涵盖工业制造、电子家电、建材家装、生活休闲等领域。组织2023年广交会设计创新奖（CF奖）评选，引导企业加快研发创新。高端化、智能化、定制化、品牌化和绿色低碳产品深受全球采购商青睐，创新成为企业开拓国际市场的新引擎。

面孔新。本届广交会"卖全球、买全球"，汇聚境内外参展商近3.5万家，其中新参展企业超9000家，既有制造业单项冠军，也有专精特新"小巨人"；既有中国高新技术企业，也有来自五大洲的世界级品牌企业。全球229个国家和地区的采购商线上线下踊跃参会，"新面孔"不断涌现，"老广交"后继有人。广交会全球合作伙伴增至186家，覆盖102个国家和地区，朋友圈越来越大。

功能新。本届广交会丰富业态，拓展功能，优化服务，充分发挥多功能综合平台作用。成功举办第二届珠江国际贸易论坛，向世界宣示中国坚定不移推进高水平开放和高质量发展的决心。海内外嘉宾围绕贸易数字化、知识产权国际合作、拓展新兴市场、投资促进等前沿话题展开研讨，发出广交会声音，讲好广交会故事，贡献广交会智慧。

广交会是一本大书，内涵丰富，故事精彩。读懂广交会，就能更好地了解中国，更好地了解世界。让广交会这本书常写常新，就要紧跟全球经贸发展大势，顺应展览业发展规律，持续提升国际化、专业化、市场化、数字化水平，全力将广交会打造成为中国全方位对外开放、促进国际贸易高质量发展、联通国内国际双循环的重要平台。

征途漫漫，惟有奋斗。展望未来，我们将秉持"广交世界 互利天下"的理念，持续擦亮广交会金字招牌，奋力书写广交会高质量发展新篇章，为推进贸易强国建设、维护全球产业链供应链稳定、服务构建新发展格局作出新的贡献。

（http://paper.people.com.cn/rmrbhwb/html/2023-04/25/content_25977623.htm）

Passage 2【参考译文】

News from Canton Fair

The China Import and Export Fair, or Canton Fair, has become a key window for China's opening-up and a great platform for foreign trade. It is also an important channel for enterprises to expand into international markets. Over the past 67 years, Canton Fair has made significant contributions to serving international trade, connecting domestic and international markets, and promoting economic development. Since the 18th National Congress of the Communist Party of China, General Secretary Xi Jinping has sent congratulatory letters to the Canton Fair twice, fully affirming the important role of the Canton Fair and pointing out the direction for its development.

The 133rd Canton Fair, which took place in Guangzhou from April 15 to May 5 in three phases, resumed its offline exhibitions for the first time after the smooth transition of epidemic prevention and control. And its online operation will run throughout the year. This is the first Canton Fair held in the year of comprehensively implementing the spirit of the 20th National Congress of the Communist Party of

China, and the first Canton Fair held after China achieved a major victory in epidemic prevention and control. The 133rd Canton Fair, as the largest one in its history, is of great significance. On the new journey of comprehensively building a modern socialist country, all foreign trade business insiders have taken the initiatives to make Canton Fair better.

New themes. In response to some new trends in international trade and new demands in the global market, the current Canton Fair has closely followed the market hotspots, adding new themes such as industrial automation and intelligent manufacturing, new energy and intelligent connected vehicles, smart living, and the "elderly economy". These themes fully showcase China's industrial upgrading, trade transformation, and technological innovation achievements to the world. It is an important adjustment to the layout of the Canton Fair exhibition areas to keep with the times, which helps to promote exchanges in emerging industries worldwide and boost innovative development in trade.

New products. This session of Canton Fair is promoting such transformation through innovative measures. Among the more than 3 million items displayed online, there are around 800,000 new products and over 500,000 green and low-carbon products. Nearly 300 events involving the launches of new products were held in fields including industrial manufacturing, electronic appliances, construction materials and decoration, and household and entertainment. The Canton Fair Design Innovation Award (CF Award) for 2023 encourages companies to accelerate research and innovation. High-end, intelligent, customized, branded, and green and low-carbon products are highly favored by global buyers. Innovation has become a new engine to drive companies to expand into the international market.

New faces. The current Canton Fair, under the theme of "Selling to the World and Buying from the World", brought together nearly 35,000 exhibitors from home and abroad, including over 9,000 new companies. Among them, there are both single-item champions in the manufacturing industry and "small giants" with typical advantages in the industry. There are not only Chinese high-tech companies but also world-class brands from around the globe. Buyers from 229 countries and regions around the world participated in the event online and offline, with new faces emerging while traditional Canton Fair exhibitors continuing to appear. The number of overseas partners of this session of Canton Fair increased to 186, covering 102 countries and regions, indicating an expanding circle of friends.

New functions. This Canton Fair will enrich business formats, expand functions, optimize services, and give full play to the role of a multi-functional comprehensive platform. The successful holding of the Second Pearl River International Trade Forum demonstrated to the world China's unswerving determination to promote high-level opening-up and high-quality development. Guests from home and abroad held discussions on cutting-edge topics such as trade digitization, international cooperation on intellectual property, expansion of emerging markets, and investment promotion, speaking out about the Canton Fair, telling the Canton Fair's stories well, and contributing to the Canton Fair's wisdom.

The Canton Fair is a big book with rich connotations and exciting stories. By understanding the Canton Fair, you can better understand China and the world. To make the book of the Canton Fair always fresh, we must keep up with the global economic and trade development trends, comply with the development laws of the exhibition industry, continue to improve the level of internationalization, specialization, marketization, and digitalization, and make every effort to build the Canton Fair into an important platform for China's comprehensive opening-up, promoting high-quality development of international trade and connecting domestic and international dual circulation.

The journey is long and we must work hard for a brighter future. Looking forward to the future, we will uphold the concept of "Canton Fair, Global Share", continue to promote the reputation of Canton Fair, strive to write a new chapter of high-quality development of the Canton Fair, and make new contributions for promoting the construction of a strong trading country, maintaining the stability of the global industrial chain and supply chain, and fostering the new development paradigm.

参考文献

[1] 李长栓. 非文学翻译理论与实践 [M]. 北京：对外翻译出版社，2008：1-13.
[2] 秦亚青，何群，何其莘，等. 英汉视译 [M]. 北京：外语教学与研究出版社，2009：1-9.
[3] 宋菁，安文婧. 商务英语口译实务 [M]. 重庆：重庆大学出版社，2015：1-25.
[4] 汪涛. 英汉口译笔记法教程 [M]. 武汉：武汉大学出版社，2012：31-94.
[5] 郑家鑫. 英汉口译红皮书 [M]. 武汉：武汉大学出版社，2010：75-76.
[6] 仲伟合，赵军峰，莫爱屏，等. 英语口译教程 [M]. 北京：高等教育出版社，2006：1-19.
[7] 张威，王克非. 口译与工作记忆研究 [J]. 外语与外语教学，2007，(1)：43-47.
[8] GILE D. Basic Concepts and Models for Interpreter and Translator Training [M]. Amsterdam & Philadelphia：John Benjamins，1995：179.
[9] WARRINGTON E K，BADDELEY A D. Amnesia and memory for visual location [J]. Neuropsychologia，1974，12 (2)：257-263.
[10] BADDELEY A D，HITCH G. Working memory [J]. Psychology of Learning and Motivation，1974，8：47-89.
[11] BADDELEY A D. The episodic buffer：a new component of working memory [J]. Trends in Cognitive Sciences，2000，4 (11)：417-423.
[12] MILLER G. Human memory and the storage of information [J]. IRE Transactions on Information Theory，1956，2 (3)：129-137.
[13] 温家宝总理在第三届东亚峰会上的讲话 [EB/OL]. (2007-11-22) [2023-10-16]. https://www.gov.cn/ldhd/2007-11/22/content_812088.html.
[14] 刘光源特派员在第四届粤港澳大湾区论坛上的主旨演讲 [EB/OL]. (2021-11-30) [2023-10-16]. https://mp.weixin.qq.com/s/nRp5wRhU1n-7ea6ta17pew.
[15] 普林斯顿大学校长2023年开学日演讲：批判思考，大方拥抱！[EB/OL]. (2023-09-06) [2023-10-16]. https://mp.weixin.qq.com/s/M2IanIJAaanYMF7aK7G_MA.
[16] "放慢脚步，弥合裂缝"：耶鲁大学校长2023—2024学年开学典礼演讲 [EB/OL]. (2023-09-04) [2023-10-16]. https://mp.weixin.qq.com/s/DyWgbwY8jqcGWUba27HVEg.
[17] Guangdong-CELAC trade volume tops 65.5 bln U.S. dollars in 2022 [EB/OL]. (2023-05-26) [2023-10-16]. https://language.chinadaily.com.cn/a/202305/26/WS6470509da310b6054fad5493.html.
[18] APEC经济体应秉持开放态度 [EB/OL]. (2023-11-17) [2023-12-06]. https://language.chinadaily.com.cn/a/202311/17/WS655718c5a31090682a5eecc7.html.
[19] 第134届广交会吸引15万采购商 [EB/OL]. (2023-10-26) [2023-12-06]. https://language.chinadaily.com.cn/a/202310/26/WS653a30cea31090682a5eaefe.html.
[20] China's foreign trade hits over $5t in Jan-Nov period. [EB/OL]. (2023-12-08) [2023-12-09]. https://language.chinadaily.com.cn/a/202312/08/WS6572ca95a31040ac301a6ddb.html.
[21] 我国工业企业利润连续3个月保持正增长 [EB/OL]. (2023-11-28) [2023-12-09]. https://language.chinadaily.com.cn/a/202311/28/WS6565ab0fa31090682a5f06ed.html.
[22] 习近平在中法企业家委员会第六次会议闭幕式上的致辞 [R/OL]. (2024-05-07) [2024-05-08]. https://www.gov.cn/yaowen/liebiao/202405/content_6949484.htm.
[23] When Brothers Are of One Heart and One Mind，They Have the Strength to Break Metal [EB/OL]. (2023-05-25) [2023-12-03]. https://www.fmprc.gov.cn/mfa_eng/wjb_663304/wjbz_663308/2461_663310/202305/t20230526_11084380.html.
[24] 石本俊，战秀琴. 商务英语口译实训教程 [M]. 广州：华南理工大学大学出版社，2017.

[25] The Queen's speech at the COP26 Evening Reception [EB/OL]. (2021-11-01) [2023-10-16]. https://www.royal.uk/queen%E2%80%99s-speech-cop26-evening-reception.

[26] 驻欧盟使团团长傅聪大使在庆祝中华人民共和国成立七十四周年国庆招待会上的致辞 [EB/OL]. (2023-09-25) [2023-10-16]. https://www.fmprc.gov.cn/web/wjdt_674879/zwbd_674895/202309/t20230926_11150287.shtml.

[27] Speech by Ambassador Fu Cong at the Reception Celebrating the 74th Anniversary of the Founding of the People's Republic of China [EB/OL]. (2023-09-25) [2023-10-16]. http://eu.china-mission.gov.cn/eng/mh/202309/t20230926_11150390.htm.

[28] A speech by the King at the State Banquet of the State Visit of the President of the Republic of South Africa [EB/OL]. (2023-12-22) [2023-10-16]. https://www.royal.uk/speech-king-state-banquet-state-visit-president-republic-south-africa.

[29] 李强总理在第十四届夏季达沃斯论坛开幕式上的致辞 [EB/OL]. (2023-06-27) [2023-10-16]. https://www.mfa.gov.cn/web/zyxw/202306/t20230627_11104618.shtml.

[30] Address by H. E. Li Qiang, Premier of the State Council of the People's Republic of China, at the Opening Plenary of the Annual Meeting of the New Champions 2023 [EB/OL]. (2023-06-29) [2023-10-16]. https://www.chinadaily.com.cn/a/202306/29/WS649cbfc9a310bf8a75d6c2e3.html.

[31] MESSAGE ON WORLD ENVIRONMENT DAY [EB/OL]. (2023-06-05) [2023-10-17]. https://minusma.unmissions.org/en/message-world-environment-day-5-june-2023.

[32] 加强团结协作,共谋亚洲发展——王毅在第七届中国—南亚博览会开幕式上的致辞 [EB/OL]. (2023-08-17) [2023-10-17]. https://www.mfa.gov.cn/web/ziliao_674904/zyjh_674906/202308/t20230817_11127940.shtml.

[33] 王树国校长在西安交通大学2023届学生毕业典礼上的寄语 [EB/OL]. (2023-07-02) [2023-10-17]. https://news.xjtu.edu.cn/info/1033/198329.htm.

[34] Secretary-general's video message to the opening of the United Nations World Data Forum [EB/OL]. (2023-04-24) [2023-10-18]. https://www.un.org/sg/en/content/sg/statement/2023-04-24/secretary-generals-video-message-the-opening-of-the-united-nations-world-data-forum.

[35] 联合国世界数据论坛在杭州开幕! [EB/OL]. (2023-04-24) [2023-10-18]. https://www.unwdf2023.org.cn/content/content_8520491.html.

[36] 李强在二十国集团领导人第十八次峰会第一阶段会议上的讲话 [EB/OL]. (2023-09-10) [2023-10-18]. https://www.fmprc.gov.cn/zyxw/202309/t20230910_11140648.shtml.

[37] Remarks by Chinese Premier Li Qiang at Session Ⅰ of the 18th G20 Summit [EB/OL]. (2023-09-10) [2023-10-18]. http://en.people.cn/n3/2023/0910/c90000-20069916.html.

[38] "Red tourism" becomes increasingly popular among Gen Z [EB/OL]. (2023-04-06) [2023-10-18]. https://www.globaltimes.cn/page/202304/1288652.shtml.

[39] 广州市人民政府外事办公室. 外国人在穗指南(2021) [M/OL]. 广州:南方日报出版社,2021:46-47 [2022-02-15] [2023-12-9]. www.gzfao.gov.cn/attachment/0/1/1529/227314.pdf.

[40] BAKKER, HENDRICA M, ELIZE, et al. Tourism and the sharing economy: policy & potential of sustainable peer-to-peer accommodation [R/OL]. (2018-09-25) [2023-10-17]. https://documents.worldbank.org/curated/en/161471537641836/pdf/Tourism-and-the-Sharing-Economy-Policy-Potential-of-Sustainable-Peer-to-Peer-Accommodation.pdf.

[41] 珠海:淇澳红色旅游人气旺 [EB/OL]. (2021-09-10) [2023-10-17]. https://www.gdzz.gov.cn/hsc/content/post_13124.html.

[42] Futureproofing tourism via digitalisation [EB/OL]. (2022-10-06) [2023-10-17]. https://codeblue.galencentre.org/2022/10/06/futureproofing-tourism-via-digitalisation/.

[43] 探访《狂飙》取景地广东江门："天然影棚"助推侨乡文旅产业"狂飙"［EB/OL］.（2023－02－10）［2023－10－17］. http://www.gqb.gov.cn/news/2023/0210/56254.shtml.

[44] Chinese cities to see tourism peak in New Year's Day holiday［EB/OL］.（2023－12－20）［2023－12－25］. https://language.chinadaily.com.cn/a//202312/20/WS6582adc7a31040ac301a8b8f.html.

[45] 寻味顺德 第三集 美味相传［EB/OL］.（2016－05－02）［2023－10－17］. https://tv.cctv.com/2016/05/02/VIDE06CSxIcN6EYc4JXHJ1kw160502.shtml?spm＝C55924871139.PT8 hUEEDkoTi.0.0.

[46] 阿里巴巴的云服务生意由于新冠疫情而风风火火［EB/OL］.（2020－04－28）［2023－10－10］. http://yingyu.xdf.cn/yd/tech/202004/11055281.html.

[47] 公司简介［EB/OL］.［2023－10－10］. https://www.huawei.com/cn/corporate-information.

[48] 苹果公司英语演讲［EB/OL］.（2022－04－11）［2023－10－10］. https://wenku.baidu.com/view/c031be1a3a 68011ca300a6c30c2259010202f378.html?fr＝income2-doc-search&＿wkts＿＝1713254134669 &wkQuery＝Apple%2BInc.%2Bis%2Ban%2BAmerican%2Bmultinationa.

[49] 特斯拉 Logo 究竟有什么含义？CEO 马斯克给出了官方解释［EB/OL］.（2017－02－07）［2023－10－10］. https://www.ciplawyer.cn/whcycycy/130120.jhtml?prid＝172.

[50] China leads company count on Fortune global 500 list again［EB/OL］.（2023－08－04）［2023－10－10］. https://language.chinadaily.com.cn/a/202308/04/WS64ccc00fa31035260b81a5fd.html.

[51] 关于海尔［EB/OL］.（2023－04－26）［2023－10－10］. https://www.haier.com/press-events/news/20230426_209045.shtml?spm＝net.home_pc.hg2020_home_live_20240306.5.

[52] 腾讯主页［EB/OL］.［2023－10－10］. https://www.tencent.com/zh-cn/about.html#about-con-1.

[53] 集团概况［EB/OL］.［2023－10－10］. https://zgh.com/overview/.

[54] Foreign companies up investments in China's manufacturing sector［EB/OL］.（2023－12－04）［2023－12－06］. https://language.chinadaily.com.cn/a/202312/04/WS656d9bc4a31090682a5f15c0.html.

[55] 华为 5G 折叠手机未来感爆棚［EB/OL］.（2019－02－25）［2023－10－10］. https://mp.weixin.qq.com/s/3V7ZlkJPsqkHPvGLvbDEfw.

[56] 日本农民培育出酸酸甜甜的"柠檬西瓜"［EB/OL］.（2022－08－02）［2023－10－10］. https://baijiahao.baidu.com/s?id＝1773085146265209684&wfr＝spider&for＝pc.

[57] Foreign media workers carry backpacks received at Beijing 2008 all the way to Beijing 2022［EB/OL］.（2022－01－12）［2023－10－10］. https://language.chinadaily.com.cn/a/202201/12/WS61de1a06a310 cdd39bc80734.html.

[58] About Apple［EB/OL］.［2023－10－10］. http://www.apple.com.

[59] 淄博烧烤为何会火出圈？［EB/OL］.（2023－06－05）［2023－10－10］. https://www.ximalaya.com/audio/639489734.

[60] 中国丝绸技术［EB/OL］.（2023－11－28）［2023－12－04］. https://mp.weixin.qq.com/s?__biz＝MzAwOTkyMTA5OA＝＝&mid＝2247535141&idx＝1&sn＝00ddda98facfa8752d38fca7bb2960f9&chksm＝9b5a3d00ac2db416438f32aec5e1095ca425378e1a2d07c41106942bca60e989978fb5169a8e&scene＝27.

[61] 2022 福布斯中国客户服务企业 TOP100［EB/OL］.（2023－10－18）［2023－12－04］. https://www.sohu.com/a/729156501_120008919.

[62] China makes impressive high quality development progress with BRI［EB/OL］.（2023－06－28）［2023－12－04］. https://language.chinadaily.com.cn/a/202306/28/WS649bc6aa310bf8a75d6c1b7.html.

[63] 海上丝绸之路［EB/OL］.［2023－12－04］. https://baike.baidu.com/item/海上丝绸之路/439948?fr＝ge_ala.

[64] 路上的车还是会越来越多，未来交通到底该怎样转型［EB/OL］.（2022－12－15）［2023－10－10］. https://mp.weixin.qq.com/s?__biz＝MzU1NTcxODQ0OQ＝＝&mid＝2247768192&idx＝1&sn＝944d19fe2bdf04dc8b 7b2015b7e638&chksm＝fbde9adecca913c896d40afa1db11594202891f912e06ba64

ca65cb38b2d35c7cc3364 aae4f5&mpshare = 1&scene = 23&srcid = 1004JessGMpl0JhYfzsQQfct&sharer_shareinfo = 07164d1a3507 fdcb966f6a0fa479f653&sharer_shareinfo_first = 07164d1a3507fdcb966f6a0fa479f653#rd.

[65] 执一不失，开创未来［EB/OL］.（2022 – 01 – 17）［2023 – 10 – 10］. https://www.haier.com/press-events/news/20220117_174923.shtml.

[66] Policy seen as booster shot for recovery［EB/OL］.（2023 – 08 – 17）［2023 – 10 – 10］. https://language.chinadaily.com.cn/a/202308/17/WS64ddd0eca31035260b81cbb8.html.

[67] "酱香拿铁"引爆全网！"年轻人的第一杯茅台"到底好不好喝［EB/OL］.（2023 – 09 – 05）［2023 – 10 – 10］. https://mp.weixin.qq.com/s?__biz = MzU1NTcxODQ0OQ = = &mid = 2247828075&idx = 1&sn = ab70249119e10a575b1ec 8c9cc089f8a&chksm = fbdf8035cca80923ee451f02a5af1ebe081bab2a8ca7c6f6d 64576327f5680400e8f2da 7e1f6&mpshare = 1&scene = 23&srcid = 1004yfnRUNdwdUYnORK xrgtT&sharer_shareinfo = 8d4f73a138 d3c5001e6a0a7daf 72144c&sharer_shareinfo_first = 8d4f73 a138d3c5001e6a0a 7daf72144c#rd.

[68] 未来之路，捷足先登［EB/OL］.（2018 – 04 – 23）［2023 – 10 – 10］. https://mp.weixin.qq.com/s?__biz = MzU1NTcxODQ0OQ = = &mid = 2247541757&idx = 2&sn = daf7f72b2d9c4082a3cfdb5ceac 39933 &chksm = fbd261a3cca5e8b5c0f6334616d5b2557172a41f6fa02eb9aab80b94edbd15b0f67f3e1548db& mpshare = 1&scene = 23&srcid = 1004MjANgEzgK98QDQhKeUxr&sharer_shareinfo = 406afdcf56c3a5cfed 2fb01089 b181fb&sharer_shareinfo_first = 406afdcf56c3a5cfed2fb01089b181fb#rd.

[69] 国货品牌迎来"泼天富贵"，"79元套餐"卖疯了！［EB/OL］.（2023 – 09 – 19）［2023 – 10 – 10］. https://mp.weixin.qq.com/s?__biz = MzU1NTcxODQ0OQ = = &mid = 2247830448&idx = 1&sn = 53c52ae8ff386c725a87ac87b527a 667&chksm = fbdf89eecca800f81d5a18c2aa39e6f2188cb438b7eb37 adbedacd8f88fdf2ab15824798af50&mpshare = 1&scene = 23&srcid = 1004RmNL88LgLjmVwEwaLlTJ&sharer_shareinfo = bfaf20ee09c68c1ce9c417be 0634e725&sharer_shareinfo_first = bfaf20ee09c68c1ce9c417 be0634e725#rd.

[70] China, US commerce authorities to establish new working group［EB/OL］.（2023 – 08 – 29）［2023 – 10 – 10］. https://language.chinadaily.com.cn/a/202308/29/WS64ed9dd7a31035260b81ed35.html.

[71] 姜荷梅. 商务英语视听说教程［M］. 上海：上海外语教育出版社，2017.

[72] 腾讯控股有限公司2022年全年业绩公布［EB/OL］.（2023 – 09 – 22）［2023 – 10 – 16］. https://static.www.tencent.com/uploads/2023/03/22/04983fdfe04453994fcaf15d92188f47.PDF.

[73] 5G 3年等于4G 5年，第一波运营商已取得商业成功［EB/OL］.（2023 – 02 – 27）［2023 – 10 – 16］. https://www.huawei.com/cn/news/2023/2/mwc2023%205g%20business%20success.

[74] 李强在博鳌亚洲论坛2023年年会开幕式上的主旨演讲［EB/OL］.（2023 – 04 – 12）［2023 – 10 – 16］. http://www.catl.org.cn/2023 – 04/12/content_85225119.html.

[75] China-Northeast Asia Expo concludes with record project investment［EB/OL］.（2023 – 08 – 27）［2023 – 10 – 25］. https://english.news.cn/20230827/b8445342566344f6396af1f36136ebaf7/c.html.

[76] 第7届中国—南亚博览会即将举办，哪些亮点值得期待［EB/OL］.（2023 – 07 – 25）［2023 – 10 – 16］. http://www.news.cn/2023 – 07/25/c_1129768048.htm.

[77] GAO Yundi. Analysis of BYD's Business Model and Future Development Prospects［C/OL］. Atlantis Press，2021：398 – 403［2023 – 10 – 16］. https://www.researchgate.net/publication/357609788_Analysis_of_BYD's_Business_Model_and_Future_Development_Prospects.

[78] 硬刚特斯拉，小鹏汽车官宣新价格体系，打响新能源汽车耐力赛［EB/OL］.（2023 – 01 – 18）［2023 – 10 – 16］. https://www.tfcaijing.com/index.php/article/page/76696872474443646978436363359466b4c2 f6f51773d3d.

[79] China's Law-Based Cyberspace Governance in the New Era［EB/OL］.（2023 – 03 – 17）［2023 – 10 – 16］.

https://www.chinadaily.com.cn/a/202303/17/WS6413a396a31057c47ebb4f0f.html.

[80] 关于恢复和扩大消费的措施[EB/OL].(2023-07-28)[2023-10-16].https://www.gov.cn/gongbao/2023/issue_10646/202308/content_6898891.html.

[81] 上半年我国服务进出口总额同比增8.5%[EB/OL].(2023-08-04)[2023-10-16].https://language.chinadaily.com.cn/a/202308/04/WS64cca144a31035260b81a58d.html.

[82] China issues first national five-year plan on modern logistics[EB/OL].(2022-12-15)[2023-10-16].https://www.chinadaily.com.cn/a/202212/15/WS639b00d5a31057c47eba49c6.html.

[83] Nation going all out to be investment magnet[EB/OL].(2023-11-07)[2023-12-07].https://language.chinadaily.com.cn/a/202311/07/WS6549e6e4a31090682a5ece5b.html.

[84] 新西兰小企业进入中国大市场,进博会"真的"不虚此行[EB/OL].(2023-09-19)[2023-10-16].https://www.investsh.org.cn/cn/investsh/ywjqs/20230919113444 79442987.

[85] Xi hails innovation forum, calls for advancing global sci-tech cooperation[EB/OL].(2023-09-12)[2023-12-08].https://en.pujiangforum.cn/en/en_news_show.aspx?channel_id=20&cateid=328&id=116.

[86] 习近平向2023年浦江创新论坛致贺信[EB/OL].(2023-09-10)[2023-12-08].m.news.cn/2023-09/10/c_1129855112.htm.

[87] GEORGIEVA K. The Path to Growth:Three Priorities for Action[R/OL].(2023-04-06)[2023-12-07].https://www.imf.org/en/News/Articles/2023/04/06/sp040623-SM23-CurtainRaiser.

[88] 李强在第二十届中国—东盟博览会和中国—东盟商务与投资峰会开幕式上的致辞[R/OL].(2023-09-18)[2023-12-07].https://www.gov.cn/yaowen/liebiao/202309/content_6904599.htm.

[89] FIGAREDO R R. Speech at the High-Level Conference on Investment in Central America[R/OL].(2007-02-02)[2023-12-09].https://www.imf.org/en/News/Articles/2015/09/28/04/53/sp020207.

[90] 1—8月我国对外投资持续增长[EB/OL].(2023-09-22)[2023-10-16].http://cn.chinadaily.com.cn/a/202309/22/WS650d49aba310936092f23249.html?ivk_sa=1023197a.

[91] 推动中国与东盟新兴产业合作[EB/OL].(2023-07-05)[2023-12-09].https://language.chinadaily.com.cn/a/202307/05/WS64a5180ca310bf8a75d6d663.html.

[92] 习近平向2023年中国国际服务贸易交易会全球服务贸易峰会发表视频致辞[EB/OL].(2023-09-02)[2023-12-09].https://language.chinadaily.com.cn/a/202309/02/WS64f53f11a310d2dce4bb3c0d.html.

[93] 员工在家办公 企业如何管理?[EB/OL].(2012-07-23)[2023-10-16].https://www.kekenet.com/read/201207/191689.shtml.

[94] 华为提出全面智能化战略,加速千行万业的智能化转型[EB/OL].(2023-09-20)[2023-10-16].https://www.huawei.com/cn/news/2023/9/huawei-all-intelligence.

[95] 习近平向2023年浦江创新论坛致贺信[EB/OL].(2023-09-10)[2023-12-08].https://language.chinadaily.com.cn/a/202309/10/WS64fff6e8a310d2dce4bb54ef.html.

[96] 如何帮助长辈融入数字世界[EB/OL].(2021-08-04)[2023-12-08].https://www.tencent.com/zh-cn/articles/2201184.html.

[97] New policies encourage foreign firms to expand operations[EB/OL].(2023-08-15)[2023-10-20].https://language.chinadaily.com.cn/a/202308/15/WS64db3d42a31035260b81c496.html.

[98] 华为投资控股有限公司2022年可持续发展报告[R/OL].(2023-06-19)[2023-10-16].https://www-file.huawei.com/-/media/corp2020/pdf/sustainability/sustainability-report-2022-cn.pdf.

[99] 格力电器官网介绍[EB/OL].[2023-10-16].https://gree.com/about/business.

[100] 京东企业简介[EB/OL].[2023-10-17].https://about.jd.com/company.

[101] Speech by Minister Josephine Teo at Future Economy Conference & Exhibition[R/OL].(2022-03-24)[2023-10-16].https://www.mci.gov.sg/media-centre/speeches/minister-josephine-teo-at-future-

［102］ 后疫情时代的中国企业：出海，走出去，寻找更多商机！［EB/OL］.（2023－01－10）［2023－10－16］. https://mp.weixin.qq.com/s/itb0E6SVyUGyhANRp5ggiA.

［103］ 义博会——中国三大出口商品展之一［EB/OL］.［2023－12－09］. https://www.yiwufair.com/cpzz/about/.

［104］ International Ceramic Expo［EB/OL］.（2023－10－19）［2023－12－09］. https://language.chinadaily.com.cn/a/202310/19/WS6531e038a31090682a5e9b7a.html.

［105］ 国际投资盛会，见证中国与世界的"双向奔赴"［EB/OL］.（2023－09－16）［2023－10－16］. https://mp.weixin.qq.com/s/faDWmJEywE3JQVzBl8aOOA.

［106］ 习近平在第五届中国国际进口博览会开幕式上的致辞（全文）［R/OL］.（2022－11－04）［2023－10－16］. https://www.mfa.gov.cn/web/ziliao_674904/zyjh_674906/202211/t20221104_10800671.shtml.

［107］ Minister Wang Wentao attends and addresses Invest in China Year Summit and Shanghai City Promotion［EB/OL］.（2023－11－06）［2023－12－09］. http://english.mofcom.gov.cn/article/newsrelease/significantnews/202311/20231103453160.shtml.

［108］ 李强在二十国集团领导人第十八次峰会第一阶段会议上的讲话［R/OL］.（2023－09－12）［2023－10－16］. https://www.catl.org.cn/2023－09/12/content_115707279..html.

［109］ Lenovo Group further invests in cutting-edge technology［EB/OL］.（2023－07－14）［2023－10－17］. http://www.chinadaily.com.cn/a/202307/14/WS64b132f2a31035260b816886.html.

［110］ 让广交会常办常新［EB/OL］.（2023－04－25）［2023－10－17］. http://paper.people.com.cn/rmrbhwb/html/2023－04/25/content_25977623.htm.

［111］ China Focus：Euro-Asia Economic Forum highlights cooperation, development［EB/OL］.（2023－09－22）［2023－10－16］. https://english.news.cn/20230922/931e11a1924443e3bd87950084f7031e/c.html.

［112］ SHEIN SWOT Analysis 2024［EB/OL］.［2023－10－16］. https://www.edrawmax.com/article/shein-swot-analysis.html.

［113］ How to Create a Winning Marketing Strategy in 5 steps［EB/OL］.（2021－05－26）［2023－10－16］. https://adrefs.com/blog/marketing-strategy/.

［114］ China's foldable smartphone shipment rises 173 percent in Q_2［EB/OL］.（2023－08－21）［2023－10－16］. http://en.people.cn/n3/2023/0821/c90000－20061005.html.

［115］ Full text of Xi's speech at the closing ceremony of the Sixth Meeting of the China-France Business Council［R/OL］.（2024－05－07）［2024－05－08］. https://english.news.cn/20240507/0c86bf580fe7420d8fbac0a6298e68c6/c.html.